TROUBADOUR:
SONG OF THE LARK

Also by Clara Pierre:

Troubadour, French translation
Der Gesang des Troubadours, German translation

A Troubador's Tale
Das Erbe des Troubadour, German translation

TROUBADOUR: SONG OF THE LARK

✠

A novel by

Clara Pierre

Grossman Press
800 Heartwood Lane, #11, Bayfield, Colorado 81122 USA

Copyright © 2015

First publication in English, revised.

All rights reserved, including the right to reproduce this book or portions thereof in any form, store in a retrieval system, or transmit in any form or by any means, electronic, mechanical, photocopy, recording, or otherwise without permission in writing from the publisher, except by a reviewer who may quote brief passages in a review.

Clara Pierre

ISBN: 978-0-9863838-0-9
Library of Congress Control Number: 2015932204

Previously translated into French and published by France loisirs, in 2001, as *Troubadour*
Previously translated into German and published by Heyne Verlag, in 2002, as *Der Gesang des Troubadours*.

Grateful acknowledgment is made to the University of Chicago Press for permission to use KEHEW, LARK IN THE MORNING a brief excerpt from English text of "Del gran golfe de mar" ("From the Depths of the Sea") by Gaucelm Faidit.

Edited by: Elizabeth A. Green
Cover Design: Cindy Coleman
Book Design: Lisa Snider
Map Design: Mark Stroud

Printed in the United States

www.troubadour-books.com

To the memory of my sister:
Clara wished that this story (and its sequel) should be available
in English

Ar hai dreg de chantar,
Pos vei joi e deportz,
Solatz e domnejar,
Qar so es vostr'acortz

Now I have the right
To sing because I see
What brings joy and delight
Good friends and gallantry.

— "Del gran golfe de mar"
Lark in the Morning, Pp 232-35
translated by Robert Kehew

TABLE OF CONTENTS

Historical Note xi
Cast of Characters xv
Map: Land of the Troubadours..xvi

I TOULOUSE

Chapter 1: Rai Mundi 3
Chapter2: Peire Vidal 9
Chapter 3: Tolosa La Rosa 21
Chapter 4: Paratge 31
Chapter 5: L'Eretria dels Preires 41

II VENTADOUR

Chapter 6: The Road to Ventadour 53
Chapter 7: Jonglaresa 65
Chapter 8: Douce...73
Chapter 9: Cortesia 77
Chapter 10: The Comborn Festivities..89
Chapter 11: Checkmate 97
Chapter 12: News from Provence 107
Chapter 13: Christmas at Ventadour 115

III MONTDRAGON

Chapter 14: In Love's Service 125
Chapter 15: Amador 137
Chapter 16: Dies irae 145
Chapter 17: Requiescat in pace..151
Chapter 18: The Hospice 159
Chapter 19: Douce's Confession 167
Chapter 20: The Road to Couthézon 173

IV COURTHÉZON

Chapter 21: Jalosia 187
Chapter 22: Chauzir..193
Chapter 23: Vidal Redux 201
Chapter 24: Acordanza...211
Chapter 25: Parley 217
Chapter 26: Attack 227
Chapter 27: Kyrie Eleison 239
Chapter 28: The Mission to Marie 243

Glossary 251
Publisher's Note & Acknowledgments 255
Excerpt: A Troubadour's Tale 257

HISTORICAL NOTE

> *Gaucelms Faiditz si fo d'un borc que a nom Userca, que es el vesquat de Lemozi, e fo filz d'un borges. E cantava peiz d'ome del mon; e fetz molt bos sos e bos motz. E fetz se joglars per ocaison qu'el perdet a joc de datz tot son aver. Hom fo que ac gran larguesa; e fo molt glotz de manjar e de beure; per so venc gros oltra mesura. Molt fo longa saiso desastrucs de dos e d'onor a prendre, que plus de vint ans anet a pe per lo mon, qu'el ni sas cansos no eran grazidas ni volgudas.*
>
> *E si tolc moiller una soldadera qu'el menet lonc temps ab si per cortz, et avia nom Guillelma Monja. Fort fo bella e fort enseingnada, e si venc si grossa e si grassa com era el. Et ella si fo d'un ric borc que a nom Alest, de la marqua de Proenssa, de la seingnoria d'En Bernart d'Andussa. E missers lo marques Bonifacis de Monferrat mes lo en aver et en rauba et en tan gran pretz lui e sas cansos.*

Translated, this *vida*, or brief biography of the troubadour reads:

"Gaucelm Faidit was born in Uzerche, in the Limousin; he was the son of a merchant. His singing voice was the worst in the world, but he made many beautiful words and melodies. When he lost his money at dice, he composed songs for a living. He was a man of great size who enjoyed eating and drinking; that way he grew fat around the stomach. For a long time he was unlucky, receiving little acclaim in his own country, so that for twenty years he wandered abroad.

He married a prostitute, who traveled with him; her name was Guilhelma Monja. She was beautiful and talented, and she took on girth like her husband. She came from the rich town of Alès in Provence, in the seigneury of Bernard d'Anduze. The marquis de Montferrat gave Gaucelm Faidit money and attire, and held him, and his songs, in highest esteem."

This, and his seventy-some poems, are all we really know about the troubadour Gaucelm Faidit. Even his dates are uncertain. Scholars place him variously between 1150-1205 (Jean Mouzat), and 1190-1240 (Robert Briffault). Blackburn and Economou settled on 1185-1215 as the period in which Gaucelm's career thrived. I have arbitrarily chosen 1176 for the year of his birth so that he could enter Toulouse at age nineteen, when Raymond's court was at the height of its glory.

Like most historical novels, *Troubadour* is a mix of fact and fiction. There is no evidence that Gaucelm spent time in either Toulouse or Courthézon, but it is clear from the poems themselves that he did know both the Count of Toulouse and Raimbaut d'Orange. He addressed eight songs to the latter, and his words give ample proof that he loved Provence as much, or more, than his native Limousin. That Marie de Ventadour was his patroness for a time is solidly documented by the many verses he made for her. But, judging from the sheer number of verses he composed in lower Limousin, his sojourn at Ventadour was bound to have been much longer than I have made it here. It is likely as well that Gaucelm stayed at courts other than Marie's: Malemort, Comborn, and Embrun among them. Though he surely did not write a *Chronica*, or epic history in verse of the crusade against the Cathars, someone did: one version exists from 1211, another from around 1228.

The reader should keep in mind that little was written down in those days. Troubadours were part of a lively oral tradition in which few people knew how to read and write. At court, a troubadour's performance was a routine part of the night's entertainment, along with dancing, juggling, storytelling, and laughter. It was deemed no more necessary to record his songs than to write down that one had drunk a goblet of wine or exchanged polite remarks with one's dinner partner. It was not until the mid-thirteenth century that the earliest troubadour *vidas* were written. We cannot even rely on them, for by that time the edges of history had doubtless leached uncontrollably into fantasy and exaggeration. (Gaucelm's *vida* is a case in point: its writer tells us that he was fat, but not that his travels took him as far as Lombardy, Hungary, and, in all probability, to Outremer.) The songs themselves were not recorded until some hundred years after the greatest flourishing of troubadour culture. It is probable, however, that Gaucelm could read and write, for he grew up in a thriving merchant town and would have had a conventional education: scripture, logic, letters. Thus he would have been able to commit to parchment a *Chronica*, had he written one.

With the exception of Douce and Gui, all the major characters in this book actually did exist. But as with Gaucelm, I have in some cases shifted their dates a bit so that they could be, literally, on the same page with one another. Bernard de Ventadour probably died about 1195, but I have extended his life span so that he could serve as Gaucelm's mentor.

Béatritz de Die is an elusive figure. She appears to have been born about 1140, and she may—or may not—have had a romantic liason with Raimbaut d'Orange. A woman of that name, a descendent of one of the seigneurial families near Montélimar who married a lord of Die, was a *trobairitz*. Four of her poems survive. Whoever she was, her name gave me the idea for the character Béatritz. Now at least she exists as a hybrid of my imagination. I have advanced her death date, allowing her to inhabit the same period as Gaucelm. As for Raimbaut, he seemed just the right "fit" to be Gaucelm's patron. Therefore, although his dates were circa 1144-1173, I have plucked him from history and moved him ahead about twenty-five years.

The Ussel family were, in fact, neighbors of Marie and Ebles at Ventadour. I have borrowed the name of Elias d'Ussel's cousin and given it to his invented son, Gui. Bertrand Marty was the Cathar bishop of Toulouse at a later time than this story. He was burned at the stake at Montsegur in 1244, along with 220 others who refused to renounce their faith.

The action in *Troubadour* condenses the period between the last years of the twelfth century and the early years of the thirteenth. It does so in order to dramatize what had already been in poignant contrast for decades: the full flowering of troubadour poetry in collision with the drastic wars that were to devastate the South and finally cut troubadour culture off at the roots. But the fiction writer sometimes has to goose the pace of history, for societies change more slowly below the surface of events than makes for good storytelling.

The general historical framework of *Troubadour* is as accurate as I could make it. However, I have invented incidents like the attacks on Montdragon and Courthézon, which are based on the frequent skirmishes against towns known to harbor heretics in the years before 1208, when Innocent III officially declared his "holy war" on the Cathars. Such quick strikes, in which a whole population might be put to the torch, prefigured the major onslaughts on cities across the South, such as the massacres at Béziers (1209), Lavaur (1211), and Muret (1213).

Where records of a public event exist, I have taken no liberties with the facts, such as they are able to be gleaned from a period so far in the past. Thus, for example, the reader may be sure that Vidal's account of Raymond's excommunication in 1208 is based on what eyewitnesses observed.

Finally, the alert medievalist may note that it was only after the Middle Ages were over that builders in Toulouse began to use brick, to which they were forced to shift when local stone quarries became exhausted. Nonetheless, the famous "rosy red glow" of the city one sees today better serves a novelist's design, and I have invested twelfth century Toulouse with it retroactively.

– Clara Pierre

CAST OF CHARACTERS

Gaucelm Faidit – A troubadour in the south of France, during the late 12th and early 13th centuries
Raymond – The count of Toulouse, also called "Rai Mundi" or "Light of the Earth"
Bernard – A well-known, older troubadour from Ventadour, now living at the court of Count Raymond of Toulouse
Eleanor of Aquitaine – A celebrated duchess famed for her "court of love," at which lovers settled quarrels
Peire Vidal – A young, eccentric troubadour at the court of Count Raymond of Toulouse, who reputedly thinks of himself as a wolf
Folquet – A former troubadour who becomes Abbot of Le Thoronet
Guilhelma Monja – A prostitute who falls in love with Gaucelm
Marie – The countess of Ventadour, who rules her "court of love" and is the wife of Count Ebles
Ebles – The count of Ventadour, husband of Marie
Douce – The young daughter of Marie and Ebles of Ventadour
Madame Audiarde – Marie's friend, who lives in Malemort, a day's ride from Ventadour
Humbert Comborn – Douce's intended husband, whose family are neighbors of Ventadour
Elias d'Ussel – A knight who lives near Ventadour
Pierre d'Ussel – The brother of Elias
Gui d'Ussel – The son of Elias and an aspiring knight
Béatritz de Die – Daughter of the Baron of Montdragon and a Cathar
Raimbaut of Orange – A count living at Courthézon;
Tiburge – Sister of Raimbaut
Alphonse – King of Aragon, a region in the northeast of what is now Spain
Goodman Raoul – A Cathar parfaite
Trencavel – Nephew of Count Raymond of Toulouse
Simon de Montfort – A northern baron and ally of Folquet

✠

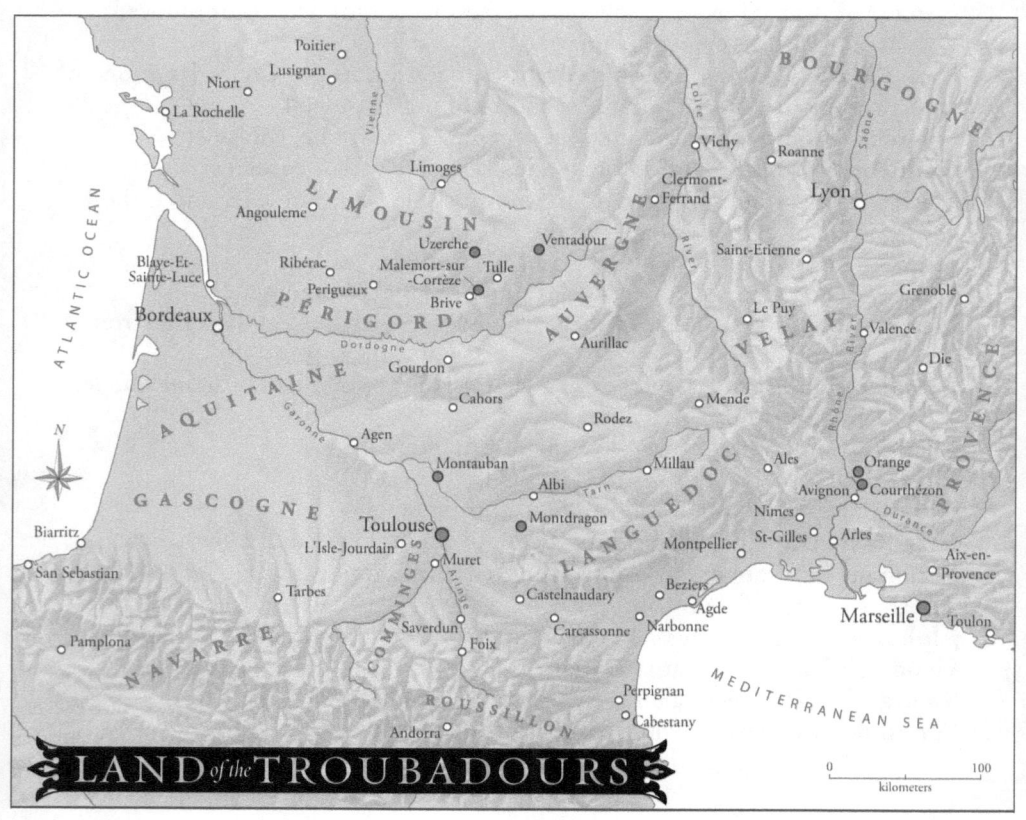

I
TOULOUSE
1195-1201

Chapter 1

RAI MUNDI

Gaucelm rode southeast into the strange lands damp with spring. Before him, the fields fell out like lengths of velvet. Uzerche now seemed to him a poor place by comparison. True, there were pigs in every yard and forests full of chestnuts, but the soil was flinty, good for growing beans and cabbages at best, nothing like this part of the south, where the land was lush with vineyards as far as the eye could see.

So this was the very heart of the Languedoc, Gaucelm thought, that great swag of country whose language he shared. Here, the finest wine was aged, the rarest pears and plums were grown, the purest southern tongue was spoken—and all of it belonged to the fabled Count Raymond of Toulouse. Gaucelm had heard tell of it in the same breath as such fairy-tale landscapes as Brittany or even Paris, where King Philip Augustus, monarch of the northern-speaking people, resided.

Yet Count Raymond's domain was no faraway land. Gaucelm was only five days from home—the town of Uzerche, in the Limousin. Saddle-weary though he was, he laughed out loud. The "great world," which everyone had talked about as though it were on the other side of the moon, was less than a week's ride to the south.

The rains this year had been plentiful enough to satisfy any season's thirst, he thought. Trenches by the roadside were still draining water. His eyes moved along the grape vines—black knobs twisted into the ground. They were not yet in bloom; their harvest would begin just the other side of summer, under the dusty, slanted sun of autumn. Like knots on a knight's quilted vest, each vine seemed to tack down the earth. The sight goaded his taste for wine—a pot of Corbières, dark as a velvet-black rose, with a slight curl to the bouquet. Gaucelm wondered if there might be a tavern close by, where he could get a drink and throw a game of dice before bedding down in Toulouse.

He shifted position in the saddle, rising tall. The thought of a tavern made him feel almost as old as his father. Now he could roll his cubes for all they were worth, and his father would never know that his son had become an expert at his own secret vice. Oh, if the Elders of Uzerche ever found out how much time Faidit of Mercer Street, dealer in luxury yard goods, spent tossing dice, they might think twice when his name came up for election to the Town Council. When Gaucelm pictured his father, pink-cheeked at forty years, he felt a swell of pride and sorrow for the burly man whom he'd left behind without an explanation.

Gaucelm had awakened at dawn, taken the packet of pies his mother had prepared, pulled down the viol from its peg and wrapped the delicate stringed instrument in an extra pair of breeches she had sewn for him. Creeping toward the door, he had squeaked open the latch while his mother waved and prayed, the farewells they'd exchanged the night before still quivering on her lips.

Slowly Faidit would have risen from bed. Gaucelm could envision him lumbering about the chamber like a big, dazed animal, muttering with disbelief, "How could you—my own wife!—have kept this news from me?" While his mother sank deeper into silence, he would have given a bull-necked roar, then gone to the window sill, shaking his bewildered head before asking "why?" over and over again. Finally, the cords in his neck would have stood out with rage, "Answer me!"

Gaucelm squirmed on his horse. He felt Ventar's dappled belly swelling in and out like a bellows beneath him. From the saddle he grabbed a few stalks of winter wheat and sucked at them to quiet his own grumbling stomach. For a long time Gaucelm had known he had to leave home—or spend the rest of his life shouldering bolts of cloth, counting coins, snipping, ripping, wrapping.

Most youths his age were married already. He enjoyed women, especially the Benet girl. His face flamed at the memory of her hard, tiny nipples against his chest, even now. But marriage? That was not for him.

So he had planned to leave, hoping that his mother, who had always praised his prowess at music, would become his ally. Even now he knew he had to prove himself to her.

The early morning sun was bright as it angled upward. In a brilliant flash, it caught the knobbed nose of Montauban Cathedral, and Gaucelm felt a jag of excitement. Within two days he would be in Toulouse: the name alone made him shiver. Count Raymond's castle would be upon him all too soon, where, at this very moment, Bernard de Ventadour might be performing. Since he'd first heard it as a child, sung by a scruffy minstrel in the main square, the tune had been his talisman. "*Can vei la Lauzeta mover*" The words seemed wondrous, like balls being juggled in the air and tumbling groundward at the end of each stanza. He knew then that his life would have the sound of singing in it. Like its namesake, the lark, the *Lauzeta* song drew him on invisibly, to the moment when his dream of paying homage to Bernard de Ventadour in person, with his own chosen composition, would be fulfilled.

He was swaying slightly to the motion, half dreaming, when a phrase came to him, then another, falling into place with words that were already lying on his tongue. He knew the signs: a song was forming.

> *E las fontz e.l riu clar*
> *Fan m'al cor alegranza*

A strange happiness flooded him.

> *Prat a vergier, quar tot m'es gen*
> **In spring each brook and field**
> **seems fresh as though with first**
> **time seeing**

Over the next two days, he spun out his song, finishing it with a tornada, a perfect loop of verse, neat as the edges his mother sewed on her linens. He counted the stanzas to remember their order, his eyes returning to his surroundings.

The yellow fields behind him now, he came upon another road entirely. He continued, hoping for a hint, a hamlet in the fold of a hill, a lone human being who might direct him. But his bearings were utterly gone. And then he saw it: a tall conical steeple on the far horizon, which, as he approached, proved to be one of many spires. The profile of a great city emerged: Toulouse at last!

It was high noon when he rode through the main gate between the fortified twin towers and asked the watchman the way to the castle. Inside the city walls, Ventar's hoofs echoed on the empty stone streets. Smoke rose from kitchen chimneys. The very air seemed crowded with the presence of so many souls—eating, breathing, snoring, snug inside their brick and stone homes.

Gaucelm slowed the horse to a walk and inhaled deeply. City of Bernard de Ventadour!

The street pointed out by a watchman took him over a wooden bridge that spanned the banks of the mighty Garonne. He heard the silver murmur of water below and set his sights on the tall, gated archway ahead. He rode directly to the castle's entrance and without dismounting, called out to the guardhouse above.

"Who's there?" a voice boomed out.

"Gaucelm Faidit, by name."

"From which country?"

"Uzerche, in the Limousin." A pause. Gaucelm waited, his hands tightening on the reins.

"What brings you here?"

"I make songs for great lords," he replied, with a bravado that surprised him.

Gaucelm held his breath. Then the man shouted, "Pass," and the portcullis rose in a sweep of chains. A stableboy came running for Gaucelm's palfrey.

The stableboy pointed across the courtyard. "The hall's there, sir."

Gaucelm took up his pack and walked, sore-legged, toward a pair of huge doors studded with metal knobs. Gaucelm pounded hard on the doors and waited. From somewhere inside dogs yapped and whined. He was about to knock a second time when a houseboy scrambled out to meet him from a side entrance.

"This way," the boy said gruffly, leading him inside.

It was the custom, Gaucelm was told, for Count Raymond to make his household rounds at the noon meal. But as he entered the hall, there was no food in sight. Instead, knights in full regalia, swords slapping their thighs, thronged the room with talk and laughter, while hall servants in livery of crimson and gold milled about expectantly, awaiting orders.

An immense fireplace arched halfway to the ceiling—big enough, he thought, to roast two oxen at one time. He felt small and scruffy in his mud-caked shoes. Four men wearing hats like squashed pillows pressed against him. In loud, confident voices, they were weighing the possible effects of a request for tax exemption. The squashed hats were members, he surmised, of Toulouse's famed city council. His father, who kept informed on political matters, had spoken often of the enlightened "consuls" of Toulouse who, like their Roman forebears, had given their city a name for independent rule. He caught snatches of conversation: salt monopolies in Narbonne, restrictions on building windmills.

Turning around, his attention was caught by a laughing cluster of ladies, their full bosoms displayed above tight bodices. His thoughts leaped—even he, lax churchgoer though he was, had heard such styles declaimed from the pulpit in Uzerche. But what did they know of fashion? Here, the ladies wore long bliauts that trailed like queens' gowns, their sleeves reaching below the wrist to reveal a graceful flouncing of hands adorned with rings or gloves and lacy handkerchiefs. And yet it was their tresses that took his breath away. Accustomed to the modest linen caps that hid his mother's brow, he was stunned by the worldly sight of hair so much in evidence. Glossy swags of it slipped from tall combs studded with pearls or were bound in nets set with glittering jewels.

Suddenly there was a stir at the far end of the hall. He stretched to tiptoe, but all he saw was a sea of heads. He heard a ripple of whispers among the crowd: "The Count!" A slight, balding figure with a page in tow forged a split through a knot of knights. The man, simply dressed in a royal blue surcoat, stopped often, laying a hand of greeting on a shoulder, pausing to say a few words to someone else, breaking off to bestow a handclasp or a quick embrace.

The women withdrew to the sides of the room, dipping their skirts and slightly lowering their heads as the count passed. He moved with such gravity, such stateliness, that he seemed not to walk at all, but to sail like a masted ship, his robes bellying out as he made his way across the floor.

The Count wore no circlet, no diadem—only a fringe of sparse hair, straight-cut. No jewels at all, no ring, no fibula. *Impossible!* Gaucelm thought. The count's cloak, incredibly, looked to be homespun.

In another instant, his whole being took fire as the lord approached him, his eyes smiling.

"You wander, I see," the Count said, looking over Gaucelm's disheveled appearance.

"And sing, my lord." Gaucelm bowed.

"And are out of pocket, no doubt?"

"I am, my lord."

"But well pocketed in front for a stripling!"

Gaucelm sucked in his stomach. It was true, his love of food was giving him a gut like his father's.

"What are you called?"

"Gaucelm Faidit of Uzerche, your lordship."

"And what brings you from Limousin?"

"I seek to be in your service," he replied, surprised by his own audacity.

"You have come a long way to find me."

"Not for one who dreams of singing for your lordship."

"Out to gain your fortune, are you? I like that in a youth." Count Raymond clapped Gaucelm's shoulders, then stepped back to look at him once more.

Gaucelm was riveted by the Count's intense topaz eyes with kindly creases radiating to his temples. Gaucelm thought of the enamel eyes set into a mosaic on the church wall in Uzerche. Wherever he stood in the église Saint-Pierre, the eyes would be upon him.

"I'd be pleased to have you stop awhile with us. I'll have someone attend to your horse and give you quarters."

"They have. . ." Gaucelm began, and then re-formed the phrase into something more suitable. "All politeness has been extended, for which I am grateful, lordship," he managed.

The Count's eyes crinkled with amusement at his formality. "Good, Gaucelm, you honor us with your reply. You hope to sing—and so you shall, before the company tonight."

Chapter 2

PEIRE VIDAL

An invited guest! Gaucelm looked around him as the hall emptied of people. Soon, he was alone.

It dawned on him that with everyone gone but the servants, he might sneak upstairs and investigate the other rooms. A single rush-light flickered as he made his way up the staircase behind the dais. Someone was singing. Cautiously he trailed the ribbon of sound, his footfalls nearly silent on the wooden floor.

A succession of columns lined the long gallery, each finished differently: one bore griffins; one, a pattern of notched crosses; another, a honeycomb design. From the top of each column rose a magnificent splay of stone cut like a clutch of stems that fanned into ribs across the ceiling. The spot where the ribs met their opposite number was marked with a rosette of stone. Gaucelm marveled at the work set so high, yet more delicate than that of any church interior he had ever seen.

From his mother's *Little Book of Hours*, Gaucelm had conjured up visions of crystal chalices and gifts of Byzantine splendor set with pearls or carved ivories, uncut emeralds the size of knuckles, golden baubles from Africa sewn onto Venetian silk. But with Count Raymond, wealth took on a different meaning. The Count had come forward to greet guests in a plain cloak, bare-headed.

Count Raymond's crown was his courtesy. Yet his rule went far, much farther than that of the real king, Philip, his cousin to the north, who sat so pitifully upon that narrow strip of land called Ile de France.

If God will only let me stay in Toulouse for as long as it takes me to learn, he vowed, *I will become the best troubadour in the land.*

He had resolved to be patient. Some days before his departure from home he heard his mother out: "A risky business," she said repeatedly, "playing and singing in front of a rag-tag audience." Then, casting her eyes upward, she conceded it would be a long time, God willing, before he would inherit anything from his father, and the small holding of land at Sauger, her own dowry, would not bring him much either. She had put aside her embroidery and looked at him squarely. "But how will you keep a shirt on your back? To start out as a vagabond, with no position in life—what can you be thinking?"

"What about Rigaud?" he had reminded her. The distant relative was a legend in the family, a lesser baron whose holdings had shrunk to a hamlet and a few fields somewhere near Barbezieux. He had given up everything to travel to Poitiers where it was said he had sung before Eleanor of Aquitaine and her spirited daughter Marie, Countess of Champagne, who together conducted the fabled Courts of Love. There, his verses were held in esteem. Having made a name for himself, he'd wooed many fine ladies but he never married.

What could his mother say to that? Though she pleaded and wept, in the end she gave Gaucelm her blessing.

He heard singing coming from one of the castle's private chambers. Strolling the length of the corridor, he listened. The singing ceased; a viol took up the tune. The faint melody stopped and started repeatedly; someone was rehearsing the same phrase over and over. The song rose in cadenzas and descended, then hammered through the closing envoi and ended. As Gaucelm moved nearer, the envoi began again, faltered, faded out. Then a voice bellowed some obscenity and an object clattered sharply on stone.

Let it be a fellow minstrel! Gaucelm prayed fiercely. He headed past a group of small apartments, almost reaching the privies, and paused outside the last room.

A figure knelt on the floor by a wooden bench. From the rear, Gaucelm saw a thicket of black hair sticking out from under a cap whose peak was set rakishly to the side. The room was almost bare of furnishings. Hearing Gaucelm's footsteps, the young man swiveled to face him. He held a broken bow in one hand.

"This is the last punishment I have in store for you, thou great snarl of woodrot!" he declared, pitching the ruined bow against the wall. The man rose ceremoniously from his crouch, then approached Gaucelm, hand outstretched.

"Sorry about the noise, my friend. My name's Peire Vidal. And you?"

"Are you the same Vidal who composed the 'Proensa Song'?" Gaucelm asked incredulously.

"The very one." He looked pleased.

"I've heard many of your ballads. I guess I thought of you as . . . older," Gaucelm fumbled, then hastened to add, "Your verses are beautifully crafted."

"I'm honored, though not surprised, that you know my little ditties." Vidal gave a small bow, then snatched the cap from his head.

"You were working on something," Gaucelm apologized. "I shouldn't have intruded."

"When the music won't behave, I am thankful for any interruption," Vidal replied puckishly. Spinning his cap on a forefinger, he commanded, "Watch this." The cap spiraled into the air and landed back on Vidal's head, tilting over one ear.

Vidal skimmed the floor in an undulation of invisible robes, bending first left, then right, greeting, nodding, murmuring.

"What are you doing here? I saw you in the great hall earlier today. Who invited you to my chambers?"

Gaucelm winced. Had he erred in following the sounds of Vidal's music? "I heard your music and knew I had to find you."

"What's your name, anyway?"

"Faidit, Gaucelm," he replied with a dash of Vidal's own mocking inflection.

"*Faidit*! Your father's not the silk and samite dealer, the one who trades at Narbonne and Limoges?"

"Yes, and Beaucaire and Ypres," Gaucelm added, his chin lifting a little with pride.

"I've heard the name from my own father who's in furs. He's met yours many times, called him 'Traveler' if I remember correctly. That's right; Faidit, the Traveler."

"He came by it justly," Gaucelm said. "Our name means to wander."

"Aha! And did you just *wander* away from home?"

"Not really. That is . . . yes. I mean, I didn't wish to be a merchant, so I left."

"Well, I congratulate you. I didn't wish to be a merchant either. What a business! With fur, everything depends upon the season, the weather, a good harvest or famine—and how many people are desperate enough to work for the few pennies you pay them to supply you with hides? It's a scoundrel's life."

All at once, Vidal took the stance of a theater announcer mouthing the title of a melodrama. "We're brothers under the pelt. The Tale of Two Strayed Bourgeois!" he boomed, setting his cap a-twirl again. They both laughed.

Vidal's cap stopped spinning and sagged on his upraised hand. "So, what do you intend to do here?"

"I sing," Gaucelm replied.

"You too?" Vidal swiftly appraised Gaucelm a second time. "Rai Mundi brooks no rifts among his minstrels, you know."

"Rai Mundi?" Gaucelm asked.

"Light of the World, Raymond," Vidal replied, laughing.

"He asked me to sing tonight. I meant to ask you . . ."

"Quick work."

"What is?"

"Already you have been asked to sing."

"Well, it would suit me better if I were prepared. I've got to go," Gaucelm said with sudden ferocity. When he played or sang for himself, he enjoyed it as he might a ripe fruit. But this evening he would have to serve that fruit to others, and the thought of it filled him with dread.

But Vidal talked past him. "I've set the devil of a difficult piece, but I may have overshot my intention. If I had any sense I'd stick to ballads. The company loves anything tuneful and hummable. Tonight I want to try an *aubade* that's been inside my head for weeks, but my voice can't carry the cadenzas. I thought I'd play them on my instrument instead, but now I've ruined *that* possibility," referring to the splintered stick he'd cast on the floor. "As you see, my bows bear the brunt of my temper. That's the third one I've smashed this year."

"I'll lend you mine. I won't need it tonight."

"How gracious! My thanks, then, I'll borrow it if I may. You're singing unaccompanied? Let's hear your piece."

Gaucelm winced. "I'd rather hear yours first, to know if mine's in the right mode."

"Mode? *Mode*? My dear Faidit, no one will hear you. No one will notice anything except your new face."

"Well, that suits me fine. I've never sung before such a *large* company. Just, you know, the usual routine: taverns, fairs, festivals." In actual fact he had never performed in front of an audience of more than two, and that only once, when some colleagues of his father's had put him up to it at St. Gilles, in the summer of the Jerusalem taffetas.

"Who taught you to play the viol?" Vidal asked.

"No one. The viol maker encouraged me. He showed me how to tune the instrument and find the chords. The rest I taught myself." He paused. "And my mother. She drilled me in Latin rhymes and had me study the liturgy. She taught me the scales and keys, hoping to bend me toward a respectable career in the ministry. I loved the music, but I hated church."

"Umm," Vidal nodded knowingly, nudging the broken pieces of his bow with his foot. He began to move impatiently around the room. "As for tonight, stop worrying. You can rely on me. But to work, sir! And where is the bow you promised me?"

The evening's guest was no ordinary cleric. He was Bertrand, a heretic elder with the status of a saint among his followers. He had journeyed from the Foix district, deep in the southwest, a stronghold of the unbelievers called Cathars, whose number was increasing throughout the land. Bertrand's reticence only added to his reputation. When he emerged from seclusion to speak, people of all persuasions gathered in his presence. Nicknamed the Pope of Foix, he was considered by many to be holy.

Two small pages, stiffly sandwiched into their livery of crimson and gold, sounded the trumpets. Hall servants lit torches in sockets below the banners of Toulouse and Foix. Standing near the entryway, Gaucelm and Vidal watched the whole company parade by. Count Raymond swept in, the Countess Joanna on his arm, his right elbow leaning out from his side in exaggerated fashion, for she was short and waddled like a hen. Vidal nudged Gaucelm, surreptitiously jutting out his chin and making muffled clucking sounds.

Gaucelm could not take his eyes off Bertrand as he followed Count Raymond and Countess Joanna to the dais. He seemed whitely transparent in contrast to his black robes, the skin of his face stretched smooth as a waxen taper. Around his neck was a strange symbol, a cross with four arms of equal length. His smile seemed to come from somewhere beyond himself. As he sat down at his place of honor, the company near him fell silent. All eyes were upon him.

Gaucelm followed Vidal to the front of the hall, where they found a place to sit just across from the dais.

A page stepped up to the platform. In one hand he carried a silver aquamanile, in his other palm a laver, and upon his forearm a white linen towel. He approached the Countess, who held her hands above the wide-lipped basin as the boy struggled not to splash water all over her fingers. She then dried her hands on the cloth, and the page moved on to Count Raymond who, already absorbed in conversation with his guest of honor, merely waved him on. Bertrand performed his ablutions perfunctorily, then wiped his fingers with care.

Once settled at their places, Vidal turned to Gaucelm. "I want a good look at this heretic," he said, "Mark my words: Bertrand is the centerpiece in a private war between Rai Mundi and the Bishop of Toulouse."

"Is the Bishop of Toulouse here, too?"

Vidal snorted delightedly. "A heretic and a bishop sharing Raymond's board in the same room? Not likely!" He gave a private little laugh that ended in a grimace. "No." He paused, savoring an imaginary scene. "But oh, how I would love it if he were!"

Gaucelm's irritation with this prankster was growing. "I don't see how Raymond can fight a battle with someone who's absent."

Vidal gazed at the neophyte beside him. "Talk," he said, as though explaining things to a child. "People talk. The message will get to the Bishop's palace before the scraps from tonight's dinner are tossed out the back door to the deserving destitute. Our Raymond is a specialist in the subtle gesture. And wait—there's a further refinement. You see, Bertrand's a *parfait*."

"A what?"

"A heretic of the highest order. The Cathars have their own hierarchy—bishops, everything. In fact, Bertrand is considered a bishop himself. You could almost call it a parody of the Pope's own order. You'll understand soon enough. Raymond's honeycomb is buzzing with Cathars."

"What does that have to do with the Bishop of Toulouse?"

"Ever hear of a pope's lackey liking heretics? Well, Raymond can't resist them. When a nice, juicy heretic comes along—especially an ecclesiastic Cathar and an intellectual to boot—Raymond can't wait to enlist him into his entourage, which is why Bertrand gets to sit at the right hand of God tonight. Now, shhh . . ."

Bertrand was invited to say grace. Gaucelm craned his neck to see the feast, a wide sea of white table cover anchored by a gold centerpiece in the shape of a ship that flashed in the light from the torches.

"The nef," Vidal whispered, seeing Gaucelm's eyes grow wide. "It holds a precious cargo of salt."

As Bertrand finished the benediction, a dog barked and the musicians began tuning their winds and harps. Then the kitchen procession commenced: quenelles, pasties, plates of peacock, rabbits, and pies of pounded meat trimmed with carved fruits. Spiced wine was offered in silver cups. Servers, pages, carvers, and cooks marched through the room to deliver their treasures, displaying them first before the count, then passing them between the shoulders of the guests. Gaucelm stared, his nostrils sniffing the warm, rich aroma.

Vidal nudged him with an elbow. "Eat and stop gaping, oaf, or you'll faint when you have to get up and sing. Besides," he leaned into Gaucelm's ear, "Don't let Raymond catch you with your mouth hanging open like some ninny!"

In spite of a rising lump in his throat, Gaucelm dutifully ate. As he swallowed the croquette and his cup of lukewarm wine, a second round of platters was placed before him. He tasted lark for the first time and though their sightless eyes seemed to stare up at him reproachfully, he had to admit their meat tasted delicious.

He raised his head and a pourer came instantly to refill his cup. But Vidal was keeping watch.

"You're approaching an improper shade of pink," he observed. "If you don't stop after this one, you'll end up like one of those songbirds on your plate, feet in the air and your head in someone's mouth."

His head was suddenly fogged by drink and excitement. To steady himself, Gaucelm reached out and fiddled with the edge of the platter before him. The room was so much larger than it seemed earlier. He tried to focus. Raymond was a blur of rough-spun blue; Joanna, a dot of gray. But who was that, next to her? The head above a corpulent arc of stomach seemed to balance precariously atop a cascade of chins. There was something odd in how rapidly and deftly he moved his head from side to side, from neighbor to neighbor, bowing, nodding, with a fat man's grace and obsequiousness.

"Who is the man sitting next to Joanna, the one with the chins?"

"You mean the whey-faced fat one? A rich troubadour," Vidal replied mockingly, "whose position is one to which we can all aspire. And I don't mean being seated next to Joanna; that is merely a result of his exalted rank. I mean that he has had his *rewards* from her, like a gray palfrey and a new suit of clothes twice a year, and other favors that we who are less enamored of her physical charms don't inquire about."

"What's his name?"

"Folquet. He hails from Marseille, that cradle of fishmongers. Shall I tell you what I find the most intriguing thing about him? The way he walks. He pushes the air behind him with cupped hands, an interesting form of locomotion."

"Perhaps it's because he's fat."

"Your inclinations are too generous. No, I insist that it's because he has much to hide. In short, he's a fart, propelled by his own bad air."

Gaucelm smiled at Vidal's crude humor. "How are his songs?" he asked.

"As bad as his air."

"And who is the old one?"

"Ah, you mean Bernard de Ventadour," Vidal said in a different voice entirely. "Raymond keeps him as a blessing on the house. He's not truly old, just past his powers. There you have it: the most distinguished wordsmith present presides at the far corner of the table, drooling, with his chin practically resting on the cloth."

Gaucelm's heart began to pound. His idol! The man with musical gifts from the angels! "But why does he look that way?"

"An illness. He no longer sings."

Gaucelm's heart seemed to stop mid-beat. It wasn't right; a prince of poets ought to look like one. He wanted to cry from outrage, from sadness. His very reason for coming now made him feel hurt and a little ashamed. He took a sip of wine but couldn't swallow.

"Am I to be introduced?" he managed as Vidal thumped him on the back.

"In due course. He's still the diadem in Raymond's crown. Presenting his guests to Bernard de Ventadour is the one little treat Raymond never denies himself." Gaucelm nodded. "To maintain the supply, he takes care to restock his gallery. He delights in *acquiring* people. Like you, for instance—are you all right? "

Gaucelm took a deep breath. "Yes, I expect so," he replied, though he was tiring of Vidal always plucking a sarcastic note.

"How will I recognize my cue?"

"First there'll be the usual mummery: an acrobat, and perhaps a rondelle or two if the guests feel up to it. Then comes the serious stuff. Last week a group of traveling actors did a satire on wives too amorously celebrated by wags like you and me hoping to get rich on their husbands' indulgence. It brought the house down. Joanna turned red as a beet, but Raymond just laughed. You see, you have to know which lords love their wives and which use them as bait to attract a brilliant entourage. It's a test of political acumen. If you fail, the results can be disastrous."

Vidal's words tripped by as Gaucelm fought down the larks. He silenced them mentally, then doused them with wine until they were mute. Vidal droned on. "Of course, Raymond loathes Joanna."

At that moment a beat like the clapping of hands accompanied by a high flute sounded through the hall and a swirl of Arab dancers appeared. Gaucelm could hardly believe his eyes: the women were nearly naked except for lengths of shimmering silk that flowed around their bodies. They spun like tops, coming to rest in unison on bended knee before the high table. Then, with a shudder of tambourines the silken girls interlaced in a series of dazzling formations, blending purples, crimsons, and golds into patterns of burning color.

Gaucelm closed his eyes for a moment. He had never seen such a spectacle. When he opened his eyes the dancers were standing in two rows before him, swaying in acknowledgment of the foot-thumping applause. Nearest to him was a girl in violet the color of crushed figs. The wisps of cloth were held to her by nothing more than a woven girdle.

Gaucelm glanced at Bertrand. The count had stopped tracing circles on the tablecloth with his wine goblet and had leaned across Joanna to rap Folquet on the chest. But the troubadour was napping on his bed of chins. Gaucelm's eyes traveled down the table of chaste bosoms and official vestments. To his astonishment, more than one pair of eyelids drooped; some heads were even beginning to nod. *The wine*, he thought, *and too much foo*d.

A plaintive chant started up on a Spanish viol. Here was a language he could understand, but the dark-skinned minstrel lagged far behind. A pair of frightened eyes flickered beneath the strange scarf he wore tightly around his head, giving him the appearance of an Arab street urchin. Gaucelm glanced questioningly at Vidal.

"The pleasures he provides are . . . other than musical," Vidal replied cryptically.

Tepid applause followed the viol's lament. Six yellow-clad acrobats burst into the hall, rolling across each other's backs, springing to their feet, and ending with a bow to Count Raymond. A midget dressed in a costume of spiky black feathers brought up the rear, juggling oranges.

"I'm next," Vidal said.

Picking up Gaucelm's bow and his viol, he made his way forward. Vidal began with a simple dance tune, using his bow hand to rap its rhythm on the hollow belly of the instrument. But almost as soon as the melody was launched, he stopped abruptly. "No, no, no!" he announced. "That's *not* what I really want to play for you tonight." Chins rose, eyes opened. Gaucelm was just as surprised as the rest of the company. Vidal continued: "What I want you to hear is part of an aubade that I'm still working on." Now he had their full attention. "I crave your indulgence over the rough spots."

It was a brilliant stroke, Gaucelm thought, to introduce an unfinished work precisely at the moment when interest in the evening was flagging.

"So my poet isn't wasting his time, drinking my wine, and roistering with scullery maids—the man is producing!" Count Raymond boomed.

Gaucelm sat forward in his seat as Vidal acknowledged the compliment with a bow. He played a melodic line on his viol, then another, until a complete stanza was formed, a lover's song. But he did not sing the tune in any customary way. Propping the instrument against his thigh, he began to speak in verse, in the voice of a young lover waking his mistress before dawn so they would not be discovered together.

"*Tant vos ai ades quiza*," he intoned. "**I have desired you so**... *eu remandrai tant quan er fait lo dos*... **and I will stay with you until the light comes, for you are the gentlest being who ever begged for love...**"

Then Vidal picked up the viol once more and replayed the aubade's melody. Gaucelm did not recognize it until Vidal reached the envoi that had beckoned him to Vidal's practice room that very morning. When the song was finished there was a murmur of appreciation before a huge burst of applause.

Gaucelm cracked his knuckles beneath the table. The larks were fighting in his stomach again. He reached under the bench for the neck of his instrument, but nothing was there, only empty space. He panicked, until he remembered his decision to sing the song he composed in the yellow fields, which he would perform *a cappella. Dieus*! Let the pain be over soon, he prayed.

Then he heard Vidal address the count: "Lord Souverain d'Argence, I beg leave to introduce a young poet new to this court whose canson will dazzle you. Gaucelm." Somehow Gaucelm rose, aware only of a blur of faces whose eyes he imagined were by now opened wide and focused upon him. The silence made his head drum.

He walked slowly toward the count and the countess. Somehow he remembered the obligatory bow, down on one knee, and swallowed hard. If his mouth was this dry, would any sounds come? He deserved this humiliation. He turned and moved to the center of the hall, as far from the row of faces as he could get. *Plaitz Dieus, guide me through this and I'll faithfully serve you for the rest of my life.*

No one stirred. The silence was intense, interrupted only by an impatient rustle of sleeves, the clink of rings on goblets, a muffled titter. Opening his mouth, he was amazed to hear his own voice, and feel his body move about, gesturing, singing to a face here, a blur there, shapes that were beginning to smile back, rapping and nodding in time to his stanzas. Gradually, imperceptibly, his fear fell away and he found himself in orbit among the sun, the moon, and all the stars. What joy! All he needed was there within his voice:

> **Why should I kill myself**
> **With pain**
> **When another lady lies**
> **Ready to comfort me?**

He sang straight to Count Raymond and serenaded the countess in a pitch, which, even to him, had never sounded so pure. In the pause between verses, the smell of roast meat and spiced wine almost overwhelmed him. He glanced in the direction of Bernard de Ventadour, and caught sight of an odd expression on the man's face, a look of beatitude as though the poet were dreaming.

Gaucelm began the last verse, allowing his voice to unfurl and fill out like a sail. The largeness of the sound seemed to shrink the room that he had thought was so vast. Now he turned and sang to Bernard, paying homage at last to the man who had given him the gift of the "*Lauzeta*," and with it the desire to lay his own song at the master's feet.

> **Clearly, for love itself**
> **My lady hath**
> **Such high disdain**
> **That I shall go**
> **Back to the**
> **yellow-flowered fields.**

Around the table faces looked at one another, then came back to rest on Gaucelm, alone in the center of the room, arms still outstretched. There was a murmur and slowly the muffled sound of winecups hitting the tablecloth in a crescendo of appreciation. Mazers and saltcellars were joined in the rhythmic applause until it became deafening. It was all he could do to struggle back toward Vidal. His friend was grinning widely and gave him a victory embrace that nearly sent him spinning. He raised his eyebrows.

"An auspicious debut, I'd say."

Gaucelm wanted only to be quiet, to breathe, and to let the moment wash over him. The flush of performing had drained from his face, leaving his hands strangely cold and numb.

A blast of trumpets made his eardrums vibrate, and he winced. The feast was finished. A press of people was coming toward him, clapping him on the shoulder, reaching for his hands, ruffling his hair. Words flew about the room as Vidal introduced him to a stream of guests whose names he instantly forgot. At last the count swam into view.

From the instant Count Raymond grasped his elbow and steered him away from Vidal, he knew the moment he'd been waiting for was about to unfold. He was oddly unprepared. The count was saying: "You have a fresh talent, my boy, and we should like to keep you here as long as you will stay. There will be a palfrey for your use. We shall provide you with something new and suitable to wear. Your quarters will not be the best, unfortunately, but please understand, the house is crowded at the moment. Vidal, I know, will show you around."

Gaucelm wished that he was better stocked with appropriate replies.

Then the count said, "Let us greet Bernard de Ventadour."

At the name, Gaucelm's scalp prickled. With the count's hand heavily upon him, they swept to the high table, where Bernard still sat. Gaucelm could see that the famed troubadour looked ill and a bit twisted. Fastidiously shaven and garbed in a robe of embroidered wool, he wore the look of someone well used to his status as a court treasure. Gaucelm felt a shiver climb up his spine as he bowed low before this man who was the most celebrated troubadour of his time. He cleared his throat and spoke, grasping the great man's outstretched hand.

"I am honored," he said awkwardly.

Bernard de Ventadour greeted Gaucelm with interested eyes and nodded vigorously.

"Your songs have paved my way to Toulouse," Gaucelm began, but the poet nodded before Gaucelm finished his sentence, and it came to him suddenly, after a dreadful pause, that the man had not heard him. He glanced quickly at the count, whose look confirmed it.

Had Bernard had heard nothing, then, of his song? Gaucelm thought his heart would rupture. It had never—not once—occurred to him that his idol might be old, let alone deaf. He had thought of Bernard de Ventadour as someone wholly eternal, like his verses, forever intact like a fly in the heart of amber.

Gaucelm waved him farewell as Count Raymond smoothly propelled him away toward the man with all the chins. Folquet was hissing at Bertrand so audibly that both Gaucelm and the count could hear his words.

"I call yours a Satanic heresy and I call you a follower of the anti-Christ!" Folquet shouted, then turned on his heels and approached Gaucelm with hands outstretched, all smiles and praises.

Gaucelm heard only the mellifluous voice, the rise and fall of cadence. Vidal was right; the man did have an odd way about him. Even as they spoke, Folquet was flailing the air loose-jointedly with downward gestures as though forcing a dog to heel.

"As one who has several verses to his credit," Folquet said, "I am in a position to fully appreciate your triumph." The fleshy handclasp was warm as the man's piggish eyes gleamed into his. "How I envy your talent, my boy."

Count Raymond excused himself, gliding toward Bertrand, who had been left alone.

"I trust we shall hear from you often," Folquet added, then turned abruptly and navigated his way out of the room, churning the air behind him. Gaucelm, rudderless, stared at his feet.

Vidal sighted him, gave a whoop, and motioned him over. Together they walked from the great hall toward the long corridor leading to the common chambers.

Vidal placed a companionable arm around Gaucelm's shoulder. "You were a triumph, my dear Gaucelm. Mark my words, you'll soon be in a position to work miracles with Raymond." But his voice was different, forced, as though he had thought over matters after his first burst of enthusiasm. "Mind you work quickly and don't let him tire of you. A song honoring him would be in order next. Imagine," Vidal went on, "no sooner have you arrived than you are lionized by the Light of the World himself. My advice begs payment, don't you think, ungrateful wretch?"

Gaucelm walked by Vidal's side in silence. As they reached Gaucelm's quarters, Vidal handed back the bow.

"I shall be honored to be your guide through the perilous streets of Toulouse," he said with the grin of a sprite. "Rest up tomorrow and savor your success. The day after, we'll leave after breakfast. Be sharp about it; no lolling around in bed."

Vidal's chatter rang on deaf ears. Gaucelm was not listening at all. He was imagining his father and mother among tonight's spectators, picturing their pride at his singing. He had made good on a wager with himself that he hadn't fully acknowledged: he belonged at court, not in a fabrics shop. He had the count's word. He would cherish this moment forever.

Chapter 3

TOLOSA LA ROSA

Vidal and Gaucelm set out at dawn for the Church of Saint-Sernin.

Toulouse must surely be the most splendid city in the world, Gaucelm thought. Even King Philip Augustus said that Paris couldn't hold a candle to it. Only the night before arriving at Toulouse he had gazed from afar at its rosy-red walls, a belfry high in the north catching the sun's rays. Now he saw the color was no mere trick of light, for it was built of brick.

At this early hour the raucous streets were swarming with students, moneychangers, Spaniards, Northerners, Africans, Orientals, Arabs, Jews. From a board-sided cart hemmed in by passersby, a cluster of men and women curiously clad in black robes were struggling to unload great round bales of wool. They did not seem like ordinary market haulers, and when he raised an eyebrow to inquire, Vidal merely said, "More heretics. Cathars, to be exact." Evidently, they were free to do business as they pleased, which struck Gaucelm as odd, even reprehensible. In Uzerche anyone who disobeyed the Church was punished by death.

The stone-paved streets hummed like the Eastern bazaars of Gaucelm's imagination, the private shops with tables opening onto walkways. Each street was named for its specialty: rue de la Poissonière, where fish were arranged on their stands in silver arcs; rue de l'Epicerie where spices were scooped from barrels and weighed on scales; rue de la Boucherie, the street of butchers; and Moneychangers Row. All seemed to thrive within the red walls of Toulouse.

As they crossed the city, each district exuded its own sounds and smells, the languages and gestures of its trade. In the tanner's quarter animal skins hung on ropes to dry like laundry, still smelling pungently of the uric acid in which they had been cured. As they walked, Vidal recounted how pilgrims arrived by the thousands in early spring to view the relics of the martyr St. Saturninus at the Church of Saint Sernin, and yet even with the city so swollen with visitors, no Jews or Arabs came to any harm. The Jews were left, unmolested, to pray in their own worship house, known as the Schola Judeorum, their strange hats bobbing, phylacteries dangling. The Arabs were sought after as physicians; some even held high positions at court. Count Raymond could be proud of his light-handed rule, unlike his northern counterparts.

"Raymond is clever," said Vidal. "In his battles with the bishop, he has managed to avoid any confrontation that would excite papal wrath. He leaves most of the city's administration to his consuls. That's why they were elected, after all."

Set off by a green tunic gone a little ragged at the seams, Vidal had his bright-eyed urchin's air about him. Gaucelm noticed his little wolf-teeth and stubby hands—not at all the kind of hands that would be accustomed to spanning an octave. Even early in the morning he moved about with odd little gestures; Gaucelm couldn't tell when he was playing the wag and when he was not.

They walked for a while in silence. Abruptly, Vidal put a hand on Gaucelm's shoulder. "You are aware that I am considered quite mad?" His voice had a queer kind of pride in it.

"Is it true that you promised Alphonse of Aragon you would keep his peace in Provence and Montpellier if he gave you a good horse?" Gaucelm asked.

Vidal burst out laughing and then began to sing, "***Drogoman senher, s'ieu agues bon destrier*** ... Is that the one you mean? Where did you hear it?"

"In Uzerche."

"So that small ditty of mine gets around." Vidal seemed particularly pleased with himself. He gave an enigmatic smile as he broke away and bobbed down the cobblestones. With a preliminary jig, he swung into a parody of his own song. "**Hey, Sir, gimme a decent nag!**" Snatches drifted back to Gaucelm: "...**Famous for my warrior's nerve, I rival Roland for bravery**... *e dormis si planamen*... **You shall sleep peacefully, while your enemies grovel before me. Hey Sir! Isn't that worth the price of a nag?**"

Gaucelm caught up from behind and lifted the cap from his friend's head. Vidal went silent.

"What happened?" Gaucelm asked.

Vidal turned. "He was amused. I had already bellowed and begged—why not try boasting? My song finally got his attention."

"Did you get the horse or was the King of Aragon too stingy?"

"He is a monster of miserliness. In short, I came back to Toulouse on foot."

Gaucelm's eyebrows lifted nearly to his scalp.

"Well, most of the way," Vidal amended.

"Where Count Raymond made you rich."

"He rewards my craziness adequately. On balance it's better here than anywhere else I've been. Alphonse's got nothing but trouble on his borders; Lombardy's all chopped into pieces. What you want is a patron whose coffers aren't drained by wars. You have to keep sniffing around. Raymond's tiffs with ecclesiastics may put him in jeopardy, but not in debt—luckily, for the likes of us."

"Does the Count write verses?" Gaucelm asked.

"I will repeat to you in four lines what I know of him in all these years. But I must swear you to absolute silence." Vidal cupped his hand around Gaucelm's ear and whispered:

> **And so the wolf who wants to learn to rhyme**
> **no one can force to say, A, E, I, O, U.**
> **He only licks his chops, since in his very sleep**
> **All he can cry is sheep, sheep, sheep!**

"Amusing, but isn't that a bit unfair, my friend?" Gaucelm pronounced with gravity. "From what you say, Raymond is one wolf who can learn new tricks."

Vidal pulled Gaucelm off the street and sat him down in the shadow of the Saint Sernin church. "You have broached a serious matter," he announced. "The man walks a fine line between heaven and hell. But I know his private sympathies and they are honorable."

Even this elf with rodent's teeth can be pompous, Gaucelm thought. His feet were aching in his soft, mud-spattered shoes.

"Raymond is smart," Vidal continued, "Rome has a watch on him, mind you, but he's not about to be found out. He keeps spies. Take the dwarf you saw last night—nice chap, good juggler. He's in the court's employ as a performer, but he's also a secret informer. He knows every safe house—that is, every heretic's hideout—in the district. He runs messages when there's trouble—and there are always rumblings around here. Someone finds a Cathar cross carved into a tree and you'd think the Devil himself had put in a personal appearance. The Church will insist on exorcising it every time. Now there are rumors of another papal delegation. Commission of inquiry, they call it. Sounds dignified, except the last one was accompanied by an armed escort.

"What sort of messages does he carry?" Gaucelm asked, still thinking of the dwarf.

"No one knows exactly, but you can imagine. Warnings. The dwarf probably watches Joanna pretty carefully."

"The count spies on his own countess?" asked Gaucelm, incredulously.

"She's the daughter of the formidable Eleanor, isn't she? Eleanor of Aquitaine, Eleanor Plantagenet, Eleanor of the thousand lives, mother of Coeur-de-Lion, Queen of England, et cetera, et cetera. And, of course, Joanna's like her mother—an utterly devout Catholic. She is trying to win her husband back to orthodoxy so he won't stand in danger with the Pope. Now you see why Raymond can't exactly afford to be an open book!"

Gaucelm bent down and fished a pebble out of his shoe. Vidal continued, "Keeping a liberal court is one thing. But to have it bruited about up north that a Cathar bishop was guest of honor at one of his soirees is quite another. Raymond has to keep abreast of Eleanor's tale-telling to *that* brood. And don't forget," he said, relishing the addition of insult to injury, "that Rai Mundi's cousin is Philip Augustus, the so-called king who sits in Paris waiting to whisper in the Pope's ear."

Gaucelm was silent. Suddenly Toulouse was not the citadel of harmony that it had seemed. The Count's castle was festering with intrigue. The realization made Gaucelm uncomfortable.

While they sat, the great plaza in front of the church quickened with the racket of vendors setting up the remaining booths. Peasants in casques and rough wool surcoats unloaded the last of their wares from wagons. There was a hush in the air, the not-quite-awakeness of early morning. In mid-construction, the rising trunk of Saint Sernin's many-storeyed bell tower shone in the new sun. Masons were already hauling their ladders and tools to the back of the building where the scaffolding stood. Vidal said at last, "Let's go in. Mass will be over before we've set foot beyond the portals."

"I didn't know it had begun," said Gaucelm, surprised.

The abbey church was dark and vast. As the door bumped shut behind them, a draft of spiciness tickled Gaucelm's nose. Decades of incense had permeated every inch of the cavernous space from flagstone to vault. In the gloom Gaucelm could barely make out the red and beige patterned brick of the transept and the once-brilliant painting over the arches. It was a rich church, as befitted its site, which Vidal explained in a whisper was said to be directly over the tomb of St. Saturninus. His gaze traveled down the long nave and stopped. No one here! No one at all except a white-clothed figure, attended by two others, half-shadowed, performing Mass. The beautifully carved choir stalls were empty.

The two stayed quietly for a while in the empty church. Finally Gaucelm looked over at Vidal. Vidal seemed to be praying. Gaucelm was so overtaken by the sight of this arch cynic on his knees that he couldn't have formed any prayer in his own head if he'd tried. Finally, Vidal got up and cocked an eyebrow in Gaucelm's direction, a signal to leave. "Now you have seen for yourself," he said, "The heretics have descended like a swarm of locusts and picked the church clean."

Outside the church, the market was alive and at the ready, stalls brimming with salt meats, green cheeses, cloth, shoes, pot herbs, beans, apples from the last harvest. Gaucelm welcomed the din. Geese honked in wooden cages, barrel-smiths tapped and hammered, donkeys brayed, and a cart mare shied as a herd of cows trotted in from the rue St. Jacques. His stomach was rumbling.

"Is there a foodshop near? Early Mass always makes me ravenous."

Vidal laughed and poked his friend's protuberance as if it were a ripe melon. They set off across the plaza. "The real world awaits!" he cried, flourishing a hand at a tumble of buildings bordering the square. Vapor rose from the soup vendor's shed where they found fresh-baked pasties. Leaning against the door they ate, surveying the marketplace.

"Now it is time for gaming," Gaucelm ventured, hungering for other pursuits.

"We'll game all you want, if you'll wait," Vidal replied. "But first, I know of a good wine shop on the rue des Changes."

They turned onto a narrow spur of the street.

"It's the only wine shop in Toulouse that is careless enough to give me credit," Vidal laughed.

"I thought the count was generous."

"So is my love for wine."

"You will stay long with him, then?" Gaucelm remarked as they entered. The low-ceilinged room was shaped like the inside of a barrel. Already it bustled with farmers and merchants doing business over pots of watered wine. Vidal flapped a hand in the direction of a bench and table.

"Dear Gaucelm, your career promises well. You will soon be living on your songs. Some enjoy court life. I do not. I like to travel and stir up a little more excitement than Rai Mundi's hive of bees can provide. In short, I am restless."

"But how can you afford it?" asked Gaucelm as they sat down. He dove to loosen the shoes on his aching feet before unpocketing his dice.

"On the contrary, he has slackened his esteemed generosity. Anyway, boredom makes money a secondary matter. At worst, I can always come back. Thankfully, Lady Fortune has not provided me with a wife. Neither am I in love, for a change. So I am free." Vidal put up two fingers; two pots of wine soon arrived.

"But where will you go?"

Meditatively Vidal fished in his pouch for dice, drawing out each one slowly before answering.

"Wherever the road leads. Preferably south. Carcassone, perhaps back to Marseille. But I will probably stay a while longer."

Vidal tossed first. Gaucelm made no move with his dice.

"Raymond's made me comfortable, but so did Barral of Marseille. No, I need some time away from Raymond's court. Folquet and I brawl constantly. I'm forced to sing in praise of Joanna, whose politics I detest. I need to be on the road."

"What about Provence? I've heard the Counts of Forcalquier are rich."

"Rich but scrapping. I'm sick of petty wars. Big expeditions are more my style. No, I'll take leave after Michaelmas. By then I'll know how things stand with Raymond and his promises. Once I've got the goods I'll go, at least as far as Marseille. The climate's better in winter."

"So, if you take up the Cross and go on crusade, you can sail from Marseille?" Gaucelm asked expectantly.

"Only if my business with Barral and, in particular, his Viscountess Azalaïs has settled down. That's the rub." He took a swallow of wine in answer to Gaucelm's puzzled look. "Let's not go into the details," Vidal said, waving them aside. "A little matter of a stolen kiss resulted in my immediate escape from the premises—and my consequent trip to Aragon, thence to Toulouse. And now you know all."

"But Barral took it good-naturedly, or so you implied in your song. "*E.lh baizei a lairo la boca e.l mento*," Gaucelm ventured.

"Aha! You always know more than you let on at first. Soon I shall call you a connoisseur of my work. Well, you are right—or so my poem says. But life said differently."

"We poets are a funny breed, constrained to untruth for beauty's sake," declared Gaucelm.

"Who said that?"

"I just made it up."

"Very pompous. More likely that untruth is put to the service of a single rhyme, which rarely achieves something so elevated as beauty. No, we are not a funny breed, but a paltry one."

Vidal gazed at the table, forgetting that the dice rested mid-game. "Provence. Saying its name makes me love it all the more. When I was there I composed this,

> *Ah! l'alen tire me l'aire*
> *Qu'en sen venire de Proensa*
> *Tot quant es de lai m'agnesa.*
> **I long to breathe the good air**
> **That comes from Provence**
> **For I love all things from there.**

"You sing it as you might sing the praises of a woman," Gaucelm said. "A landscape, though, is not as complicated. If you love it truly, you can sing about it well."

"*Un*like a woman." Forefinger in the air, Vidal interrupted. "Though landscapes never *lie* in the manner of women. You can't make love to the land though you can *proclaim* your love to it. As for me, between the two, I prefer . . ." he studied the dice, then rolled them out with a flourish," . . . both."

"But a woman, though she lies, can still be laid."

"Well said, my dear Gaucelm, you're quite the wit, aren't you?"

And so the conversation continued as evening subsided into dusk.

The two men finally pocketed their dice and left the wine shop, hurrying to the outer walls just in time to watch as the sun burnished burgher's house and hovel alike with its rich gleam.

Vidal turned to Gaucelm. "Let's go to the Chantier quarter, what say you?"

Not certain what that was but ready for anything, Gaucelm cried, "Let's!"

They set off down the silence of the long stone street. Once or twice, Gaucelm stepped up to a window where, unnoticed through the half-open shutters, he could watch a housewife lifting a spit off the fire or putting a trencher down before her husband, while their children quarreled in a corner. Houses leaned like drunkards against the protective city walls. Few lamps lit the rooms, for this was the oldest part of Toulouse, inhabited by transients, small tradesmen, and those who were down on their luck.

They came to the poorest section, a motley collection of shelters. With a low bow, cap in hand, Vidal introduced the newcomer to a part of town for which he obviously had a special affinity. "This is the heart of the Chantier," he said, "where blacksmiths, tinkers, and shepherds once encamped. Now it's a colony of women—widows, many of them. The streets ring all day with the cries of their children and are noisy at night with their customers. Do you follow me?" He looked pointedly at Gaucelm.

"Most are always hurrying from laundry vat to shack. They all know each other's business. They know how it goes with husbands, lovers, children, money, jealousies, employers, and disease. There are rules and there are courtesies."

A whole world ruled by women! Before Toulouse, Gaucelm's imagination had feasted on great nobles, splendid castles, fairs, and open plazas, where princes ruled and merchants traded. But never had he dreamed of an enclave of women who ran their own affairs—for profit. Here in darkened rooms, behind lamplit windows, women traded their bodies for silver.

Lured by the scent of singed meat and smelly lamps, he heard voices, whispers, and laughter inside the shacks. He pictured warm, close bodies rolling together, a glimpse of white flesh by springing candle flame.

Girls, some whose small sharp breasts and coltish limbs proclaimed they had not yet done with growing, lolled at their windows, calling out prices. But each time Gaucelm pulled away from Vidal to look closer, his guide would disapprove.

"Not her, she's an ogress."

"That one's nothing but a bunch of chicken feathers under her shift."

"She's got the clap, take my word!"

Then Vidal pointed to "the Charioteer." This, he explained, was his secret name for her. Barely sixteen or so, a slender brown girl with gazelle thighs, she sat with perfect composure outside her shack, her shoulders outlined high and square like an Egyptian's.

"I'd put my money on her," he said on a whim. Without reflection Gaucelm agreed, happy to be relieved of making a choice.

"How much? And where will I find you . . . after?" Gaucelm asked anxiously.

"Two's enough. Ask for Guilhelma."

Gaucelm watched Vidal skip off into the night and then turned to look at his new acquisition. He came close, as though to inspect her. She sat up straighter. He tipped his palm toward her so that she could see the two coins, a gesture that he hoped would encourage her to make the next move. Duly, she motioned him to follow her inside. *Good*, he thought, *it was the right amount of money.*

The room was tiny and smelled of straw. She lit an oil lamp, one hand sheltering the flickering wick, and bore it to a table so low it might have served as a stool. On it rested a jug and two earthenware pots. Gaucelm's eyes darted into each corner of the room but discovered nothing to sit upon except a straw-filled mattress occupying the middle of the floor. She spread a cover of stained homespun on top of it and here they sat side by side, facing the table. Gaucelm noticed bootmarks and footprints in the packed dirt around the bed and a shiver hiked up his spine.

They were not touching, but he could feel the air between them. She was so thin he could almost smell her bones. She was still sprouting, still only a beginning. An imagined complicity stirred something within him.

She offered him wine, which he drank thankfully, though it had gone sour at the edges. As she bent forward, he caught a whiff of perfume suggesting lemon and with it, a deeper scent of cultivated disdain. She turned toward him expectantly. Her hair was wild. Massed in stiff curls and rank with dried pomade, it rustled like leaves when she moved her head. He longed to comb it out until it was soft.

Mechanically, she began to pull the bliaut over her head. Gaucelm did not utter one word until he caught sight of a diagonal scar running from shoulder to spine.

"What's that?" he asked, with a sudden intake of breath.

Her face did not change; it was as though she had never heard the question. She resumed undressing, but as she bent to remove her worn leather slippers, Gaucelm took her hands and replaced them in her lap.

"How old are you?" he asked.

"I have no idea."

"Were you born in Toulouse?"

"Oh, no!" She shook her head and rustled all her curls. "In Africa."

"Go on," he said. "Tell me. Your parents."

"My mother died when I was born, and I was bought by Arab dealers in Bougie . . ."

"Where's that?"

"I'm not sure. In Africa somewhere. All I remember is being pushed onto a slave ship. There were thirty of us. They said we were bound for Spain. They fed us some sort of mush. There was so little to drink, we had to fight over the water jugs. One of the boys broke into the hold and found only sacks of dried bark and sealed oil urns. Nothing to eat! So, when the boat stopped at Marseille, I got off."

"Just like that?"

She shook her head gravely. "In return for favors," she said.

He could hardly imagine such a thing. "I, too, left home to be free," he said. He eyed the scar again with unease, knowing that "free" in her case meant something quite different. He ran his finger along the angry mark, and saw how the hair on her forearms stood up. On impulse he buried his face in the sweet smell of her neck, nipping the skin so that she giggled with excitement.

How many times, he wondered, had she done this before? He knew next to nothing about being with a woman. Fear seized him. He was conscious of his own sweat as he pulled fiercely at his britches. She drew the rough chemise over her head, the wings below her shoulders springing out like taut bows across her muscular back. She was not pretty. Gaucelm watched her from behind, transfixed by her simple gestures.

She was his to do with as he liked. Suddenly fired, he leapt into her from behind, the way Vidal said these women liked. He turned her frontwise and then rammed her hard. Her eyes were closed, for which, when he remembered later, he was grateful.

When the storm in him subsided, he fell back onto the mattress cover. Curled up, knees to chest, he was faintly aware that a piece of straw was poking the underside of his shin, but too drowsy to do anything about it. A potent odor rose from the straw mattress, making him sneeze. His mind drifted with satisfaction above the rich compost of human desire beneath him. His member reawakened, riding above his thighs.

"How much for the second time?" he asked, cocking his head to look at her. It was difficult to sound experienced while in such a ridiculous posture, propped in this manger like some barnyard animal. She hooted at the question.

"With me you always get a bargain, at least two for the price of one! For all I care you can fuck yourself senseless—unless there's a line at my door."

Gaucelm sat bolt upright, gathered his britches and hugged them to his chest. He stared at her in disbelief, open-mouthed at her foul declaration. Then he collected his shoes and the rest of his clothing, while she busied herself with whatever it was these girls did to prevent children. He caught a whiff of vinegar and from the corner of his eye saw her crook a knee and insert a piece of cloth inside her. His head reeling, he pulled on his clothes and left without a word.

Gaucelm walked along the echoing streets of the old quarter, reliving it again and again. *Dieus*, a vision of her kept coming back to him: the almond-dark eyes, widening, narrowing, the silence of her lids closing, the neat fringe of black lashes.

He felt even now a residue of shame, as though he had used a battering ram to open a door which already stood unlocked.

Suddenly he thought that he was going to faint. His stomach was churning, empty, acidic; he hadn't eaten since the morning's pasties on the square and felt sick. He reached for his purse and realized, with dread, that it was gone. He bent over in the street, retching, sweat dripping from his brow. The little fox! Like a child lost on the street of whores, he tried to remember the name of Vidal's putana but could not.

His insides convulsed, he spat out spoiled wine, and slowly a name formed on his lips: *Guilhelma*. He dragged himself down the street. The oil lamps had been snuffed out so the shacks had no eyes to light his way. Stepping up to the nearest window ledge, he shouted: "Where can I find Guilhelma?" A voice in the darkness yelled back: "Three down. The door with the vines hanging over it."

Gaucelm struggled on, his head spinning, until he saw the outline of twigs above a lintel. Too weak to knock, he slumped in the doorway and passed out.

At dawn Vidal almost fell over him. He would never have recognized this roll of soggy brown tunic had it not been for Gaucelm's familiar shoes.

"God's eyes, Mother of Mary, and I'll be damned!" He tested Gaucelm with a jester's toe. When there was no response, concern coursed through him, and he wrested the sleeping head from its entanglement of hood and tunic. Gaucelm opened his eyes resentfully, feeling the bilious lining of his mouth. His head pounded like a hundred hooves thundering across his field of vision.

"Did she beat you, or what? Are you drunk? Speak, man!"

"Hungry," Gaucelm muttered and coughed.

"You look like a sorry beggar. You'll catch a fever, lying there in your own piss. Come, Guilhelma will fix you up—is there any gruel left?" he called into the shack.

Someone came forth in a thick swish of skirts and removed his tunic. With a pair of arms hooked under each armpit, Gaucelm felt himself being dragged through the doorway and deposited on a stool in front of a table. His head fell to his arms as he struggled to make sense of the evening's events, how much to tell Vidal, and how much to consign to his own remorse.

"Look for his purse." Guilhelma spoke like a provincial.

With an expression of disgust Vidal fished amongst his damp clothing. "Gone," he said.

"The little bitch always knows the newcomers. She can't resist. You'd think word would get round and they'd stay away from her, but there's always a greenhorn in the lot. Full of bad wine, too, I'll wager."

After two bowls of gruel and a jug of water, Gaucelm felt more like himself. In the lamplight, Guilhelma Monja slowly came into focus. Round and sturdy, she moved with a competence older than her years, yet her face was rosy as a girl's. Was she seventeen, perhaps? She wore her heavy, dark hair knotted loosely at the base of her neck. She leaned over him to take up his plate and he sensed the abundance of her breasts, could smell the wheatflour deep in the skin of her forearms. No, he thought, not a girl. No matter what her age, a woman.

Guilhelma's broad face framed intense, deep-set brown eyes beneath brows that seemed ready to take flight at the slightest change of expression. Her nose had a proper Roman bump; the chin was straight in profile but pouched like a child's when she bent her head forward. Her mouth was plump, dimpled on either side, and for some reason that Gaucelm could not have explained for a whole kingdom of lost purses, the sight of her made him feel completely restored.

"No harm done!" said Vidal cheerfully, clapping him on the back.

"By whose measure?" Gaucelm grumbled. He was stiff from lying on stone for so long. Vidal's "Time to be off!" seemed annoyingly premature. He had no wish to be anywhere but here. Being fed gruel, and watching Guilhelma as she moved about her small house would have kept him happy until nightfall.

Once outside, Vidal was like a drummer in the dawn, beating out an *estampida* – an ancient dancing tune whose infectious rhythm Gaucelm had known since childhood – and coming down hard on the vowels.

"**KalENdaya MAya, ni fuelhs de FAya**," he sang happily, executing little steps between verses.

"Does she always make you break into song?" Gaucelm asked, staggering along the cobblestones, barely erect.

Vidal ignored him and continued to sing, "**Ni chanz d'AUzelh, ni flors de glAYa!**"

Da-dee-dee-DA-ya, dee-dee-da-YA-da, Gaucelm continued in his head. Then over the bump—*pros domna guaya*—he loved the refrain *chanz d'auzelh*, how the words hummed against his teeth like moths against a candleflame, sizzling wings of zzz's, then the breathless continuo of rapid lines—one, two, coming—and the final, perfect click of rhymed finish.

"*Non es quem playa*," Gaucelm sang aloud in spite of himself.

Fog shrouded the river in pink, steamy light as they approached Saint Sernin and the empty marketplace. Their voices were shrill on the damp air. With the sun barely edging above the city's rim, they roused the citizens of Toulouse with their song, their heels marking out rhythms with a swift, metallic beat on the cobblestones.

They turned the corner into the main square and the singing stopped. Gaucelm's heart gave a mighty lurch; Vidal let out a groan of disgust. Before them, three severed heads, oozing blood, had been set upon pikes. Two were ragamuffins, their black hair matted, their foreheads smeared with mud. The third, raised slightly higher than the others and staring out blankly, was the sightless head of Bertrand, the Cathar heretic.

Chapter 4

PARATGE

Heretic! As the years passed and the new century approached, this word would ring out over the gentle slopes of Languedoc with increasing frequency.

"Heretic!" whispered the villagers on market day, barely audible above the shuffle of wooden clogs and the flap and squawk of hens. Heretic! clanged the bells at dusk, from Albi to Foix. The word became the very currency of fear, fought about and gambled over in wine shops and inns, spoken in brothels and shouted in street fights. Like the drone of cicadas at midday, rumors rose to a pitch.

"The Pope's cracking down," said the priest.

"A sure omen of the Apocalypse," said the herdsman.

"It's nothing less than the final wrath of God," said the plowman.

"A bad sign for our Raymond," said the weaver.

But in spite of portents, prophesies, and occasional panic, the century turned, and the year 1200 was rung in without incident.

One summer morning in 1201, nearly six years after his first sight of a severed head on a stick—a head that had nodded greetings, said grace, bestowed praises only a few nights before—Gaucelm awakened in a sweat, his heart beating like a trapped bird, the eyes of Bertrand staring at him in the dark.

Following the martyrdom of the Cathar elder, Toulouse had gone suddenly silent. Heretics no longer preached in the streets. Count Raymond retreated into his court like a beetle into its carapace. The bishop was triumphant. In time, the horror of Bertrand's death was forgotten by most. But often over the years it came upon Gaucelm suddenly, rousing him from sleep. He saw the head on its pike, and heard Vidal's breath escape in disgust: "Those papal thugs really mean business this time!"

Gaucelm's scalp prickled now, just as it had then. He felt curiously haunted still by Bertrand's presence, the long white fingers, the oval nails. At such times as this he longed for his mother and the tisane she would bring to his bedside as a boy when he woke up crying from a nightmare. He had grown from a timid weed into a robust figure now held in Count Raymond's high esteem. Yet he sometimes caught himself in childhood reveries, longing for his mother's soothing touch.

He felt that he alone was prey to the vision of Bertrand. He had become, over time, consciously alert, watchful, while those around him—including Raymond—chose to ignore the rumors running rampant throughout the countryside. And so, in those pre-dawn hours when his fears doubled themselves in the darkness, words began to take shape. Slowly, they formed the start of a long composition that quieted him. The longer he held the song in his head, the less Bertrand's eyes haunted him.

In his years at Toulouse, Gaucelm had traversed the orbit of Raymond's power, at first behaving like a subject—a serf who found himself by good fortune in the count's magic fiefdom—then becoming more like a son. Increasingly, they had spent time together touring Raymond's estates and visiting neighboring courts, and with each day he saw the count in action, Gaucelm had come to love him even more. He couldn't have said just when the bond settled down over his shoulders like a protective cloak, imbuing him with a sense of Raymond's confidence. But he remembered when he first heard Raymond use the word *paratge*, acknowledging an equality that transcends rank, a recognition of merit in the other.

It was the autumn after Vidal had left. Gaucelm emerged with other worshippers from early morning chapel after a resoundingly dull service. The trees were already half-stripped by late fall winds, and Gaucelm felt his mind floating in a chilly blur. The gloom of winter was approaching; he hated that endless, dark season.

Raymond caught up with him. "Old Odo did drone on and on. That refrain of yours kept entering my head: '**vos vei acordatz totz, los pros e-ls malvatz**'—*that you grant to everyone whether they are worthy or unworthy*. You say it so much better than the boring priests."

"It's not church language," Gaucelm mumbled. "It's the priest, Odo."

Raymond rambled on, not having expected a reply. "Perhaps it's because the church has never learned the meaning of paratge."

"What?" asked Gaucelm, gripped by his winter-bound mood.

"Come, sit here for a moment. Let the others race to breakfast." Raymond motioned him to a stone bench. Gaucelm felt cold about the ears and noticed that the count, as usual, wore no head covering.

Paratge, Raymond explained, was a quality he sought in each of his lieges from foot-soldier to manservant. But in all his dealings, he had found it most readily in Gaucelm, his troubadour.

Gaucelm's attention surfaced suddenly, almost audibly, like a sea creature breaking through a crust of ice.

"It is your phrase '*acordatz totz*'," Raymond said. "It urges us to reconcile differences, to encourage generosity and open-handedness. *You* have that same gallantry, something many others strive to learn, this open-mannered way. It has nothing to do with station. If I could teach it, I would make it my prime legacy."

Gaucelm sat in awkward silence though he felt his insides leap like a torch. Looking at Raymond, he thought, *Here is a veritable king, and he considers* **me** *gallant?*

"No one is in a better position than I," Raymond continued, "to know that true aristocracy is of merit, not of rank, or riches, or even power. Furthermore," he paused, both arms outstretched, "paratge keeps people and tradition alive, always absorbing new teachings, new men, new ideas. Without it, you kill off what you value most."

Raymond gathered his robes. "Can you imagine what Odo would make of all this? At least you understand. You *do* understand, do you not?"

Gaucelm merely nodded, at a loss for what to say in the wake of Raymond's impromptu declaration of trust. The Count gave him a thwack on the belly. "What I like about you is your way of drinking things in. Let's go and get a scrap of breakfast."

It was then they cemented their brotherhood of like-mindedness. The two of them, so far apart in age, class, and experience, found themselves warmed at the same fire.

From that day on, Gaucelm knew he had the freedom to compose and sing as he liked. He thrived in the light of Raymond's favor. Along the way he had a crack at the usual adventures and games, song tournaments, prizes. He even collected his leaden pilgrim's badge and set off for Compostela in northwestern Spain, but along the way he found the country of the Gascons to be rich in bread, wine, and garrulous women, and he left the other pilgrims well before the Pyrenées. His exploits on the way home were a tribute to all he'd been taught by Vidal, that antic lover of life's pleasures.

The blank pages of Gaucelm's life filled in rapidly: women, fore and aft. Launched under Vidal's tutelage, Gaucelm liked them every possible way: hard and full of muscle and fight; nut brown, round and fat, the kind he could sink into and wonder at all there was inside; thin ones he chewed and spat out like chicken bones; young girls already half gone with drink and too many babies at home. The taste of women was never enough. If his blood was up, he liked to take them in fields rather than cities, where they paid toward the rent of their miserable shacks. There had been bad ones as well, crones who left a sour taste afterward and made him sick to his stomach.

He learned about women's curious ways, how they brewed decoctions from willow leaves, or pennyroyal, or rue, how they drank a cup of the evil-smelling stuff to prevent conception.

Near Bayonne there had been a smooth brown girl with a golden braid to her waist, and so slippery inside that he came hard again and again until she screamed that she was pregnant, and then went limp. She had begun to bleed, and cried. He'd stopped and put his arm around her and given her coins from his pouch. But she'd refused the money and lay there panting so desperately, he was afraid she would bleed to death. He stayed with her all night, wrapping her in his cloak. By morning she had gone.

There had been other journeys. Two summers after Vidal left, Gaucelm, impatient for the road, had gone north to campaign with Arthur, the young Duke of Brittany. But forty days in the mud had caused him to set off for Paris as soon as his obligation was over. In Paris he met the duke's uncle, the fabled Richard the Lionheart. They spent much time together; as a lark they had even composed verses in tandem.

"Whose *is* it, then—yours or mine?" Coeur-de-Lion had asked, referring to the tenson of which they'd each contributed a stanza.

"Mine," Gaucelm had sung back, "since I finished last. He who ends it, keeps it."

"No, mine," replied Richard in clever quatrains, "since if I can capture the English crown, I can certainly claim a brace of doggerel verses!"

The light-hearted side of the famed warrior's nature won Gaucelm's affection, and he was sorely tempted to accompany Lionheart in his ongoing tussle with King Philip of France. But in the end, his yen for Languedoc tugged at him. Northern mud had given him a new appreciation of sun-blasted Toulouse.

He had missed Guilhelma. After their first meeting, she was the only woman he had frequented in the Chantier. Now he found himself often savoring little things to recount to her. On his trips he stored away incidents in his memory to tell her about later: *I must remember that for Guilhelma—she'll be amused.* He found himself longing for her comforts, their talks and meals and nights together.

The sweet curve of her mouth with dimples on either side haunted him. She had entered his songs: he called her "amia." They'd trade stories about Vidal, how he taught her to toss dice. He'd said to her, "Anyone who can count can play and a woman can count as well as any man, so why shouldn't it be a woman's game too?" Somehow her anecdotes about his friend made Gaucelm miss him less. Guilhelma became his refuge, companion, lover. In her he found a listener. Gradually he got into the habit of singing to her a verse or two of a song he was working on and she, able to keep the strophes in her memory, would prompt him when he forgot the rhymes.

One night after Gaucelm's return from Brittany, Guilhelma invited him to come for a proper meal. "A *week* hence? Why not sooner?" he'd asked, unaware that it would take some days' worth of customers to furnish her pot with the meat and vegetables needed for a proper stew.

Her week was prosperous. When Gaucelm arrived on the appointed day, a plump hen sat in the cauldron and there were apples enough to roast for dessert. She had baked a leavened bread at the Chantier's communal oven, and it had come out high and golden as a cathedral's dome.

"I can cook a banquet's worth," she said when he expressed surprise at the feast she had prepared. "I can even chop wood for that matter. My father was a woodcutter."

"Where?" Gaucelm asked, curious now about where she'd grown up.

"Near Alès. Do you know it? A market town, in the Marquisat of Provence."

"In Provence," Gaucelm mused. "Yes, I must have passed through it with my father, then."

He did not wait to begin on the apples. With his knife busy and his left hand full of bread, Gaucelm's thoughts turned to a question that had been nagging him. He blurted out, "What's it like . . . having so many men come to you? How did you happen to . . ."

Guilhelma was perfectly matter-of-fact. "What else can you do for a living if you're a woodcutter's daughter in a poor fiefdom? For Andussa's lands are not rich. There are five of us in my family—my parents and two brothers. My father and my older brother were in the woods all day long. My mother worked on the estate, pulling roots in the open fields. We ate turnips and onions in the lean months when even bread was scarce. Once, all of us in turn spent an entire winter spitting blood. My mother and I made infusions and poultices from plants when we thought my younger brother was going to die; he grew so thin and white. But I was always robust."

She stopped short, surprised at Gaucelm's interest. After all, *his* father was a merchant, Vidal had said, and a wealthy one. Gaucelm had even been schooled in Latin. But he leaned forward, urging her to go on.

"Ever since I was old enough to cry when my parents quarreled," she continued, "and knew my brothers would leave home as soon as they could, I wanted to go to Uzès. So I did, a year after my menses began. I wasn't disappointed in the place. It's a thriving town with a great market. My older brother took me there and found me lodgings with a weaver. The weaver was poor, too, but his wife was kind and she took special interest in me. As for employment . . . well, I had to pay my board somehow. So I explored the town and discovered the shack quarter. It was easy. The women there were a good sort, pressed for a living like me—laundresses, cooks, unmarried all of them, some with an infant to feed or an old relative to support. Most had family in the neighborhood. One had a lame leg; another was weakened by child-pox and couldn't find work in the fields. But by and large they were a healthy lot."

"And you learned . . . from them, how to . . ." he stumbled.

"Yes," she said, "how to use rags soaked in vinegar and when to start counting after the bleeding-days. Soon they were coming to me for my magical potion."

"What's *that*?"

She gave him an uncertain look as though weighing whether or not to tell him. "I add mentha," she said. "That way it's sweet-smelling. Mint, you see, stops the seed. There are many such plants."

Gaucelm nodded. A frown crossed her forehead. "Some of the girls from the country are so ignorant!" She threw up her hands and leaned back in the chair. "One told me, 'Drink the man's urine before, and it will prevent conception.' Nonsense! I know what works and what doesn't. So far I've never had to use wormwood—after the fact. The worst, though, is hazelwort. It poisoned Artema, killed her and the babe."

Gaucelm turned aside. He was unsure whether he wanted to hear more, but she continued.

"Maybe I was lucky," she continued, "I made out well from the start. When there was money sometimes, I got a chicken, a length of wool, or a dozen eggs instead. And the stories! They were almost payment in themselves. Some of my men were traders, merchants. Uzès is a crossroads, you see. I learned about the world from them, and they showed me what they wanted in the straw. It was no book education, but I learned everything I needed to know—and more."

"More?"

"Any common putana knows how to spread her legs, but that barely pays the rent! Beyond that, it's what you . . . well, what you . . . *devise*. It's the extras that keep their interest up."

"And their purses open."

Guilhelma gave him a mysterious look and bit her lip. "You could say I learned my job well."

"Did you ever see your parents again?" Gaucelm asked.

"I've had no news of them since the day I left."

"What about your brothers?"

"I heard tell they joined d'Andussa's forces, from a man whose business had taken him through Alès. I never saw him after that night."

Gaucelm had never known a single thing about any woman before Guilhelma, with the exception of his mother, of course. Now he sat opposite this woman with a history all her own.

"How did you come to Toulouse, then? And why did you leave Uzès?"

"I wanted to see more of the world than a market town. I'd heard Toulouse was a great capital, with many cathedrals. So when a group of pilgrims came through on their way to Spain, I joined them. I set up shop in the Chantier right away. And it's brought me more than I expected to see in a lifetime. Here, we meet men from Raymond's court, like you. Uzès was mean pickings by comparison – mostly poulterers, vegetable dealers, shophands, an occasional tradesman. Toulouse regulations are strict, though. I have no quarrel with the city fathers—we call them the wise consuls—but they make sure we're watched, you know. Still, when they arrest us our clients bail us out—men of experience, they are—men of all professions and colors who've roamed the world and know what life's about. Men like Vidal, men like you."

"And some, like me, come back?"

"Some, but usually it's in, out, and up! Though many a time I've grown to like a man's face and wished for more."

Gaucelm fiddled with the last bite of his apple, holding it aloft on his knife. He fixed his gaze on the morsel, not quite daring to look at Guilhelma. For the first time during the meal he had no response. In his mind's eye he saw them all, a long parade of men winding in and out of her room, one dragging his shirt over his head, another fastening his breeches and pulling up his boots. Did they leave her lying on the straw, bed-clothes crumpled under her, the dark strands of her hair spread across her face?

He let his knife drop onto the table and got up. He stood with his back to Guilhelma and in a voice unlike his usual one, he said, "What if I want you for mine alone?"

It was Guilhelma's turn to be silent, but only for a heart's beat. Then on impulse she pushed back her stool and went to Gaucelm, folding her arms around his ribs, resting her head between his shoulder blades. "Of all the men who've said that to me, there's none I've wanted to answer . . . except you." She drew him around so that she could speak to his eyes. "Only you," she said again. "But then . . . what would I do for a living?"

Irritated by the question, Gaucelm pushed her an arm's length from him. "What do other women do? Could you not be a midwife or a wise woman, with your knowledge of simples and herbs?"

"The little I know would never suffice," she said. "It requires years of experience, and before that, an apprenticeship. Have you noticed," she asked coyly, "how midwives and herbalists are mostly married women? Besides, I'd never make near enough to keep body and soul together."

He sat down at the table again and stared at his knife. "You're a practical woman, Guilhelma—I admire that. You know how I live from season to season on Raymond's bounty. Aside from the suit of clothes and the horse he provides, I have only a viol and a lute to call my own." He picked up his knife, speared the last piece of apple and ate resignedly. "I suppose I can lay no claim to you, although I hate the sound of the truth when it interferes with what I covet."

He turned in his seat to look at her. A swag of raven hair had slid from her knot and rested on her shoulder. She smiled at him, and it was a smile of such sweetness that he rose and gathered her fiercely in his arms, making her laugh and plead for mercy at the same time. Instead, he carried her to the bed.

It was not yet daylight, but in his quarters the very air seemed to grow thinner in preparation for the first rays of dawn. Gaucelm knew he would not fall asleep again before morning began its climb along the stone wall behind him, gradually picking out each fine thread in the tapestry which hung above his head. Much was on his mind.

His nights had, finally, been freed of terrors. Instead of Bertrand's unseeing countenance, he dreamed contentedly of Guilhelma. He could almost sniff the bread she would bake for him in the Chantier oven, making the whole street smell delicious as she carried it back to her shack. In the three years since their first dinner together, she had become more of a mainstay than he was willing to admit.

Gaucelm still thought of himself as a man of the road, a troubadour who sang and journeyed—and whored—as he pleased. That was just the problem.

Thanks to his travels, Gaucelm's songs had spread his fame beyond Toulouse. When his old companion-in-verse Richard Lionheart was shot dead by a Limousin crossbow two years ago, Gaucelm's planh, "***Ai, Dieus!* what sorrow and what grievous loss** . . ." was sung everywhere, north and south alike. So in Toulouse, as his work and reputation grew he had less time for the Chantier. In truth he became uneasy about anyone from the castle discovering him there. It was all very well for a man just passing through—a traveler—but he had his future to think of, and that future was to be at court. He belonged to Raymond's retinue; Guilhelma belonged to the shacks.

Her very name unsettled him in some way. He had come to feel, in spite of himself, that this was some sort of sign. Her name, the scent of her hair, her very presence engulfed him.

There was danger in Toulouse. He could not ignore it. He had been struggling with a long poem. As the plan of it took shape, whole phrases came to him, dropping into place like flagstones set into a floor. Still, doubts sometimes bit at his heels.

Sighing and pulling the bedclothes about his ears, he asked himself for the thousandth time: who was he to be alarmed, when no one else seemed to be? What was he to the Cathars, that he should defend them? And who was he, an unbeliever, to complain about the excesses of the Church Triumphant?

That he loved this city was, he supposed, reason enough to send out warning signals. He understood all too well how things stood with its citizens. Unlike country folk, the people of Toulouse had learned to withstand the winds of change; they were no chicken-brained peasants! The city was becoming so accustomed to the Pope's fits of outrage, they heard them as one hears whispers or the faint sound of matins in half-sleep. Besides, everyone knew the faces of these so-called heretics—they were as familiar as friends. And it was precisely in such familiarity, Gaucelm reasoned, that the danger to the city lay: it had grown used to heretics.

Unbeknownst to Gaucelm in his early morning reveries, the citizens of Toulouse awoke that very day to the sight of four heads reduced to charred bone on a pyre set up in the square. When news reached him, he sprang into action. Gaucelm did not have to see them for himself; he had lived with the skull of Bertrand in his dreams for years. Now the germ of his song took on a life of its own. He set to work in earnest, spending whole days in the practice room he once shared with Vidal.

Gaucelm had not attempted a piece on this scale before. The work, which he secretly called "*Eretria deis Preires*"—"Heresy of Priests"—was ambitious. It was slow going, but nothing had given him such a surge of excitement since the day he'd arrived in Toulouse, a boy unwashed behind the ears and ignorant of politics. He'd grown accomplished at his role, at wooing and charming the court with his ballads and cansons, his pretty aubades. None of these were inconsequential, but he had played the courtier long enough. Moreover, his subject was now at hand. It was time to try something different: a political poem.

At first he had cast about in his head for models. All he could fish from memory was the blood-curdling *sirventés* of Bertran de Born's that ended "***e dijas li que trop estai en patz.***" How could he echo in his own song the majesty of that ringing line "**and tell him he has lived in peace too long**"? It was exactly what he wanted for his new "*Eretria deis Preires*" although the subject wasn't war, but priests.

If only he could ask Bernard de Ventadour for help. The poor man's heart had failed him again a year earlier, causing half of his face to sag, but leaving his hands free of affliction. Gaucelm would see him sitting for hours in the practice room, not quite playing but, watching his fingers on the strings of his viol, first pursed and bunched, then splaying out, marching across the lines of tightly drawn gut. *At least he could still strum a continuo*, Gaucelm thought. His fingers were capable of dancing that rounded motion which always reminded him of someone plucking flowers near their roots.

Because of his deafness Bernard spoke little, but when he did, he uttered the most banal sentences with such force, he seemed to make up in effort what he lacked in substance. Afterward his eyes would close momentarily, the left side of his mouth would droop, and he would enter a world of imaginings beyond the reach of ordinary mortals.

Eventually, having wrestled alone with the coblas for a week, Gaucelm went to the elderly troubadour for advice. Bernard responded like a man saved from drowning. His shrunken figure sat upright and seemed to gain strength for the first time in Gaucelm's memory. Like a bird fluffing out damp feathers, he took on new life.

By mouthing words in an exaggerated way, Gaucelm found he could "feed" Bernard the lines that needed work. "***Dels bels digz honratz/ e-1 bens dirs es vertatz*** . . ." Gaucelm mimed.

Bernard paused for a moment and then clapped his hands. "Wonderful!" he said slowly. "well-fashioned . . . opening . . . strophe . . . hear again." Gaucelm complied, and Bernard hunched forward, repeating, "Well formed . . . even perfect lines . . . require proper . . . placement. Finely-tuned words . . . most suitable . . . tornada."

". . . ***bens dirs es vertatz***? But that's how I begin!"

"Try placing . . . at end."

Gaucelm put off Bernard's suggestion for as long as possible. He dreaded that the old master song writer was right, because the change would unravel his entire poem. He'd be damned if he'd see his "*Eretria*" turned upside-down in the blink of an eye. Going over the main themes had become his delight, his secret obsession. He had stitched them together, piece by piece, the way a seamstress would construct a great quilt. So at first he balked at each suggestion, but held his tongue until the change sat well with him. All the while, he traipsed back and forth to Bernard's quarters with fresh ideas, fresh versions, fresh problems. The more technique he acquired, the more Bernard flourished, and the two quickly became inseparable. In the end he always came to Bernard's view, and now with his mentor's help, Gaucelm labored on the new tornada. He reversed the lines. Then, slowly, he mastered the intricate rhyming of the coblas.

"It should be . . . like weaving," Bernard said, "whole sense . . . caught up in . . . last turn of phrase."

When Gaucelm finally got it right, Bernard nodded his head in approval, and the old man took him by the hand. "Immense talent . . . my boy. You have . . . the gift. What . . . do with it?"

Gaucelm was overwhelmed—the praise he had longed for six years ago had come at last. He was so flooded with joy that Bernard had to repeat the question.

"What . . . you *do* with it?" he asked again.

Gaucelm, recovering, was astonished by the query. "Do with what?" he stumbled. He found himself focusing on a wrinkle in the old man's neck where the autumn sun illuminated a single long, white hair. "But, just what I've been doing—compose. Refine the art." He bent to repeat the words directly before the deaf man's eyes. But Bernard sat motionless, poised for him to continue.

Working his mouth so that the words emerged like big letters, Gaucelm pronounced, "I would like to be the best trobar of all. Next to you." Bernard still did not react, as if he hadn't yet heard what he was waiting for.

"Maybe better, perhaps . . ." Gaucelm took a breath before he said, "than you."

"Good," Bernard nodded, satisfied. "You are . . . capable. But there is risk . . . a danger . . . not to audience, but you . . . composing courtly verse . . . You must go . . . beyond . . . old conventions."

"But this . . ."

"You . . . difficult subject . . . *Eretria*." But . . . new forms as well. What means . . . to be finder, trobar?" Gaucelm looked puzzled, as though someone had given him a riddle without an answer.

"One day," Bernard went on, "you . . . discover what is . . . be a poet." He glanced again at Gaucelm to make sure he was listening. "A *poet*," he emphasized, in a deaf man's loud voice, "not someone good . . . at rhyming verses. You already know . . . difference."

Chapter 5

L'ERETRIA DEIS PREIRES

On the thirteenth of September, legates of the Holy Father entered Toulouse and forcibly removed Aymar, a Cathar priest. The warning was clear: Aymar had been banished by papal interdict after refusing to take an oath of loyalty to the Church. The Cistercian abbot who headed the Papal delegation was none other than Folquet de Marseille.

Until now it had been a puppet show. The hands that stole away Cathar lives, that stacked the faggots and struck the flint which caused the pyre and its Cathar victims to burn—those hands belonged to no one anybody knew. Not in Toulouse, that city whose citizens enjoyed the advantages of their own Raymond's enlightened rule.

Where would a person even begin to look for someone to blame? Toulouse was a city run by powerful burghers who had forged their right to worship as they pleased, and were famously protective of that freedom. Toulouse was a city in which even women could take part in government elections. And if their Raymond was sometimes tolerant to a fault, it could never be said that the citizens of Toulouse weren't open to fresh ideas.

But on that brisk day in the autumn of 1201, the hands revealed themselves, the strings were visible at last, and the puppet show was over.

Oblivious to court chatter, Gaucelm worked in a blind fever. An immediate request from Raymond had put him in a dither. The count wanted something new and he wanted it tonight. *Impossible*, Gaucelm thundered silently. He hated composing under pressure: it gave him stomach gas. He felt indignant, like a viol maker commanded to assemble an instrument in a day; he could fit the parts together, but how could he be sure that it would play properly?

Gradually, as Bernard's high regard came to mean so much to him, Gaucelm realized that he was growing tired of pleasing Raymond. When he had first arrived in Toulouse, all he could think about was gaining a place in Raymond's court. Then he wanted to do everything with the count, to lead the life of luxury and adventure that he had dreamed of. He had taken every advantage of those opportunities yet still felt dissatisfied. As he grew close to Bernard, he realized that his cansons had always been what mattered most.

What did Raymond know about composing, after all? Could he even imagine that his troubadour had something really provocative up his sleeve? Now Gaucelm had to cram the tornada into finished meters as though all it required was a touch here and there, a little polishing.

No longer able to bear his own cramped quarters, Gaucelm wandered fitfully into the great hall, where at least there was some space to compose and fume and stamp out rhymes. The presence of others was exactly what he needed; here, the medley of musicians and housefolk attending to their duties drew off some of his annoyance.

He was surprised to see Bernard there so early. He sat in his accustomed chair with a lute on his lap, beckoning Gaucelm to attend him. He mouthed the words "full accompaniment tonight," then pointed to a pile of instruments near his feet: harp, mandore, psalterion, rebec, and a shiny new six-string viol. Gaucelm had no idea what to make of this.

"We . . . play my lark song . . . tonight," Bernard announced importantly.

The "*Lauzeta*," of course! Gaucelm clapped his hands in delight. Bernard was no longer an old man clinging to the past, repeating his well-worn favorites as though to reassure himself that he had not yet passed into history. His face was like a child's, full of anticipation. But wait, Gaucelm thought, if the "*Lauzeta*" required a full accompaniment, perhaps he ought to play his "*Eretria*" on the Moorish guitar instead of his viol. Gaucelm preferred the Moorish guitar's rounded back—so like a woman's buttock—to the slabsided Latin version. Distractedly, he bent over the pile of instruments and picked the one that pleased him.

"In Folquet's honor," Bernard continued. Gaucelm nodded absently, his hands settling on the string of the instrument. Then he heard Bernard's words, as he so often did, in echo.   "*Folquet*?" He wheeled around full-face before Bernard. "Folquet the Fat?" He was astonished. "He is coming to dine tonight?"

It was Bernard's turn to nod; he did so expectantly, pleasure registering in his expression. Clearly no one had thought to bring the old man up to date on the abbot's politics.

Gaucelm turned away, muttering, "What's that pious bag of air doing back here? Why has no one told me? What is Raymond *up* to?" Unthinking, perturbed, he faced the old troubadour. "I thought he'd been kicked upstairs to some high-and-mighty diocese . . . wasn't it Le Thoronet? I heard he'd even *married* . . ." It all tumbled out too rapidly for Bernard, who raised a hand. Gaucelm, seeing a "what?" forming on the poet's face, placed an impulsive forefinger over the man's mouth, forestalling Bernard's request for an explanation.

"You are playing the "*Lauzeta*" then? Good!" Gaucelm repeated, changing the subject, enunciating brightly, forming the words for Bernard slowly once again.

"I . . . lead apprentices," the older man corrected. Gaucelm's hand slid down to his elder's shoulder, which he patted with affectionate respect. Acknowledging the small attention, Bernard reached up to clasp Gaucelm's hand in his own. Gaucelm, consumed with impatience and curiosity about Folquet's reappearance, merely gave the bony shoulder an extra pat. A hasty misgiving about the political repercussions his song might have flown though his head, but he did not dwell on it. Instead, he took comfort in knowing that Raymond, from long experience in adversity, had become so clever at launching exotic and conflicting views with such soothing finesse that court objections were nearly always overcome. Raymond would encourage rather than quell the prospect of a little heated discussion, as long as it remained civilized and didn't get out of hand.

Gaucelm began to rehearse in earnest. He would need another run-through with the young jongleur he had trained to sing the partimen sections; he could finish the accompaniment for his tornada afterward. He practiced until the chapel bell rang vespers.

Early autumn sun streamed slantwise through the arched stone windows of the hall. A glance out at the furiously smoking chimney of the kitchen indicated that preparations inside were in full swing. The great hall was being transformed into a banquet room as houseboys spread rushes on the floor; trestles were dragged out and set up in a great semicircle and the boards were covered with white linen. A bearer carried in the ceremonial nef of salt.

Gaucelm felt the familiar flicker of apprehension. Even after all these years he sensed tremors of anxiety before performing. Doing so for Folquet only made him more nervous.

Dear Raymond, Gaucelm thought. Recently he'd seemed so—aged. But Folquet's presence tonight certainly proved that Raymond still relished walking the fine line between liberty and perdition. Doubtless he thought it would be enlightening at best—politic at least—to invite the pompous bastard. That was Raymond's style, anyway. On the other hand, Gaucelm mused, Raymond was wily enough to want Folquet as an ally in spite of their ideological differences. Rumor had it that the Pope was considering Folquet for high office.

Before Gaucelm could rehearse the tornada to his satisfaction, the dinner procession had begun. Folquet, more blubbery than ever, spooned the air toward his backside as he progressed across the floor. He was wearing the white cloak of the Cistercians, his face wreathed in smiles. The trumpets flurried their brief announcement, Folquet said prayers, pages scurried. Gaucelm, in brow-to-brow consultation with his jongleur, ate nothing, barely conscious of the hum around him.

At the high table, Raymond was conversing with Folquet about a Spanish mystic who had just completed a treatise on pantheism. Folquet dismissed it with a wave of his jeweled hand, "My dear Raymond, who needs Ibn Arabi's scholarship these days, especially in thirty-four volumes? He has wasted a lifetime studying the ancients, which is all very well for keeping libraries filled. But I see it as a sign that the Arabs are witnessing the setting of their sun at last."

Folquet's ringed fingers toyed with the wine cup, "Mysticism only serves to keep their strange gods alive—which is, no doubt, their intention. At this rate they are going to intellectualize themselves into extinction."

"Our loss," said Raymond, on reflex.

Folquet bit the bait, "What new do they have to offer our world? Yet another Sufi hermit writes a tome on satyrs and horned devils while we are having every kind of trouble just keeping one God alive!" His rings knocked sharply against the tabletop as he leaned toward Raymond's shoulder to make his point. He hissed, "They are living in the dark ages, my dear man—fooling around with alchemy, heating smelly metals in black pots, hoping to abolish evil, or some such nonsense."

Folquet sat back in satisfaction. "Really, Raymond, I would expect you to show more evidence of enlightenment! Darkness is all around us. We don't need to go peering into cauldrons to find demons. Satan is running free all over the countryside—especially your own. Ibn Arabi's Pan-headed deities exist where they are doing the most harm—in the minds of your subjects, and *not* safely tucked away in books!"

Raymond listened impassively, nodding in occasional assent, a smile playing about his lips. He scanned the arc of his table. Folquet's pontifications were tedious, Raymond thought, as his mind wandered to other guests. He was delighted with the number of foreigners present. A Greek was speaking Latin to his neighbor with the lovely hiss and slide that his native tongue lent to every language not his own; young Peire Cardenal, who had started dirt poor and whose mendicant passion for verse had led him halfway around the world, was telling tales of his travels in faultless Provençal.

Raymond's gaze traveled to his troubadour, who sat at a table across from the dais. Gaucelm had none of the courtier's grace and never would. He indulged every appetite to excess. He ate and drank too much, and the results showed in his girth. He was about as far from the classical code of moderation—of *mesura*—as man could get.

Still, he possessed the rare quality of paratge. And so he had allowed Gaucelm's talent to declare itself. It had been obvious from the first, to Raymond's practiced connoisseurship, that the youth would be a singer of *fin' amor* someday. He had watched Gaucelm grow out of his provincial innocence into a somewhat hotheaded adulthood. True, he still took events like the Bertrand affair and all the rest of the Pope's medicine much too seriously—but that only made him more fond of the young man.

Enough reverie, he thought. The count rapped on the table three times: "My lords, gentlemen, ladies. We are in familiar company tonight. Most of you know Folquet, whose verses have inspired much conviviality at this table. Tonight he has returned in new ascetic garb, but we trust that his mood can be revived, in spite of his status a while back as a responsible family man—and now as the good Cistercian he has become." Laughter reeled through the room. "I have entrusted this task to Gaucelm who, under inordinate pressure for which I take full blame, has completed a satire . . ." Joanna reached around and plucked the back of Raymond's robe fiercely. "*Bernard*," she hissed.

"My apologies," Raymond announced. "I am sure Gaucelm will permit experience to precede youth. We have grown so used to the presence of Bernard de Ventadour in our midst that we forget he is no more the silent treasure of our kingdom. He has begun to play again, and for that we all rejoice. Tonight he will lead the accompaniment of his own great song . . ." He looked at Joanna; she nodded him on. ". . . **Can vei la lauzeta**." Bernard was helped to the center of the room by two apprentices, one of whom carried a sturdy chair into which he settled the old man. The other presented him with his lute.

Gaucelm took a deep breath, feeling oddly nervous. He noticed how matter of factly Bernard began to tune his instrument, as though he had been doing it all along and this was not the first time he had played before the court in years. He admired Bernard's self-contained gestures and the way he held the lute as though it were part of his body. He noticed with concern how Bernard's fingertips wavered slightly, but Bernard readjusted his seat and pulled the instrument closer to him so that it nestled in the hollow between chest and stomach. This was how the old troubadour could "hear." He was tuning by the vibrations of the lute's belly against his own. As he adjusted the strings his fingertips became steady.

The two apprentices were ready. One would sing and play harp while the other, who had fetched his viol, was prepared to join Bernard in the instrumental passages. Now Bernard plucked out the introductory phrase and the young boy's voice emerged pure and sweet.

> When I see the skylark move
> His wings for joy against the sun's light
> And forgetting lets himself fall
> From the sweetness that pierces his heart
> Ah! such an envy I feel
> For those whom I see rejoicing,
> I marvel that in an instant
> My heart does not melt from desire...

Gaucelm was rapt, captive as always to the magic of that first stanza. Like someone at a pantomime who already knows the routine, he drummed the beat with his fingers and mouthed the words before they were sung. "*...enveya m'en ve*," he breathed in, sucking the words against his front teeth. "*...veya jauzion!*" he whispered at the end of the phrase. Unconscious of anything but the line of the song, he hummed along, to the growing annoyance of his neighbors.

> Alas! so much I thought I knew
> Of love, and I so little know.
> I cannot keep myself from loving
> Her from whom no favor will I ever have.
> She has taken my heart, my all...

It was wonderful how those words moved, flowed, into the next line after that heart-stopping catch in the throat of "*Ai, las! tan cuidava saber d'amor, e tan petit en sai!*" how it rushed into "*car eu d'amar no.m posc tener*," and then that change of key, that slide into the minor mode of "*celeis don ja pro.*"

Gaucelm sighed with the desire to be able to do it that *well*. He marveled at the song all over again, the song that had brought him here in the first place. His eyes still fixed on Bernard, he sat back in his seat with pride and relief. Now he could simply enjoy the performance. He closed his eyes. In an invisible arc above Bernard's head swooped his lark, the songbird that fell to earth because, being so in love, it forgot to fly. The phrases were drowned in love:

> I have no power over myself
> Nor had I any since that hour when
> She let me look into her countenance,
> Into that mirror which pleased me much.

Listening to the words with eyes shut, Gaucelm began to hear them differently. He knew the song had been made for and about someone real, but as a youth he had thought of her merely as a disembodied inspiration, for her name never appeared in the verses. Now it dawned on him who she must be. He could put a name to her, a famous name to all who knew the great families of the Pays d'Oc: Marie de Ventadour. One uttered Marie's name in the same breath as that of the fabled Eleanor of Aquitaine; both were known for their ladies' courts, their courts of love where women were said to rule. Gaucelm had heard tell of the games they played, the tests of love they devised for the young knights in their thrall, the decisions they rendered on matters of romance. He thought it a queer idea but it stirred him with excitement. Yes . . . she had to be "la contessa" of Bernard's song.

Listening, now, to the *"Lauzeta"* as though it were newly springing from Bernard's lutestrings, Marie de Ventadour emerged as someone who lived and breathed, Bernard's early love. Bernard from Ventadour. She had given him the name of her castle, if not her hand. She was married, Gaucelm recalled, to a count with the strange name of Ebles. How grand she must have seemed to the young Bernard.

Clapping roused Gaucelm from his musings. Bernard was finished. It was his turn. Raymond rapped on the table for attention. "Now for Gaucelm's satire," he announced. "It is called, I gather, '*L'Eretria dels Preires*,' and I am sure we will all be amused."

With a heart full of gratitude toward Bernard, Raymond, and the whole company in this room—a heart bursting with happiness for this moment in his life, Gaucelm stepped forward. He knelt, and began on a high-spirited parody of obeisance to his patron. "**O Light of the World**," he intoned in Latin, but Raymond broke in good-naturedly, "Do stop your flattery and give us poetry instead of classical rhetoric, Gaucelm. We are in need of something sweet after eating all that grisly game."

"Spare us!" a disgruntled Folquet muttered audibly in Raymond's direction. "Your troubadour is paid to supply the wit in this household, is he not? Though a ditty in that 'sweet' voice of his will give me indigestion for certain."

"All right then," said Raymond, "perhaps he will sing something sharp instead. Or something sour. Who knows?" Raymond cocked a conspiratorial eyebrow at Gaucelm who was still on one knee before him.

"A thousand pardons for my voice," Gaucelm said, determined to rise above Folquet's barb. "I have never heard it disparaged with so much politesse." He rose and faced Folquet. "Where I was born, in the Limousin, a poet makes words, not voice. However, your grace, since I do not have a jongleur to sing my words, my own poor vocal cords will have to do."

"My friends, enough!" Raymond raised his hands. "Have I gathered together the most famed poets in the South to have them spend their evenings, and ours, in verbal jousting? Sing, Gaucelm! We will judge your words, not your tune."

"Then fill my cup so I may swallow wine instead of insults."

"Done, and well said," laughed Raymond, motioning for a servant. "Now amuse us!"

Gaucelm propped the Moorish instrument on his right thigh and began:

> *Tan m'abelis per slatz reveillar.*
> *Que s'es trop endormitz...*
> I delight in wakening solace,
> for these days it sleeps too long.
> Awaken, you who call yourselves Christians!
> Wake up and watch how your priests live
> – richly – on the farthings of believers.
> Our clerics like their wine red,
> their women white as snow.
> They emulate the Pope in wealth of dress.
> They buy costly horses from the East.
> Did God ask poor folk to slave to the end of their days
> and die fasting so priests can feast on pheasant?

A muffled crash rang out as Folquet's sleeve knocked over his wine goblet. All eyes followed the red pool as it crept along the tablecloth. Folquet did nothing to stop it.

Gaucelm continued his song. It was a long piece, which had turned out more or less to his liking in spite of a couple of clumsy rhymes. When he finished there was a heartbeat of silence, then ragged clapping, then nothing.

Folquet looked grim. "Tell your verses to the Cathars," he said, turning to Raymond. "It's bad enough to have to listen to an old man praising adultery. But," he nodded in Gaucelm's direction, "with poets such as *this* in your court, you risk excommunication!"

He stood up to leave. "This is no satire. It is heresy!" he declaimed ponderously. "Your failure to suppress this kind of outrage will earn you an anathema from the Pope!"

It was Raymond's turn to rise. "Some think me too kind," he said. "But I pride myself on my judgment of men. This time I was clearly wrong. I have invited a hypocrite into my hall! How dare you—you who called yourself a troubadour like the others, who praised women like the rest, you who were nothing before you came to my court, and lived on my hospitality. How dare you threaten *me* with the Pope?"

Folquet waved a dismissive hand toward Raymond, further enraging the count. "My God, man, we have relatives among the Cathars. They are harmless people who want to live in peace. If you want to lick the soles of the Pope's feet, go ahead. But will you risk your carcass in a war for him?"

Pointing a finger at the troubadour turned cleric, Raymond fumed, "You are a fool, Folquet!" He swept his arm across his body in a wide arc, gesturing to the entire great hall. "Have a look – this court is famed for its openness. If it were otherwise, you wouldn't find yourself at my dining table tonight. I won't tolerate human cruelty, especially when the ends are so obvious. I won't have turncoats in my presence either. So get out!"

A torrent of words filled Folquet's cheeks, but incredulity blocked their release. Constrained to sputter and spit, he wheeled around, and bobbed his way across the hall. At the arched doorway he turned, pointed directly at Gaucelm and hissed, "Poetry mixed with politics is a lethal draught. Let this be fair warning!" Then, in a voice only half meant for Raymond, he repeated his admonition, "Make no mistake. The Pope shall hear of this!" and left the room.

"How dare he!" Raymond exploded, dropping into his seat. He shook his head back and forth, then sank his forehead into cupped palms with a groan.

Joanna was frozen with fury. "You see where this sort of bravado leads!"

Gaucelm remained where he was, the guitar still resting on his thigh. He glanced swiftly in Bernard's direction. The old man had taken in every move. He had raised both arms, like a prophet in despair. He seemed to sway back and forth. A flash of fear for the poet's frail heart swept through Gaucelm. He looked to Raymond for a sign, but his lord sat oblivious to company, music, manners. Gaucelm dared not move; he hardly breathed.

What would Vidal do? He imagined the sprightly figure poised beneath Folquet's window, serenading the fat abbot with his own raunchy love songs composed long ago in his troubadour days. Folquet would be pacing back and forth in his chamber wringing his pudgy hands, a victim of his own words, unable to do anything but hurl insults at Vidal's tousled head. And Vidal, in parting, would say: "We had no idea you had such a hidden talent for austerity. No doubt the Virgin now replaces Barral's wife as the object of your affections. Perhaps you'll spend your time doing penance instead of the Pope's dirty deeds!" But the little scene failed to comfort him.

In the morning Raymond came directly to Gaucelm's quarters. Without apologies or long speeches the count dismissed his troubadour. Gaucelm was stunned.

"You are freed from my protection," Raymond said, "but when this business blows over you will again be welcome at my court. Perhaps I've been living on borrowed time. I might be negligent, blind, or both, but I choose to believe I am right. And I am certainly not afraid of a couple of windbags, though their titles be pope and abbot. We will endure, Gaucelm. We always have." They embraced and kissed cheeks. When Raymond held him at arm's length for a last look, Gaucelm saw tears in his eyes.

Gaucelm rolled his vest inside his cloak and pummeled them into his saddlebag along with the boots from Brittany and the crucifix from Paris. Fury stung at him like an insect. Why had Raymond let Folquet get the best of him? Had he lost his edge? Was it weariness? He could talk a fine case for generosity of spirit—until the enemy stared him straight in the eye.

As Gaucelm gathered the last of his belongings, his rage dulled to a terrible disappointment, slowing his movements and pulling at him like a giant undertow. He sat down on his bench for the last time, his fists clenched to his eyes. He'd been too blind to see this side of Raymond until now. The man rode with the tide. The part of him that calculated loss against gain was willing to banish a friend after one misstep. It was a transgression of everything Raymond had said about paratge. For six years he had been Raymond's man, his troubadour, his . . . son. Now it was over. He wept.

It was not finished with Bernard, however. Gaucelm could not leave without saying goodbye to the man who had so recently turned his childhood reverence into love. He wished that he had not been so slow to penetrate the barrier of Bernard's deafness. But if the "*Eretria*" proved to be Gaucelm's undoing, it had also breathed new life into Bernard de Ventadour.

On this account, a feeling of gratitude ran like an invisible thread through his anger, propelling him down the corridor to Bernard's chamber. On the way he composed, for the deaf man's benefit, a fragmentary account of his meeting with Raymond, and a parting speech: "Understand, '*escotatz*'. . . he has betrayed my loyalty. Believe me, I shall strive continually to live up to your example. '*Senher, amic*' . . . you are always . . . *e.l. miels trobar* . . . what the Tuscans call *il miglior fabbro*."

The moment Gaucelm entered the elderly troubadour's quarters he knew that Bernard already understood what had happened. Seated in his chair, he held out his arms to Gaucelm who, fighting back tears, let himself be enclosed by Bernard's farewell embrace.

When they drew apart Bernard asked, "Where will you go?"

"Ventadour," Gaucelm said softly.

Nothing could have pleased Bernard so much as the sound of his own birthplace on his protégé's lips. "But I must warn you," he jutted a finger into the air, "about Marie. It is true, what the songs and legends say. I was in love with her. She was too young for Ebles and I too old for her. They say Ebles had me banished, but don't believe it. He was a more tolerant husband than was good for him. He liked to see his wife's youth and accomplishments praised at his court. He liked to encourage other poets, for he was one himself, a master of the *trobar clos*. His largesse even drew Folquet . . ."

"*Folquet?*"

"He followed on my heels at Ventadour. Now, he was of a suitable age for Marie. By that time I had gone north, crossing the water to be in Eleanor's service. Ah," he said pensively, "that green-eyed duchess, England's fair queen. It was a new world for me; I left Ventadour behind, and all that happened there. I know only what I heard afterwards: that Marie and Folquet intrigued together."

"*How so?*"

"She was much the politician, even as a young wife," Bernard said thoughtfully. "Ah well, that was long ago. It must be sixteen years or more since I laid eyes on Marie."

The old troubadour shook his head in silent remembrance, then turned to his protégé. "Salute her for me, and Ebles as well, if he lives still. This is the right time for you to go there; we all seem to gravitate to Ventadour to hone our skills. He clasped Gaucelm's shoulder, "Be a poet, not a versifier. You have it in you." The old man sought Gaucelm's eyes and held them in his gaze. "See that we do not lose you from our ranks."

At Bernard's words Gaucelm forgot his little speech of farewell and clung to the old troubadour, unable to withhold the beginning of tears.

"Mark you well, Gaucelm," Bernard said solemnly, "I'm no soothsayer, but I know a real poet when he comes my way. There's room for but one in every generation. I believe that art will hunt you down like the hound of heaven and it will find you in the end. Go with God, my boy."

Gaucelm just managed to kiss Bernard's hand as, flushed with tears, he slipped from the chamber and out across the courtyard. With the look in Raymond's eyes and the feel of Bernard's bony embrace still stinging his heart, Gaucelm went in search of Guilhelma.

II
VENTADOUR
1201

Chapter 6

THE ROAD TO VENTADOUR

It was full autumn. Guilhelma heard every swish of the mare's legs as they brushed over the thickly covered path. She leaned her cheek against Gaucelm's broad back and looked down: below was a broad trail of wet and brightly colored leaves. She liked to see the seasons change, and loved autumn best of all. Contrary to the Church calendar, so far as she was concerned, each year had two beginnings: Candlemas, which was the Virgin's Purification in the dark month of February, and Michaelmas, at the end of the harvest in September. The latter heralded the highest of holidays: the mysteries of All Hallows and then the feast days of Christmastide. But the cycle of seasons kept her anticipation sharp, since it brought new causes for celebration all year around.

The coming of autumn obviously had done nothing of the sort for Gaucelm. She had given up trying to talk to him as he seemed bent on being morose. He was still mired in fury over his satire on priests.

That pig Folquet! She had known him in the old days; he could never get enough of it. Back in the time before Vidal, even, Folquet had started coming to her whenever he was in Toulouse. And if she was occupied with a customer, he took who he could find. It made no difference to him. All he saw in a woman was a place to put his desires—his demands, to speak rightly. Some men were light-hearted in their wants, some would chase her around the room, playing at pursuit. Some, it was true, kept their boots on and were rough in the straw. But it was men like Folquet who made her job heavy and joyless. He always did it in the usual way, treated it like a duty to himself, a servicing of his nether parts. Afterwards, to make things worse, he would hang about and buzz her ears with his awful verses.

And he had religious theories, too. Like so many of the young men who fancied themselves poets, he had leanings which he liked to call heretical. Admired the teachings of the Cathars, he said.

Guilhelma had heard it all before, mostly from students. In Folquet's case, she secretly thought that all his anticlerical posturing made him feel self-important. But then he went away, and it was many months before he came to her again. When he returned, he had changed his beliefs as well as his ways. He appeared chastened in his religion—he wore the white robe of a newly-ordained Cistercian—and he was even more full of himself than before.

That was when he began to be violent towards her. The first time he tried to lash her wrists together she fought him tooth and nail. Then he turned more gold out of his pouch than she had ever seen, and she relented. But soon it got so that he slapped her face or ripped her clothing almost every time he visited the shack. It got so bad that she tried to refuse him, but he wasn't one to take no for an answer.

She sighed in relief that those days were over, even though the boar always *did* pay well. Thinking of Folquet, she leaned forward and whispered in Gaucelm's ear, "The more distance you put behind you now, the better." But he only grunted, so she left him alone. Best for him to stew in his own juices, she thought, for as long as he could stand it.

Guilhelma looked up into the aspens, shot through with gold beams of light. *In autumn the world seems slanted*, she mused. *In summer everything's low and flat. Spring is a puff heavenward.* Wistfully, she thought of the grape harvest which they'd be preparing now near Toulouse. The vineyard troughs would be dotted with homespun kerchiefs bobbing above the long blue bunches that sometimes split their skins at the picker's grasp. She pictured her plum tree ripening on the back wall of her house in the Chantier. Then soon, in the south it would be time for geese to spread their wings in V-formations overhead, time when fruits simply rolled at her feet. *How could I have gone away now*, she thought, *at the doorstep of winter, on the threshold of that darkening time so thick with things to come?*

Guilhelma had realized something was wrong the moment Gaucelm set foot in her shack. She was aware that Folquet was in town; the Chantier often got wind of such news before anyone at court. In fact, her street smelled faintly of bloodhounds—two men from Folquet's entourage had already paid her neighbors a visit. But she was unprepared for the sight of Gaucelm on her threshold, looking wild and sleep-starved.

"You're in worse shape than the morning Vidal found you on my doorstep," she exclaimed. "Whatever's happened to you?" He explained about the "*Eretria*," repeating Raymond's last words to him though it pained him to do so, then recounted his farewell to Bernard.

Guilhelma sat bolt upright on the bedstraw, listening. She did not interrupt; she was used to hearing a man out. For Gaucelm, she would listen all night. He went on talking in a tumble of words as if he were desperate to have a plan, anything to move ahead, to take him out of Toulouse.

"Bernard has counseled me about Ventadour. Ebles holds a great court there. Bernard said that he learned more about composing from Ebles than from anyone. He said all the great troubadours have passed through Ventadour." Gaucelm paused to catch his breath. "I suppose it's my turn now."

"And how far is this place?" Guilhelma asked. She hated the thought of losing him, of his leaving.

"A week's ride, perhaps. It's no farther north than my birth city, Uzerche." And then suddenly he asked her: "Will you come with me?"

Her heart leaped at the idea. All she knew of the wide world was what her clients had told her. It would be an adventure, whatever it brought. She slipped from the mattress and began to walk around the room. *How will it be to leave all this?* She wondered. *Leave friends, clients, the familiar streets of the Chantier, the profession that put bread on my table?* But with summer drawing to a close, business had slowed. Perhaps, after all, she had had enough. She went to a low wooden cupboard, lifted the carafe of watered wine and poured herself a drink. She gulped some, then offered the mug to Gaucelm. Nay, she was tempted.

Gaucelm pictured for her the deep gorges of the Corrèze and the tangled paths that lead out of them, the gnarled woods, the rocky precipices, the winds that blow trees into fantastic shapes, the pounding waterfalls of the north. He had been in country like this before on his way to Brittany. There was nothing like it, he said. It was exciting, dramatic, wild.

"And Ventadour?"

He pulled his stool close to where she stood. "Have you ever heard tell of the courts of love?" he asked.

"Like those of Eleanor of Aquitaine in Poitiers?"

"Ah, hers were famous. She must be an old woman now," he replied. "But at Ventadour, too, there is a great lady, Countess Marie, the Wife of Ebles."

"Does she hold such courts of love?" Guilhelma asked, her eyes widening. "What do they do there? Are there tribunals? Do lovers plead their causes before a judge?"

"The judges are women," said Gaucelm, warming to a subject he had only heard about. "And they hand down decisions. But they are not in earnest. It's . . . oh, a kind of sport. I remember talk about a case at Raymond's table. It went like this: Is it more desirable for a lover to kiss his beloved on her belly than on the lips?"

"You're not *serious*!" Guilhelma fell onto the bed, legs in the air. "And what did the women judges say?" she giggled.

"It was ordained that the belly is sometimes more beautiful than the mouth, and far cleaner. If I remember, the consensus was that kissing of the belly should be promoted as an act of reverence to the very root of life."

Guilhelma was rolling on the mattress, shouting with laughter. "Who told you this?" she gasped. "I don't believe it."

Before he could answer, she stopped laughing and sat up, her face composed. Slowly, she walked across the room to his stool.

"I will!" she said. Then, with a whoop, she set about pulling her cloak and skirts from the small wooden cupboard and folding them into a bundle. She wrapped a loaf of bread and a string of onions in cloth, then tied it up with two firm knots. With a forthright glance in Gaucelm's direction, she knelt to retrieve a small wooden box from beneath the straw mattress. She opened its lid, counted out separate stacks of gold and silver with great care, before reaching under her skirt to shove all the jingling coins into her stocking for safekeeping. Then, she lifted the winged brows of her bright dark eyes and said, "I'm ready."

She surveyed the horse's back. There was nothing but a blanket tossed behind Gaucelm's saddle. She was to ride pillion, then. Hiking her skirts fore and aft, she swung up and settled in behind him. She asked the mare's name. "Ventara," he said.

They rode northeast from Toulouse. Within view to the west on the second morning was Gaucelm's old landmark, the snub-nosed dome of Montauban cathedral. The next day they could just see the town walls of Cahors, before they crossed the Lot River at St. Cire and began a slow ascent through the forests ringing the gorges of the Dordogne valley. They were four days winding along precarious paths leading, sometimes, they knew not where.

Guilhelma's attention returned to the hush, hush of hooves. She was brimming with questions she dared not yet ask. Instead she kept her sights on the rustling multicolored leaves of the forest floor gliding beneath the mare's belly. It was growing late. As they rode out of the woods, Guilhelma glimpsed an ice blue curve of river in the distance.

On the horizon she could distinguish the spires and walltops of a town. As she watched, the sun sank slowly, leaving the skyline capped with gold.

"Shall we stop there?" she pointed across Gaucelm's shoulder.

"We'll stop when I say," came his reply. She wanted to kick the backs of his calves like a belligerent child; instead she only let out a sigh.

As they neared the small town, Guilhelma squirmed in the saddle, anticipating a hot evening meal. Wisps of smoke hung lazily above its walls as though supper had already been cooked and eaten. *People must go to bed early here*, Guilhelma thought. How unlike Toulouse! The hills gave way to stony bare patches, as the mare and her cargo approached the town gates. Strangely, the barbican stood wide. As they entered, a pungent odor overcame them.

Gaucelm drew his mare to a standstill and looked around. The houses were poor, worn away, their roofs shabby and lichen-grown. A weaver's hamlet, perhaps. But the village, he saw, was deserted. The streets ran with cats. From some godforsaken perch a mad mocking bird scolded incessantly. Gaucelm dismounted, leaving Guilhelma to stare at the sights around her. He entered a house whose doorway swung open at a touch; not even a stale piece of bread remained. The place had been abandoned, but not hastily. There'd been time to load up belongings for a complete escape. He left the house quickly, motioning Guilhelma to follow him on the horse. Had there been a plague, a drought?

Gaucelm turned into the small square below the village church and stopped abruptly. Two charred bodies were slumped atop a pile of cold wood ash; one was still half-lashed to a partially burned wooden support. Guilhelma rode up behind him, but she couldn't cry out. Her eyes were riveted to the corpses. Backing off from the stink of decomposed flesh, Gaucelm felt consumed by a mix of anger, curiosity, and desire for vengeance. He knew who these victims had been. They were almost certainly Cathars who had been protected by the village for a long while. No wonder these citizens, having been "taught a lesson" by the Pope's charges, had decided to flee.

Gaucelm picked up a raw stick and, covering his nose with one hand, prodded the ashes. Something, a piece of metal, fell to one side with a light clink. He scratched it out from beneath the pile: a silvery Cathar buckle. Holding it between his thumb and forefinger, he gingerly examined its workmanship. Then he rubbed it on his jerkin and slipped it into his pouch.

Suddenly he was hungry and anxious to move. His mare sniffed the acrid air and began tossing her bridle restlessly. Guilhelma remained transfixed. Gaucelm remounted, and without being urged, the mare headed down the dark streets at a canter, nostrils twitching. They emerged gratefully into the twilight, and neither spoke as they watched the horizon grow dim.

Just before nightfall they came to a stream lapping gently at the foot of the folded hills. No other town was in sight. Gaucelm removed the mare's bridle and tethered her to a tree trunk. She snatched hungrily at the grass, shaking her mane free. Without a word, Guilhelma walked alone to the riverbank, where she found the last of the summer's berries. She scrambled and picked and gathered, the job of putting a meal together helping to banish what she had just seen.

Clambering up from the river, she found Gaucelm poking along the ground for nuts. He was no longer listless, but full of energy. Guilhelma fed him berries and showed him how to peel the young pine buds and nibble out their soft cores. The river served as their wine. They made love defiantly under the silent sky, their hunger for each other heightened, perhaps, by the sharp night air and the sheer luck of being alive. Afterward, she nestled into him contentedly, and they listened to the mare snuffling as she dozed on her feet.

A sharp jab underneath his ribs prompted Gaucelm to fish through his clothing for the pouch. He fingered it open, pulling out the Cathar buckle. Reaching across Guilhelma's back, he held it before her eyes. She sat up. Then solemnly, he folded her fingers around it. "With this token may the Lady Fortuna bless our path to Ventadour," he said ceremoniously, and sealed his words with a loud kiss.

Guilhelma opened her palm and ran her thumb over the buckle. "It's pretty," she said. But she thought, *I will never wear this . . . it's not a trinket for display.* She wrapped the heretic buckle into the folds of her belt. Then she rested her elbow in her skirts, hands over her eyes, remembering the ruined corpses.

"Gaucelm," she began, "I can't help seeing . . ."

". . . the pyre," he finished for her.

She shook her head in bewilderment. "I don't believe the Cathars are evil people. Not the ones I saw in the market every day. They look like hard-working priests in those black cloaks! And down in Weaver's Street everybody *knows* Aimery's wool is the best around. They aren't like other tradesmen, squeezing out of you whatever they can get. Gaucelm . . ." she nudged him. "Do *you* think they are evil?"

"I don't understand heretics. They don't eat meat and they won't fight. Vidal told me they don't hold by the sacraments and that they think marriage is an invention of the devil . . ." Gaucelm said. ". . . they could be right! Beyond that, I don't know exactly what they believe. But I do know that if Raymond isn't afraid of the Cathars, neither am I."

He rolled onto his back and gazed into the night sky. *At Raymond's court,* he said to the stars, *such fears had no place. Until Folquet.* Stretching, he turned to Guilhelma. "Let's sleep." Though the earth was damp under them, the mare's body close by gave off warmth and they drowsed, cradled in the roots of a great oak tree with Gaucelm's cloak spread out beneath them.

Gaucelm had dozed off when Guilhelma suddenly sat up.

"Gaucelm."

"Mm?"

"I've been thinking about Folquet."

A groan. "By Saint Stephen, why *now*?"

"Perhaps seeing that village. The pile of ashes . . . they were once people, Gaucelm! And all that's left is the metal buckle you gave me."

"Mmmm . . ."

"It just struck me . . ."

"What?" he opened his eyes, half-annoyed.

She bent over his ear and whispered loudly, "You've been saying all along that Raymond betrayed you after six years as your patron, dismissed you because suddenly he's afraid of the Pope, afraid of trouble, afraid of Folquet. I was thinking, Gaucelm. There must have been an ultimatum from Folquet. *Excommunication*. Gaucelm?" She shook him by the shoulder.

He rolled over and murmured wearily into the darkness, "Excommunication is always in the air—it's nothing new, my girl."

"But consider, Gaucelm: why his sudden change of heart? Do you think for a moment that Raymond would have made the slightest move against you—"*Eretria*" or not—if it hadn't been for that pig? Folquet's a schemer, believe me. I know his kind. What else could Raymond do but bid you goodbye? Mark me—I think Folquet's out for *your* skin as well as Raymond's."

Now fully roused, Gaucelm elbowed himself up, bunching the cloak uncomfortably beneath him. "Fine, let's say he's after Raymond. That makes sense. But why me? Aren't there plenty of songsters who make political poems and sing them openly? What about Cardenal's diatribe against Dominic and that lot . . . or just about anything Vidal has set to music, for that matter? Aren't there enough anti-clerics around to keep Folquet busy? Why not some *big* game? Why not a troubadour Cathar? Why *me*?"

She grinned. "You can do the one thing he can't."

"Make love?" Gaucelm dove down against the shallows of her body.

"Make great verses, silly. I mean the real thing, famous songs that are sung to the far ends of Languedoc and all the places you've traveled to. Songs like the planh you made for Coeur-de-Lion . . ."

"But why should Folquet care, when he's so good at his own game?" he whispered directly into her ear. "Why should he care, when he's Abbot of Le Thoronet? He made a push for it and won. Now he can run his own show. Why would he be jealous of me? He's got power—isn't that what a man like Folquet wants?"

"Who's to say what a man wants in the deepest part of his heart. I think he wants you both dead."

Gaucelm sighed, anxious to dismiss the question. "Look, we know he's good at politics. I'm good at words. I think that's a fair division of labor, don't you? But *whatever* you think, I'm exhausted. I must sleep."

The final leg of their journey took them through the wildest country Guilhelma had ever seen. Gaucelm was not mistaken about the winds. As soon as they entered the Corrèze valley they were smitten by gusts. On the heights it was worse. They could battle these winds to exhaustion, like an enemy. On foot, on horseback, it made no difference. Unrelenting-winds wailed at them like the tirade of a personal insult. Abrupt winds blasted them off their feet, sending them scrambling for any upstart bush where they could only gasp, waiting for the next explosion of air. Winds teased, more treacherous than any mistral. They could make people crazy.

On the last morning they emerged from thick forest to find themselves on a precipice of sheer rock. They stood on the edge of a drop so dizzying that both of them stopped breathing for a heartbeat. Below, so far below that Guilhelma might have threaded it through her hair like a ribbon, a shining river flowed. Gaucelm let out a cry, circled the mare without even allowing Guilhelma a second gawk, and headed straight north, keeping in sight of the water.

Once on the road he asked directions to Ventadour, but merely got vague gestures to the north. There was mention of a waterfall, then a lake where the river they had been following emptied out. "At the top of the lake the river changes its name to Luzège," said a woodsman. "Then you know you're nearing Ventadour." When Gaucelm inquired about the approach to the castle, the man raised his eyes heavenward and made a roof with his fingertips. "It is steep. Bona fortuna!" he called as they rode off.

"Before nightfall," Gaucelm promised, "we will be in view of it." But neither was prepared for what they saw as they rounded the curve of the next foothill. Straight out of a slab of rock rose the high, square keep of Ventadour, its machicolations etched sharply against fields spreading to faraway mountain peaks. The tower and its surrounding wall stood out in a burst of late sun which lit its profile with copper. Here on its stilt of rock, its foundations buttressed by stone outcroppings, Ventadour castle presented a formidable sight. Nothing but a thunderbolt from on high could dislodge it. Blazing autumn trees, wildgrass, and cedar scrub grew right up to the base of its enceinte. Below lay slope on which a few houses tumbled together for protection inside their own wall, their mean outlines already sunk in shadow. Gaucelm gave a low whistle and turned Ventara's head up the path toward the castle.

When the pair reached the crenelated bulk of the gatehouse, the day was already dark as the inside of a well. Winter came early to Ventadour. By the time the garrison managed to haul the stout timbers from their iron sockets, Ventara was snorting for grain and the travelers were chilled to the bone. Finally the great gates swung loudly inward on iron hinges and the twosome rode wearily into the courtyard.

At Ventadour, the season of lighted lamps had begun. Its castle, low-built against the bailey wall was fully lit under the steel sky of the Corrèze, and seemed to dance like a twinkling, granite ship in the dusk. Oil-wicks illuminated the chambers with an orange glow. In the chapel, torches blazed for vespers. Only the arrow loops in the keep were dark.

As Ventara was led off to the stable, a house page dragged open the castle doors, then fled as they brushed shut behind Gaucelm and Guilhelma. They found themselves in an empty room, on the threshold of a castle as foreign to them as another country. The hexagonal pavings of the long corridor before them rang out like struck flint with the footsteps of knights passing in the distance.

Where they stood, the air was still. But as they turned a corner, they sensed all at once the wind of wings beating off stone. No silks or furs were spread about this reception chamber as at Raymond's; only a single magisterial weaving kept the drafts from those who waited to enter the main hall. Cold moved through this castle like a day-ghost.

Tired from the long last leg of their trip, the visitors waited for what seemed an eternity for someone to notice their presence. At last the house steward, a goateed, affable little man, darted up to ask their names. Gaucelm begged leave to be presented to the countess in the morning, as they were weary from their journey. But just as they were being shown to their quarters which were, the steward explained, beyond the great hall, a burst of trumpet notes sounded. The company began to assemble for the evening meal. Proceeding down the corridor behind the little man, the two mud-splashed newcomers attracted a flurry of notice.

A woman—tall in an emerald bliaut trimmed with dark brown velvet—disengaged from her partner and clapped a hand on her diminutive steward.

"Pons, have the grace to let us know who our guests are!"

There was no mistaking the authority of her tone. Marie de Ventadour's face, though it wore an expression of warm greeting, was big-boned, stony. A span of graying hair was parted and pulled so tightly to the sides of her forehead before being overtaken by her wimple that it corrugated her brow. Her eyes, frank and full of intelligence, seemed to register all the details of the travelers' sorry appearance in one glance. Dancing low at her left side, the one unmistakable focus of her attire was a festoon of keys on an iron ring whose chain she fingered constantly. Her hands were long, transparent, and bony.

As a flustered Pons turned to his charges to repeat their names, Marie motioned to Ebles, her dignified, white-haired consort, to join her. A young girl walked beside him, a child of fourteen perhaps. As they approached it was clear by the accord with which they moved together that, though the daughter shared her mother's blue-grey eyes, she was the light of her father's eye. Her face was a perfect oval framed by streamers of the brightest golden hair Gaucelm had ever seen. Tired as he was, his mind filled with the memory of the yellow-flowered field, where he'd been so deliciously sidetracked on his way to Toulouse. Gazing at her in wonder, he realized he'd been holding his breath; he let it out with a short sigh that, under the circumstances, could pass for fatigue.

"Our welcome," Marie said, as her husband and child joined her. A brief silence encircled the three of them like a moat. Marie stood, impenetrable, at the center of this little group. The arm she brought to rest on her daughter's shoulder pressed down upon the yellow hair so that the girl flinched. Guilhelma stifled a sympathetic breath. Pons bent toward Marie, announced their names then wavered back, uncertain whether the information he had imparted would cause his mistress displeasure or satisfaction.

But Marie was pleased. "Gaucelm Faidit!" she cried. "Your songs are well known to Ventadour. You do us high honor by your presence! From Toulouse, then? You'll have much news for us. We are most eager to hear how Folquet fares—he was my special pet, you know. He has been making quite a reputation for himself, I gather." She winked triumphantly across at her husband. "And *dear* Bernard, my prize. You must know that he grew up here. I suppose you are a fair trade for him . . . we shall see. Now, you must be qu . . . qui . . ."

Her sentence sputtered and stalled. Gaucelm's breath leaped in his chest: *perhaps she's about to faint!* But her grey eyes, wide open, continued to rest on his. A wave of time went by in silence. Gaucelm dropped his gaze to the floor, then glanced furtively at the girl, at her father, at the steward's pointed little beard. No one made a move.

". . . be quite worn out from your ride," Marie resume brightly. "Isn't it lovely country, our Corrèze?" Her face gave no sign that anything unusual had happened. As Gaucelm recovered his focus, he muttered something about the ravines, to which Marie, all graciousness, replied, "There is a saying that he who makes it through the gorges of Luzège earns the right to st-st-s . . ." Gaucelm stared in confusion a second time. ". . . stay here forever."

She turned briskly toward Guilhelma. "And now, who is this?" she asked.

"My jonglaresa, countess," Gaucelm heard himself reply. He had not planned to say anything of the sort. He had been hoping that there would be no necessity to identify Guilhelma at all. But he was overcome with the desire to impress, and the designation simply formed itself on his tongue. Jonglaresa. Why not? Marie de Ventadour would never have to know Guilhelma's true calling. He collected himself, then, and spoke her full name, Guilhelma Monja, hoping that there would be no further questions. Names flew in the air all at once.

"Viscount Ebles, lord of Ventadour." A nod of greeting, "Lady Douce de Ventadour." The grave child executed a little dip without her mother's prompting.

In small, staccato moves everyone was introduced. It was a sort of dance, the intricacy of which exceeded anything Gaucelm had encountered in Raymond's less formal presence. He stole a glance at Guilhelma, but her expression betrayed no surprise at being called "jonglaresa." Rather, she looked—was he mistaken?—as though she was enjoying his invention.

Marie, meanwhile had cast a shrewd eye on Guilhelma. "As an advocate of female participation in the musical arts," she was saying, "I congratulate you. But surely, accompanying Gaucelm does not take all your time. Pons!" From the gloom of the great hall the butler slithered sharply to her side, his flat belt-knife slapping the folds of his saffron yellow cotte. He reminded Gaucelm of a fast-moving crab. "You will know, Pons. Can we put to use an extra pair of hands? Does Alba need help in the kit . . . kit . . ."

Guilhelma took a deep breath. She once had a client so afflicted and knew that the only thing to do was count heartbeats, freeze the expression on your face, and wait. But instantly, Pons clasped his hands and nodded his chin so that the tip of his beard grazed his adam's apple. "She will be *most* grateful, my lady," he said.

They were excused from supper. Pons, having been instructed to bring them a joint and some wine, first removed a torch from the wall armature and lit them to their quarters.

Guilhelma had never before slept on feathers. Nor had she ever found herself protected from the roughness of a coverlet by such a sheet of gossamer-woven stuff. She was bursting with pleasure at her new surroundings and with her new secret identify. Jonglaresa. Why not, indeed? But for now she would make herself useful in the castle kitchen. Next to her Gaucelm gloomed away, unmindful of the luxuries of goose down and white linen.

"What kind of homage did she think she was paying in that speech about Bernard, 'my prized troubadour'? He hasn't been in her court for nearly a dozen years. Is she living completely in the past? And my being a 'fair trade'! Why, she spoke of me as though I were a lap dog, an ornament to be bought and sold."

"She was only trying to be welcoming," Guilhelma said.

He looked at her with a rebuttal on his lips. But his words melted at the sight of her familiar profile in these strange surroundings. Her wide-boned open face with its full mouth was utterly serene. He propped up his head to study her.

"Smile," he commanded.

"Why?"

"Just smile."

"With you behaving like a gravedigger, why should I?" She turned toward his elbow and smiled. He took the first and last fingers of his free hand and placed their tips lightly on her dimples. "They grow deep when you do." He began to hum.

"Sh-sh, you'll wake the others," she said.

"The others, my sweet neophyte, will still be in the hall awaiting the ends of her sentences and warming up for their word-duels. I can only imagine the sort of games she teaches. Folquet seems to have learned them well enough." He rolled toward her again, reaching across her back to squeeze the edge of his hand into the secret place between her breasts. She smiled again, though he couldn't see her face.

"Did you notice that *girl*?" he muffled into the pillow.

"The daughter, Douce."

"I didn't get what she was called." *So her name was Douce*, he thought as he called up a glimpse of grave eyes, an arm's length of golden hair.

He yawned and turned his face away, pulling the coverlet higher to his chin. Then, for the first time he noticed the fresh scent of linen and promptly fell asleep.

Guilhelma lay awake long past compline, alert to every noise. Muffled voices and the bass throb of a viol drifted along the corridor from the great hall. Gaucelm's rumble of snoring was borne quickly aloft under the high ceiling—the very air seemed to swallow sound. By turning her head to the left, Guilhelma could see through a narrow window into the night sky. The shadows of branches moving back and forth across the floor revealed that there was more than a sliver of moon. Very slowly, so as not to wake Gaucelm, she eased away from the bed.

A shudder went through her the moment her feet touched the flagstones. She pulled out the chemise from her pack and smelled the dear southern scent of dried lavender from its chilly folds. Unworn since last winter, it quickly warmed to her skin as its familiar length slid over her head and about her. Before crossing to the window she drew on woolen stockings and flicked her shawl across her shoulders. She shivered once again, then gingerly placed her elbows on the window's stone casement. Afloat in black and silver clouds like a ghostly ship, a moon so low that she could see its contours shone suspended above the castle.

They'll find a place for me in the kitchen, Guilhelma thought. *Will there be great feasts with peacock and venison, and special celebrations on Saint's days?*

Guilhelma pictured the gangling, well-meaning lady whose speech impediment had shocked them both. *She seems like someone precise in her accounts, difficult with the staff, and impervious to private misfortune,* she thought. *It's hard to imagine her giving birth to a daughter such as Douce. I'll wager that she hunts with the men and gives her daughter Latin lessons daily.*

The cold outside air smelled fresh, with a crystalline edge. Guilhelma, recalling their steep ascent to the castle in the dark, imagined them now to be high up among the whispering trees. She thought of the featherbed, but made no move to return to its inviting depths. She felt exhilarated, as though she had stepped out onto the roof of the world. There'd be plenty of time for sleep. This night was special. She rested her head on her arm sideways, so she could keep the moon in view, and reflected on how her whole life had quickened the instant she heaved herself onto the back of Gaucelm's horse and ridden out of Toulouse, away from the succession of customers, the piling up of coins, the business of never knowing what she'd be doing next, with whom, or when. All that was behind her; now she belonged to the clouds. Even the moon seemed closer from here.

A rustle beneath the window startled her. She raised her head from her arms and peered straight down into the courtyard. In the small, beginning light of dawn, she saw a slight figure hurrying along the pelouse, a cloak, a half-hidden basket. Then, she caught a glimpse of yellow hair streaming from the confines of a hood. Guilhelma recognized the silhouette: it was Douce.

Chapter 7

JONGLARESA

When Countess Marie, née Turenne, the grande chatelaine and ruling presence of this remote, stern castle, married Ebles de Ventadour, she had as her dowry nothing more than her youth, an ancient Limousin family name, and all the instincts of a literary hostess. For these, and her intellectual talents, she was welcomed at Ebles' hearth, where she was considered well-matched to a court that had bred and protected songsters, troubadours, poets, and jongleurs of merit ever since Ebles' grandfather's time.

Marie became someone for whom the word "commanding" might have been invented. She was the eldest of three sisters, the famous "las tres de Torena" whose high-mindedness was serenaded by the warrior-troubadour Bertan de Born. Some called her looks distinguished. Now in her thirty-sixth year, with an aged husband, Marie could look back on an alliance that had brought renewed glory to Ventadour. She had fostered the brilliant gifts of the troubadour Bernard, the grown son of Ebles' oven stoker and the castle's baking woman. Early, Marie believed Bernard was destined for great acclaim as a love poet. Therefore she took over his education, though she was much the younger.

Bernard remained at Ventadour for many years, in the light of Marie's affection; some say it was loyalty, and some say love. But when he had the temerity, nearing forty, to fall for Eleanor, the green-eyed Duchess of Normandy who had become queen of England, Marie put him out. After Bernard's exile she became even more imperious and meddlesome, falling into an obsession with this woman she had never met, prying gossip from visitors about the queen's fashionable assemblies at Poitiers. Upon these famed "courts of love" Marie sought to model her own. And in time she devised her own version, though she could not pretend to duplicate the queen's cosmopolitan elegance. Like Eleanor, Marie attempted to form a circle in which the female voice ruled unequivocally in disputes over questions of the heart. Ebles, who was now much too old for combat of any sort, wisely let his wife lead the way. "Never as a lord" had become the motto of her court. There, women simply ran things.

At Ventadour, the dark, iron dawns were so icy they made toes curl.

When the chapel bells sounded, Guilhelma rose and splashed water on her face over the washbasin. It was a punishment, this half-frozen water, but better than having to draw it herself from the well. With a disapproving glance at Gaucelm's sleeping form, she tied on her kerchief and trod softly down the corridor.

She peered at the inner courtyard through one of the long, narrow windows. Two house servants were dragging in wood to lay fires in the great hall. A thin spindle of smoke drifted up from the chimney of a round building—that must be the kitchen. Walking across the courtyard, she could make out two wells, one overgrown with winter weeds, the other with its top ajar.

Guilhelma could see nothing beyond the high stone bailey surrounding the courtyard. Next to the castle the square, severe tower of the keep rose above her like a citadel. The sight of it so close up took her breath away. The morning chill had begun to mount her skirts, mocking her woolen stockings. She made for the little round house with its signs of warmth, and pushed open its heavy wooden door.

Inside was pandemonium. An inferno of heat, a bustle of bodies, flying curses, retorts, instructions, the grind and clash of pots and pans, the clatter of wooden soles on tile, the sizzle and buzz of searing fat. Squinting into the clouds of wood smoke, she spotted an older woman. A nappe of white muslin was folded low over her brow, concealing her hair. Her shoulders were solid as hams, her forearms thick as rolling pins, and brawny.

Before Guilhelma could count to terce, the woman presented her with a wide wooden board and a brace of chickens ready for plucking. Steadying one bird by a firm grip on its feet, Guilhelma dutifully set to it, feather by feather.

"I see you know how to handle fowl."

At Guilhelma's nod, the woman tipped the finished poultry from her own board into a vat resting by the hem of her long apron. "I am called Alba," she said matter-of-factly. "I am the head cook. When your chickens are done we'll string them up."

With sinewy hands, the woman swept a pile of onions onto the counter before her and attacked them, stem end first, with her knife. "I know a fresh face when I see one," she said as she chopped. "I've been here twelve years come next Candlemas. Started in the laundry, then here, cutting vegetables, cleaning fowl, splitting and pounding the meat. Where're you from?"

Guilhelma decided to say, "Toulouse."

Alba's eyes narrowed. "You don't sound like a city girl. Where were you born?"

"Alès."

Alba smiled broadly. "So you're a real provençal, *sen venir de Proensa*, eh?" She began to hum a snatch of southern song. "Ventadour has all sorts, from everywhere." *What a strange way of talking*, Guilhelma thought, her eyes fixed on her chicken. "And you?" she ventured.

"From right here in Ventadour."

"The castle?"

"The village. And it makes a difference, my handsome young lady. It takes an outsider to see a place from a bit of a distance, don't you know?"

Alba returned to her chopping. "We're preparing the usual for tonight: twelve brace of fowl, three sides of meat, maybe more."

"But that would make a supper for . . . fifty!" Guilhelma exclaimed.

"Just so," Alba nodded approvingly. The girl knew her sums. "Oh, it's work, all right! But Ebles is rich. You'll see, the larder's stocked with fine sugars, almonds, honey, all sorts of nuts and dried fruits. Even rice and figs from the fair at Limoges, in their season. Ah yes, when the household's full, it's nothing but run, run, run all day long. And that's most of the time."

No wonder they have two wells, Guilhelma thought. She shook her fingers free of feathers, wiped a hand on her neighbor's towel, upended the bird, and reached inside. As she felt for the warm, slithery innards, her gaze traveled around the kitchen. Already she felt at home in this din. She was used to brawl and bustle. Only here, people knew exactly what lay in store for the doing: twenty-four chickens needed to be plucked and dressed; after that, the vegetables. Later, the hot fowl would have to be hacked from its bones, the meat sliced. Stewpots needed tending. This, she decided, was more than agreeable. It was perfect.

For a hair's breadth she saw herself in charge: the poulterers, the soup cooks, the realms of root cellar and storage rooms below where, she supposed, lay barrels of flour, wine, and oil, and the larder with all its sweet treasures. She could almost smell the winter apples, the bacon curing, the cheese and honey in their crocks. She heard herself delivering commands to each servant, from sullen scullery maids to the burly boys who were loading the spits and keeping the fires going. She'd oversee every move. She imagined the orderly procession of platters as they exited from her care, made their way across the yard, and were greeted in the great hall amidst a storm of applause.

Guilhelma had just scooped the last handful of innards from the second bird when her stomach gave a growl. As though to echo her hunger, Alba said, "Now that you've finished, we'll lay breakfast."

Space was cleared at the huge worktable. Up came beakers of wine from the cellar. Jugs of water drawn from the well sweated in the warm atmosphere. Hunks of the last night's bread were rolled onto platters, while the largest, flattest pieces were put aside for trenchers. Everyone seemed to accept Guilhelma's presence as though she had merely been away for a stretch. She followed Alba, pulling a stool to the table. "Is it always this busy so early? When do you get any time to yourself?"

"Child, you'll have time on Doomsday, when the castle stands empty. That's the truth!"

Is it *ever* empty?"

"When they're all out on an overnight hunt, or on progress, you'll get a chance to draw breath. I welcome those days! But they never tell you beforehand. One morning you'll just wake up and hear the packhorses being led into the courtyard and the clatter of the carts being hitched. Once they're off, the first thing I do is take a long walk around inside the bailey. I pay the cats a visit, walk in the herb garden, check on the warrens and rabbit runs. I go to the dovecote in the back of the stable to watch the birds fly in and out. Mind you, this happens three or four times a year."

"You must have many guests who come from afar?"

"Oh! The castle is full to bursting at holidays, and plenty of other times when you're least prepared. Before you can blink an eye, a hundred people will be sitting at the table waiting to be served. We've had archbishops, kings, all but the pope himself. Then, it's non-stop, morning till night. No sooner is breakfast over than we start with dinner. The horns are blasting before the food has even been put on serving platters, and they'll be finishing grace before we're halfway up with the soup." She leaned toward Guilhelma's ear. "When you get your training in this kitchen, the whole world becomes an emergency!"

Just at that moment the kitchen door opened and closed with a wheeze and a bang.

"It's our little miss!" Alba said as Douce entered her domain. "She's come down for some sustenance before chapel, I'll lay a bet on it. Wouldn't you know we've got nary a scrap from last night—it's all gone out to the almsman!" She bobbed her head as Douce approached, then made off to thread the spits on the hearth.

The girl's golden hair separated at each shoulder like a parted curtain. Her tunic, embroidered in triangles of red and gold, stood out stiffly from her slender form. Below it a skirt of lightest linen twirled above her toes. She wore the composed air of a child who had performed some grand duty to her utmost satisfaction. Her fingers brushed the edges of tables, paused at the rims of cauldrons, toyed with the odd spout, handle, lid, without really registering their presence. Then she spied the kitchen cat, and made a lunge for him. "Gris!" She called as she caught him by the tail, scooped him up and carried him to a stool by the fireplace.

Breakfast over, the kitchen began to clear out in the lull before preparations for the noon meal. Guilhelma rose from the table and went back to her place, where a basketful of turnips awaited her. Her eyes rested on Douce by the fire, and then on the row of dried herbs suspended from the beams above the hearth.

Suddenly Douce was at her elbow. The child picked up a turnip and tossed it from hand to hand.

"Do you sing his songs?" she asked abruptly.

"Whose?"

"Your husband's."

"Gaucelm's, oh yes. No, I mean. No. He sings his own."

"Do you play the lute, then?"

"He does. And viol."

"You mean, you can't sing?"

Guilhelma dug the tip of her knife into a turnip. "I can sing."

"Do you make up your own songs?"

"Some," she murmured.

"Then sing me one!"

"Ah, sometime. Not now."

"Now!"

Guilhelma turned to face Douce, suddenly annoyed by the child's impertinence. Hands on hips, she declared, "I have turnips to ready for the stewpot, missy. Don't you know there's a full house tonight?"

"Now. *Please?*"

"*Dompna, Dieus Maria!*"

"I'll help you—if you'll sing to me." Douce took a knife from the utensil pile. Guilhelma feigned exasperation, but secretly she was pleased. She placed several turnips, before Douce.

"Here you are, young lass. Now, take hold of one this way and mind, gouge out every root, like so." In silence they worked side by side, Douce concentrating hard on the turnip. Guilhelma glanced at Douce, hesitated, then ventured, "Wasn't it you, last night, out there on the pelouse with a basket?"

The girl's knife rested motionless in her hand. Her eyes grew intense, then narrowed like those of a frightened rabbit. She bent over her turnip again. "Sing to me now," was all she said.

Guilhelma thought for a moment, then began the wisp of a song the weaver's wife in Uzès used to sing long ago when she worked around the house.

> **The other day beside a hedge I came across a lowly maid,**
> **the daughter of a peasant man.**
> **Her cap and gown were trimmed with fur,**
> **and woven were her blouse and vest . . .**

"You *can* sing!"

"Hush, child. If you want a song, be quiet, then."

"I am *not* a child. I am nearly fifteen. They're going to make me marry soon."

"Marry who?"

"Oh, someone . . . a Comborn."

Guilhelma was silent. Then Douce declared, "You have a pretty voice. Sing again. Please." Guilhelma cleared her throat. It was not such a bad idea to carry a tune while paring vegetables.

Neither of them heard the door wheeze open when Gaucelm entered. He stood stock still as Guilhelma sang,

> **...si cum filla de vilana,**
> **cap e gonel' e pelissa**
> **vest e camiza treslissa,**
> **sotlars e caussus de lana.**

She paused after the verse and took a breath. Then, aware of a presence, she turned and saw him. His face was red, his expression at once amazed and flushed with pride.

"Why didn't you *tell* me?" He bounded over, then rested his chin on her shoulder from behind her.

"You never asked," she said with mock indignation. "I can frame a song as well as any trobairitz or jonglaresa." She crooked her elbows like an outraged fishwife. "Vidal never said a thing? Why, the old pelt, the *mareng villein* . . ." Gaucelm put a stop to her peasant expletives with a hand over her mouth which became a kiss. "And don't you know," she resumed when he released her, "he taught me himself, which is more than you ever tried to do!"

"All the same, some instinct must have whispered the idea in my ear. Don't you remember how I introduced you last night?"

"*I* remember," Douce interjected, ". . . jonglaresa!"

"And I thought I was making it up," Gaucelm said.

"Aren't you going to finish what happened to the maiden?" Douce pleaded. But sensing that her place in Guilhelma's attention had slipped, she merely announced, as though Gaucelm were not there at all, "You shall sing in the great hall. I'll see to it."

"No."

"I want you to! Is that Bernard's song?"

"Bernard . . ."

"Yes, *our* Bernard. He goes by the name of Bernard de Ventadour. The famous one. Mama says his mother worked for us right here, in this kitchen."

"No, it's not his. I think it's one of Marcabrun's." She looked at Gaucelm, who nodded.

"Who is this Marcabrun?"

"A Gascon who hated women," Gaucelm answered.

"Then my mama would not like him," Douce proclaimed, and turning neatly on her heel, she flounced out of the room.

Gaucelm came around and faced Guilhelma. Tipping her chin with a forefinger he said, with his biggest and most bumptious grin, "Now I understand why Vidal always said that the kitchen was the most important place in a household. You find out *everything* here. What are we going to do with you, my girl, now that we know you can sing? I can't have you upstaging me in court. But by Saint Stephen, I always knew you were a woman of parts!"

"Say Mirepoix."

Over by the window in the waning light, Guilhelma studied how Gaucelm formed his lips. When she repeated "Mirrrepoix" he went slack as though all the stuffing had gone out of his body. "How am I going to teach you to be a lady if you can't follow directions?" Exasperated, he sat down on the featherbed. "If Douce has her way and you're to make your debut before every noble in the region, you must not sound like a peasant"

It had begun some days ago with Gaucelm teasing her about her singing in the kitchen. Winding himself in her shawl, he'd minced around their quarters twirling an imaginary circlet of keys. He meant it as a gentle reproach. As he saw it, Guilhelma had been putting on airs ever since Douce opened up the prospect of her performing in the hall. Part of him applauded her bravado as well as her voice, but enough was enough. He was irritated with her behavior in general, in particular, her preoccupation with Marie and Ebles. In the short time they had been at Ventadour, she had made her presence felt far beyond the kitchen. She had quickly mastered the household's schedule, and offered her little services where they were most appreciated.

She made it her business to draw Ebles' bath and to attend at Marie's levee. She reported that Ebles slept in a bed covered with fur and camel hair throws, and his washing water was always heated twice at the kitchen hearth before being carted to his room. She found dried rosebuds in the pantry and took them to Marie, saying they made a soothing solution to bathe in. She thought of things like that constantly. Why, she knew more about the workings of Ventadour than he, by St. Stephen! In the time it took to bat an eye, Guilhelma had become the reigning queen of the servants' quarters.

He got up from the bed and made another attempt with her. "Try to stop rumbling your r's, and don't put g's on the end of words like *marrain*. You called Vidal a '*mareng villein*' this morning, remember?" Guilhelma merely cocked an eyebrow at him as though to say well, wasn't I right? Gaucelm's schoolmasterish expression dissolved into laughter. "That's exactly what he is of course—you had him perfectly—a bad boy up for a spanking!"

It was Guilhelma's turn to get serious. "Just what do you mean, 'rumble my r's'?"

Gaucelm took a breath, paused, and collected himself. "Right. Now we'll begin again. Mirepoix."

"Mirrrepoix."

"No, like this . . ." Gaucelm pulled back his lips so that she could look into his mouth to observe how he formed the syllables, as though the secret rested there. "Not like this: Mirrrepoix." His tongue indulged in a rattle of r's over the word's middle hump. This seemed to stump Guilhelma, and she was hesitant to try. "*Dieus Maria*," she said, "my tongue is doing the same as yours: Mirrrepoix! I don't see the difference."

"You don't *hear* the difference!"

"Explain it, then. Don't just say, 'Mirrepoix' over and over as though I hadn't heard the first time." Gaucelm sighed again. He thought for a moment, then said, "You have to get *up out of* your r's . . . don't just lie in them and let them roll over you. You'll drown in r's one day! Try: Roussillon, Perpignon. . ." He listened to her say the words. "That's better. Now can you hear it? Per-pi-gnon. Not Perrr-pig-non. Good! Mire-*poix*. Pierre. Try Pierre."

"Pierrre."

"Oh, *Dieus*!"

She broke off and went for his middle at once. "It's lucky you've no r's in your name. I'd make you suffer for them!" He held her at arm's length, protecting his stomach. Unexpectedly, she turned and walked right out of his grasp. "Besides, if you want me to be a great lady, you'll have to treat me like one."

"And what might that involve, pray?"

"Gold, perhaps?"

"How so, exactly?"

"Well, you're the one she'll favor: with her gold, if you play your cards right, and behave. But mind my words. It will cost you. She will tempt you to become her most ardent admirer. And then what do *I* get?"

"You have mine."

"Your what?"

"Admiration. It isn't every troubadour who has his own jonglaresa."

"Aye, and thank you very much," she replied. "But your esteem will buy me nothing."

Now he lunged at her, laughing. Grasping her by the shoulders, he said, "Do

I detect a whiff of envy here? Don't you know how lucky you are? Your Gaucelm has housed you in a castle, where you are fed rare delicacies. But all this does not come free. You are right. Your Gaucelm is no lily of the field. Like any professional songster, he must earn his bread by praising his patroness to the skies and proclaiming his love for her."

"Love! Since when does a professional singer have to be in love with the lady he praises?"

"I didn't say *in* love. But it helps to *seem* so."

"Gaucelm! You surprise me," she twitted him. "Be in love with her gold, then, but make your poems to *me*. Just be careful that she doesn't fall for you in the end. Rich women with old husbands need followers, and ugly women are never as wary of flattery as pretty ones."

"And where did you pick up all this fine wisdom?"

"In bed."

"Smart girl."

She is that and much more, Gaucelm reflected. He had to marvel at how she was rarely awkward in company. She was as confident among nobles as she was with servants. "I am Guilhelma as well to lords as to scullery maids," her presence seemed to say. There was a new self-satisfaction in her bearing since their arrival at Ventadour. Often he watched her as she dressed, taking special care with her bliaut, buffing her ankle boots to a soft sheen.

The daylight was nearly gone. Gaucelm undid his belt and stepped out of his tunic. It was remarkable how people of every age gravitated toward Guilhelma. Douce, for instance. He had begun to realize that she spent nearly every morning in the kitchen with Guilhelma.

"Douce seems to fancy you," Gaucelm remarked as he raised both arms to pull off his shirt.

"Poor child. Imagine a mother like Marie, can you? With Ebles away so much and no brothers and sisters, Douce needs somebody. Besides, when I'm with her no one can give me orders."

"Clever of you." Gaucelm walked to her, hugged her head to him, then scrambled into the bed. "Get between the covers, woman, and warm my feet!"

"Sing me a song first."

"I'll make *you* sing a song."

"Only for gold!" She attacked him feet first, plunging under the covers to bite his toes. He roared, she flailed at his stomach; he kneeled in the middle of the coverlet and pounded her with a goosedown sack until feathers drifted to the floor and both collapsed on their backs. "Silence!" came a bellow from the corridor. "Save your screechings for All-Hallows Eve, will you?"

Chapter 8

DOUCE

As winter beckoned and Gaucelm and Guilhelma settled in, Marie was quick to see a solution that would free her even more for her own pursuits. Guilhelma had become her daughter's newest curiosity and Marie encouraged their companionship.

During their time in the kitchen together, Guilhelma and Douce went about their business like sisters born in the same household. The girl's relish of her own expertise at practical tasks was one of the qualities that led Guilhelma to feel at home with Douce.

When Gaucelm and Guilhelma came to Ventadour, Douce was no more than a hairsbreadth this side of childhood. Not yet 15, she was already a beauty. Eyes, nose, ears, little pointed chin—each feature in itself was exquisite, but together their arrangement had a kind of heart-stopping perfection

But her looks deceived: the transparency of her manner and her solemn oval face belied her firm hold on everyday affairs. Douce knew court ways as well as any habitué and played her role of fair-haired princess with some arrogance, assuming that it was for her, and not for her famous mother, that the knights rode out. War meant no more to Douce than table chatter of tourneys and border disputes. At meals she wore the air of a girl who enjoyed playing adult games but could retreat at will to her own world.

Gradually, *Guilhelma* had forgotten that the yellow-haired girl who spent so much time at her side was the daughter of a count. The hospitable clamor of the kitchen dissolved all differences of rank.

But Guilhelma's refusal to explore beyond the confines of the castle grounds kept Douce on the lookout for another accomplice. By November she had found one: Gaucelm. One morning while the others were at Mass, she discovered him pitching horseshoes beyond the postern gate, in the outer yard where the farrier's forge roared. He was talking loudly to himself, declaiming something in a singsong voice, and so immersed in his own words that her presence made him start. "Dieus!" he shouted in surprise. "I thought no one came out here. Least of all *you*, my lady."

Her body was narrow all over. She seemed to glide just a little above the earth, the petals of her bright hair floating down her back. Her dream-like walk was reminiscent of an apparition, this wraith with ankles so slender that gazing at them made one feel weak inside. *This is the way all beings might look if only God the Maker were able to get it right every time,* Gaucelm thought.

"I prefer just Douce, if you please."

"Na Douce, then."

She giggled. "Just Douce."

"Pax," he grinned. "Douce. You win."

"Will you teach me?" She made a throwing motion.

"Gladly. But allow me, before we begin, to count stanzas." Aloud, he ticked off rhyme endings on his fingertips. Douce watched in fascination as he silently mouthed the words, memorizing them to his satisfaction. Only after she persuaded him to explain his odd method of composition would she let him begin her instruction in the game of horseshoes.

From that moment on, Douce came to adore the troubadour freely. There was still enough child in her to enjoy his other forms of play. Not for him the indoor activities of winter-bound knights. When he had to he could manage chess well enough, but the games of open air and wine shop were more to his taste. The thought that she would ever be like her mother—solid, impassive, someone who issues commands—seemed impossible.

Neither the sturdy poet nor the willowy girl saw reason to keep their outdoor play from anyone at court. So far as Douce was concerned, no young knight or page would have time to engage her in such nonsense, and her father's idea of fun was limited to hunting. As for Gaucelm, he sensed that having a bit of rough and tumble was something most proper young ladies missed, and would regret later in life. So long as Guilhelma was instructing Douce in household matters, and no one else was doing it he put himself in charge of the girl's outdoor education. They invented endless variations on beggar's chase and pick-a-penny. She pretended that she carried a magic shield and that no knight—not even a Comborn, the family whose son she was slated to marry—could touch her. By mid-November Gaucelm was showing her how to shoot with a bow and arrow behind the stables.

Marie got wind of her daughter's unconventional education. Spending time in the kitchen with Guilhelma was acceptable, but cavorting with a troubadour was utterly intolerable. Unable to contain her rage, Marie strode out past the barn and discovered the two aiming an arrow at the back wall of the stable. When she saw how Gaucelm stood at Douce's left side, one hand resting on the girl's shoulder, the other outstretched protectively to meet her daughter's grasp on the bow, Marie shrieked. The pair turned in astonishment, letting go of the wooden instrument whose arrow looped lamely to the base of the stable wall.

"Maman . . ." Douce seemed to go limp, dropping the bow onto the stiff grass beneath her feet.

"I don't want any explanation of this behavior," Marie said coldly. "Gaucelm, I hold you responsible for this . . . tra- tra- trans- transgression! I will not stand for such goings-on. Douce, I will speak to you later. You, Gaucelm . . ." She paused, as though unsure what discipline to impose. "You will hear from me!" With that, she marched back across the stubble to the comfortable warmth of the castle.

When she found life too taxing, Douce appeared to hear something—music? conversations?—that no one else heard. Annoyance faded from her face, supplanted by a mask of composure. At such times—and now was one—she chose to keep her thoughts to herself.

"Gaucelm?" she said, breaking her silence.

"Mmmm . . ."

"Guilhelma says that one day you just left your father's house and never went back."

He was stumped for a reply at first. Then he said, "There's no livelihood for singers and poets in Uzerche . . ."

"I know. I mean . . . what was it like to just leave like that, in secret?"

"It wasn't a secret from my mother."

"But your father . . ."

"Oh, he was over it in a week, I'll wager . . ."

"But . . . not seeing him again?"

"I'll go back one day," he said. Then, "Why do you ask?"

"I mean, what did it *feel* like to go away from them, thinking you might never ever see them, or Uzerche, or your house, or anything . . . familiar?"

"Why do you ask such a question?" Gaucelm repeated.

"I only wanted to know," she replied after a time. He respected her silence.

"Ladyling," he murmured, meaning to chide her teasingly for not allowing him to call her "lady." At first she stared straight ahead, puzzled. Then she shifted her gaze to him, acknowledging that in this singular form of address, he had declared his affection for her.

Chapter 9

CORTESIA

By the end of November, evening fell swiftly at Ventadour. Outside the arched window of Gaucelm's practice room, the moon shone full and distant in a sky streaked with brindled clouds.

Gaucelm bent over a small square of parchment, scratching at it with an unpracticed quill. It was years since he had attempted to make the volatile mix of dusty black pigment, water and gum do his bidding on a greasy surface, which kept curling up every time he tried to smooth it with his palms. He moved the candle closer. "Esteemed Parents," he had scripted with difficulty. "Know that, after six seasons as troubadour to the Count Raymond of Toulouse, I sing now for the Countess Marie at Ventadour. Be assured that I am well . . ."

As Gaucelm wrote, the nib caught in the parchment, launching a string of black beads across its surface. Gaucelm let fly a staccato of oaths. Had he given in to his mother's hopes, by now he'd be a cleric, Gaucelm thought ruefully. And the forming of letters would be everyday business, not the intermittent, unholy torture it was. *Dieus*!

Pons entered. "The countess would like to see you right away," he announced portentously, "in the solar."

The summons took Gaucelm by surprise even though he had lived with the certainty of her displeasure over the bow and arrow incident for the past several days. He had never been to Marie's private quarters; he knew only that her rooms occupied much of the castle's uppermost story. Blue moonlight paved the stairway as he slowly mounted the steps. Aggravation over the spilled ink only heightened his anxiety about what Marie had in store for him. She was capable of anything, including his dismissal.

He was shocked to see her without her coif. Marie de Ventadour stood within the flickering reaches of candle flame, which illuminated the silver in her hair. He found himself unnerved by the sight of grey-brown strands cascading down her back. He was used to her in a headdress and chinstrap so tight that it threatened to throttle her stutter. Without it, Marie looked very much alive, and alarmingly naked.

Wasting no time on pleasantries, she said, "It is time I told you that I know about the '*Eretria*'." Gaucelm, having labored to put that painful incident in the past, was so taken aback at its mention that he merely stared at Marie.

"Playing with fire, were you?"

When he had recovered sufficiently to trust his voice he replied, "I don't think of it that way. Neither did Raymond."

"Raymond? What about Folquet?"

There was an ominous silence. Outside the casement window sharp branches scratched like cat claws against stone.

"You nau- nau- naughty boy. Surely you understand: I must know everything about those to whom I extend my patronage, past and present. In particular, I like to keep myself informed of Folquet's doings. And I do not like to hear of his being slighted—especially by a troubadour whom I took under my roof in good faith. Such a naughty insult cannot go unheeded." She smiled at him as though they had some unvoiced agreement.

Naughty. Was she flirting with him? Had she decided to forget about the bow-and-arrow business? He was baffled, but for the moment his curiosity overcame all else. "How did you find out about the '*Eretria*?"

"Silly boy," she repeated, to his annoyance. "From a certain dwarf who knows all about orthodoxy—and its transgre- gre- gressions." Gaucelm remembered Raymond's message-carrying dwarf. Marie was saying, "With me, gathering information is never an act of idle curiosity. I am interested in the extremes of human nature. If I want answers, I get them. Now please sit down."

She motioned him to a high-backed chair before the fireplace, then stood so the firelight danced at the skirt of her russet surcoat and played with the keys that swung from its embroidered belt. "I had already designed a way to even the score with you. My plan was to send you away for a while on a . . . on an errand. But when I . . . disturbed . . . you with my daughter the other day, I knew I had the perfect pu- punishment to fit the crime."

At the word "punishment," Gaucelm started. But Marie put out a hand gently as if to stay his fears. "Do not think of this as punishment in the usual sense," she said, lowering her voice to calm him. "There is enough betrayal and deceit at loose in the world. Men, in particular, are too quick to judge and take action. I pride myself on thinking things through – that is a woman's way. I have my own brand of justice. As for your assignment, I think you will not find it unpleasant at all. Whether you do or not depends on your deepest nature." She finished with a complicit smile, enjoying her careful choice of words as much as his bewildered expression.

She began to move about the solar, pausing by a table heaped with little pots, sealing wax and silk binding cords. She meandered, picking up first one object, then another, withholding the details of her plan. Gaucelm waited, inhaling the room's clean scent. Nothing, however, could ease his discomfort.

Finally she announced, "You will set out at first light for Malemort castle. There you will find a woman whose friendship I value, Madame Audiarde. She will interest you, for she is learned and enjoys discussion. She is, as you will see, a beauty. But I must warn you that she has been without company ever since her husband left for Outremer after the harvest." And with a peculiar smile, she added, "I honor your sensibilities by giving you no further instructions. I leave the results of your encounter to Lady Fortuna." Gaucelm found himself even more mystified than before.

Marie walked to a table where a large ledger lay open. *Of course she would do her own household accounts*, Gaucelm noted abstractedly. *She wouldn't trust anyone else.* Marie ran a finger down one page of the register before bending to open the lid of a large wooden chest. With a sweep she drew from it a pelisse of some plum-colored stuff lined in fur, and handed it to Gaucelm. "You will be needing this against the cold," she said abruptly.

The gift presented, she wandered to the other side of the fireplace. Aimlessly, she picked up a black knight from the chessboard and twirled it in her fingers, coming to stand before Gaucelm. One more thing," she said, "You must bring me a sign of your success with her."

"Such as?" Gaucelm asked, puzzled.

"I leave that to you," she said and smiled.

Now it was becoming clear: he was to be on loan to this Madame Audiarde de Malemort, an offering from the Countess Marie. A pawn, perhaps, in a game invisible to him. Still, he had expected worse. How could he complain? A troubadour's life was a series of barters, a constant exchange of services for goods. Filled with relief, he was mostly stung at having to start so early in the morning without a decent night's rest.

"What more can you tell me of the lady of Malemort?" Gaucelm asked.

"You need know nothing except what I have already told you. Once you are there, leave everything to Arman, her butler." Gaucelm was unsatisfied but resigned, and rose to go.

Puzzled, intrigued, his worst fears allayed, Gaucelm thought about how to explain his sudden departure to Guilhelma as he started down the stairs. He was finding it hard to put what had just transpired into words that she would understand.

There was a taste of snow on the air as Gaucelm set out before dawn, mounted on one of Ebles' destriers. He was glad of the new pelisse, though its loose sleeves lined in reddish fur confounded him with their weight. They would take some getting used to in the saddle.

Like most byways in this inhospitable land the road was not promising, and at such an early hour before prime, Gaucelm traveled it alone, except for the wind. There was no respite from the winds of the Corrèze, and along his way to Malemort he would know them all.

But the sight of Malemort castle at the end of the day was enough to make Gaucelm forget his journey's discomforts. Unlike Ventadour, the structure appeared to be newly finished; its stone had a whitish, crystalline cast, as though it had been from some lunar landscape. Gaucelm could see from a small rise that it was constructed in the shape of a trefoil. He had heard tell of such curiosities but had never seen this kind of triangular, clubbed fortification. It seemed to him to possess a perfect logic and strength. He kneed his horse to a canter and sped toward the trinity of gleaming towers with a thrill of expectation.

The gate had been raised, as though his presence was expected. A stableboy ran for his destrier as soon as Gaucelm rode into the yard. When he had dismounted, the boy gestured him on to the castle's entrance. There Gaucelm was admitted with a minimum of inquiry and ushered, as though by prearrangement, under a sculpted marble portal and into the main hall. Its ceiling was so unusually high that his immediate impulse was to look up. Far above his head a progression of cross vaults spread out like a forest, with richly decorated capitals too high to see in detail. There was a strange silence at the heart of this hall. Standing there, Gaucelm felt an unaccustomed equilibrium, as though his body had been placed in the exact center of a space almost mystically proportioned. When he so much as cleared his throat the sound carried without echo.

From far down the corridor a woman's step could be heard. And then she appeared.

The moment Gaucelm laid eyes on Madame Audiarde, a line of verse came into his head and lodged itself there. The voice said *ruby red, hoarfrost white* just as his lips were whispering greetings over her hand. A single, splendid, dark red gemstone blazed at her throat. And then, sure enough, his sight registered the bodice below it, which was not just rimmed with embroidery, but entirely constructed from it. The fine openwork was interlaced with silver threads so that Gaucelm's impression was of a cascade of gossamer snowflakes.

Had this delicate creature actually been born, and then—surpassing other mortals—grown into such inconceivable loveliness? Or had she simply appeared one day, fully formed, exactly as she now stood before him, a swan-necked angel with flashing eyes, two curly blonde locks straying from her white coif? The hand above which Gaucelm had bent was weightless, blue-veined; the wrists were tiny. But her voice, though mannered—inflected, even—in the precise way of women who were used to directing servants, left no ambiguous tremor in the air. It was a voice conscious of all its musicality, a voice made for pleasure.

The butler Arman was helpful, as Countess Marie had promised, bringing Gaucelm his bread and watered wine the next morning. d

Nor was this pantomime lacking in elegant backdrops. Madame Audiarde's rooms upstairs were as spacious and unadorned as Marie's solar was cluttered. Because of the clover-shaped construction of Malemort castle, the walls were curved like those of a round keep, and needed no tapestries to preserve warmth.

As he entered, Gaucelm was conscious of a sharply aromatic scent rising from the hearth. Madame Audiarde stood before the crackling logs, one hand outstretched, the sleeve swept back from the fine bones of her wrist. Her palm brimmed with spiky dried herbs. These she cast upon the fire in small pinches, as though she were tossing grain to geese.

"Mmmm, a delicious smell," Gaucelm remarked.

"I like the sizzle as the flames take it up."

"What *is* it?"

"Rosemary." She flung the rest of it into the fire and waited until it blazed in a surge of sparks.

"Come, let's sit and have a cup of wine. I want to hear all about Ventadour, and about you."

She motioned for him to draw two chairs close to a low table. Today, he noticed, she wore an exquisite bliaut of pale spun silk. Its girdle was fastened by a clasp in the shape of a scorpion set with jewels. Gaucelm took note of this Cleopatra-like foil for her fragility. On the table was a footed flagon, its handle chased and inlaid with ivory, two silver cups, and a bowl of pears. Gaucelm inhaled the warm, heady aroma spiced with cinnamon and ginger before taking a sip.

Suddenly there was a piercing scream from somewhere across the room. Gaucelm gave a violent start, sloshing wine into his lap and retracting his legs as the stuff seeped into the wool of his stockings. "By the Cross!" he exclaimed, recovering enough to forsake an earthier expletive. Madame Audiarde's laugh rang out like a descending scale of chimes as she skimmed across the room, thus saving Gaucelm the embarrassment of coping with the spilled wine in her presence. "I've forgotten her hood!" she cried. "Chanute, darling!"

She flung back her sleeve and held her arm close to an ornately carved wooden pedestal. A pure white gyrfalcon hopped onto her bare wrist, causing a little bell attached to its leg by leather jesses to jingle. "Come," Madame Audiarde called to Gaucelm. "Come and meet Chanute." He stumbled across the floor, brushing the remaining drops of wine from his cotte. "Her name means 'white-feathered' in the local patois. She's rare, an albino." Gaucelm eyed the bird with misgiving. "Darling, talk to our new friend. Show him how smart you are." At this, the falcon fanned out a wing to the farthest pinion. Gaucelm recoiled instinctively, but Madame Audiarde took no notice. "When she mantles like that it means she's at ease. She likes you."

"Good," Gaucelm said.

Madame Audiarde picked up a leather hood ornamented with white plumes. It resembled a war helmet fit for a miniature Zeus or Hermes. "She was brought to me as an eyase, straight from the nest. When she got to be full-grown I tried her in the field, but she refused to fly at anything. Albinos often have bad sight, you know. By then it was too late to train her with the lure. But the Virgin be praised, for she's kept me good company." Gaucelm eyed the bird's saber-curved beak, the pale talons fitted like spurs into its claws, and finally its red eyes, cold and vigilant. He was not persuaded that this bird was tame—it was as wild a thing as he'd ever seen in captivity—an instrument of warfare.

When it came to hawking, Gaucelm was at a loss. In truth, he feared attack birds—even kestrels, harmless little things that a mere villein could own. The first time out hunting with Raymond he had seen a jerfalcon kill an enormous crane on the wing. He had watched with fascinated horror as the falcon skimmed its prey near the ground, then drove its talons deep into the crane's body. Try as he might to admire their warrior's skills, he could not warm even to ordinary peregrine falcons, which still looked fierce to him, and long-winged hawks he found positively terrifying.

"What do you feed her?" Gaucelm asked, to be polite.

"Fresh-killed pigeon is what she likes best, but she'll eat rabbits and rats if there are no small birds about." Below the perch Gaucelm noticed an open cage filled with sand and bird droppings, whose odor the fireborne rosemary effectively covered up. "Does she mind being confined?" he continued, in an effort to impress her.

"I take her out and cast her on a leash every day. She goes everywhere with me, except near the hawk house. I want her to know that she's unique, so I keep her away from the others," she murmured, stroking the bird's wing feathers. "And you are special, my darling, aren't you? Tomorrow you shall have your bath. You adore that, don't you?" She said to Gaucelm, "You must come with us. I let her wash in purest rainwater, which collects in an open cask by the stables. Now, Chanute, back to your perch." The bird hopped from Madame Audiarde's wrist onto the pole. Her mistress placed the little contraption over the falcon's head. Like an executioner's hood, it shut off the bird's sight. "Now," declared Madame Audiarde as she fastened the delicate leather thongs under the hood, "we'll have no more interruptions."

As he lowered himself into his chair Gaucelm eyed the pears hungrily, but she did not offer him one.

"How do you find Marie?" Madame Audiarde asked as she sipped her wine, not really expecting an answer. "You came to her from Raymond's court, I understand. You knew Marie's precious troubadour Bernard, then. I never laid eyes on the man," she paused. "She wouldn't let him . . . stray. He was *her* rare white falcon, you see. Do *you* think he was in love with Marie?"

She sighed. "**Ai, bon' amors encobidal cors be faihz, delgatz e plas..,**" she intoned, glancing at Gaucelm. "That says it all, though, don't you think? How can a man sing of sweet love long desired, a body gently made and narrow, if passion doesn't rule his heart? . . . Would you like a pear?"

She knows Bernard's verses well, Gaucelm thought as Madame Audiarde rose and went into another room, bringing back a slender lady's knife into whose handle was set a band of carved porphyry. She selected the most densely speckled fruit, pressed it with her thumb to test its ripeness, then cut it through the middle. The look of her fingers on the knife with its handle of purplish stone, the veined milky alabaster of the bowl, the pears' muted bronze—all this, he had to remind himself, was only a day's ride from the ringing gloom of Ventadour's stony halls.

She handed him half of the pear. Its stem end was pursed as a crone's lips; its skin felt grainy and rough in his hand. But its cut surface was a dazzling white, already forming sweet beads in the wake of the knife blade. Without stopping to sniff, Gaucelm bit into it greedily.

He did not want to talk about Bernard—it was Folquet who worried him. "Bernard was long ago," he said. "It's Folquet de Marseille she speaks of now."

"Folquet! Ah, but he was another matter. He was the one she chose to do her bidding—Marie's love ambassador." She hesitated as a thought illuminated her face, "Of *course*. How stupid of me not to see at once. If it's Folquet she's talking about, that explains why she's sent you."

Indeed, why? Gaucelm thought, struggling to conceal his anxious curiosity.

She smiled at him furtively, watching his response. "What an apprenticeship Folquet served! A quick study he was, too, in the hunting field, in hall—and in ladies' chambers. Made himself useful everywhere." She paused, looking pointedly at Gaucelm. "He knew by instinct what was wanted of him. Produced some better than passable verse, when the demand arose."

Gaucelm swallowed the last of his pear, coughing slightly as it slid down his throat.

"And now, Marie reports, he's become Abbot of Le Thoronet. Folquet!" Madame Audiarde continued. "I can hardly imagine it. A wolf in Cistercian clothing! Well, such men have been known to end up bishops—popes, even."

Gaucelm wondered if she had heard about the '*Eretria*' and if so, was she signaling her approval?

"Another pear?" she asked sweetly. Madame Audiarde fondled the fruit remaining in the bowl and made her choice. "I wonder whether Folquet has renounced the . . . the niceties of love, entirely?" She glanced at Gaucelm, but his expression revealed only bewilderment. "I do hope he hasn't," she resumed, "for he was an expert, in his own fashion. He had an understanding of—let us say, nuance—and a way with equipment, if you understand me?"

Gaucelm rose nervously and looked about the room. *Folquet, an expert in the arts of love? Unimaginable!*

Madame Audiarde picked up a book with a carved ivory cover, opened it and held the book out to Gaucelm. "Read this," she commanded.

The frontispiece bore the author's name: Andreas Capellanus. So this was his famed *Book of Love*, Gaucelm realized, as he skimmed the kidskin vellum page. "The Eighth Principle," he read from the Latin text haltingly. "No one should be deprived of love without the very best of reasons."

Gaucelm looked up at Madame Audiarde. "It's hard to disagree with *that*. What makes him make such an expert?"

"Read what he says before that part," she declared. "It starts 'Love is a certain inborn suffering . . .'"

". . . derived from the sight of and excessive meditation upon the beauty of the opposite sex . . ." Gaucelm completed the sentence. "But why *suffering*?" he complained.

"Is Andreas not talking about spiritual love, *amor purus*?" she responded, "but continue."

Aloud, he read, ". . .which causes each lover by common desire to carry out all of love's precepts in the other's embrace." Gaucelm realized he was beginning to enjoy this conversation. "Ah, so he speaks of both," he said.

"Spiritual love and that of the body," she said, touching his shoulder. "But enough of Andreas Capellanus. Which do *you* think is the greater, and which the more ennobling?"

"That is easy: love made by two bodies is greater than that which is fabricated by the spirit," he answered.

"Then what of this proposition: that the love between two human beings, duly consummated, may lead to love's embodiment—in spirit?"

Gaucelm laughed and closed the book. "But," he countered, "if we go by what Master Andreas says—that love is really the desire for passionate embrace—does not true love then amount to spiritual *adultery*?"

"Very clever," she said. "A lawyer's argument. Have you thought of taking up the profession?"

If he was not yet adept at verbal jousting as prelude to a woman's favors, it was at least good entertainment in itself, Gaucelm mused. Malemort may be no court of love, but a morning spent with Madame Audiarde was a lesson in cortesia. "If not adultery, then what do you propose? Is there such a thing as spiritual marriage?" he asked in jest.

To his surprise, she turned suddenly serious. "I don't believe in that sort of nonsense," she protested hotly. Already, bright pink triangles had risen in her cheeks. "How would 'spiritual marriage' be different from the attitude of our present Pope? Or even of the Church itself? There is no more ardent supporter of chastity than the entire Holy Mother Church."

Wisely, Gaucelm held his tongue.

"This is a Church that fears women and defiles them by its words, in its scriptures, and in the mouths of its clerics," she fumed. "When there were still preachers who could draw a crowd—if it was your habit to go to church—were you not treated to endless fulminations against women? Words said against her wantonness, her adornment, how she inflames with the fire of her lust all who behold her, how she marks men forever with her desire . . ."

"Well, yes . . ." Gaucelm started to answer, but she paid no attention.

"Really you'd think the priests got a kick out of that sort of thing themselves. I think they *enjoyed* it!" she said, elated with her own argument. "Poor fools, what do they know about women anyway, driven to revel in their ignorance in public? And no doubt give their public a rise, too!"

"Such speech might be construed as heresy," Gaucelm said, taken aback by her vehemence.

"Then let it be!" she answered without hesitation. She paused, then, and moved toward the hearth. "But, pray, who are you to talk of heresy? Malemort is not so remote that news of Raymond's court fails to reach us."

"You know of my little misadventure?" he said cautiously.

She surprised him with a smile. "Misadventure? I would say it was an act of courage albeit a foolhardy act that may one day cost you dear."

"I thought from what you said that Folquet was no enemy of yours."

"Let me explain something, Gaucelm. I was drawn to Folquet, and he to me, for very—specific—reasons." He waited, but she did not elaborate. "I could not know his true sympathies then, for he had not yet begun to play a part in politics. I make no secret of my own views, however, and they run absolutely counter to what Folquet stands for. Everyone knows that the Church is corrupt. Anyone can see that the Pope prefers to find scapegoats in infidels and heretics rather than put his own house in order."

Gaucelm breathed deeply and let his shoulders relax. He could feel the tension leaving his body. With Madame Audiarde he felt a license to practice once again the cynicism he had acquired in Vidal's presence. "Perhaps such a solution is not self-serving enough for the present papacy," he suggested. Her laugh was her assent. Then, sensing that he might learn something by playing the innocent, he was prompted to inquire, "Do Folquet's politics deter the Countess Marie?"

"Oh no," she answered. "Quite the opposite. He's her man. She lives to see him rise in the world. His position with her was always different than his with me. From the start he was her vassal, and only incidentally her . . . gift to me . . ."

Gift, thought Gaucelm, set off-balance yet again. His heart gave a strange lurch as it became clear that he was following directly in the footsteps of the man who had promised to denounce him to the Pope. "Does Marie often share her courtiers with her women friends?"

"More than that, Folquet was her *creation*, as I said. She took pains in shaping him. That's something entirely different. It's outside even the rules of cortesia. Our friend Andreas Capellanus would probably not approve."

"Then," he said, abashed, and still slightly mystified, "I guess it's all right, my being here."

She stepped forward and touched his cheek. "It is more than all right," she said softly.

"You intrigue me, my lady," Gaucelm said, regaining his composure. He spoke straight to her eyes, which still blazed with conviction and reflected firelight. "I must go," he added suddenly, "before I confuse *amor purus* with—what were your words?—the fires of lust. Thank you for our talk. I haven't had such sustenance since I left Toulouse."

Precious creature! he almost gasped as he took the stairs at a gallop and made for his quarters. Silver threads and scorpions and jewel-bright eyes. No, he decided, she was no snowflake, there was nothing ethereal about her. She was both delicious and intelligent, a woman of independent views. She was perfect in her own way, brittle, perhaps, offering the slight, preliminary resistance of cooled spun sugar. She was no illusion of white gossamer, as he had first supposed.

Though he was prepared to exercise patience if the game to which he was now party required it, the invitation to Madame Audiarde's bedchamber came that very night. It was delivered by the noiseless Arman, who materialized shortly after compline.

He was instructed, once up the familiar staircase, to go through the room where they had talked that morning, past the albino falcon and directly into Madame's private bedchamber. As Gaucelm paused at the top of the stairs, he could see that a flare had been lit to guide him through the dark sitting room. Chanute rested on her perch, hooded and silent. Beyond was the room from which Madame Audiarde had earlier fetched her knife. The door was ajar, emitting the scent of tallow, and a brightness so intense it stung his eyes. He entered.

Light bounced from dozens of candles flickering at both sides of the bed. Upon it, clothed in a robe of white samite with the ruby like a spot of blood at her neck, lay Audiarde de Malemort, her wrists and ankles bound to the bedstead. Horrorstruck, Gaucelm stared at her slight form pinioned like an espaliered rose against a wall. When his heart quieted he reached toward her feet to free them. "Don't," she said. "Come here." Her gaze followed him closely and marked his every move.

When she saw the panic in his eyes, she laughed softly. "Mother of God," she said. "There has been a misunderstanding. What has Marie told you of my appetites . . . or what *hasn't* she?" His look was uncomprehending. "Nothing?" she asked. He shook his head. His attention was fixed on the silk cords that held her wrists in the dancing light of the tapers. "Who tied you up like this?" he asked finally.

Madame Audiarde laughed again. "Come closer, Gaucelm," she said gently. "Later you may untie me, if you wish." Then, almost as an afterthought she asked, "Do you like me?"

Gaucelm stared into the tiny, bobbing flames as they reflected off burnished surfaces of hammered gold and liquid silver. Every piece of plate in the household must have been assembled to hold the banks of wax candles. "Yes," he whispered. His surprise had vanished at her sweetness, and slowly his awkwardness changed to something else. He said, "Madame, so long as I am a guest under your roof I remain your liege. I wish to do as you say."

"Come, then. See what I have for you. Sit here by me on the bed. Now look." She lifted her head and nodded a little to the left. Resting on a low stool was the same lady's knife she had used to slice his pear. Gaucelm reached for it. "No, not yet," she said. "First, let me see you. Stand up." He rose from the bed. "That's right. Now begin with your boots. The laces," she instructed, watching him fumble at the leather thongs. "Stockings." He pulled the black wool chausses from his calves. "Your cotte." He undid the fermail at his neck and drew out the pin, then passed the blue silk garment over his head. Madame Audiarde observed his tousled curls with pleasure. "And now the shirt." This, Gaucelm was not able to achieve so gracefully as he wished, for it was tight-sleeved and unfastened at the side. Then, without her urging he undid the cloth belt and let his linen underwear slip to the floor. He stood naked before her, his sex erect.

"*Now* pick up the knife," she commanded. He bent toward it, hesitated. "Take it in your hand," she repeated. He paused, then moved to where her wrists were bound to the bedstead. "Not yet, Gaucelm." This time she did not laugh. "Open my robe." He parted the white samite folds and found her naked thighs beneath. "Begin at my ankles," she instructed, "and let the dagger caress me."

At her words his whole body contracted with fear and excitement. "Go on." He placed the metal blade against the inside of one leg and inched it along her tender flesh, not daring to look at her face. But soon he heard her breath coming fast, and his eyes travelled up to see the ruby rise and fall rapidly at her throat. He watched her then, speechless, his hand moving slowly, all the muscles of his frame tensed.

Suddenly her breaths came more quickly and she asked him to look away. Gaucelm struggled to master himself, watching the darting flames until she was restored to calm. But he could not do it, could not stop himself, and in a heartbeat he was astride her, under the white folds, riding her until her hands formed fists in their silk cords and drummed against the bedposts and his heart seemed to explode in his throat. Then his body eased and he subsided into her, rolling aside slightly to let her breathe.

But it was not over. She moaned a little and he thought he heard her say "hold me." Pressing himself down upon her, he wrapped his arms under her and pulled her close.

"No," she cried suddenly. "*Hit me*!" He sprang away from her, then, rocking back on his hips, and stared at her face in disbelief. All tenderness was gone from her; between clenched teeth she hissed, "Hit me! hit me!" Gaucelm, desire drained out of him, looked wildly around the room, saw the door, thought to escape. But she persisted, her voice rising to a scream, and finally, not knowing how else to quiet her, he did it. He slapped her across the jaw. She went slack under his blow; her fists unclenched.

The silence that ensued filled Gaucelm with cold. In all the times he had been with women he had never experienced anything like this. It was comfortless, eerie, like a pause in battle. But it bore none of the signs of a truce or even a standoff from which enemies might walk away satisfied, honor intact. It was as if both sides had fought and, almost coming to terms, had instead gone back to being foes again.

"You may release me now," she murmured finally. Like a sleepwalker, Gaucelm picked up the dagger where it had clattered to the floor. He cut the silk from her wrists and she sat up slowly. Taking his head between her hands, she kissed him on the forehead and fell back on the cushions, asking him to free her ankles. Then, like an infant, she curled onto her side and settled herself for sleep. Gaucelm, fingers shaking, did not stop to button the waistband of his drawers. He forced his sweaty toes into the wool chausses and threw shirt and cotte over his arm. Then he yanked his boots off the floor by their laces and tiptoed from the bedchamber of Madame Audiarde de Malemort as fast as his stockinged feet could carry him.

Chapter 10

THE COMBORN FESTIVITIES

On the morning of Gaucelm's departure for Malemort, a messenger from Archambaut, Viscount of Comborn, set out for Ventadour.

Marie's day had not gone well. She had just completed evening rounds, and she was cross. The candlemaker was nowhere to be found; she suspected he was lying drunk somewhere in the village. Alba had reported pilferage of flour, which meant they would be short the entire week, as the miller's delivery didn't come until Friday. Walking briskly across the courtyard, Marie barely looked up as the clip-clop of hooves sounded ahead of her. But the edge of a light blue caparison over the horse's flanks caught her eye: the Comborn colors! She went in by a side door and made for the great hall, entering just as a messenger in full livery was leaving the room.

Ebles sat on his favorite bench, his chessboard before him. A scattering of knights had discreetly distanced themselves at a far corner of the hall. "It seems that our daughter will be married at last!" Ebles announced triumphantly as Marie reached his side. "The Comborns are ready to negotiate a dowry."

"When do they arrive?"

"Tomorrow night."

"What exactly did the messenger say?"

"That Archambaut wishes to parley. That he will be accompanied by Guischarda, Humbert, and a small entourage—"

"How many?"

"He didn't say."

Marie sighed. How could she assign bedding without knowing their number? "What age is Humbert now, about nineteen?"

"He didn't say. The man was only a messenger, Marie."

She snorted with impatience. "Was there anything else?"

"What more would you wish?"

True enough, Marie conceded. The Comborns were rich. They were descended from the viscounts of Limoges, and their fiefs, which lay a full day's ride to the west of Ventadour, extended across the whole Garonne valley. From Ebles' father's time the two families had been so linked by events that they seemed to share a common destiny. It was natural, then, for Comborn to seek Ventadour in marriage. From Douce's twelfth birthday she and Ebles had talked of such a match.

The news of their imminent arrival threw Marie into a flurry. She was being asked to work a miracle in no time: a small supper party for tomorrow night, and a grand banquet with invited guests after the parley ended. In between there would at least be an afternoon of hunting—a blessing, since everyone would be out from under her feet. Still, that gave her exactly two days to arrange for a feast of no small importance. It was almost insulting that the Comborns had not given them more warning. Under normal circumstances she would have considered her choice of invitees with care. As it was, she would have to send out messengers immediately, without pondering the full play of her guests' variegated interests and possible clashes.

Cornils, she counted on her fingers—three. At least five Turennes, her own people, whom she could rely on at times like this. Certainly her two sisters, anyway, with their husbands, unless Guiraut had gone abroad after all. Then Lemozi de Brive, who was charming with ladies and—happily—almost always available. It irritated Marie that she had packed Gaucelm off to Malemort at exactly the wrong moment. But how could she have foreseen that this really quite major event concerning Douce—and all their fortunes—would be on hand to enliven the dreary last days of November?

Neighboring landowners would have to be invited whether or not they could come at such short notice. That meant the Biartzes, Arnaud de Tintignac and that awful wife of his, and the Glotons from Egletons. Also the Ussels, however much she regretted Elias's failure to run his affairs intelligently and keep up his small property. Yes, at the risk of reigniting the border dispute he had with Ebles, Elias would have to be asked. And if Elias, then his son Gui and the brother—Pierre, was it?—would have to be included. Those two would merely swell the ranks, but Elias—this much could be said for him—would cut a fine military figure at her table.

Now the entertainment. That promised to be a real problem with Gaucelm gone. Douce had been at her about Gaucelm's woman, Guilhelma, claiming that she had a good voice. *Well*, Marie thought, *perhaps now is the time to try her out*. It wouldn't be the first time that Ventadour had turned up a golden sou from the servant ranks. As to dress, a pity there wasn't time to have a new bliaut made up. The bolt of brilliant blue samite she had ordered from Provins last spring would have to stay rolled up in her wardrobe.

The messengers had to go out at daylight. Suddenly, an idea for a pièce-de-resistance at the banquet came to her. Old Alba would have to be persuaded, but it was guaranteed to make the Comborns sit up and take notice. The negotiations might rest in Ebles' hands, but the show would be all hers.

Early the next morning, every washtub was full of linen and every vat bubbled with sheep fat for fresh candles. The candlemaker was dragged from town and admonished to keep a strict eye on his tallow troughs.

Inside the castle, house servants polished plate. Village wives were brought in to help with the cleaning, while their husbands pulled weeds in the courtyard and rolled it smooth. A cart was dispatched to Egletons for whatever flour could be found. Excitement filled the castle and the village as word spread of Douce's probable engagement. From field hand to barnyard, from cellar to solar, villeins and servants knew: their little miss would soon be joined with the powerful Comborns from across the Garonne valley.

As soon as she heard, Guilhelma went to the kitchen. By the look of things she would have no rest until nightfall, but she was as excited to be swept into the preparations for the great occasions as if it were her own affair.

If only Douce would leave off pestering her! A little after the chapel bells rang terce, the girl had burst into the steaming kitchen, her face red and tear-streaked. Guilhelma had just begun on the first batch of fowl, which would be quartered as soon as they came off the spits, and she merely glanced up. Douce turned away, scanning the room for the comforting presence of the cat. "Gris!" she called, clapping her hands, but no animal responded to her summons. Too dispirited to search for him, Douce gave Guilhelma a reproachful look and went to sit by the hearth where, head down, she hugged her knees to her chest.

At last Guilhelma finished with the spits and mopped her face with the towel that hung from her belt. A scraping of stools announced that the other servants were preparing to eat their noon meal. Instead of joining them, Guilhelma jerked the towel from her waist and picked up her shawl. She needed to breathe and rest her legs even more than she needed the bread and cheese—and she did not wish to ignore Douce. She motioned the girl up from the hearth and out into the kitchen garden.

The two huddled on the cold stone ledge by the pot herb border.

Douce sat up straight, looking for all the world like a schoolgirl who wished to please, but suddenly had nothing to say. Guilhelma spread her square hands, palms up, on her skirt and waited for Douce to speak.

On certain matters a gap would always separate the two. Guilhelma was a villein. Her life, from the moment of her birth, was destined to be as different from Douce de Ventadour's as night from day. How could she possibly understand what Douce feared was coming?

"I *won't* marry. I don't want to marry anyone," Douce said at last. "Certainly not someone with the awful name of Humbert."

Guilhelma suppressed a smile. "Is there someone else?"

"There was, but . . . oh, it's so complicated. It's so impossible!"

"What is he called?"

Douce hesitated, then thought, *It will mean nothing to her.* "Gui."

It had happened in the spring, over a year earlier, all because of the border dispute. Gui d'Ussel had just left service as a knight apprentice in the household of Arraut de Cornil when, on a green May morning he rode with his father to Ventadour.

Then in his sixteenth year, Gui had acquired the bearing of someone who was on his own for the first time. His stride, as he went forward to greet Ebles, was brisk, his expression alert as a young fox's.

The eternal wrangle over land with the Ventadour neighbors had been a fixture of his childhood. But its subtleties, its twists and turns, preoccupied him little. Much more vivid to him were the rumors circulating at Cornil just as he was leaving: there was trouble in Provence. Soon after Elias and Ebles were hunched in discussion over claret, Gui excused himself, bent on mingling with Ebles' knights and discovering what they had heard about the unrest in the South. The first person he glimpsed on leaving the hall was Douce.

She saw him across the courtyard. He slowed as they approached one another.

Those eyes! Dark as violets, so unlike her father's lupine eyes. They nodded politely. How handsome he was! His chin was neatly cleft; the bow of his upper lip showed a bit of its velvet. His cropped black curls swept back over his ears like the helmet of Achilles. After he passed, she turned to catch sight of his long torso as it curved into the sword belt slung low on his hips. How perfect he seemed.

It was well into summer before she saw Gui again. The fields in dispute were already knee-high in bracken when he and his father rode across them to meet Ebles in anticipation of a final accord.

By now Douce knew that she was in love, and she was determined not to show it. That night at supper she was sure no one noticed anything at all uncommon about her. In fact she was livelier than usual; her talk glowed. She curtseyed to Ebles, parried his observations, carried and fetched for her mother, allowed Elias to pour her wine, and never so much as glanced at Gui. The effort exhausted her. Moreover, it was stupid, all this chatter of harvests, taxes, tithing, tournaments.

After the dogs were fed and the lamps extinguished, Douce bade good night to her parents and mounted to her room, resolved to pray.

"I had almost stopped thinking of Gui until this morning," Douce said to Guilhelma. "And now he'll be coming with his father and uncle tomorrow night. But it's true, what I said: I never want to marry. No matter *who*."

Guilhelma stared at her. "No young woman with any sense refuses a marriage like the one you're being offered. How else do you expect to provide for yourself?"

"There are ways for a lady to live on her own," Douce said mysteriously. Guilhelma shouted with laughter at the picture which immediately came to her mind—the incongruity of Douce setting up shop in the Chantier quarter. Douce turned to frown at her.

"What's so funny about a religious order?"

"*You*?" Now Guilhelma was incredulous. "Come, Douce, it's not worth shutting yourself up forever just to avoid marrying someone called Humbert!"

"I've been thinking about it for some time," Douce said, her voice cool, as though she suspected Guilhelma of not taking her seriously.

"Thinking about what, exactly?"

Douce hesitated. "Do you promise, absolutely *swear* to tell no one, not even Gaucelm? This is a life-and-death secret."

"I promise."

"I met a wisewoman." She paused, then her words came in a rush. "She can cure a person taken with fits. She makes her own medicines, like you. I take her plants and dried herbs. She belongs to a secret religious order."

"So that *was* you, that night, with the basket on your arm!"

Douce grabbed both Guilhelma's work-worn hands and squeezed them in her own. "You must never, never tell," she pleaded.

The door to the kitchen swept open and Alba's voice rang in the courtyard. "Guilhelma! Where is she? Guilhelma, are you there?"

Douce grimaced at having her confession interrupted. Guilhelma rose suddenly, full of guilt at her absence, then walked briskly toward the kitchen. Obviously this wisewoman who had a way with herbs was exerting some power over the girl. Secret order indeed! The old woman probably knew a good thing when she saw it, particularly when it came from a castle. But Guilhelma felt a surge of faith in Douce, and told herself that in any case marriage would rid her mind of such crazy religious notions. Girls got strange ideas at this age, and all she could do for Douce was listen, and remain as steadfast as possible.

Guilhelma paused and hugged her shawl close as she watched Douce sprint across the courtyard. If she can move that fast, she thought, at least I've helped to lighten her heart.

The grey shadows of Ventadour seemed to cast a spell on the Comborns and their visit from the moment of their arrival. On the morning of the banquet everything went wrong at once. Alba had balked when Marie revealed her idea of a pastry cage filled with live birds for the table's centerpiece. Nonetheless, a dozen song sparrows and magpies had been netted on Marie's orders and brought to the kitchen, where they were housed overnight in a contraption made of twigs. The cats, including Gris, were banished to the yard as a precautionary measure. The candlemaker and the poulterer were ordered to take shifts sleeping in the kitchen to see that the captives didn't peck each other to death.

Even from behind bars, the birds had managed to turn the entire kitchen upside down. Always the first to enter in the morning, Alba was greeted by a cacophony of bewildered chirping as the creatures slammed their wings against the lashed twigs of their prison. The candlemaker had fallen drunk on his watch and had to be sloshed with cold water before he was fit to stagger back to his shop.

There were other mishaps. After terce the shamefaced cellarer reported to Pons that most of the wine had turned, and would have to be boiled with spice and honey to make it potable. The cellarer got a thrashing with the back of Pons' hand for keeping the wine undrawn past its time, and two unfortunate pages, a cupbearer and a dispenser who happened into Pons' line of fire, got a tongue-lashing in the bargain.

Just before compline, when the final batch of wine had been heated and the last piece of venison struck off its spit and onto a platter, Marie calculated that the guests had been kept waiting long enough. She signaled to Pons, and the company took their seats. Guilhelma, wishing she had something pretty to change into, merely pulled off her apron, splashed some water on her face, and sat on a stool at one of the long tables that Marie had assigned to upper servants of the household. Hands folded in her lap, she watched as though she were in church while the chaplain said grace.

The hall looked very grand, she thought, with the pale blue arms of Comborn displayed above the dais and those of the other families on either side. The head table was laid out with silver, the visitors' gifts had been set in a row on the sideboard, and the trumpeters were in full livery. She could just glimpse Douce at one end of the high table, her presence there a concession to her new status as bride-to-be. She looked miserable.

Once Pons entered bearing Alba's pastry cage followed by a procession of dispensers and pages—all familiar faces—Guilhelma breathed more easily. Then the unthinkable happened. Just as Pons moved forward to bow before the guests, one of the dogs got up and sent Pons sprawling. Guilhelma watched open-mouthed as the cage slid from the platter, its apple garnish thudding to the floor. Servants on either side of her moved to help, but the situation was beyond repair. Birds escaped with piercing cries from their pastry prison, just as Ebles' pet gyrfalcon swept down on them. A tidy massacre! The guests whooped with amusement at the unexpected entertainment, until the rafters rang. Guilhelma was by turns shocked, dismayed, and, finally, diverted. Soon she could barely stifle her laughter. The uproar was terrible: hawk screams, bloodied birds scattered over the floor straw, dogs barking, warm wine running across the linen and seeping into the trenchers.

On impulse, Guilhelma rose from her seat and walked to the front of the hall, where she stood before the dais. At no one's bidding she did the only thing it seemed natural to do under the circumstances: she sang. It worked like magic. Before she was into the fourth verse of "*Tant ai sofert*" the worst of the mess was mopped up and the pages and dispensers were bringing the platters from the kitchen in something like their right order.

Guilhelma sang on, in an infinite ascension of notes. Alcohol quickly had its effect, masking everyone's embarrassment. Once the final echo of her song sounded from the walls Guilhelma curtsied, and sought Douce's nod of approval from the far end of the table. But the girl was staring at someone else. Guilhelma followed her gaze and understood immediately. She saw thick black hair framing the features of a young angel, and knew this must be Gui. From the look on Douce's face, Guilhelma was certain it all spelled trouble.

Before she could make her way back to her seat, the guests were clamoring for more song. They were beating their cups on the table, asking, pleading for another. She came forward again, this time assured and smiling in triumph. Now she gave them the pastourelle that Douce had liked when, on that day in the kitchen, she discovered Guilhelma could sing. By now, Guilhelma knew, she had her audience's rapt attention. For her last song she would do one of Gaucelm's, the "*Be-m deu plazer.*"

Gaucelm caught a few winks of sleep and saddled up before Arman and the rest of the household awakened. Cantering back to Ventadour a day earlier than Marie expected him, he felt even more confused than on the morning he had left Raymond and ridden out of Toulouse with Guilhelma. Were there signals he had failed to pick up from Marie, hints that his "punishment" was to be unusual, if not exactly cruel? Had there been the slightest inkling of what was to follow—of candles and silken ties and the jeweled lady's knife? He recalled Marie's flirtatiousness, her odd smile as she explained his mission, hovering over the little table piled with seals and ribbons. Perhaps he'd been still too in awe of her to see how she had practically been tasting Gaucelm's encounter with Madame Audiarde.

By now, though, his awe had turned to anger. He had been used by two women playing sexual games on the board of courtly love. Those "rules" set down by Andreas Capellanus were just an intellectual excuse. It dawned on Gaucelm that there was probably no such thing as courtly love at all. At least, not at either Ventadour or Malemort. But being tricked by women was what rankled most. Who now was the whore, he or Madame Audiarde?

To steady himself he fiddled with a few words to begin his poem, the form of "proof" he had chosen to present to Marie. It would have to be pure artifice. That, at least, she could appreciate. How could he speak in verse of what had actually happened in that bedchamber? He was still haunted by Madame Audiarde, by "ruby red, hoarfroast white," and thought he might weave it in somewhere. He tried a stanza on cortesia, lifted more or less intact from the fragments of Andreas that he had read aloud. But the stylized Latin prose of the *Book of Love* didn't lend itself to any song he was in the mood to sing. Finally, he shouted out "*Dieus, ges longuas non posc soffrir l'afan!*"

God, I can't go on with this for long! was what his heart was telling him. He felt split in two. *I should have stolen her dagger!* he thought. *Then I could have just handed it to Marie and let her make what she could of my 'proof'!* That Marie might jump to the conclusion that he had killed Madame Audiarde made him laugh, but the dagger would have allowed him to put something over on both of them, for a short while at least. Marie of course would have to be told the truth soon enough, and then she'd demand the details. Of course! *That* was what she was after, wanting to be part of it, the old voyeur.

He'd give her the details, all right, and spare her nothing for sending him on this fool's errand. He'd let himself be angry at her in verse—why not? She might, given her perversity, enjoy it. He decided on a tenson, but not the usual kind, with stanzas alternating between two different voices. His poem would be an argument, as a tenson was designed to be, but he would compose a dialogue with *himself.* He was so delighted with this innovation that he kicked Ebles' destrier to a gallop. One eight-line stanza of his own true thoughts, answered by one describing what went on in the bedchamber with his ruby red, hoarfrost white lady. Smarting with injustice but delighted with his plan, the first line came easily: *Aissi me tol mos covinenz e.ls fran.* **She takes my precious covenant and breaks it.** After that he could go on:

> *Si.m fos grazitz mos chanz ieu m'esforzera*
> *e dera.m gaug e deportz e solatz,*
> I'd be encouraged if I could like what I compose
> for then I'd feel happiness, satisfaction and repose...

It was turning out to be a simple enough matter. He needed only two more stanzas. By the time he rode up the scraggly path to Ventadour he had completed his song. He was still memorizing rhyme endings as he threw the reins over the destrier's head and led him into the yard.

Once a stableboy had taken his horse, Gaucelm headed for the castle. He was astonished to see light streaming onto the pelouse. Torches burned steadily behind every stone-rimmed window and arrow-slit. As he approached he knew from the thud of music and clapping issuing from the hall that a banquet was in progress. But when he reached the threshold of the hall he found himself in the presence of a hushed court.

Multicolored banners hung high above the heads of a multitude, whose silk and samite robes were motionless above the head table. Pairs of eyes beyond count, belonging to faces he did not recognize, stared at the point below the dais where Guilhelma stood alone. His whole being was riveted as she sang his own words: "***Be-m deu plazer, car sobre las genssors es sos rics cors de simpla captenenssa...***" He felt his pulse quicken wildly. There was no mistake—her voice was rich, wonderful. It vibrated with a fierce kind of pride. How right his instincts had been that first night when he'd introduced her to Marie! Guilhelma was graced with the talent of a born jonglaresa.

He sensed again the mix of triumph and jealousy that shot through him when he had first heard Guilhelma sing. Of course there had always been jonglaresas. Some were even famous, like Alamanda, but he had never seen her perform. Come to think of it, in all his years of travel, he had never heard a woman sing at court. Mostly they frequented inns and taverns. In the alehouses up north, they were usually egged on by a crowd and then had to beg for a sou afterward.

Gaucelm could not take his eyes from Guilhelma. What little instruction Vidal had given her made no difference to the natural quality of that voice. It was generous even in the upper registers, and its base was like her, full and sturdy. It had plenty of range, and—he could not describe it otherwise—her notes had colors in them. The high ones, "*sos rics cors*," were silvery; her lower registers made him think of a dark velvety blue. When she descended in the scale the sounds turned molten, as though a flame had been lit somewhere deep in her belly.

It was thrilling to hear her. Why, Gaucelm mused as he stood listening, had she never taken advantage of her gift? Well, *he* should certainly do so. Here was proof that she showed off his words to advantage, presenting them better, in some ways, than he. After all, composing was one thing, the art of the jonglar or jonglaresa was quite another. He wondered whether, given such musicality, she had the talent for inventing verses as well. But no, that was not for the likes of her. A few ladies of the nobility composed, but they were so rare that even the name they were called—troubairitz—sounded foreign to the ear.

Nonetheless, he decided to encourage Guilhelma. Having settled this in his mind, he waited until she finished singing and then went forward to the front of the hall. Startled, Guilhelma caught sight of him and moved eagerly in his direction. After the strangeness of what had happened at Malemort, he was happy to see her. Still, the slightest bit of envy tinged his welcoming kiss.

Chapter 11

CHECKMATE

Gaucelm slept through prime the next morning. He awoke groggy and unsure of where he was, as though he had been away from Ventadour for a very long time. Guilhelma, he realized, had probably gone to the kitchen even before chapel. Last evening's fiasco would have given Marie reason to castigate the servants and insist that they redouble their efforts. He would corner Guilhelma at her station and propose that she escape for a walk with him during the noon meal, when she would least be missed. He had to talk to her. When there was too much going on in his head she helped him to sort things out.

He found Guilhelma washing up from breakfast, and he waited while she scrubbed the pots in readiness for the midday meal. Miraculously, the kitchen was as tidy as though the banquet had never taken place. "God be praised, most of the company have left," she said. Her expression was briskly triumphant, showing no sign of fatigue.

At noon, as the door closed behind them, they heard a light wind seething in the treetops. "It feels like snow," Gaucelm said. Guilhelma pulled her cloak tighter in the raw air, wrapping both arms like a mummy's within its folds. She was glad of the extra layer the kitchen apron made around her waist. They passed along the frozen, rutted path that led beyond the stables to the postern gate.

Once Gaucelm made fast the heavy bolt behind them, they paused and surveyed the world of Ventadour. "Oh!" Guilhelma exclaimed, pointing into the distance. A dusting of white crystals softened the sharp ridges far below them. They were poised above a gorge of great depth, a precipice so steep that Guilhelma ventured to look directly down only once. To keep her head from swimming she forced her gaze across the swooping undulations of land to a point where the ravines gave way to level ground and fanned into fields.

"My first snow," she murmured.

Vaulting gusts began to shake the trees on the crag where they stood. Gaucelm stamped impatiently. He hated the desolation of this place, the dense black trees, the faraway thunder of rushing waters, the cold, and, even worse, the menacing, rocky, impassible ravines empty of towns, houses, all that warmed human existence. Above all he hated the ceaseless winds of the Corrèze. They had dogged him to Malemort and back. Their memory and the new snow made him instantly sorry he had suggested this walk.

He blew on his bare hands. "Let's go back," he said, "before the wind turns us to stone." He hugged Guilhelma around her waist.

"Now then, tell me . . . what happened at Malemort?" she asked.

"Aren't you cold?"

"A little. But I love looking at snow. It's miraculous."

"Well then," he said, resigning himself to the chill. He talked about Madame Audiarde, leaving out her exquisite attractions and concentrating on the oddities of her household he thought would amuse Guilhelma: the silent Armand, the white falcon. When he mentioned Folquet she started slightly, as though his name had put her on the alert. Guilhelma stopped him. "What really happened to you at Malemort? I mean in the bedchamber, with this Madame Audiarde?" She gave him a knowing look and locked his shifting gaze into her steady one.

His reticence gave way and he told her everything, silken ropes and all. As he spoke he watched her face uneasily until her eyes, wide with curiosity, began to narrow. "What made you stay, then? Why didn't you just leave the moment you saw her tied up? Or did the candle flames bewitch you?" It made him nervous, the way she stared at him as though he were a stranger, her cheeks flushed, her eyes like flint, her bare hands clenched.

"Orders," Gaucelm replied. "It's simple. I obey Marie or we have nowhere to sleep. To get the benefits, you play the game. Until you can call your own shots you do what you're bidden in order to stay alive. You of all people should understand that. I couldn't *just leave*," he said scornfully. "Marie is nobody's fool. She demands proof that I carried out her command." The explanation made perfect sense to him as he voiced it. Relief cleared his head as it always did when he confided in Guilhelma.

"What *kind* of proof?"

"What she had in mind, I'm sure, was some token. The little knife would have filled the bill nicely, if I'd had my wits about me. As it is, Marie insisted on leaving it to my ingenuity, so what she'll get instead is a song."

That seemed to satisfy Guilhelma. She changed the subject. "And Folquet. Who told you about *his* being there?"

"Madame Audiarde. But Folquet was Marie's protégé, remember. She told us so the night we arrived, as though it was something to boast about!"

Guilhelma clutched her cloak closer beneath her throat and bent her chin into its folds. Folquet—it was beginning to make sense. Stung as she was by Gaucelm's acquiescence to Madame Audiarde's wishes, there were odder matters to consider, like Folquet's twisted sexual proclivities. *So that's where he had his start,* she thought, *in the bed of the vixen Gaucelm had just been delivered up to, and for the same reasons!*

Folquet had always puzzled and infuriated Guilhelma. She knew him first as the son of a rich Marseille merchant, then as a striving troubadour and a married man. He had continued to come to her as a novice monk, and then as Abbot of Le Thoronet. She had not purposely kept her dealings with Folquet from Gaucelm. It was just that there had never been occasion to bring up Folquet's name in *that* context. In fact, she'd always assumed that Gaucelm knew Folquet had been one of her "regulars."

Everyone knew. In Toulouse it was practically a matter of civic pride that the Chantier received men of the cloth like potentates. They (and leading merchants, of course) got the best and most hygienic treatment. Some said it was unfairly preferential. But when the word was out that a legation of priests was on its way, fair or not, the decks were cleared for them, so to speak. Local clients were hustled out a little earlier than usual; street drunks and common layabouts were whisked off to temporary quarters in one of the almshouses, and there'd be nary a disreputable character in sight. No, the Chantier of Toulouse was known far and wide for such niceties. In return, visiting clergy showed their appreciation—they were generous and always paid their favorites in gold. Particularly Folquet, as he gained in riches—and, she remembered ruefully, in girth. She quickly became his putana of choice.

Now, with this revelation of Gaucelm's, the pieces fell into place: Folquet had learned his perverted ways right here, under Marie's tutelage! So this was how the "court of women" worked, and this was what was meant by "playing the game of love." Well and good. But that Marie had sent Gaucelm out for instruction just as she had sent Folquet—that made Guilhelma recoil.

There and then, Guilhelma recounted her past with Folquet to Gaucelm, and it was his turn to be furious. "You? Folquet?" He was shocked, in spite of what she thought he knew of the realities of her former occupation. "Folquet!" he railed against her. "How *could* you? Why Folquet, of all swine!"

There was little she could say. It was useless to remind him that she could hardly pick and choose who came to her bed, so long as they could pay. No child of privilege could be expected to understand this, and experience had taught her simply to withdraw from such issues. But Gaucelm's outburst bewildered her. Since he held Folquet beneath contempt, jealousy was out of the question. It dawned on her finally that, having lived at Raymond's court when he wasn't travelling, he might well know next to nothing about the Chantier. So far as she was aware, he had not set foot in the quarter on "business"—except to visit her—after that first night. Obviously she would have to set him straight on the conventions of her old profession, and on Folquet's peculiarities of behavior. Later.

Mercifully, Gaucelm's fury soon returned to Marie. He was incredulous at her motives: claiming that snake Folquet as a minion made her more than a virtuoso of deceit. To put it bluntly, it made her a procuress. Defiantly, he looked up at a sky gone suddenly grey with the threat of more snow. "I'll have no more of it! Let's leave Ventadour," he said, turning his back on the fields. "I've had a bellyful of trickery. What is there to keep us here?"

"Nothing. Except for the benefits you just mentioned. A roof. Bread." Guilhelma, too, felt divided. Gaucelm's encounter at Malemort, the revelation of Folquet's sojourn there, Marie's intrigues—it all put her in two minds about everything she had taken for granted only a short time ago. Now a gulf seemed to open before her. But to return to her straw mattress in the Chantier, to give up all she saw before her to become a woman alone again at the mercy of any man who came along; to leave Douce and Alba and three square meals a day in spite of the occasional kitchen frenzy. No, it was unthinkable! The castle might be a slit-eyed old fortress and its mistress made of stone. Nonetheless, she could afford to either ignore Marie or toady up to her, whichever suited her purpose. Leave Ventadour? Never! And especially not after the thrill of singing in the great hall last night.

The only person who stood between squalor and her own bright future was the man who stood next to her, numb with cold and resentment. She might as well tell him now. "Wait," she said, a finger beckoning from her cloak. "There's more. You might as well hear the rest, about Folquet." Impatient, almost, to have his anger assuaged, Gaucelm turned toward her.

"More than half a dozen years ago, when Folquet first frequented the Chantier, he was composing verses, trying to establish himself as a troubadour, as you know. Well, like any amateur he saw himself as a free spirit and he made a regular nuisance of himself at my place, reciting his doggerel and drinking my wine when I should have been tidying up for the next customer. He would go on about the heretics who called themselves Cathars and how their beliefs interested him." Gaucelm gaped at her. "I'm not saying that he actually joined their ranks . . . I wouldn't know anything about that. Even then I could see that it was part of a pose. But he made it his business to know the young ones, especially the jongleurs and musicians about town whose companionship he sought out."

Gaucelm could hardly contain himself. "Didn't I hear you say, not so long ago, that you'd never had a heretic in your bed?" His grin was mischievous.

"Never *knowingly*, Gaucelm. Mind you, I have no proof. More than likely it was a flight of fancy, a rich young man's fling with a fashionable idea. You know yourself how many artists as well as tradesmen are Cathars. I guess that he wanted to be part of their circle."

Gaucelm pounded his right fist into his left hand. "I can hardly believe my luck. This is too good to be true!" and he raised both arms in triumph.

"I have no *proof*, Gaucelm," Guilhelma again warned. "There's no way to use this against him."

"Nevertheless. . ." Gaucelm said, ". . . nevertheless," and she knew he was beyond listening.

As they walked in the direction of the castle, Gaucelm suddenly stopped dead and stared at her.

"Does Folquet know *you* know?"

"About . . . ?"

"About his Cathar sympathies, of course."

"He must. After all, he talked about it at my place. I encouraged him. It was less boring than hearing him recite those awful ditties of his."

Gaucelm's face fell. "That *could* spell trouble."

"Why, by the mother of God?"

"If he ever got wind of an allegation against him on that score, it would all come back to roost. Toulouse, the Chantier, a woman named Guilhelma Monja . . ."

". . . and," she said without missing a beat, "if he knew you and I were together, he'd go straight for *your* throat." They entered the castle enclosure in glum silence.

Guilhelma was not surprised to find Douce waiting for her when she returned to the kitchen. One look at the girl's solemn face told her that something must have happened and she, too, wanted to talk. But Guilhelma had used up her quota of free time; the others were already back at work. "Quick, catch up with Gaucelm! Maybe you can interest him in a round of horseshoes."

"Why?"

"His spirits are low."

"So are mine."

Guilhelma sighed and motioned Douce to the fireplace where they were less likely to be overheard. She began adding herbs to the pots that Alba had filled in her absence.

"So *that* was Gui, last night at the high table."

"Yes," Douce said. Then she burst into tears. Guilhelma dusted the herbs from her fingers while Douce cried on helplessly, her back heaving beneath Guilhelma's protective arms. Finally she raised her head and announced, amidst a strangle of sobs, "It is all settled. With the Comborns. For Whitsuntide next year. I can't, Guilhelma. I *won't!*"

"Have you spoken to the lord your father?"

Douce merely gave her a look. She wiped her eyes with the backs of her hands and stood up. "I have made up my mind. If I can't have Gui I won't marry anyone. I shall join Madame Belot's secret order."

"So that's her name, the wisewoman?"

Douce nodded. "Will you help me leave Ventadour?"

Guilhelma ignored her plea. Along with her curiosity about this Madame Belot she recognized a faint stab of jealousy.

"How did you meet such a person?"

"The widow Belot? With old Daniel, on rounds in the village," she said impatiently. "Promise, Guilhelma! I need your help."

Guilhelma sighed again. Fond of Douce as she was, she could do nothing to help the poor creature. It was absurd, she thought, how the moment she herself was happily situated, doing steady work that she liked, and on a full belly, the two people who meant the most to her were threatening to leave Ventadour. She turned to Douce.

"Love can change, you know."

That got Douce's attention. She raised her head and stared at Guilhelma. "I can see that you love him," Guilhelma continued. "Now you love him passionately with your whole heart. You believe that love will last in you. But I've seen enough of life to know one thing: do not expect it to be the same forever. That's the mistake everybody makes. Love changes." Guilhelma could almost hear Douce's silent rebuttal: *What makes this servant woman think herself so wise in the world's ways?*

Douce said, "Either there's love or there isn't. Gui is who I want. He is perfect, Guilhelma. You have seen him with your own eyes. You *know* that we belong together! Sometimes I feel he *is* me . . . that we can't tell each other apart."

"And Gui?" was Guilhelma's response. "What does he know of all this . . . 'perfection'?"

Douce's annoyance turned to gloom. Guilhelma was right. Gui knew nothing of her feelings. There had been only glances across the table, a smile, his eyes on hers. Douce turned and got up from her stool. *That poor child is in for a hard time*, Guilhelma thought as Douce left the kitchen without another word.

Once all was in order for supper, the staff cleared out until the chapel bells rang vespers. Guilhelma walked slowly across the courtyard, unable to take her eyes from the snow. She bent down and scooped some into her fingers, not noticing how numb it made her bare hand. She suspected that Gaucelm would be venting his fury at Marie in that song he had promised her, and she found him, predictably, in the practice room, tending to his wounds in the way he knew best. She sat on a stool and listened.

From the moment he left Guilhelma at the kitchen door, Gaucelm had resumed composing as though a fire had been lit beneath him. But the tenson that had come so easily as he rode from Malemort now seemed weak. He eliminated all but the quatrain beginning, "*Aissi me tol mos covinenz.*" He liked those lines for their emphasis: "**She *takes* my covenant and *breaks* it**!" The words cooled his head a bit.

Once he had decided to be more forthright, the phrases flew from him. When he heard the door open he was prepared to resent Guilhelma's presence, but she sat quietly and did not interrupt, so he could not object. The moment he finished, he asked her to tell him whether or not his words had the delicious irony he intended. "*No m'alegra chanz ni critz d'auzels*," he sang.

> **Since neither songs nor sounds of birds
> Can rouse your heart, I must have sinned.
> Lady, tell me why my pleas
> Fall on deaf ears —
> Or must I forfeit joy, no more to sing?**

"Get up off your knees," Guilhelma suggested when she had heard the tenson all the way through.

He looked at her. "I'm not *on* my knees."

"I mean to Marie, silly. You are too modest. Don't plead. Play *her* game. Play it *her* way and you stand a chance to win. Keep doing it your way and you're sure to go on losing."

He was stunned. Why did this damned peasant wench always turn out to be right? She was telling him to say what he could not have brought himself to put into words. Something, some stubborn scruple, had acted like a catch throughout the whole tenson—this he now saw. The verses harped on a single note.

But here was Guilhelma telling him to try something else, to turn it around, to play into Marie's strategy, get her attention, dare to say what he felt.

It was worth a try. He felt suddenly intrigued with the idea of fighting fire with fire in deadly earnest, putting himself on the line. Could he bring it off? He gave a great sigh and, beating time against the wall with his bow, started over. First he scrapped the birds, then the pleas. Next, he decided to announce his departure from Marie's service, casting it as a *fait accompli*. That gave him his tone, and he launched into the body of the piece as though it were a saga in the manner of the old-fashioned *laïs*.

"**New in northern lands, I came to Countess Marie's Ventadour,**" he began. He saw Guilhelma nod in approval. Then a rueful twist on the obligatory conceits about his patroness's great reputation. Finally, a surprising turn: "**From this moment I am forced to flee you like any duplicitous lover. I ask pardon. I entreat your forgiveness. Take pity on me!**"

He glanced at Guilhelma, hoping that this had done the trick. Evidently not, for she got up and began to pace the room.

He flung his bow to the floor in Vidal's old gesture, and before he could retrieve it he had another inspiration. He mouthed the words, "**I have cheated.**" He sat still, the bow motionless. No music came. Instead, he was relishing the sight of Marie's face when she heard this word, *cheated*. He, a self-accused *lauzengier*—a common liar and slanderer—was there anything worse to admit to in the entire canon of courtly love?

The phrase grew tendrils, and before he knew it he was reciting two new stanzas aloud. He looked at Guilhelma. At first, silence. And then she burst out, "You are clever, my Gaucelm! That should do it; you'll win her over on your own terms, just wait! There is nothing for her to say but renew the tie if she doesn't want to lose you." Deep down she was not so sure, but she would hold her breath and try not to think about having to leave Ventadour.

At supper that night the numbers were so sharply reduced that the atmosphere in the great hall was almost intimate.

An overnight snowfall had caused the Comborns' early departure. With a day's ride ahead, the Biartz entourage also left at dawn, but the Tintignacs and the Glotons, all closer neighbors, said their farewells after a substantial breakfast. The Cornil lands bordered on Ebles'. They would stay on for a bit to give Arraut de Cornil more time with his godson, Gui. Marie's own people, the Turennes, would remain for the rest of the week. It appeared to Marie that the Ussels would linger as long as the stores of cellar and pantry held out, so she had countermanded yesterday's order to send to Egletons for more wine.

As Marie took her place on the dais for supper, Gaucelm was aware that she had changed into her everyday dark green bliaut and her hair was once again concealed by a wimple instead of bound with the circlet she had worn at the Comborn banquet. It was not hard to assess her mood: he had never seen her more relaxed. The lines of habitual vexation, normally accentuated by the tightness of her headdress, were hardly visible. Despite the chaos unleashed by captive birds flying about the great hall, she was, he surmised, riding the wave of a satisfactory conclusion to Douce's engagement.

Unable to muster much of an appetite, Gaucelm barely noticed Alba's fragrant stew. But frequent glances in Marie's direction told him that she had already ingested two helpings, and drunk more than her usual single draft of watered wine as she chatted vivaciously with her brother-in-law Guiraut.

As it happened, Gaucelm was in luck: he had finished the tenson just in time.

Immediately after supper, Marie sent for him. He was surprised to be called to her quarters so soon, but he reasoned it was better to get this business over with now rather than later. He was about to undertake the biggest risk of his life, and he knew that if he dwelt on it overmuch, his resolve would sink to nothing.

He reflected on Guilhelma's part in this venture as he walked toward the solar staircase. The woman wanted to remain at Ventadour—that was clear. Yet she was urging him on in a reckless move that might send them both on the road again. Anyone else would have encouraged him to bend a knee, deliver the conventional words of praise, and consider himself lucky to come out relatively unscathed. But not Guilhelma. Was she—the idea shot into his excited brain—was she planning to get him expelled while she stayed on? He rebuked himself instantly, but his thoughts were disordered as he entered the solar.

This time there were no preliminaries, no perambulations from desk to chair, from fireplace to chest, by which she had given Gaucelm the opportunity to observe and admire her. This evening her bearing indicated confidence that such evidence of her power was already in effect, and that no further effort was required to win his esteem. On the contrary, two red spots revealed her excitement. She was fairly burning with curiosity, Gaucelm saw, but before she asked for the full account of his Malemort venture, she had to know one thing: "Why did you leave a day early? Was Madame ill?"

Gaucelm took a deep breath. "You have entirely misjudged me, Lady."

Marie stepped toward him, as though to inspect the intent of his words more closely. "Sit," she said.

"I prefer to stand."

She looked at him, puzzled. Then she turned to the fireplace as though to dismiss him. "What do you mean, *misjudged*?"

Gaucelm paused. "I understand reprimand and even corporal punishment, where appropriate, my lady. But not torture."

Slowly she turned toward him once more. "Gaucelm." She had done a complete about-face; her countenance was full of sympathy. "Gaucelm . . . oh, my dear man, it was only a *game*. I was so sure you would find Madame Audiarde a *diversion*! Of course I was cross with you. Surely you did not expect otherwise. But those who take their chastisement at the hands of Madame Audiarde cannot consider themselves . . ." Here she hesitated then advanced, both hands outstretched as though in a peace offering, ". . . anything but privileged!"

He made no reply.

"Very well," she let her arms drop back to her sides, "we'll dwell on this no longer. The matter is finished, except for one thing: Have you forgotten our agreement? You have brought proof of your little love-lesson from Malemort?" Her look grew eager again.

"I have not forgotten, Lady." And with that, Gaucelm sang Marie his resignation in four stanzas of verse.

Her expression, at first confident of hearing the spicy details of the scene she had arranged for her own delectation, quickly angered. Gaucelm continued to recite, watching as the lines bracketing her mouth deepened, and the red flush at her cheeks darkened in outrage. Then she abruptly turned on her heel and went to stand by the fireplace, her back to him. When he finished his tenson he withdrew from the solar with a bow, though she did not see it. She did not turn around, nor did she call him back. Instead, as the chimes struck compline, she dispatched Pons to Gaucelm's quarter with a bag containing thirty pieces of gold.

Not until after Guilhelma grabbed him and they broke into a mad dance around the room did the entire force of his venture come over him. Was he getting drunk on risk? He decided then and there to exact the full measure of his price from Marie. He marched up the staircase again, knocked at the bolted door of the solar, demanded fifty pieces, and got them on the spot. Along with the coins, he received a look from Marie that said, "Good. Now that the score is even, on to the next round!" He had won. She acknowledged it, and he had to admit that she had been spirited in defeat. She did indeed play by the rules, even though they were of her own devising.

He thought about it as he descended the solar stairs. He had begun by being intrigued and then despising the sport of idle women as much as he had once despised the hunt, a sport of idle men.

Now that he knew he could play a winning hand with the likes of the Countess of Ventadour, however, it was no longer the game itself that he disliked so much as something deeper. It was not her bizarre efforts at his corruption he could not forgive. He burned, in spite of his victory, with his first humiliation at the exercise of female caprice.

Chapter 12

NEWS FROM PROVENCE

On the second morning after the banquet, Ebles de Ventadour, enveloped in a miniver-trimmed mantle, sat in his armchair in the great hall. He was in his element, entertaining the remaining knights with stories of the Eastern crusade. War, for Ebles, meant leading a thousand men over the plains of Asia Minor against the swarthy, raggle-taggle Infidel who fought back any way it could, including tooth and nail, hand-to-hand in the dust.

He leaned forward, his elbows on the table which had been cleared after an early breakfast. "We were outnumbered just outside Jaffa. There were only two of us—myself and a German—and it was lucky for me that he had an axe by his saddle. As we galloped up the rise, this German and I, we were surprised by three Moslems on horses singing out an Arab war cry at the top of their lungs and waving those broadswords with curved blades that looked for all the world like scythes . . ."

"What did it sound like, their war cry?" Gui D'Ussel's bright, upturned face signaled that he wanted to hear the real thing. Ebles obligingly gripped the arms of his chair with both hands and, screwing up his eyes, let out a high-pitched "ye-eee! ye-eee!"

All movement in the hall stopped. Marie, who had been doing her conversational duty with Gui's uncle Pierre, froze in mid-sentence. And so Ebles found himself the triumphant center of attention, a state he had not enjoyed since his return from the Eastern crusades eight years before. Marie's stunned expression gave him a little tremolo of pleasure.

Ebles coughed and settled back into his chair. Having put in a lifetime of soldiering abroad and in the North, he well knew that for these young knights, his tales of war in the limbo before their departure gave them a foretaste of their own future.

"I suddenly realized," he continued, "that those three Moslems were going for our horses. They got the German's first, but not before he'd released his axe from its fitting. I managed to run through one man and unhorse another; the third fled. In the end there we were—the three of us on the ground, axe and sword and saber flying. We took the axe and made short work of the last Moslem, that German and I!"

As he spoke, it dawned upon Ebles that some of his dashing young listeners might not even know what sea he'd had to cross to get to the East. After a while, he detected signs of mere politeness beneath masks of rapt attention. Soon, most of them drifted away. Gui d'Ussel remained, as did his rotund uncle Pierre and Arraut de Cornil, in whose household, Ebles knew, Gui had just completed his service.

"Pons! Where is the cellarer?" he called.

The steward, waiting in attendance at the hall's entryway, slanted over to Ebles' side. He reported that madame the countess had cancelled her previous order.

"Nonsense! Send a cart to Egletons immediately! How in the devil can we keep a roomful of men amused without something to drink?"

Pons skittered back across the floor.

"And Pons!" Ebles called once more. "See to it that we have something to eat..." He waved his hand in a vague, dismissive gesture. "Pasties. Anything Alba has lying about!"

His eyes fell on Elias. It was already more than a year since he and Elias had sat a whole day in the study upstairs, hammering out a solution to their boundary problem. Elias had managed to remain clearheaded in spite of continual refills from the cellar. When, near sundown, he had left in a huff, Ebles marveled that the man could so much as stand.

All morning, he noticed, Elias had not been among his listeners. Perhaps he was holding forth elsewhere on his own battle scars, of which, Ebles conceded, he bore an honorable number. When all was said and done, he had to admit that in recent years, despite the boundary business, he'd come to think of Elias as a decent sort. He was good company at chess and knew a respectable claret when he got it (which, often as not, was at this very table). He was strict in his religion and composed passable verses, though no tradition of "trobar" could ever be said to have flourished at Ussel as it had at Ventadour. Since his wife's death, of course, he'd been father and mother to Gui and so far as Ebles could tell, the boy was none the worse for it. Seemed clever. Had curiosity, a rare enough quality in youth nowadays. Engaging good looks. He was honest-seeming, though untried at heart. Too bad, in a way, that a match between Douce and the lad was out of the question.

The Ussels were hardly a family to be reckoned with. Not that there wasn't plenty of land. Elias had Ussel castle and Charlus as well. But that was exactly what set Ebles' teeth on edge: the D'Ussel holdings were old, if not quite venerable, and Elias had squandered his inheritance. Even in peacetime the Ussel estate was slovenly run, its tenants sickly and complaining. Instead of managing his fields and granaries, Elias was apt to spend half his days out hawking and the rest drinking red wine with those cohorts he called "poets," though Ebles had never heard a line of their verse recited anywhere. Charlus, too, was practically a ruin.

One had only to look at him: it was clear to anyone with the merest field experience that Elias' talents were lying fallow until they could be put to use, in battle. From his shaggy locks to his rough and ready boots, he was the quintessential soldier.

Pons advanced with unaccustomed dignity into the hall, the food forgotten, his face flushed with import. He announced that a troupe of itinerant actors and minstrels had led their horse-drawn wagon up the path from the village, where they had spent the night.

"They seek employment, my lord, and beg permission to encamp outside the postern gate."

"Tell them," Ebles said with a wide sweep of his arm, "that they may stay as long as they like, provided they agree to entertain us every night!"

Pons remained, hovering. "They bring news, Count."

"Well, what is it?"

"They have come from Provence. It seems that Alphonse of Aragon is arming his supporters around Montdragon against Count Raymond of Toulouse."

Knights, their swords bucking at their sides, came quickly across the hall. Clustering around the table, they pounced on this piece of information like starving dogs.

"Alphonse the *Arrogant* would be a better name for him! I say back to Spain with the man, the flat sword against his rear end!" Pierre d'Ussel exclaimed.

The Turenne contingent regarded him coolly. "Oh, Alphonse is an upstart, sure enough, though now that his coffers are loaded, some say his claim is older than Raymond's Marie's brother-in-law," Guiraut remarked.

"Of course!" another Turenne agreed. "Being rich these days means you can get away with just plucking off any piece of land you fancy. And there will be plenty of lackeys around who'll risk their necks to fight for your claim no matter *how* suspect it is!"

Gui came forward on his stool. "But Raymond is also rich," he ventured, "and, I have heard said, risky in his enterprises . . ." The Turennes turned to look at him as though he were a schoolboy speaking out of turn.

Elias d'Ussel appeared amidst the clash of voices. Ignoring his son's comment, he addressed Guiraut, "And Raymond's no upstart; that's the problem. *His* misfortune is that he's no soldier, either. Fighting doesn't run in their blood, those counts of Toulouse."

"Which is exactly why," Pierre nodded toward the Cornil knights, who'd said nothing as yet, "we need your assistance."

Elias picked up the theme. "Will Turenne stand by and watch Raymond defend Montdragon alone? Will my lord Arraut de Cornil?" He planted his feet in a wide stance, a warning to all who knew him that an exhortation was on the way.

To stay an imagined onslaught of objections, Ebles raised a conciliatory hand. "Well, whoever gets the best of it there'll not be much bloodshed. The men of Provence hate a skirmish, most of all Raymond."

Marie, alerted by the escalating voices of Ebles and Elias, came forth. "Why don't we ask Gaucelm what *he* thinks? He's as well acquainted with Raymond as anyone—"

"But my dear, what does our troubadour know of politics? Wars aren't fought in practice rooms."

"I should like to meet the man," Elias said.

"Then you shall. And perhaps he will give us some insight into what Raymond is likely to do. Pons!"

Like an unearthed mole, Gaucelm blinked in the doorway of the great hall. On top of the familiar scents of straw-swept stone floors and dogs slumbering close to the fireplace, he sensed the sharp, acrid odor of metal. It was a northern smell, in which steel predominated: Ebles' men, unlike Raymond's, wore their swords at all times.

These knightly gatherings were not to his liking. Faces he did not know turned toward him. He wondered what Marie had in store for him now. It was not beyond her to enjoy public humiliations. According to the rules of their little game, hers was the next move.

"Gaucelm Faidit!" Marie pronounced his name with a flourish. "We look to you to break the impasse in our discussion. Has Pons told you . . ."

". . . Nothing, my lady."

"Ah, then I shall recount the news," she said. "The Spaniard, Alphonse, is laying siege to Montdragon. Raymond must fight back or lose his land. If Montdragon falls, all of Provence could follow."

Raymond! Gaucelm fought the impulse to simply leave the hall. He did not want to think about Raymond, let alone speak of him.

"You were six years with Raymond," Marie said, "and one of his inner circle. What do you think he will do?"

Ebles added, "Have you any idea of his defenses? Number of catapults? trebuchets? Are his men kept in practice? Or are they caged in his court like ornamental cockatoos?"

"I have no opinion on the matter, my lord."

"Gaucelm," Marie said, "we are not asking you about politics. We'd merely like to hear your assessment of the man himself. You knew him as well as anyone in Toulouse." Such obvious flattery put him on guard, but real concern sounded in her voice as she continued, "We'll hold you to nothing, Gaucelm. We ask because we—Ventadour, that is, Ebles, our knights, as well as Elias, Arraut, Guiraut, all of us—might find ourselves embroiled in a crisis that could endanger our lands, perhaps our lives. In your opinion, how is he likely to react? Will he sit tight or take action?"

Gaucelm fought down the impulse to shout, *The man is a traitor! He will do whatever it takes to save his own skin.* Instead, he recalled Vidal's words as though the wise imp were whispering to him, "Listen, Rai Mundi is used to playing cat and mouse with the Pope."

"Raymond walks a fine line between heaven and hell," Gaucelm said. "His politics are . . . inconsistent."

Puzzled silence was broken by an insistent voice. "But Raymond's not the point! Don't you see, it doesn't matter whether you can trust the man. He has no choice but to defend his lands—and ours too," Elias said. His tone was urgent. "Let Raymond join the South together while there's still time! Provence is not so prideful as to prevent an arrangement with him . . ."

". . . nor, if it comes to that, an arrangement with Alphonse to defeat Raymond," one of the Turennes interjected.

"Possibly," Elias answered. "But if I were to toss on it, I'd bet on Raymond to make the first move. An alliance with Provence could only work in his favor. Look at what he has to defend! It's not in his interest to have barriers between Toulouse and Provence, and Ventadour, for that matter. *I* say, since we all speak the same language, why not make the bond official!"

"So you *have*, Elias d'Ussel," said Ebles leaning back in his armchair, "many times. But look at the realities. Raymond is in double jeopardy. He's got the Pope on his back and this Cistercian abbot nipping at his heels about the heretics. Now on top of it all, he may have to battle Alphonse for his share of Provence. Ask me, and I'd say he's in deep enough trouble without forming a front against the Spaniard and the church to protect a band of ecclesiastical outlaws!"

"It's true, Elias," Marie said. "Such a muster of forces would be extremely suspect. It would look like an alliance against the Pope. At least that's how it could be construed by someone in Folquet's position, and by others who see the Count of Toulouse as a protector of heretics."

"When I was at Cornil," Gui interjected, "in the service of my lord Arraut, I heard mention of barons, even counts, who are themselves Cathars—not that they whisper it abroad, of course. Is it possible that Raymond is . . . " he faltered, then continued, ". . . could *this* be why the Pope points a finger at him?"

Arraut de Cornil winced. The Turennes stared in disbelief and Ebles just shook his head.

"I wish I could say that I knew Raymond as well as the countess implies, well enough to entertain the idea of his being a heretic," Gaucelm said, gazing at Gui, "but I can't."

The lad asked questions instead of delivering opinions like edicts. Though he could not be much younger than Gaucelm, there was a naivete, a deference in the youth's demeanor that made Gaucelm feel almost protective. The young man's guileless conjecture about Raymond was shrewd, but innocent.

"I can say this. Raymond has a spy, a dwarf . . ." Gaucelm stopped. Marie knew of the dwarf, but did anyone else at Ventadour? He swallowed hard, decided he had to continue. ". . . he can identify every Cathar safe place around Toulouse and south of it, down as far as Foix. It's also rumored that Raymond has hidden Cathar bishops and *perfecti* when they've been in danger. But I suspect this is not news to anyone who knows Raymond's liberal leanings."

"A dwarf," Gui murmured.

Marie looked sternly at Gaucelm, but remained silent.

"So then, if it does come to war, what will we be fighting for?" Gui asked. "Land or a band of heretics?"

"Both!" shouted Elias.

"Elias. Gui!" Ebles sat forward like a referee intent on preventing a fight from getting out of hand. "It will never come to that," he said. "Raymond can't afford any maneuver which might escalate into a war against the Pope."

He turned to Gaucelm. "Well, now that you've heard everyone else speak out, what do you think . . . will Raymond send soldiers to Montdragon or won't he?"

"Sire, I think he is likely to do so," Gaucelm said quietly, as though to Ebles alone. Silence descended on the great hall. One or two knights stole glances at Ebles. Deflated, the old man shrank back in his chair.

"Raymond and Folquet and the Pope be damned!" Elias burst out. "We waste time talking about what might happen, and all the while the enemy is right under our noses! These Spaniards have preyed on Provence long enough. Let's rout them! We'll raise the troops ourselves! This is only the beginning. Mark my words, Ebles de Ventadour, your troubadour is right. Raymond will make his move at Montdragon. And before we are through, the whole South will be at war!"

Gaucelm watched the craggy knight motion the youth to him and quickly leave the hall. He followed them out. Elias heard footsteps behind and turned impatiently.

"So you'll be going off soon, then?" Gaucelm said to Gui.

"I'm not yet a knight, actually," Gui said, with a glance at his father.

Elias slammed a fist to his forehead. "We must remedy *that* in short order! We'll have the ceremony here. Today."

"Will my lord Arraut de Cornil confer my shield?" Gui asked.

"As his godson, you should ask him. God be praised, he's likely to be here still. We'll need Ebles and the chaplain will bless what arms you have—what *do* you have, Gui, beside sword and helmet? Hauberk?"

Gui shook his head no.

Elias thought for a moment. "Surely Ebles can lend you a hauberk and spurs."

"If I may suggest . . ." Gaucelm interrupted, "just yesterday I noticed a suit of mail at the farrier's, out by the postern gate. It looked to me to be nearly finished, though it may be spoken for."

"Excellent," Elias said. "We must throw ourselves on Ebles' generosity once more. You'll need a lance and mail gloves as well, Gui. I'll give you my surcoat. The smithy's over there . . ." he pointed beyond the stables, "Go quickly and see whether he's finished the hauberk, then find Arraut. I'll talk to Ebles directly. Now off with you!"

Gui nodded, and pivoted so that he faced Gaucelm. With a smile in his dark eyes and a little military bow, he echoed his father's words: "I am honored." Then he started for the postern gate at a run.

"Sacrificiis praesentibus quaesumus, Domine, placatus intende: ut et devotioni nostrae proficiant, et saluti ... O Lord, we beseech Thee, look down favorably upon these present Sacrifices: that they may profit us both unto devotion and salvation . . ."

Before sundown, all were assembled on the porch of the castle's chapel. As the temperature dropped, a light snow began. It dusted the chaplain's black robes, and settled into the weave of Marie's cloak. She presided silently, her back straight and immobile. Guilhelma leaned into Gaucelm's side for warmth. Douce huddled next to Ebles, wrapped in the hooded cloak that Guilhelma knew she wore on her secret visits to the wisewoman, Madame Belot. Soon Gui, in his white wool surcoat, was the only one against whom the snow was invisible.

Following custom immemorial, the sacred part of the ceremony took place in private, at the chapel altar. When the chaplain, followed by Gui, Elias, Arraut de

Cornil, and one of the Cornil knights bearing helmet, lance and shield, crossed the threshold into the chapel, Guilhelma saw Douce drop her gaze. Guilhelma could have sworn that Douce's hand brushed tears from her eyes.

After a short time, Gui emerged and stood under the portal, surcoat swept back to reveal his armor, newly donned and blessed. The snow fell gently on his silver helmet draped with chain mail to protect his neck and throat. The hauberk, unfinished at the bottom, nonetheless hung far enough below his knees for protection, and his legs were bound in sturdy leather chausses. Arraut de Cornil's shield was strapped to Gui's left forearm; his right hand held the lance with the Ussel colors, azure and white, affixed.

With the other men assembled behind Gui on the chapel porch, the chaplain recited his injunction: "Thou, Gui d'Ussel, shall keep inviolate the faith which thou owest first to God and afterward to liege-lord and commonwealth. Protect both against the enemies of Christ with all thy strength and prowess."

Guilhelma could read the exultation on Gui's face. He was eager to fight this usurper Alphonse, to restore the southern heritage to its own soil and free it from foreign tricksters who couldn't even understand the language of their enemy's battle cries. Her throat constricted as she watched Gui take formal leave of his father. Was he thinking of Douce as he turned his head—there!—in her direction?

The girl raised her eyes to him in that instant, and Guilhelma caught a glimpse of wet cheeks. During the brief moment that they stood there in the falling snow, she pictured Gui as Douce must be seeing him, mounting his destrier and galloping off, clothed in his new knight's pride.

Chapter 13

CHRISTMAS AT VENTADOUR

It was the Eve of the Shepherds: tomorrow would begin the year's high feasting. In the winter fields around Ventadour the wolves howled. But for their voices, the night was utterly still, the stars coming down just to outstretched fingertips.

Gaucelm, now reinstated in Marie's favor, had been delegated to organize the Christmas ceremonies. He was presiding over the setting up of extra tables in the great hall when the door opened, flooding the inner court with torchlight. A cheer went up as Pons and a tenant farmer's son carried in the Yule log. With ritual flourish they paraded it three times around the hall. Then with much stamping and puffing, they tugged it over to the fireplace, where at last it rested.

"Now where is she?" Gaucelm wondered aloud, for Douce had slipped away. At that moment she was in the cowshed twisting greens and berries into the goats' collars. These she had fashioned earlier from rope wound with bright bits of cloth scavenged from her mother's sewing corner. Two by two, joined at the neck with ribbons, geese, goats, and chickens would march into the hall to a trumpet fanfare immediately after the minstrels' masque. Gaucelm credited Guilhelma with all this enterprise: the animals were her idea.

It had been a matter of expedience. From the day Gui left, Douce had chattered so incessantly about him, that Guilhelma suggested Marie put the girl in charge of decorations for the feast. The plan worked like a charm. She was kept occupied mending banners, consulting with Alba about sugared almonds for the table, pinning down Pons for the Yule log expedition and a thousand other details. The animal procession, however, was an innovation, and it met with some resistance.

"But," Douce had retorted over Marie's strenuous objections, "they have more right to be present than we do, since it was *their* stable the Baby Jesus was born in!" Marie sighed and gave in; it was better than having the child moping around the servants' quarters all day long.

Unlike the others, Gaucelm never thought the parade of animals odd. He had in fact composed the music for their entrance, and had been rehearsing Douce for the pastourelle she would sing once her flock was gathered before the high table. Now that the animals were ready, Douce was at a terrible pitch of excitement. Lest one of her creatures extricate itself from its fancy-dress, she shouted for a stableboy to watch her charges until time for their entrance.

Satisfied that all was well, she hiked up the glistening saffron silk of her skirt and flew back to the hall, where the entire household had by now assembled. This was the moment for lighting the log along with the ash of last year's, and for the distribution of Christmas portions. Gaucelm gave the command. Her cheeks flushed, Douce smoothed her skirt and took a handful of coins and the flask from Pons. She placed coins on one end of the log and spattered the other end with wine, as Pons skipped forward to light it. Everyone watched as the dry bark blazed up. Then Gaucelm, arms spread, asked for silence and gave over the proceedings to the chaplain.

". . . and God protect this house and all its inhabitants from Evil in the coming year. May we increase in joy: *Dieus nous alègre.*" Tenant farmer families with their children, the household staff, pages, Ebles, Marie, Douce, guests, Gaucelm and Guilhelma all stood with bowed heads until he finished intoning the solemn words.

Shyly, the farmers fell into line to claim their holiday portion of a loaf and a pitcher of wine from Ebles. They were followed by those house servants who rated the addition of figs and almonds. Each inclined his head and mumbled thanks as he received his gift, then shuffled away, filling the corners of the great room in preparation for the summing up of the year's work and events.

Ebles stood to speak, majestic in his miniver-trimmed mantle. He droned on about matters of harvest, taxes, debts, births, deaths, salary raises, and pensions. Douce squirmed as Ebles concluded his speech. The tenant farmers with their families, the villeins, and yard servants withdrew. To table at last! Though supper would be meatless in preparation for tomorrow's profligate feast, her breath quickened at the parade of trays piled high with pies and fish stews, and roasted eel. Later there would be platters of pasties with bits of lamprey tucked into the flaky, hot dough. Then would come junkets and luce, special Christmas cakes filled with sweet flawns; after that, the medlars and Alba's sugared nuts. The inside of her mouth puckered at the thought.

Where would Gui be keeping Christmas? Douce wondered. Would he be in barracks with the other soldiers or in a lord's great hall? Would he go to confession tonight, before Mass? Would he be all alone now at prayers? She envisioned him small and solitary, kneeling in some nameless chapel, one hand on the helmet resting beside him on the cold flagstones. Or would he be riding a mission, under the stars, his hair whipping out like a black flag in the wind?

Gaucelm got up. Tonight his song seemed to be made for her alone and though she knew better, she allowed herself to think so while its enchantment lasted:

> **Love that holds me, holds me bright**
> **Body gentled, radiant**
> **Pleasured often, love yields best**
> ***Ai, Seigner Dieus, merces!***

His gravelly baritone sometimes made her giggle; tonight, though, tears welled up at his words and with a burst of warmth she thought, *How I do love Gaucelm. Tonight I love everyone in the whole wide world.*

Then it was time for family and house servants' gifts. Unlike the Christmas portion which was everyone's due, presents spelled out one's value to the household. Once a year everyone became a child of Marie de Ventadour, receiving praise or blame according to her wishes. A slight—a silver coin instead of gold, gloves instead of an expected new suit of clothes—could create a stir. A boon in the form of boots, a sugar loaf, a horse, or a sword elicited an audible sigh of satisfaction. Tempers were barely restrained until after dinner, when recipients could get together among themselves to compare fortunes and favors.

As always, Pons and his predecessor, the elderly retired house steward, came first to the head of the table where Marie sat, and bore away their identical bolts of dyed blue cloth with dignity. When it came Guilhelma's turn, Douce felt her stomach tighten. She had helped choose this gift. She watched with anticipation as Guilhelma drew the beads from their silk pouch, giving an audible gasp of pleasure. They were discreet and of even size, alternately quartz and amber. Guilhelma held them to the light and to her claret bodice. Then she thanked Marie in a rush, and bore them aloft to her place, where hands reached to feel their weight and assess their value. The admiring murmurs conceded that Guilhelma's string of beads added up to a vote of high confidence from Marie.

In spite of all Gaucelm's efforts to keep order, the hall buzzed furiously. Pages and lower household servants with their families were still to be rewarded. By the time it was the children's turn, their squeals of pleasure were practically inaudible in the hubbub. Tops, balls, and dolls rolled under the trestles. The dogs, not yet fed anything but scraps, were in a fever of excitement, bounding after the bows and arrows just bestowed upon the pages, panting and wrenching at the toy swords and boardgame pieces flying in all directions. The moment Ebles's dog leapt onto the high table and made away with a swipe of pie, things had clearly gone too far. The children were banished, leaving their parents to collect what belonged to them from the confusion of toys.

The silence was momentary. Goblets were refilled, and then came the cry of "Let's have the tale of Griselda!" The minstrels gathered in the entryway. This was their moment.

Douce earnestly hoped it wouldn't be a nativity, like last year. Everyone knew the story, and there was too much solemnity about it.

She was reassured by the appearance of a creature in horns and tail who wove his way through the company, saluting and greeting, prodding ribs and poking a cleric's front here, a headdress there. Snatching a fish bone from the long table, he waved it for attention and began a recitation in a whisper, almost a hiss. When he got to the part Douce liked best—his pronouncement of the omens of the night—he was properly sinister, punctuating his speech with little flicks of his black tail. Last, he admonished his audience to confess in chapel before the evening was up, warning against the spells he could cast should they neglect their souls, and reminding them to keep the lantern wicks straight and the cats from miaowing until the morrow, as these were bad signs.

At that moment Pons came scuttling in and whispered something in Ebles' ear. Ebles half-rose, then seemed to search the crowd for someone. He pointed to Elias, pressing the steward in his direction. Elias got up directly and went out with Pons. Ebles followed, his face grave.

They were barely noticed, except by Douce and Gaucelm, who nudged Guilhelma. A silence fell on Douce, though it was coming time for her procession of animals. She fought off wild thoughts, her mind black as an unlit stage against which the figure of Gui emerged in the strangest guises. One instant he appeared to be licked by flames. The next he was glowing in a white surcoat just like the Prince in the burlesque. But how silly. It was probably nothing to do with Gui at all.

Still, she did not like the look on her father's face when he returned to his seat. If it were a matter concerning Elias alone, why that distracted frown? Ebles leaned across and whispered two words to Marie. There was no mistaking her mother's look as she sought her child's face. Douce's mind closed in terror: Gui, then! She ran to Ebles, stumbling over the remaining confusion of toys on the floor, her skirts catching at the table corner. Her cheeks flamed with the demand, "Is it about Gui?" But Ebles was unmoved. "Nothing, child. It's nothing you must know." And as though to lend credence to his words, he rose, went out, brought Elias back, and sat him down.

Douce had always trusted her father; there was no reason to change that. And yet she could sense that there was something profoundly amiss. To quiet herself, she went to sit between Gaucelm and Guilhelma. The masquers took no notice of these interruptions. A torchbearer led in tumblers, whose buffoonery was totally lost on Douce. Gaucelm, sensing something awry in her mood, tried to distract her with instructions on her pastourelle. "Give me the rhyme endings," he prompted, and began "***Volria...amia...que sia***..." But they had carefully rehearsed them before; that made her all the more suspicious. She wondered whether Guilhelma had told him anything of her feelings for Gui. Guilhelma patted her hand and whispered directly into her ear so that no one could hear, "It can't be Gui, or his father would not have returned to the table."

To stave off her confusion and fear, Douce decided to go early to the cowshed and check on her animals. She maneuvered past the long benches, climbed round the dogs, and slipped out of the door near the fireplace where the Yule log blazed. She hesitated, and on impulse returned quickly, bent down, and scooped a bit of the ash from the floor of the grate into her palm. Then she left the room unnoticed.

It was magic; if anything could, this would keep him safe, and dispel the demons gnawing at her. She knew the peasants often mixed Yule ash in their medicines, or kept it all year in their huts to ward off fire. When she got to the cowshed she saw a sparrow hawk had got loose from its perch and was mocking his four-footed inferiors from the rafters. One of the goats had chewed through its collar, but the rank and file of Douce's procession was otherwise intact. They looked charming. She was suddenly impatient to start, and she woke the stableboy, sending him up to take the cue from Gaucelm.

Behind Douce the line of reluctant beasts made its way across the threshold of the great hall. When the first pair of white sheep peered in at the crowd and refused to budge until coaxed by one of the tumblers, Douce feared that her animal performers might fail her. But once the music of the tumbler's finger cymbals had enticed the sheep, eyes blinking, into the middle of the hall, the geese and the goats followed in a rush, straining at their collars and dragging their mates across the floor.

It was Gaucelm's processional music which saved the project from chaos. It opened with a trumpet fanfare played by two young pages whom Gaucelm had taken on as apprentice musicians. The deliberate beat contrasted with the aimless milling around of the animals, as if Gaucelm had composed it with the maintenance of strict order in mind.

Encouraged by her audience, Douce managed the pastourelle with aplomb, though she left out a verse without realizing it. Then the animals were led out by the stableboy. Guilhelma squeezed Douce in her arms and Gaucelm offered her wine, which she drank breathlessly. The two pages blew their trumpets again to announce the end of the celebration.

No one at Ventadour would tell her the truth, as though they thought her too young to accept what they called "life." She suspected Ebles and Marie were conspiring to keep her on the straight and narrow path labeled "Comborn." Whatever the reason, nothing could be more painful to Douce. To find out what had happened—for by now her suspicions were truly inflamed—she decided to ride to Ussel the next morning after Christmas Mass. She would take Guilhelma with her, and they would carry coins, toys, and holiday bread in pouches slung behind their saddles. In case they needed it, Douce thought of a noble alibi: to visit the sick of a neighboring village at Yuletide.

But things did not fall out quite the way she had planned. Alba, always delighted when her "young miss" came to visit, stiffened when she glanced out of the kitchen window and saw two horses with Guilhelma, instead of a stableboy, at their bridles.

"Where are you off to with the bread at this crack of dawn, then? Is Daniel going with you? It's not his usual hour . . ."

Douce put the bread down on the cobblestones and watched Guilhelma gather her skirts in her left hand. She flung her right leg against the saddle, then inched herself up into it, her fingers anchored in the horse's mane. Douce hastily followed suit, and they clattered out of the courtyard, leaving the bread behind. Never mind! A puzzled Alba, watching at the window, would retrieve it.

Douce had not been to Ussel since her childhood. But all was different now: this was Gui's home. Her feelings revolved wildly within her at the prospect of seeing it. Soon, though, she understood what her father had meant when he spoke of Elias d'Ussel as a wastrel. Once they had come into full view of the castle it was obvious that the keep, alone of all the buildings within the enceinte, was intact. The others looked as though they had been laid siege to years ago and never repaired. The long stable was of wood, and part of its roof was missing. The storehouses were mounds of crumbling stone. When Guilhelma gave an audible sniff, Douce knew what she was thinking: *you couldn't call that kitchen more than a cookhouse attached to an outdoor oven.* It was disgraceful. And there was no such thing as a chapel anywhere to be seen. While the gatekeeper set off to find the steward, Douce's heart sank with knowing that this semi-ruin was what Gui must someday inherit.

A steward opened the keep's iron-hinged door to them. Bent with age now,

Isarn was pleased but baffled to see Douce, whom he did not recognize at first. "But my lord left this very morning for Montdragon," Isarn said in his deep burr. "The young master has been hurt bad, though the page from Die who rode through here yesterday said nothing of a mortal wound, God be praised! Did the lad not stop at Ventadour? I sent him on with the news."

Douce nodded. And where, exactly, in the town of Montdragon would Gui be? she wanted to know.

"From what the page said, the young master's lying in the house of the lady Béatritz de Die." Wanting to be helpful, Isarn told Douce all he knew. "Now, the lad also said that the old baron of Montdragon, her father, may have been killed. His castle is hard by the Rhône River, you see, and the page heard tell that it had been ravaged by Alphonse's men, the Devil take them!"

"Who is this Béatritz de Die?" Douce cut him short.

"Aye, and well might you ask!" Isarn replied with relish, for he held his own opinion on matters. "Dieus knows what care she may be taking of maister Gui, she with her crazy politics and her religious ideas! Even up here it's known how she tried to run Raimbaut's kingdom . . ." But Douce had heard enough. She motioned impatiently for the old steward to come and cup hands under her foot so that she could remount.

Douce waved her thanks at Isarn as the horses turned in the courtyard and made for the gate. Guilhelma shook her head. There would be no stopping Douce now. She knew the signs: the child's color had risen and her face was all alight. Once on the road, Douce reined in and slowed alongside Guilhelma's horse. "When does my father go on circuit? Do you have any idea?"

"You know he never tells his household till the day itself arrives," Guilhelma answered. "But if I had to guess I'd say before the month of January's out, because I heard the countess your mother speak to Alba on Shepherd's Day morning about using up the flour stores so they won't spoil in the New Year."

"January! I can't wait that long . . ."

"Look, child, you can't just ride off as you please, either. Especially in the middle of winter, and with Provence under siege. I won't have it!"

Douce gave her a look intended to put Guilhelma in her place. "I'll get a page—Pieter—to escort me."

"*That* scoundrel!"

"I can't be waiting until the household's cleared out. I shall leave tomorrow."

"Douce, Douce. You can't just vanish like that! They'll send the entire world out after you. You know perfectly well how much trouble you'd be courting alone on the roads such as they are, with just a page along—and one who speaks a tongue no one understands, at that!" Guilhelma stopped to take a breath. "Where will you sleep that's safe at night?" she continued. "Montdragon is a week's ride from here at the very least! And I can tell you, child, that even when there's no warring, the byways are full of brigands who'll slit your throat for a mere purseful of pennies or a flask of wine. You'll be risking your years for a boy you hardly know, who may even be dead this very moment as we're talking. And who you'll never be allowed to marry even if he lives! Come to your senses, child!"

They rode for a while at a walk, along the sunlit wintry fields. By the time the sun's rays were level over the hills, Douce had made her plan. Once she'd scolded that page Pieter for not minding his duties last night it would be clear as day that he owed her a favor. She would bribe the gatekeeper. She and Pieter would leave well before dawn, she wearing Pieter's second suit of clothes.

She turned to Guilhelma. "I'll need bread and wine for a week's journey, and meat if you can put your hands on some before tonight's dinner. If they seem suspicious in the kitchen, any leftovers from yesterday will do. If Alba makes a fuss tell her it's for Douce's pile. She'll think it's for one of my visits to the village. I'll leave a pair of saddlebags inside the pantry door. Please have the bags filled just before matins. I'll have Pieter collect them and take them to the stables while everyone's in chapel. But mind they're ready *before* matins." She remembered the toys and the coins. "Oh, and give what's in these pouches . . ." she tapped the bulge behind her saddle ". . . to old Daniel. He can distribute them to the needy as well as I can. It's his job, after all."

Guilhelma was exasperated. "I can't let you do this! What if your mother and lord Ebles find out that I allowed you to go? Think of *me*, Douce. And at least let Gaucelm . . ." Guilhelma's voice trailed off; she saw it was no use. Douce stared straight ahead between her horse's ears.

Finally she said, "If either you or Gaucelm come with me I'd be missed that much sooner. I need time to *get* there. What would be the point if they're all on my heels before I've even crossed the Luzège? Surely you can understand that?"

"Merciful heaven," Guilhelma sighed to herself, put out by Douce's tone of voice. After a while she said resignedly, "You'll need a torch and a packet of candles." Douce turned to give Guilhelma a grin. For the first time in ages she was absolutely sure of what she was about to do. She kicked her horse on toward Ventadour.

III
MONTDRAGON

1202

Chapter 14

IN LOVE'S SERVICE

An arrow sang so close by the young knight that his arms flung wide in astonishment. Then a second arrow found its mark in his gloveless outstretched hand. He sank soundlessly from his horse as though executing a cartwheel with faultless precision. Not even the flutter of an eyelash betrayed his fall.

When Gui finally opened his eyes, he awakened to pain, his head throbbing against a tight strip of cloth instead of a helmet. Without knowing it, his body had been fighting the black angel on its own behalf. Gui located his limbs gradually, the way one gropes toward parts of a darkened cave. He looked across his arm, moving his right hand, then gazed over his chest to the left. He saw his left hand lying bandaged in the dim light like an animal asleep beside him, but he felt nothing in it. Panic rose inside him; he drew himself up on his left elbow to look at it more closely. The deadened creature sat, somnolent and useless at the end of his forearm. He fell back exhausted, with no more will to explore.

He was nearly asleep when a rustle of skirts and the clink of crockery roused him awake, suddenly alert to the smell of hot milk and bread brought by the shadow of a girl. And then he saw her face in the early light. It was Douce.

"You *here*?" he whispered.

"Shhh," she put a finger to her lips. "Don't try to talk." She moved away quickly, not daring to touch him, and leaned against the wall, faint with relief. He was going to live. She came to his side and took his right hand timidly.

"You fell after an arrow went through your hand. You hit your head on something and lost a lot of blood. Béatritz says you've been in and out of consciousness since well before Christmastide. It's the third day of Our Lord two years into the new century." She paused. "Gui?"

He rolled his head in her direction, but his eyes remained closed. "Does my father . . ."

"He knows. He stopped here on his way south.

"Where is he now?" Gui struggled through thick lips. "Who told him?"

"Béatritz told him. We are in her house. Your father has gone to raise troops south of here," she repeated. "That was before I came." His expression remained expectant. She watched as his desire to hear more fought sleep, but eventually he gave way to it. When she heard his even breathing, she sat back on her heels and sighed. It was senseless. Soldiers at loose ends, spoiling for a fight. The tears swelled. It was as stupid and heartbreaking as a casualty after a cease-fire. Alphonse's men had taken only Montdragon castle in the skirmish; Béatritz said the real battles were yet to come.

As Gui slept, Douce settled into a cross-legged vigil by his side. Slowly the half light of morning yielded to day. She watched as a beam of sun fanned out over the windowsill and inched across the stone floor. She moved her eyes along the light until they reached the tumble of straw that served as her bed. The tapestry folded on top of it seemed so incongruous. Béatritz had rescued it from the castle along with a fur throw she had been using as a blanket. Gui was lucky to be in this woman's care, Douce thought. But how humiliating it must be for her, daughter of the old baron of Montdragon, to be shunted off into one of her father's rental houses, visiting him in his castle only by permission of his captors. Yet Béatritz' manner gave no hint of discontent.

Douce's gaze drifted back to Gui. A single black curl had escaped the linen strip that bound his forehead. She touched it with a forefinger, recalling how his hair resembled a cap of glossy bird wings. She took her hand away slowly; the curl refused to lie flat. She smiled at the thought of how once, in an awkward moment at dinner, he had tried to train one unruly lock behind an ear, and it kept jumping forward. His eyes, over whose closed lids she held watch, had been merry with wine that day, staring shyly at the table whenever they'd met hers.

But here in Béatritz' snug quarters she no longer had to summon up memories. She could feast upon his face to her heart's content. Still, it pleased her to recall how, after he had left Ventadour, the mere thought of his fresh cheek and the tiny upturned dents at the corners of his mouth excited her to the point of folly. In the midst of trimming a wick or biting the thread from a hem stick, she would pause and a wide—and, she supposed, idiotic—smile would come upon her lips. She thought of how his knees must look beneath his hauberk, oval and hard as stream-smoothed stones, his calves knotty and tough as a colt's. He made her giddy. In the past few months he had turned her whole life upside down.

From outside came the familiar clap and swish of leather soles over gravel, then the heavy grating of clay on stone as a milk jug was set down on the doorstep. The wooden door creaked and swung wide as Béatritz entered.

The fire reared up on the hearth when a gust of sharp air all but blew Béatritz into the little room. The fire settled. Gui stirred in his sleep. Sweeping off her cloak, Béatritz gave it a shake, showering crystals everywhere, then hung it on a peg.

"The stalls will be up again by next Sabbath," Béatritz announced, patting her coiled hair into place. "Everything's nearly back to normal. They're saying that the market will open after Mass as usual. Now how's the patient?" She glanced in Gui's direction, then crossed the room to the fire and stretched her long-boned hands before its heat.

"He came awake. He recognized me. He spoke!" Douce announced.

Béatritz ran from the hearth and wrapped both arms around the girl, then laid a hand on Gui's forehead. It was cool to her touch. "Praise God," she said.

Everything about Béatritz was lithe, almost feline, from her tawny skin faintly lined by the sun to her sparkling green eyes. She wore a black homespun dress and a belt of woven gold that crossed at the ends to hold a talisman, a curved, milky green stone nestled in a golden oval.

"Has he eaten anything?" Béatritz asked. "The milk in his bowl hasn't been touched."

"No. I brought him that and some bread, but he fell back asleep," Douce said.

Béatritz poured new milk into the bowl and knelt beside Gui. With an assurance that made Douce catch her breath, she raised his head with one arm, and put the bowl to his lips almost before he had time to awaken.

"You see?" she nodded in Douce's direction. "Pretend you're feeding a baby. Don't ask. He'll drink by reflex. See, there!"

Gui lapped weakly at the milk, reaching once to hold the bowl himself. But soon he gave up and allowed Béatritz to feed him.

"Did I die?" he whispered ridiculously.

"Almost," she managed to smile.

". . . is Douce . . ."

"She's here," Béatritz replied.

His eyes closed again. Gradually his expression grew calm. Then suddenly, he pitched forward and vomited milk over the coverlet. Douce ran to fetch a basin from the cupboard. He vomited again and again, leaning into the pressure of Béatritz' arm around the bandage at his temples. At every assault of his stomach he flinched, as though rivers of pain were flowing through his limbs. Finally he lay back.

On the third day after Douce's arrival, Gui was strong enough to sit up. The aching in his head was no longer constant. Lying in this room asleep for days, his body had learned something of the twilight between life and death, dream and waking. This was suffering of an exquisite kind that had nothing to do with the wound in his hand and it pleased him in a peculiar way. All his knightly composure had vanished when he lost consciousness. His invincible shield, the lance he had held before him with its colors flying, had let him down.

Gui, fussed over by these two nurses, was being restored to health. He could identify and move each of his muscles in the sound parts of his body. Eating became an exquisite preoccupation; he realized that all his life he'd merely inhaled his food without tasting it. He waited with absolute faith in Douce's ministration for his hand to wake up, but it remained numb. Gradually he had to admit that he was in no great hurry to get well. The natural process would return him to soldiering soon enough, he reasoned.

Were it not for Douce's curiosity he would have put the battle behind him. But she prodded him to speak.

"What was it *like*, Gui?" she pleaded. "Were you afraid?"

"It wasn't a *war*, you know, just a . . . silly scuffle."

"But over *what*?"

"The castle."

At his words Béatritz scraped a stool across the floor and sat by the side of Gui's pallet.

"When I got down here nothing was happening. There were only a few of Raymond's men here," Gui continued. "We were freezing in our tents with little to do but sharpen our swords and wait. I got so cold that I spent most of my time grooming the horses, just to be near the heat they gave off."

"Was there a surprise attack, or what?" Douce asked impatiently.

"Well, yes . . . but not on us. I'm still not sure what happened. I'd guess that Alphonse's men were restless and their commander gave the signal for them to take the castle. All I know is that word got out at the very last moment and de Brial—that's my officer-in-charge—roused us at dawn. Most of my division was up at the castle by daybreak, but we were *it*. No one else showed up! Alphonse's troops had already forced the castle and accepted the old man's surrender."

"The old man you speak of is my father, the baron of Montdragon," Béatritz said quietly.

"Dieus!" Gui's good hand flew to his face in surprise. "How do *I* come to be here?"

You were brought to this house by two soldiers, and you've lain on that straw for over a fortnight."

"Then I pray your forgiveness . . . but who are you, exactly?"

"I am Béatritz de Die. My surname was Montdragon before I married." Gui was too stunned to say more.

"How did you get your wound?" Douce insisted.

"Wait," he said to her. "How did *you* know to come here?"

It was only after Douce recounted all the details of her adventure—Elias's sudden departure from the Christmas table, the journey to Ussel with Guilhelma to learn of Gui's whereabouts from Isarn, the old steward—that Gui could be coaxed to resume his story. "After the baron's surrender . . ." Douce prompted him.

"Well, when it was clear that we were too late and the castle was won, we started to ride back to our encampment. But the damned Aragonese wanted more. They were aching for a fight. They *had* to make something out of it to prove their stuff. It wasn't enough for them to take a defenseless castle; they had to make a noise about it. So they started going wild, shooting arrows into the air, rioting and yelling. I remember being furious that de Brial had routed us from the straw for *this*. All I wanted was to go back to camp as fast as my horse's legs would carry me and dive back under my blanket. Then, suddenly, I heard an arrow and felt myself falling—and that was all."

The three were silent for a long while. Gui, gazing at the two women by his bedside, felt tears expanding in his throat. He was sure he would cry if he did not speak. "Thank you," he said gently.

In a few days Gui insisted on trying out his legs. Anchored by Douce and Béatritz on either side he jacked himself upright, but his limbs splayed out when he tried to stand alone.

"Like a newborn foal," laughed Béatritz as he groped for her arm and sank to the straw mattress again. Then he chastised himself and resumed his efforts, but it was clear that one leg must have doubled up under him when he had fallen from the saddle; it wanted to buckle when he put any weight on it. For the time being, at least, his confinement was assured.

In the weeks to follow, Béatritz became their link to the outside world, and they dubbed her Angel of Light. Bringing water from the three-headed fountain in the market square or wine from Mathilde the tavernkeeper, she would deliver the news: how a patient had escaped from the leperhouse, or how a man was arrested on the street of Jews for dressing in women's clothes. Sometimes she went farther afield to the hut of the simple-woman, where she procured sage and rosemary for Gui's dressings and physic for his bowels. And still, she made daily visits to her father. Though Alphonse's men spared his life at the surrender, they had nonetheless made an example of his subjugation, forcing the old man to depend on his daughter for food.

Douce marveled at Béatritz's self-possession. Here was a woman who had no need of chatelaîne's keys to exert authority over her little kingdom. Logs burned smartly on the grate; there was always soup in the kettle; bread, milk, and wine appeared in the cupboard as if by magic, even when the market was closed. For Gui's benefit the brazier burned herbs instead of charcoal, the scent of juniper and sage rising on the vapors. Flagstones were swept and bedding was folded neatly every morning. Above the hearth Gui's bandages fluttered gently like white pennants from the beam where they were hung to dry. Chamber pots and poultice basins, scrubbed and upturned, waited in a far corner. Béatritz reigned over this little space. Douce sensed that her life had gone badly awry, that she had been forced to choose a different path than that of the conventional noblewoman.

One afternoon, while Gui drowsed longer than usual, Douce thought of Ventadour. She saw her parents plotting a great wedding feast for her marriage to Humbert de Comborn. Since her sudden disappearance, they must have been frantically trying to discover her whereabouts. Would Guilhelma keep her vow of silence? She shivered with the pleasure of her secret: it excited her to be the runaway princess.

Whatever happened now, Douce knew that it would be more tolerable than being thrown on the mercy of a man she had seen only once, who would always be away fighting while she was forced to act as steward for his vast estates. Anything would be better than to be confined with one child after another, directing servants, playing mistress of the house at dinners with a hundred guests.

A voice roused her from her thoughts.

"It is as if I am still dreaming every time I awaken and see you," Gui said drowsily. "I would be injured again if it meant having you here."

"You must be feverish," Douce replied, blood rising to her face as she crossed the room to his pallet. "Here, let me feel your brow."

She brushed her hand lightly across his forehead, lingering there only long enough to know that Gui's words were not the ramblings of an incoherent man. His face felt cool—and yet exhilarating—to her touch. She longed to caress the cleft of his chin, the outline of his lips.

"But you must return to Ventadour soon, mustn't you? I was at your betrothal to that Comborn . . . Humbert?" Gui said. "Your parents must be making preparations for the wedding."

"I will *never* go back to Ventadour," Douce said more emphatically than even she expected. "And I will *not* marry Humbert Comborn!"

He laughed. She was a headstrong girl, that Douce de Ventadour. Since their first encounter, he had thought of her as the girl with hair like spun gold. Now she was here, sitting beside him. As if it had a mind of its own, his good hand reached up and stroked her hair.

It sent shivers into her scalp and she giggled, biting her lip. It was intoxicating.

He turned her head and kissed her mouth. "Then marry me," he whispered.

She leaned into him, feeling his chest hard against her back, imaging the branches his breastbone made, and, longing to touch him there. She turned around gently and put her fingers below his throat, inside his lisle chemise. Could he sense—even see—the heat under her skin?

"Lover," she murmured, "*Amador.*"

Their breathing almost halted at the same time as they crawled, eyes shut, into each other's bodies, burrowing like small blind animals toward warmth. It could all be over in a minute, she thought as they clung together, and what would be the harm?

Except that the roof would certainly collapse on top of them. They would be struck down by Almighty God, sword in hand; or worse, by a grimacing skeleton wielding a scythe. She pulled away from him slightly to look at the small, dear cleft in his chin; she wanted the sight of those violet eyes up close.

If they did not stop, all would be finished for them, she decided. She would be doomed to a life of confession, burdened perhaps with a child, unable to wed; he would be prevented from taking the Cross, his sins uncleared.

And so they hovered there on the edge, faltering, not falling, holding and losing their breath at once, not quite daring to leap. Outside, the muffled scrape and crunch of leather across stone went unnoticed. They sprang apart only as the front door swung open to let in a freezing gust.

"Snow!" Béatritz announced unnecessarily, as a thin trail of it swirled in over the entryway.

The rest of her exclamation went indistinguishably out into the evening as, with her back to Douce and Gui, she pounded her slippers on the doorstep to loosen the icy clumps from them. Douce had recovered herself and was on her feet by the time Béatritz had shaken the flakes from her cloak and hung it on its peg.

As Béatritz gave her full attention to restoring sensation to her frozen feet, Douce scurried to the fireplace and urged the fire back to life. Then she abstractedly set about laying supper.

A sense of dislocation lingered in the little room. There was something strange in Béatritz's demeanor as she sat on the hearthstones in her stocking feet. She seemed very still and private. Was she aware that she had interrupted something?

"I have news," Béatritz said, finally turning toward them. "Disturbing news. I don't know what to think about it. I have never spoken to you of Raimbaut. Or have I mentioned his name?"

"I know the name somehow," Douce said. "Was it he who gave up his seigniory to the Hospitallers?"

"It wasn't exactly..."

"My father calls him a dangerous man," Gui interjected.

"A dangerous man," she said, laughing. "Oh, yes, he is *that*! But why does your father think so, Gui?"

"Is he not an ally of Alphonse?" Gui asked. "Doesn't he support the house of Aragon against Toulouse in all this stupid land grabbing that's going on? My father says he's the last hold-out in the whole south, that he'll never volunteer *his* forces for the southern cause until it's too late."

"Let's get things straight," Béatritz said firmly. "Whatever your father has told you, Raimbaut didn't 'give up' Orange. He was forced to divide it by his uncle's legacy. That's why he lives at Courthézon. And the reason he's under Alphonse's protection is because of the Hospitallers..."

"Oh, damn the Hospitallers! They fancy themselves statesmen, but all they are is rich!"

"... and the reason my father's still alive is that a year ago, when it was already clear that trouble was brewing, I threw myself at Raimbaut's feet. I begged that, should it come to war, my father might be spared. And Raimbaut did this knowing how my father loathes his leanings toward Alphonse. He did it for me!" Béatritz was near tears. "Oh, I tried to make him see the foolishness of taking up arms against Toulouse. The man is not made for waging war—he has almost no troops! And now it's all in vain!" She drew up her knees and rested her head on them, her face turned away.

Gui hobbled over to her and put an arm around her shoulder. Béatritz righted her head and patted his hand.

"Come to the table," Gui said.

She gave a sigh and rose. "There's more. You might as well hear it..."

"Only if it doesn't upset you," Douce said. She finished filling the wine jug and set it by their places, next to the bread. From the firehook she lifted a pot of cabbage and onions still bubbling in wine and brought it to the table.

"It's good for me to speak of him to those I care about," Béatritz said. No secrets remain among us now, after all. Pour me some wine, Gui, and let's eat."

"Tell us about him from the beginning," Douce said. "The stew needs time to cool."

"Let me start with telling about my husband. I was married to my lord the Count of Die at the age of thirteen, by my father's wishes. Almost from the first we were estranged—he stayed in Outremer for years at a time while I, still almost a child and too inexperienced to run my husband's estates, came back here to live," she said. "My mother had died bringing me into the world, and with my two brothers in the East, my father remained in Montdragon to oversee our properties and the townspeople.

"Weren't you lonely?" Douce asked.

"We had company from time to time. I was busy. To keep myself cheerful I made up verses and sang songs. And fortunately, I am very fond of my father even though we argued politics incessantly. As his hostess I ran the kitchen, and the laundry, and the wardrobe, and kept a fine household."

"As you still do," Gui said, picking up his spoon. He glanced hungrily at the stew pot.

"Try it at your peril," Douce warned. Gui put down the utensil. "How did you meet this Raimbaut?" he asked impatiently.

"You shall hear," Béatritz said. "One night some itinerant minstrels gave us an evening of song. I rose early the next morning, before they left. All night I had been driven to distraction by a verse they had sung whose lines ran so cleverly that I couldn't sleep for trying to reconstruct it. I had never heard such wit set to music."

"How does it go?" Douce asked.

"I'm sure I can't remember. Yes, wait . . ."

> *Escotatz, mas no say que s'es*
> Listen, but ask me not
> What it is you hear.
> *Vers? estribot? sirventes?*

She paused. "The rest escapes me now. But it was a most accomplished poem whose stanzas each closed with a phrase in prose. Its creator had invented a new style of composing—just like that!"

"And the author of this marvel was of course none other than Raimbaut, Count of Orange." Gui announced the obvious with a flourish, and helped himself from the pot at last.

"How does it end?" asked Douce, blowing on a ladleful of stew before filling Béatritz's trencher.

"The poem or my story?"

"The poem."

"Something like, 'If anyone asks who wrote this, say it was he who can pull surprises out of a hat only when he knows not what he is doing.' But my words do his no justice."

"So once you found out who he was, you wanted to meet him," Douce encouraged, pulling along the thread of the story.

"And I did manage it, with the unwitting help of my father. A cousin was to be wed in Avignon, and I begged my father to take me. I asked that we make our route through Orange in order to see the famous Roman amphitheater and the triumphal arch. I found out all I could about these ancient ruins, and impressed him with my enthusiasm for the subject—it is part of our heritage, is it not?—and he readily agreed."

"My father has seen them," Gui commented, his attention surfacing from the steaming vegetables on his trencher. "He speaks of the arch with reverence, as though it were a church!"

"Orange is magnificent, but uncanny, full of the ghosts of Caesar's soldiers. The stones echo still with their armies, their construction works, their forums and market squares. Just a short way south of the city lies Courthézon, a poor place by comparison. But that's where Raimbaut's court is, and there we spent the night."

"Was Raimbaut present?" Douce asked.

"Yes, luckily for me, or I would have counted the trip wasted. He was a genial enough host to us. My father thought him reserved, but courteous. To me he seemed the perfect knight and poet."

"You fell in love on the spot," Douce declared, smiling.

"I think I was already smitten," Béatritz said, "by the poem. Had he been a monster, I might have felt let down, but after hearing his song it would have taken a lot to dissuade me from him. The problem was that my father and he got into a . . . discussion . . . that night."

"Politics," Gui knowingly remarked.

Béatritz turned to him. "I mentioned the Knights Hospitallers before. You're aware, that the counts of Orange are firmly under their thumb. I learned after our visit that in spite of his title, Raimbaut's only outright holding is tiny Courthézon itself. The rest is in bits and pieces, most of it given over in debt to the Hospitallers or shared with his aunt and other relatives."

"And the Hospitallers are pawns of Alphonse!" Gui finished his stew with a slurp.

"Let's say, to be polite, that they are under the protection of Aragon and its king," said Béatritz, still sipping at her broth.

". . . who just attacked Montdragon. I *see*," Douce said. "You fell in love with the enemy!"

"It wasn't so simple as that, though it sounds more romantic the way you've put it."

"With all these strikes against you, however did you get to know him?" Douce asked.

"Ah, well. Since my father would not welcome him in Montdragon, I found many reasons to pass through Courthézon on my way to Avignon. After her marriage, my cousin's family grew with a speed which I found both happy and providential. There was always a new child on the way and plenty of work for an extra pair of hands. Naturally I traveled with an escort, but I always stayed with Raimbaut. We enjoyed each other's company—in *every* way—and in the end we made no secret of it."

Béatritz abandoned her stew and broke off a piece of bread, rolling it between her thumb and forefinger until it hardened into a pellet. "Not that our liaison made any difference at Courthézon," she went on. "Raimbaut was—is—a widower."

"But your father," Douce put in. "Didn't he suspect . . ."

"Of course. How could he not? He'd seen my face that night at Courthézon. Yes, he knew all along about our liaison, but it made little difference to him. Wise man that he is, he supposed that sooner or later I would fall in love out of loneliness, if nothing else. What made Raimbaut a thorn in my father's flesh was that this man's ties with Alphonse and the Hospitallers put him at odds with every just cause. The baron of Montdragon could not harbor a traitor to the family name under his roof! He had no choice but exile me to one of his properties in town—and thus you found me."

"But what happened with Raimbaut, then?" Douce asked.

Béatritz put down the bread and sighed. "Put simply, I came to understand that no mere woman would usurp his heart. Not enough to lead him to abandon a forced alliance with Aragon and switch his support to the South. He could not be expected to risk his meager holdings for the love of a married woman whom he had no hope of making his wife." Béatritz took a mouthful of wine. "So you see, the affair was doomed from the beginning. And the bitterness that came between us—the three of us—turned out to be the poison of politics." As Béatritz finished her story her eyes filled with tears.

"I'll clear," Douce said quickly, getting up from her stool.

"Thank you. You are learning how to manage vegetables, Douce. That was a good supper. Now Gui, may we have a little music? So long as the lamp lasts I want to work at my loom."

Douce put the stewpot back on the firehook, covered the wine jug, and scraped the trenchers into a pail. She found herself flushed as she thought how much alike the two of them were. Béatritz had been the victim of an arranged marriage such as the one she herself had so narrowly escaped. Béatritz, too, had sought out love for herself and taken the consequences.

But Douce could not fathom how, in spite of all her misfortunes, Béatritz seemed perfectly in charge of her fate. She had felt—acted on—the same passion that Douce felt for Gui, yet the loss of that love seemed to endow the woman with confidence.

That night Douce couldn't sleep. The evening's revelations were hard to digest, like a banquet of many dishes. Then, just before matins, she heard a light tap at the door. Immediately there was a stir from Béatritz's bed, followed by the soft flop of her fur coverlet and the faint brush and drag of cloth moving over the straw. A pause, and the heels of Béatritz's boots met the floorstones with a familiar "cloc." She must have gone to bed fully dressed.

Douce held her breath. Without the help of a candle Béatritz was proceeding across the floor as slowly and confidently as a sleepwalker. The almost inaudible scrape of her fingertips against the wall and her sharp intake of breath indicated that she had found what she was searching for. From the squeak of straw as it was raised from its hook, Douce could identify the basket that hung by the beam to the side of the entryway, the one Béatritz used for marketing. For an instant the opening door let in a luminous wedge of snowlight; then softly it closed and Béatritz was gone.

Douce sat up, wide awake, as the muffled boom of matins drifted across the white-capped town. Her own Sabbath eve trips to deliver food to Madame Belot sprang to her mind. Those missions had given her the incomparable feeling of doing good—secretly. Somehow she was sure that Béatritz was involved in similar activities. *Perhaps,* she thought, *that was why we were drawn to one another.* She smiled at the memory of how she had tricked Alba into putting aside extra scraps from the kitchen and leftover wine from supper, saying they were for her charity visits with Daniel the almoner. To this collection she would add at the last minute a few stalks of dried herbs yanked down from the kitchen beams. But though "Douce's pile" grew, Daniel saw only a portion of it. Little did he know that quite apart from her dutiful rounds in his company, she had a standing appointment with the widow Belot.

Cynics said of this woman that she heard voices and could bewitch people. But that she had real healing powers was beyond any doubt. She could cure a body taken with fits; Douce had seen it happen. On the day she first met Madame Belot, Douce had made the rounds alone, Daniel having been called home to a bedside in his own family. The widow Belot was already at work in one of the Ventadour tenant cottages when Douce arrived. The woman placed both hands on the forehead of the tossing, frightened child until he was calmed. Then, taking powder from the pouch she wore on a leather thong around her neck, she rubbed some into his chest and thence into each limb. Soon, the convulsions ceased.

What impressed Douce almost more than the cure was the fact that this sturdy little gnome who lived near Egletons came on foot a half-day's distance to perform her magic on the sick. After the boy sat up, Madame Belot told Douce of her work in the village of Ventadour and the ongoing need for bread and wine and especially chamomile and rosemary for her powders and poultices. Douce arranged for her to come every Sunday at matins to the back gate of the outer enceinte of the castle, and there she would wait for whatever provisions Douce had managed to steal. In exchange the widow Belot had brought her special gifts: once, a tiny cross in an exotic shape, its arms of equal length and bound by a circle; another time, a little bag of herbs which she said was a love potion. Now, as the church bells died on the cold air, Douce felt a pang of remorse. Madame Belot would have come at exactly this hour. But since the New Year she would have made the journey to no avail, for in her flight to Montdragon, Douce had forgotten the old woman entirely.

Chapter 15

AMADOR

At Ventadour, everyone was suspect. The interrogations went on for days after Douce failed to come back by nightfall on Christmas morrow. The stableboy got a thrashing from Marie when he couldn't tell her whether Douce had slipped out on horseback or wandered off on foot.

Ebles, tiring of his wife's complaints, sought refuge in his study. She followed him.

"That boy isn't fit to tend horses," Marie fumed. "Up to the brim with wine, as usual. Full of pasties as a stuffed pig. Really, you'd think the whole world had permission to stop functioning on holidays. And that's the very moment everything goes wrong, of course."

"You'd better look to your poet," said Ebles. "I'm sorry to say it, but I think Gaucelm will have to go if that wench of his won't talk. What Guilhelma's *not* said is enough to convince me that she knows plenty."

"The influence she has over that child has always made me nervous," Marie exclaimed.

"Have you asked *her* about Pieter?"

"That good-for-nothing is long overdue to be sent home!"

"How can you send home someone who's absent?" Ebles went to the window and looked across the courtyard in the direction of the stables. "They say he hasn't been seen since he led in Douce's ridiculous Christmas parade of animals."

Ever since Guilhelma had recounted Douce's escapade to him, Gaucelm's mind had been made up. The episode with Madame Audiarde still rankled. He'd had his fill of Marie's games. He was restless. Without Douce, he suddenly realized, the castle was unbearably gloomy. A plan was forming in his head.

The first part was clear to him: find Douce. Then, he wasn't sure; perhaps go to Marseille. The court of Marseille would be swarming with as much intrigue as Ventadour, but as a rich port town it might offer more in the way of patronage. Besides, it was just possible that Vidal was there. He waited a week, and then he told Guilhelma to pack their things.

"So!" Guilhelma was outraged. "And what about me? You have little enough regard for *my* position! Where else would I be likely to find such favor in a household? Who else will reward me with jewels at Christmastide, and with the care of the daughter of the house? Is all my work to go for naught?" Abruptly, she turned her back on him lest he see her angry tears. "*You've* got no reason to complain either. You had your due from her, in no small wise thanks to *me*, I might add. No, I'll not budge until Marie herself orders me out."

He grasped her shoulder and wheeled her around. "But think of Douce," he pleaded. "What if the child is in trouble? She might have been attacked and robbed and left to die on a road somewhere. She could have been kidnapped, violated, turned loose in a forest. What if she never got to Montdragon at all?"

"You know I am worried about Douce, but going after her will jeopardize our place here," Guilhelma cried. "If they know I had anything to do with her leaving, they will turn me out—and you too!"

Seeing how adamant she was took some of the iron out of his resolve so he gave the matter time. By the second week Guilhelma had relented. "But only," she bargained, "if we come back straightaway, with or without Douce."

They rode out the next morning in broad daylight with no goodbyes. Gaucelm was silent until they were more than a league away from Ventadour and the village chapel chimed sext in their wake. He told himself that he would never come back north—not if he could help it—but he kept his thoughts to himself. Guilhelma bobbed behind him on her nag, her heels doubtless digging the animal's flanks in a way that so annoyed him. In deference to her agreeing to this journey, he made no comment.

By the time they stopped to eat at the side of the road, Gaucelm's dark mood had lifted; some bread and a leg of roast mutton, which Guilhelma had tied in a kerchief, revived his spirits completely. It felt familiar, sitting on his cloak there on the frozen ground and soon, after some wine, Guilhelma was laughing.

"Gaucelm, what will we tell them when we get back? A sick parent? An unexpected inheritance? The truth? Oh, but it *is* good to be away from that harpy for a while."

"Come, woman. There's no time for dallying. South, to the warm lands! To Provence, where figs and olives grow wild, or so I hear. Is it true?"

"In summer, silly." She turned to him as he stood to leave. "What do you have against the North? Weren't the skies of Toulouse bright enough? What does the South hold for you, anyway?"

"It is warm *all* the time!" Gaucelm replied. *But first we'll find Douce.*

In Montdragon time seemed to stop while the snow continued to fall. A low gust had picked over the fields, leaving the haystacks like forlorn brown islands in a white sea. Along the roads poplars bristled with ice, their branches ready to shatter in a burst of wind.

The three hermits, snugly lodged, were content as moles; even Béatritz had not been able to venture out for two days, not since the night of her secret mission. Through the windows crept a flat winter light, pale as whey. Gui had been amusing himself the whole afternoon, plucking with his good hand at an old gittern that had belonged to Béatritz' father. The strings on the instrument were intact, but its dried-out wooden body made the notes sound hollow. Undaunted, Gui tried tucking the flat edge under his chin. While Douce pressed down for the chords, he plucked the strings. The sound was barely tolerable, so they abandoned the joint effort.

Béatritz had been working at her hand loom and keeping an eye on Douce. The girl's movements were swift and blithe; she seemed enamored of the merest household task—and she was asking the silliest questions.

One moment she was astir with plans: the next, she was silent as a stone. She approached Béatritz that morning with, "Am I what one might call beautiful, or just pretty? Or neither? I think my mother plain, but Ebles handsome. They say I resemble him." And the next hour she would worry, "Do you think Gui notices at all what dress I wear? I have only the two. How I wish I'd brought another pelisson! He never says anything." Then, as they cleared the table of the noon meal, she followed Béatritz around, whispering whatever came into her head. "Do you think men like women to jest with them?"

Just being in her mercurial presence brought Béatritz back to the first careering, giddy days of her own love for Raimbaut. Reliving that time, she was able to forget his betrayal for a bit. She had made love to the man, cared for him, composed tensons and partimens with him, hawked and danced and drunk wine in his company—and in the end, he had refused her. She dared not dwell on what had come to pass as a result, the loss of everything save her birthright, her father, and—mercifully—whatever remained of her sanity.

Suddenly, Gui began to sing the first stanza of a lament and her heart lurched.

> *A chantar m'er de so qu'ien non volria,*
> *tant me rancur de lui cui sui amia....*
> Of matters moored to silence must I now sing
> though I'd rather not—so bitter do I feel toward him
> whom I love more than anything;
> With him my fine courtesy's in vain,
> Worth nothing are my beauty and my virtue.
> For I have been tricked: he has treated me
> To treason as though I were worse than nothing to him!

It was hours before nightfall—too early to weep unnoticed and in earnest. But hearing Gui's song brought back the memory of her own longing, which she had fashioned into verses addressed to Raimbaut.

> *sapchatz, gran talan n'auria*
> *qu'ied.us tengues en luoc dell marit....*
> Know you well that I would give all
> To have you in my husband's place....

She rolled the words silently on her tongue and set to her weaving with fierce concentration. But the tears welled nonetheless, distorting the threads on her loom into a convex blur of blues and purples. Head down, she bit her lip. *God makes us wait*, she said to herself. *His will be done.*

Then Gui began another refrain:

> Away from her I say to her made words;
> Within her gaze I know not what to say...

He sings of me, Douce thought, swooning at the mere idea.

"I love Arnaut Daniel," Béatritz said. "I think he's my absolute favorite of the great ones."

"Not Bernard de Ventadour?" Douce asked.

"Some of his songs surpass Bernard's best."

"Sh..shhh.." hushed Gui. Douce closed her eyes in dreamy anticipation. Gui sang the refrain again, then began to make up his own words to Arnaut Daniel's tune:

Na Douce,
I owe to you my very life—
And so I have been thinking of the day
When I shall rise to bear a sword again.

This vow I've made,
The only promise I can give—
To take the Cross and sail to Outremer.
With Thibaut's men I'll fight the Infidel

And win your own bright honor as my bride.
—Away from her I say to her...

The remembrance of her own first love was too much. Béatritz let her loom slip to the floor and moved to a far corner of the room. There, she seemed to pray.

On the third evening of their snowbound confinement, they were eating wheatcakes ravenously, like prisoners living from one ration to the next, when Béatritz heard the ping of a pebble hitting the wooden shutters above her bed. She got up from the table and looked through the window. By standing on tiptoe, she could just glimpse a lone figure in a black cloak as it disappeared around the corner of the house.

"What is it?" Gui said, as Béatritz rushed to the door. Gui stood up, soldier's instinct at the ready. "Someone's out there," she said. Douce and Gui followed her.

But when they looked out onto the darkened snow there was no one in sight, not even the track of new footprints.

"What do you want?" Béatritz called into the twilight.

From the back of the house came the answer, "*In nomine Spiritus*, it's Goodman Raoul!"

She breathed with relief.

"Are you alone?" he asked, drawing back his hood. He stopped abruptly when he emerged from the darkness and saw Gui and Douce standing with her at the door.

"It's all right; they are as family," Béatritz assured him. "Give me your cloak."

Gui and Douce glanced at each other in bewilderment as the man walked between them and into the house.

"I must not stay," he said, warming himself by the fire but not relinquishing his cloak. He was tall, a man in his sixth decade at least, and he wore his hair in a fringe like a monk's. The rush of light on the floor placed him in shadow, revealing little of his face but a long nose and deep-set eyes hooded like his cloak, and the bony fingers of one hand clasped to his throat.

"There are many to be warned," he said. "Before tomorrow a great stake will be lit at Mornas."

Béatritz' hands flew to her mouth. "Dieus!" she exclaimed.

"Mornas!" Gui shouted. "Has Alphonse taken it too?"

"He has," said Raoul, drawing his hood forward. "And now I must go."

"Béatritz lowered her hands. "How many . . . how many are being held?"

"We're not sure yet. Some say twenty."

She winced. Gui hobbled toward the goodman in disbelief. "Twenty!" he exclaimed. "How can you win a town the size of Mornas and hold only twenty prisoners? Either they're hired mongrels or Alphonse's men are fumblers. Twenty men! I've never heard . . ."

"Which direction are they headed?" Béatritz asked.

"We just don't know," Raoul replied solemnly. "Seems they're all over the area, waiting to make the next strike. Montdragon may not remain safe for us much longer. They left us alone the first time, but once the dogs find out about Mornas, what's to keep them from coming back here?" He started for the door, "You've heard that Folquet of Le Thoronet made another great call to arms against Raymond?"

"Oh my God," Béatritz said.

"Three days ago, from an abbey of white monks near Avignon. Word is he's organized a lay movement against us called the White Brotherhood."

"I can't believe it," Béatritz murmured. Gui began to pace the room on his limp leg.

"Folquet is a fanatic," she said.

"Exactly. And so must Alphonse be. It's not enough for him to leave Montdragon and Mornas little more than skeletons—he is bent upon reducing *our* number in the bargain!" With that, Raoul made the sign of the cross, gathered his cloak about him, and left.

"White Brotherhood!" Gui snorted in disgust. "What does that mean? It sounds like a secret society, something up to no good, like the Hospitallers. Folquet is a cunning bastard, full of hocus-pocus."

Douce was trying to remember something. "Didn't Raoul say 'against *us*'? That could only mean one thing . . . Béatritz?" But Béatritz had fallen silent and was kneeling before her little shrine in the far corner. She recited the Prayer of St. John, then the six dobla in a low voice. She kissed her Gospel and rose, directing her gaze to Douce and Gui.

"There is much I have to say to you," she began, "but first, do you know what the 'endura' means?"

They shook their heads.

"Then tell me if you recognize these words: 'If anyone loves the world, there is no love for the Father in his heart. For all that is in the world is desire of the eyes and pride—things that come not from the Father but from the world. And the world and its desires shall pass away, but he who does the will of God shall endure forever. Have mercy on us'!"

"That's what Madame Belot used to say when I gave her food from my basket," Douce blurted out. "'Have mercy on us.' At the time I thought it was a strange way of thanks."

"Belot. There are Belots here in town. They are Cathars . . . one of . . . one of *us*. Or, should I say, I am one of *them*."

From Douce there was a sharp intake of breath.

"Lord in heaven, help us!" Gui exclaimed. "Then you're a *heretic*!"

"I am a Cathar, Gui."

"But it's a *heresy*!" he insisted.

"That's how the world chooses to look at us. There are ways other than those of the world. Come. Douce, take away the dinner things. We must talk."

Gui glanced at Douce, his eyes full of alarm. But she seemed unperturbed; her initial surprise at Béatritz's news had changed to curiosity, something close to excitement.

They drew their stools to the table. "First, you should know that there is a Cathar hospice just north of here, deep in the hills beyond Montdragon," Béatritz began. "Aragonese troops may well comb the lands about this area if they have the least suspicion of the hospice's existence."

"So we're all in danger," Gui said angrily.

"There is a risk," Béatritz agreed. "I couldn't, in good conscience, keep it to myself any longer. That's why I asked Raoul to speak freely before us all. Look, I know it isn't fair for me to have put your lives in jeopardy. I've grown to love you both so much, but I won't keep you here against your will."

Gui frowned darkly. The woman had rescued him and ministered to him; she was as close to a mother as he'd ever had. On the other hand, if they'd unearthed heretics in Mornas, what was to prevent them from doubling back to Montdragon to be sure none were overlooked? What started as a tug-of-war over land could easily turn into a witch-hunt.

But where would he and Douce go? He wasn't even sure he could mount a horse!

"Please, Béatritz, begin at the very beginning," Douce said. "How did you become a Cathar? What is it like to live as one? Is there anyone I've met in town with you who is one too?"

"Our little hospice is where it all started, for me. I found comfort there when I had to move from my father's castle and I no longer had his protection, nor Raimbaut's. A woman I knew in town, a tradeswoman who had served the castle's needs faithfully for many a year, told me of the place, giving away nothing about it other than a description of the person I should ask for. Mind you, this tradeswoman took a risk, but she knew my plight and she knew my character. There are many who sympathize with us—many in this town and elsewhere—who are not themselves Cathars. Luckily for me, she is one of these.

"And so I found the hospice and I stayed. You have no idea how different everything is inside that modest building! Honesty, patience—all the virtues we struggle to live by in the real world—are just taken for granted there. From paupers to the greatest ladies in the land, we are all equal in faith. Many of the nobility, names you would recognize—not the least of them Esclaramonde de Foix—are known to have given themselves over to it, along with their fortunes. It's a strenuous calling, but it has given me great joy. Just doing the daily chores the faith requires . . ."

"Like what?" Douce wanted to know.

"Like finding safe lodgings for our parfaits when they travel and preach. Like taking food to the sick and needy. The time I've spent at the hospice has taught me everything I know of any value: Scriptures, the tenets of the faith, the way to live. It can bestow a pride in our culture that many lack before they join. It's made me see my religion as something almost daring. The hospice is a place of perfect love, so perfect that the world *outside* it soon seems odd and wrong, especially now."

"Don't you suppose the world has always seemed so?" Gui suggested.

"No." Béatritz put her hands on the table and stared at them for a moment. Then she shifted back to practical matters. "What I have told you must remain among us. No one knows of my faith but Raimbaut. My father will die soon. When he does, the castle should be mine, with a nice swathe of land surrounding it. If the Aragonese clear out and it does fall to me, I shall give it all to the Cathar diocese that it too may be converted into a hospice."

"And what will happen to you?" asked Gui.

"Béatritz gave a sigh. "I? I have long been on my own. It's been many months since I've had word from Raimbaut . . ." she said absently. "Oh, I don't know, I don't know. Who's to say where his politics will lead him? After this town was taken, I waited. I thought . . . but he sent no one to the castle, only word that my father was to be spared . . . no inquiry about me. Perhaps he does play both sides, favoring Aragon or Toulouse as the winds blow. But I fear that he and I are divided forever."

Gui looked at Douce as she put her arms around the older woman's shoulders.

"You see what I mean," Béatritz continued. "The world is a shambles. Nothing is as it was, not since a year ago last Yule. That day we were feasting at Courthézon and Raimbaut gave me this." She pried the milky green stone from her belt and pitched it onto the table, where it made little rocking motions and finally settled. She stared at it and suddenly burst into tears.

"Forgive me," she said, "but there was nothing this year except burning and killing . . . I shall never forget *this* Christmas. Every joyous thing from the past is gone. Perhaps our parfaite at the hospice was right when she said that we Cathars are destined to be martyrs of disorder."

"Come," said Douce. "Have the last portion of wine. It'll cheer you."

"*You* cheer me," Béatritz kissed Douce's cheek. "But I have warned you both. I want to say one thing more and it's terribly important. If I am discovered, if anyone has reason to suspect me, if I am—God forbid it—denounced as a heretic, *take care you do not know me.*"

Gui groaned like a soul in pain, and got up to pace the floor once more.

Only now did it fully dawn upon Douce that, thanks to her association with Madame Belot, she too had been helping the cause.

This, then, was the bond she had been sharing with Béatritz, unbeknownst to either. This heresy . . . was the root and center of Béatritz' life, that private source of sustenance which Douce had observed and envied in her. She put her forehead down on her palms right there on the table, beside the empty wine carafe. Instantly, Béatritz was at her side, stroking her hair. Then she went back to her place at the table. Presently she reached across and tipped the girl's chin up from its resting place, searching Douce's eyes as she did so. They were dry, serene, almost radiant.

"I see," Béatritz said softly. "Perhaps I am forgiven after all."

Chapter 16

DIES IRAE

Béatritz awoke to plopping sounds as slabs of snow fell from the roof. The blizzard had finally stopped. Raoul's news was fresh in her mind. This renewed threat to all she held dear—the hospice, her father, Douce, and Gui—Instilled a sense of urgency. There were errands to be done.

She roused Douce, and after a meager breakfast of leftover griddle cakes, they set out for the castle. Each carried an empty jug to be filled at the town well. Being snowbound for nearly a week had left them low on everything but flour. Water, wine, and bread had to be carried to the castle. On the way back they would replenish their own larder. As they walked ankle-deep in snow toward town, Béatritz made a mental list, folding a finger to her palm for each item: onions, carrots, dried cod for the stewpot, apples. And lamp oil.

"The townsfolk will be out in droves today," Béatritz said as they came onto the main street. People were milling around outside the wine merchant's shop in clusters, talking. A sense of foreboding prompted Béatritz to approach a man she knew from the reeve's office.

"Nicol, has something happened?"

"Nought here, my lady. But there are reports of a papal legation in Orange. The Pope's scattering his emissaries around the countryside the way a farmer sows grain, isn't it so, my lady? And there are rumors that the Cathar bishop in Orange has fled. Thanks be, Montdragon is quiet so far. In my opinion, we're not important enough for the Pope to bother with."

"A legation to Orange!" Béatritz echoed. "Is there any word of the count's movements?"

"Only that he has sent some soldiers to Mornas, my lady. Count Raimbaut isn't much given to soldiering, they say. My guess is this shows he's cast his lot with the Aragonese, at least if the rumor's true, my lady."

"Nicol, thanks. Come Douce, we must hurry. First to the well, then the baker's. We can't tarry here."

Douce looked at Béatritz with concern.

"What does it mean . . . about Raimbaut?"

"It means that after all, in spite of my pleadings, he sides with Aragon."

"With those who take Cathars prisoner?" Douce said solemnly. "Oh, Béatritz, I am so sorry."

Gui awakened to an empty house. The revelations of the night before raced through his mind, chilling him more than a winter blast. A heretic! Béatritz was a heretic. He and Douce had to flee, to leave this place as soon as they could. If the Cathar hunters came back, they would be condemned along with Béatritz, burned for beliefs that were not theirs.

Sun poured into the little house. The storm had passed. The women were out about their errands. Like as not, Béatritz had gone up to the castle, no doubt taking Douce with her. *I have to build my strength*, he thought. *I must get to my horse.* He released the door latch, blinked at the dazzling sun, and limped to the stalls at the back of the house. There his destrier whinnied him a welcome.

He let the horse nuzzle his shoulder for a bit and then, with a flash of pain that startled him, he swung himself up, not bothering with pad or bridle, and rode into the sunlight. Today would be the first test of his fitness.

Shielding his eyes, he guessed at the direction of town by the spindles of chimney smoke rising lazily into the sky. Everything snapped into focus in the sharp air: his own breath, birds squawking in the bushes, the big trees still muffled in snow. Beneath his horse's hooves fresh deer tracks had bitten cleanly into the snowy path.

As he approached Montdragon, he grew increasingly tired. He found his way to the main street nonetheless, his good humor unchanged. But soon there was no denying his fatigue, and within the hour he had to turn around, his mission unaccomplished. He rode slowly back, half afraid at what he had done, and cursing his limbs' refusal to do his bidding. Once inside the destrier's stall he slid off and losing his balance, slipped sideways into a pile of dung. He quickly scrambled to his feet, his helpless hand oozing fresh blood through a thick layer of manure. He swore at himself for his clumsiness and went to wash as best he could.

Returning, Douce and Béatritz caught him scrubbing his boots, left hand dirty and bloodied, at his side. He flung down the rag in disgust.

"Let me see that hand," Béatritz demanded. She examined the wound carefully. "I shan't test your bravery by cauterizing it a second time, but we shall have to cleanse it all the same." She turned to Douce: "Get the rosemary solution." To Gui she said, "I'm going to have to bind it up again."

Béatritz pulled a stool to the table and waited while Douce got the poultice ready. Before Béatritz had even wrung out the cloth he gritted his teeth against the sting of rosemary and vinegar and looked to Douce. "What word is there from town?" he asked, forgetting for the moment about the purpose of his disastrous excursion.

"No, first tell us how you hurt your hand," Béatritz said. "That is a nasty wound, and it smells of manure."

Gui grimaced, unwilling to reveal his foolishness. "I . . . I walked out to the stable . . . my destrier . . . pushed against me . . . and, and I . . . lost my balance on this godforsaken leg . . . I don't know what cut my hand."

"Oh Gui, you shouldn't . . ."

"I know," he cut her off. "Now tell me about town."

Douce's expression was serious. "The news we have is not good." As Béatritz worked the poultice into Gui's wound Douce told him what they had learned. "How many men would Raimbaut have taken to Mornas?" Gui asked.

Béatritz lifted her head. "Oh Gui, no. He won't be there himself. It's not his style, leading men in battle."

Gui hid his scorn. "He'd be in Orange, then, greeting the Pope's legation?"

"No, he'll be in Courthézon. Orange is a thorn in his flesh, divided up as it is. He's never there. He hates the place." Béatritz finished applying the poultice and re-examined Gui's hand. Satisfied, she thumped the cork back into the rosemary solution and stood up to get a bandage. For a moment she lingered, her eyes fixed on Gui. "We've lived through worse than this! I remember once when we had to evacuate the hospice, all fifteen of us. Each one went to a different safe house. Our parfaite had only minutes to give us instructions, but it worked beautifully. No one was captured."

"Safe houses?" inquired Gui. "You mean hiding places for Cathars?"

"Home of sympathizers," answered Béatritz briskly, putting the corked container back on the shelf. "Usually croyants. They have pledged themselves to take in any Cathar who's in danger, for as long as necessary." She drew down a linen strip from a rafter over the fireplace and went back to sit by Gui. Lifting the poultice from his hand, she placed it in the basin Douce held out to her.

"How do you know which houses are safe?" Douce asked. Béatritz began to fan the wet solution on the wound with her hand. Gui winced.

"The hospice keeps a map. We know the routes and the houses by heart. Even to the family's name and occupation. It's part of our indoctrination."

"And what if you make a mistake?"

"You can't. Each house is marked."

"How?" Gui's eyes widened. Béatritz hesitated for a second.

"Don't tell if you shouldn't," Douce interjected.

"I trust you with this secret precisely because of your association with me. It's my gift to you, and it might make the difference between life and death. You both have seen the sign without realizing what it means: it's a cross whose four branches are equal, enclosed in a circle."

Douce instantly thought of the curious little talisman given her by Madame Belot.

"Where do Cathars worship?" Douce asked.

"In people's houses, members of the faith, sympathizers."

"May I come with you to a service?"

Béatritz rose and took Douce's head between her hands for an instant. "Of course," she said, and went out to clear snow away from the house well.

"You can't!" said Gui once Béatritz was out of earshot. "The laying on of hands, the fasting, the endura, the kiss of peace—stuff and nonsense! It's not for you. Do you want to become a martyr too?"

"I'm only curious." She paused. "Gui, what *are* we going to do? How long can we stay here this way?"

"Lady, I have no answers. It can't be long before I heal well enough to leave," he said. He drew his stool close to her then kissed her forehead, her nose, her mouth from which no words came. And when the tears welled in her eyes he kissed them too, following them with his tongue as they traveled her cheeks. Feeling that her head would burst from simple love, she rested it in Gui's lap. She said nothing still, though her whole body spoke to him tenderly. Inflamed with purpose, he continued, "I *shall* go. I have my right hand still, and it has always served me well enough."

"Amador, dear friend," was all Douce could say, taking that hand in hers.

Gui awoke two mornings later with fever. Béatritz commanded him to stay in bed. The wound had festered, as she had feared. As she unwound the bandage, telltale red streaks were visible up Gui's arm, which was swollen up to the shoulder. She should have had the wisdom; she knew to cauterize his hand in spite of wanting to spare him the pain. Disquieted, she left Douce instructions to force her patient to drink and eat. She was going to fetch the surgeon, who would know whether cutting was necessary.

Douce sat beside Gui, his burning hand held to her cheek. He had refused all but water, which he drank for her sake. Now he slept quietly under a cool towel that she had wrapped around his forehead. In the early light of that winter dawn his features resembled those masks carved in stone on the tombs in great cathedrals. He looked so still and small. The little hollows at the corners of his mouth twitched; she kissed them gently, and waited.

When the church bells struck noon there was still no sign of Béatritz. Douce returned Gui's hand to his side and covered him with the quilt. She got up to fetch the Scriptures from their shelf, and a piece of bread and suddenly felt dizzy. Never before had she been so alone. She would pray. She could not find the right words; the ones she had learned as a child failed her. She put down the book and opened the door to look out. A low sun in the winter sky offered no comfort.

It took only a moment to throw on a cloak over her dress. She stopped by Gui's bed to check on his quiet breathing, then left the house and went around to the stall, where Gui's destrier stamped in his anxiousness to be ridden again. Douce took Gui's saddle from its double peg and heaved it onto the horse's back. When she coaxed his bridle on she felt him tense the muscles in his neck and resolved to ride him gently, for her own sake.

The roads were packed hard with snow, but the town streets had been swept. "Which way to the house of the surgeon?" she asked the first citizen she saw.

"You'll not find him in now!" came the reply. "Like as not, he'll be down at the marketplace. There's trouble again from Alphonse's men, haven't you heard? They're holding a host of heretics in the square for questioning – you've never seen such a commotion!"

A fear rose in Douce that almost made her faint. She pressed Gui's horse to a fast trot, driving him until his heavy-shod hooves struck sparks off the cobbles. The marketplace was thronged with bleating goats and chickens clucking in cages, with fruit sellers, city officials, ecclesiastics, tradesmen, and a ragged tail-guard of curious townspeople. Her eyes searched frantically for Béatritz's crown of heavy hair, but she saw no familiar face in the crowd, not even Raoul's. She reined and sat for a moment to catch her wind. She could see the prisoners directly across the square, the only listless figures in the whole moving mob, surrounded by Alphonse's occupying force. Surely Béatritz had noticed something was amiss and headed off to the castle. Only then did she see that the town was in ruins.

Montdragon was a skeleton, as Raoul had predicted. Its outer walls had been broken through in many places, its moats and ditch lay filled with rubble. Windows had been knocked out of the church, gaping holes that opened onto the marketplace. Before her was the familiar three-headed fountain where she had so often gone with Béatritz to draw water. But along the street of Jews there were no rebuilt stalls. Instead, the vendors had spread their goods on blankets. Behind them, torched houses stood like empty corncribs, slats leaning every which way, roofs tumbled in, innards exposed to the sky. Wood fires sent up smoke at street corners where the houses had burnt to the ground. From the low murmur of voices came an infant's cry of hunger.

Then she saw three mounted soldiers enter Montdragon's central square quietly and without resistance. Not expecting any sign of protest, the three addressed their black-clad prisoners. Alphonse's men tightened their ring around the group of men and women, some of whom were kneeling in prayer, half hidden in their cloaks. A white-robed ecclesiastic intoned names. A tall prisoner in black suddenly cried out against the mounted soldiers, asking to see the clerk at the prison. The ecclesiastic in white was saying something about the price of scorning the Church's mercy. One of the heretics actually laughed.

Some compulsion drew Douce on toward a little knot of prisoners at the edge of the square. There was a quiet in their midst which pulled her to its vortex as though these miserable souls were the only pool of sanity in the haphazard mob. They were not pleading with the soldiers, not struggling to get free. They spoke little among themselves, as if they knew that it was only a matter of time, silent in the weary knowledge of what awaited them.

And then Douce saw Béatritz. She had risen from her knees, her cape had fallen away from her neck, and the coil of burnished hair slid free. Douce sat helpless in horror.

"Béatritz," she called. The older woman looked up. An arm, bared and striped with scarlet weals, emerged from her cloak. "Béatritz!"

But the familiar upraised palm signalled silence.

Béatritz turned and met her friend's eyes for a long moment. Her face was strangely calm. She then closed her eyes, motioning silence again with her hand. Douce remembered Béatritz's words on the night of Raoul's visit: *Take care you do not know me*, and her lips froze.

Before the prisoners were led away, Douce wheeled about and rode out of the marketplace, pushing Gui's horse at full speed until she reached the house. She jumped off, tethered the horse to a ring and ran across the threshold. She needed Gui's help desperately. Her heart sank as she saw that he was not awake, but in the throes of some fitful sleep. His body was swollen, his face bright red, and he was breathing with difficulty.

A terrible fear exploded inside her. She woke him, held him, kissed his eyes and mouth. She hugged him in a rage of tears. "Don't die. I love you. I am with you." She felt his heart beat fast as a bird's. She saw him open his eyes, try to speak her name. And then she felt his heart no longer. He was quiet, smiling. She held him silently, her face against his, still hot. Gui was gone. Beside her lay a young knight, dead.

Chapter 17

REQUIESCAT IN PACE

The rain came, pale and cold.

It ran from the toes of Gaucelm's calf boots, thin-soled with wear. He kicked his heels from the stirrups for a moment to stretch his legs. Smacking the drops from his new blue hose, he cried, "So much for the grand sun of the South!"

"Did it ever occur to you that God is punishing us for Douce's disappearance?" Guilhelma said.

Gaucelm grunted, "You perhaps. I had nothing to do with the business, as you well know. Besides, I'm sure God saves his punishments for greater sins than that. Still, as we've been deluged for nearly five days straight, he could at least give us fins." He gazed at the grey horizon. "What do you have in mind for us, Lord, a second Great Flood?" Then, warming to his complaint, he raised his fist skyward and roared, "Seigneur, in return for this hardship with which you have afflicted our travel I beg you—allow me to commit a sin I enjoy, a really magnificent sin, one which I would have the privilege to plan and execute at my leisure, a sin of such scale and audacity that you would be obliged to dump torrents upon my head, not this measly, endless drooling, this drivel you call rain!"

Guilhelma giggled.

"And furthermore, Seigneur," Gaucelm continued, "since we're on the subject, the rain isn't all you've inflicted on us. It's those dreary hill towns you've put in our way on every precipice. Oh yes, they look like fortresses for angels from down here. Very pretty. But climbing them stone by stone is a different story. And once we reach the top all we find are the same moronic humans as on the flatlands: petty nobles and the poor slaves of their fields and kitchens. Why, Seigneur, could you have not built some cities on the plains hereabouts—well-spaced, so that we could have a decent roof over our heads and something hot for supper without mounting halfway to heaven each night?"

Dismounting to rest the horses, they peered through the slanting drizzle into the valley below. A slow, steady downpour marched across the fields, advancing like a steel-lanced army. Soon, Gaucelm and Guilhelma were drenched, swelling rivulets of water encircling their boots. They stood fast while the water sucked the gravel from beneath their feet like undertow.

"It's a wonder the stone foundations of the houses aren't washed out," Gaucelm said as they remounted and began to plod downward. It was nearly vespers before they found a monk in a remote priory who would give them lodging, for a fee.

By morning the sky had cleared. The monk waved them in the direction of a town called Joyeuse where, he said, they would find a stream that joined the Ardèche. Joyeuse was happily named. There they found a simple cookshop where they breakfasted and fed the horses before the last leg of their journey.

By now the gorges and grottos of the Dordogne, so wild and treacherous to cross, were only a memory. Well behind them were both the tedious flats of the Lot valley and the rainswept peaks of the past two days. Ahead they could see low hills basking in winter sunlight, their soft flanks sloping to the great plateau where the Rhône flowed. At its edge, they were told, lay Pont Saint-Esprit, and across the water from Saint-Esprit would be Montdragon. Only two days' ride farther south, Gaucelm estimated, was Guilhelma's home country in the Marquisat of Provence. But their mission urged them forth to find Douce.

In Saint-Esprit the market vendors were in full cry. The pair clopped along the "street of gold" named for its moneychangers. Here they exchanged their coins for new currency struck in Orange and stamped with the likeness of its handsome count, Raimbaut IV. They filled their saddle packs with leeks, beets, dried fish, Valencias. It was the first time Guilhelma had seen barrels of olives since she left Alès. While the épicier had his back turned, she scooped her hand through a barrelful of the oily fruit and smiled with the pleasure of it, holding up her fingers for Gaucelm to lick.

"We had Spanish olives in Toulouse," he said. "They're tarter, greener."

"*These* are real olives, allowed to ripen till they're black," she said. "Their oil is golden, not greenish. You'll see."

They bought a demiard for Douce, and some fruit for Gui.

"I shall make us a proper southern stew," Guilhelma said with anticipation.

They remounted and passed a Jew selling hazelnuts from his tattered cap. At the edge of town worker's shacks and bordellos were piled up against one another. They rode across piles of slop and refuse—what Gaucelm called "the town's digestive system"—and held their noses. The walls of Montdragon were now visible just beyond the bridge.

"No more dried beans and turnips, then," Gaucelm sang as they left Saint-Esprit. "From now on, figs and pears, nougats and marchpane, new wine—and *sun*!"

Their mood sobered as they reined in before the gouged-out city walls of Montdragon.

"The place looks deserted," she said as they surveyed the decimated enceinte.

"Where were you told to look for her?" Gaucelm asked.

"The old steward at Ussel said only the house of Béatritz de Montdragon."

Gaucelm approached the first figure he saw for directions. The soldier only shrugged and spat. Gaucelm persisted, his voice urgent but the rough fellow in his battered mail shirt gave no indication that he understood. They rode into the square where a display of strange banners drooped listlessly from the portals of the church. A platform stood empty below the banners, draped with black cloth. There was no movement but a swirl of smoke as it blew from several woodfires. Here and there figures crouched over pots. There was a scent of boiling meat, the low whimper of children.

Gaucelm dismounted and approached a disheveled young man slouching by one of the woodfires.

The reply to his question was a cynical snarl. "Who knows who's left since they took the heretics? They'll burn the church itself next!" Then the voice softened: "If she's one of *them*, there are still some in hiding."

Gaucelm hesitated before asking, "When was the burning?"

"There was none. Yesterday they were tried and led away, God knows where. It's enough, by Christ's blood, it's enough now! The evil eye has turned upon us all. *They* have their faith to die for, but it's time the rest of us were left in peace. Who are you?"

Gaucelm didn't answer, but unfastened his pack and handed the man a bunch of leeks.

"Blessings on you," the man said.

They continued their search through the city, knocking at every likely house. Guilhelma's panic widened as she plodded after him. Gaucelm only became more determined in his mission, thrusting his head into every window shamelessly.

When they at last came to Béatritz's house, Gaucelm's routine question died on his lips as Douce rushed out and enveloped them in a storm of embraces, cries of relief, and tears. Guilhelma saw how wide yet deep her eyes looked, how pale her face. Douce uttered not a word, but led them both by the hand to where Gui lay under his quilt. Guilhelma bent to pull back the coverlet.

"Dear child!" she exclaimed and glanced at Douce. The girl opened her mouth but could say nothing.

"Where is Béatritz?" Gaucelm asked, taking her by the shoulders.

"Dead," she said. "Béatritz was a heretic." Then Douce collapsed.

Guilhelma and Gaucelm, one on each side, rolled out their bedding and gently lifted her light body onto it. Guilhelma pulled the fur throw from Béatritz's bed and tucked it around her. When Douce inhaled Béatritz's presence near her closed eyes, the pounding in her heart subsided, and she fell into a deep sleep.

A fever burned in her. They took turns holding her hand; awake, she did not utter a word. Asleep, she spoke her dreams. She grew certain the room was crowded with evil creatures. The air was thick with whispers that rose to high-pitched clicking like crickets in the cold. Nothing seemed to be in its right season: the Christmas mummers mocked her; the white boy knight with his crown askew came back to haunt her. Trees broke into blossom and she laughed aloud. She woke often in a sweat, with the sound of wings beating above her head. Guilhelma's hand was always there, or Gaucelm's; the candle burned on.

"I shan't, I shan't! First I want to be measured," Douce mumbled. "Measure me!"

Guilhelma heard her plea over and over again. *The child thinks she's home in Ventadour being fitted for a dress,* the older woman thought.

But in her dream Douce was dazed and dirty, fleeing marauders who had attacked her parents' village. Inexplicably, she knew she needed wings and found them in a shop. The shopkeeper, dressed in white, with black hair down to her waist, told her she had to bathe before she could be measured for wings.

"Now!" Douce insisted. "Now!"

But the woman marched her toward the baths. As she did so, she noticed that Douce had a pair of horns on the back of her head, and became afraid. She lifted a crucifix from the wall and hooked it onto one of the horns.

Douce awoke screaming.

Gaucelm stood by awkwardly as Guilhelma lifted the child in her arms. Douce pitched back and forth, sobbing like someone crazed.

"Here, I'll help you take the pain away. Give it to me, give it to Guilhelma." And she rocked her like an infant until Douce fell asleep once more.

The next morning Guilhelma said to Gaucelm, "I must prepare Gui's body for burial. Go into town and find a priest and the gravedigger. Tell them to get things ready for a funeral this afternoon. Then bring back a strong youth. If you can find one with a cart, so much the better. And Gaucelm . . ." she added, ". . . see that Gui is well-coffined. Talk to the cooper yourself. Don't leave matters to the gravedigger." Thus instructed, Gaucelm set out for Montdragon.

With a glance at the sleeping Douce, Guilhelma began her work. She bathed Gui's body in snow water, crossed his arms on his chest, and wrapped him first in his own cloak, then in the coverlet that Douce had thrown over him. She was so engrossed in her task that she did not hear Douce waken, but as she straightened from tucking in the corners of the coverlet, she saw Douce sitting up in her bed, completely composed.

"Dear one!" she said, startled. "How is it with you?" Quickly, not waiting for a reply, Guilhelma took from the hearth the gruel she had made and brought it to her. Famished, Douce spooned it straight from the pot.

"There, kitten," Guilhelma said, well pleased. "There's more to be heated if you want it."

"I'm much better, thanks," Douce replied almost formally. She propped herself on one elbow and regarded Gui's body calmly.

"Guilhelma, remember what you told me once at Ventadour, that love can change? I didn't know exactly what you were talking about then. Now I understand." *It is true,* she thought to herself. *Perhaps Gui's religion and mine were never meant to be the same.* He had laughed at Béatritz's account of the endura and the kiss of peace; those things were not for him. But to the bewildered Guilhelma she merely said, "Now that he is gone I must do his living for him, in *my* way."

Guilhelma's thoughts, meanwhile, were running along a different channel. Half afraid to broach the subject, she murmured, "Surely, he died nobly . . ."

"His hand was shot through by an arrow."

"Ah well, then," Guilhelma sighed in relief. "He died in battle."

Just then the door flew open and Gaucelm entered, blowing and stamping from the cold. Seeing Douce recovered, he threw out his arms and ran to embrace her. He sat on her bedstraw, one arm enveloping her shoulders, while Guilhelma admonished him, "Really, Gaucelm, Douce will catch her death from you! Take off that cloak. Have you found someone from town to give a hand?"

"He'll be here shortly," Gaucelm said, struggling free of the cold-stiff folds of his woolen cloak and casting it on the floor. "Now tell us, Douce, what was going on in that head of yours while you slept. What was it that set you writhing like a contortionist?"

"I must have been dreaming," she said sweetly.

"Paaagh! It looked as though you were fighting the very Devil . . ."

"When I woke from it I realized I'd been given a task." Her voice was earnest, low. She looked first at Guilhelma, then at Gaucelm. "I must go to Count Raimbaut, in Courthézon and tell him about Béatritz."

"Tell him *what* about her?" asked Gaucelm.

"How she died." Her gaze traveled around the room, coming to rest on Gui's still, swaddled form as evidence of her mission. Then she looked over at Béatritz's bed, her chair, and her loom. It was only when she allowed herself to recall the sight of Béatritz herself—so recently alive and mending the very cloak she had worn to her death—that Douce's whole body caved in anew.

When her tears stopped, she faced Gaucelm and Guilhelma. "You can't imagine her expression as she looked at me just before they snatched her away. Her face was absolutely serene. Her eyes were full of trust. She sought me out . . ." Again Douce could not prevent her tears. But this time her face cleared quickly. "She was so competent in everything she did. Making a fire, mending, dressing Gui's wound." Douce felt suddenly much better, as though in sharing Béatritz's virtues, she could almost possess them herself. "And she had the most wonderful hair—honey-colored, and she wore it like this." Douce grasped a handful of her own and coiled it briefly at the crown of her head. Gaucelm smiled at the gesture, that of a young girl yearning to be grown up.

"Also, she was in love," Douce was not certain she could manage this part without breaking down again. Guilhelma arched her eyebrows expectantly. "With Raimbaut, Count of Orange," Douce finished.

Guilhelma looked blank, but there was a sharp intake of breath from Gaucelm, who said, "A thorn in Elias d'Ussel's side, that one. But a good man for verse."

Douce seemed not to hear Gaucelm's comment. "So you see why I must go to Raimbaut, why I must tell him how radiant she was before her death, and how much she still loved him. Otherwise he will never know."

A squeak of wheels sounded outside. "That'll be the town lad," said Gaucelm, getting up with a grunt. "My ears tell me he's got a cart and . . ." he answered Guilhelma's inquiring look ". . . he *said* he'd bring a litter."

Guilhelma peered from the window. "I hope he's strong enough; he looks barely twelve. What did you offer him?"

"I gave him a few coins I had in my pouch, with promise of more to come. The gravedigger's fee is eight coppers. There's not a priest to be found in all of Montdragon. I searched the church, crypt to steeple." He opened the door, then turned to Guilhelma. "I wish we'd thought twice before buying out the greengrocer's in Saint-Esprit," he said. "I've got little enough of the new coinage to last us until we're on the road again."

"What we bought from the greengrocer at Saint-Esprit will keep us alive until we *are* on the road," Guilhelma replied firmly.

Douce rose quietly and went to the cupboard. While Gaucelm and the townsboy negotiated the litter through the entrance as Guilhelma held the door,

Douce knelt and reached for Béatritz's little gospel of St. John, then shut the cupboard.

Gaucelm's helper was a wiry lad in a leather jerkin and breeches. He let it be known that he was called Ulf after his father, a builder of no small reputation in town.

With Gaucelm as a captive audience, he extolled his father's qualities even as they lifted Gui onto the litter. Guilhelma took Gui's sword from the hook where his cloak had hung. Douce ran out to hold the horse steady while Gaucelm and Ulf transferred the body from the litter into the cart. Guilhelma placed Gui's sword next to him and ordered Douce back inside.

"We'll be outdoors all afternoon," she said. "Mind you wrap up well against the cold."

Gaucelm went to the stable, to saddle Gui's destrier. After a series of muffled grunts and commanding "Ho!"s, followed by "whoa, boy, steady," Gaucelm managed to position the saddle and pull up on the woven hemp girth until it felt tight against the horse's stomach. For a moment Gaucelm stood with his back to the stall door, out of harm's way, and surveyed his accomplishment. Then, on impulse, he circled the destrier, flinging the stirrups up and across the saddle tree from both sides. Gui's horse would be ceremoniously riderless for all to see.

Gaucelm grabbed the reins close under the bit and led the horse from the stable into position, a respectful eight paces or so in back of the cart. Ulf clambered astride the cart horse, bade the women climb in and, with a flap of the reins, the little procession started off. They moved cautiously along the packed snow, in a solemn line, beneath an iron gray sky: horse and cart, Douce and Guilhelma facing each other across the body, Gaucelm at the rear leading the destrier.

When they came to the church graveyard, the digger was hard at work upon the unforgiving ground. Seeing that there would be time, Gaucelm brought the destrier up ahead and asked Ulf to hold both horses while he searched the church again for its errant priest. As he walked away Douce cried suddenly, "I'm coming with you!" and sprang from the cart. "Wait, Gaucelm!"

He turned, she caught up, and they entered the church together. Douce made straight for the apse, then knelt in prayer. Gaucelm watched in silence as her lips moved with the utterance of words he could not hear. When she finished, he said, "Come and help me find a priest. There must be one somewhere in this godforsaken town."

But when they came out of the church Gaucelm could see across the snowy yard the figure of the gravedigger leaning defiantly on his shovel. Next to the freshly dug grave was a casket which Guilhelma appeared to be eyeing with disapproval. As they drew closer, Gaucelm saw why: the gravedigger had produced a box of raw planks. In his zeal to find a priest, Gaucelm had neglected Guilhelma's advice to order directly from the cooper.

"There's been a heap of dying hereabouts," the gravedigger was protesting, his free hand rising to indicate new heights of carnage, "and not one box of seasoned wood to be found in the whole of Montdragon. Every breathing soul wants a good burial for their dead. But it's wartime, sir, and not even gold can get you what there's none of." Gaucelm said, "So be it. We live in difficult times. If it weren't for this wicked war, Gui would have had a proper burial at Ussel."

"If it weren't for this war," Douce declared, "Gui would be alive. Let's do his funeral the way he'd want it. Ulf, put the body in the casket." She nodded to the gravedigger. Then, from a pocket inside her cloak, she took the Gospel of St. John. She opened to a place marked by Béatritz and her eyes widened in astonishment. The text was almost miraculously appropriate. She scanned it twice, just to make sure that it truly did promise a life after death, then handed the book to Gaucelm. "When they have put Gui in the grave, please read this," she commanded him softly.

The two townsmen did their work, and the little group witnessed Gui's disappearance into the open ground. Then, heads bent in impersonal grief, the helpers rejoined the circle as Gaucelm read, "'My kingdom is not of this world . . . Verily, verily, I say unto you, the hour is coming, and now is when the dead shall hear the voice of the son of God: and they that hear shall live." Glancing up between the lines, he caught sight of Douce's hand emerging from the folds of her cloak to seek out Guilhelma's. Otherwise she stood stiff as a crozier. He noticed that she did not look again at the grave; when he could glimpse her face he saw that it was suffused with tears. *By now*, he thought, *her brave facade, her little charade of authority has come to an end. Poor thing, it must have cost her dear.*

Gaucelm, satisfied that they had done as well by Gui as circumstances permitted, paid Ulf and the gravedigger their coppers. Pulling the stirrups down from the saddle, he helped Douce and Guilhelma mount the destrier. Then, walking forward to grasp the reins under the horse's head, he gave the signal and the funeral party set out for the house.

On the morning after the burial, Guilhelma decreed that the whole house be cleaned from top to bottom. Every stick of furniture, every tub, sack, and stool was placed outside while she scrubbed, dusted, mopped the flagstones with vinegar and aired the bedding. Kettles of water boiled on the fire, clouding the air with steam. Finally she spread fresh rushes on the floor, trimmed the lamp wicks and lit new candles. By suppertime, it was done.

Douce lent a hand sporadically. To Gaucelm she seemed right enough, neither weepy nor inclined to dwell overmuch on the little household items which could so easily bring forth the enormity of her loss. He gave her an account of Ventadour gone topsy-turvy after her escape. He told her of Marie's fury and Pieter's disappearance. This last bit of information seemed to amuse her.

"You mean he never went back to the castle?" Douce asked. "Well, that's no surprise to me. He hated it there. He just wanted to go *home*."

But there were moments later that night when Gaucelm began to worry about her. Once or twice he caught her examining the forking bones in her hands so closely that her eyes seemed to bore right through the skin. To his inquiry she merely replied that this was the closest she could come to seeing herself from inside. Then she let her hands travel over her ribs, wondering out loud what it would be like to see her skeleton and whether she would recognize her own bones, the shape of her skull. Would she be able to say "that one's mine" if it were heaped in a pile with others?

Gaucelm was aghast, but not wanting to alarm her, he only said, "What a curious idea. I've never thought of that." It made him nervous, this kind of talk. It made him impatient to leave Montdragon, with its smell of death. Guilhelma, he felt sure, would know how to handle Douce.

Later, he cornered her at the other side of the room by the hearth. "Her grieving is driving her mad!" Gaucelm said.

"It's like the tail end of a fever," Guilhelma reassured him. "You remember how she talked nonsense in her sleep. It's not harmful. It's her right, after what she's been through. We must let her be. She has to drift awhile between heaven and hell."

But slowly, like a shape emerging from clouds or firelight, Douce saw the meaning of the dream about horns and the crucifix, as though Béatritz herself had spoken it directly into her ear: *Take your faith and find the hospice*. With her goal as certain as the Grail, there was only the question of *when*, and that was up to her body. She would have to rely on her own judgment, in which she had very little confidence at the moment. Until she did, she would have to content herself with imagining the place.

"Just north of here, deep in the hills beyond Montdragon," Béatritz had said.

Meanwhile, she ate. Guilhelma concocted leek and onion pies, beets in sugared vinegar, beans ground and worked to a thick paste.

The question of time continued to torment Douce. She still felt dizzy when she got up from her bedstraw and her legs had grown thin like pieces of string. She knew that Gaucelm wanted to be on the road again. Though he had said nothing about leaving, she could almost hear his impatience buzzing in her ears. How far was it to the hospice? She would have to make the journey on foot. How long would it take to get there? It was futile to make calculations without any idea of the distance involved. Still, she could not help seeing the hospice over and over again in her mind's eye. She imagined a simple cottage invisible from any road, and protected by hills. The sight of it was what she lived for.

Chapter 18

THE HOSPICE

Finally, on the morning of February Kalends, the first day of the new month, Douce knew the time had come. Gaucelm and Guilhelma had ridden the destrier into town to buy flour and wine and to see that the grave had been properly filled and marked.

Even before the sound of hoofs faded, Douce had wrapped a piece of bread in a cloth. Remembering the gray, chill weather of Gui's funeral, she put on every layer of clothing she possessed. Her shock, when she opened the door, was pleasing. The air felt soft, almost like spring. Melted snow dripped from the roof. The sun was out. Back in the house, she took off an outer skirt of heavy wool and an underblouse, leaving only her chemise and the homespun bliaut under her cloak.

Mindful of the potential distance, she decided to ride Guilhelma's horse. She had divined her route by a mixture of instinct, common sense, and the echo of what Béatritz had said: "north of here, deep in the hills" If she got lost today, she thought, she would come back and try again the next time she found herself alone. Trusting, then, to what amounted to blind luck, Douce's plan was to join the high road until it went west into town. She would skirt Montdragon, branching off to the north just beyond it, and ride until she saw hills.

Everything around her rustled and whispered as she set out. Branchfuls of snow slid heavily to the ground, choking the already mud-filled ditches, while the green-black fans of fir trees, newly released from their snow loads, seemed to wave her forward ceremoniously.

The horse's footing was precarious over mounds of melting snow and the glassy remains of splintered ice. They picked their way around the great muddy trenches rutted with wagon-wheel tread that ran down the middle of the road. Even so, she was happy to be by herself, freed awhile from Guilhelma's overweening care and Gaucelm's inquiries into her state of mind. On the road she could be what she wanted, outpacing the deaths of her dear ones.

But her imagined innocence did not accompany her for long. As she was about to turn north off the high road she saw a man on horseback coming toward her. She hoped he would pass her quickly, knowing perfectly well that the roads were never safe. Now she cast down her eyes, but the rider slowed his horse ominously. With mounting dread, she grasped the reins tightly, aware of little more than her pulse throbbing as the rider pulled his horse alongside her. When she could muster the courage to raise her head, she found herself looking straight into the eyes of Goodman Raoul.

"What a miracle you escaped!" Douce cried, taking in his monk's fringe, his deep-set eyes.

"It was luck. At least, partly," Raoul said, still breathing hard. He leaned forward to give his horse a gentling pat. "My job is to warn others of our faith when there is danger. I had crossed the river and was already beyond St. Etienne when I heard about Béatritz. She is a terrible loss to us. When things quieted down, I went to see her father, the old baron."

"How did he take it?"

"The man is poorly, and a bit befuddled." Raoul said, shaking his head slowly. "He didn't seem to understand what I was saying. He kept asking why he was shut up in his own castle. I think he expected to see Béatritz come in at any moment with some wine and food."

Douce nodded sadly.

"And where are you bound for, young miss, out on the road alone?"

"Béatritz told me of a hospice, a place where they took her in and gave her protection."

"Are you in trouble, then?"

"Oh, no!" Douce said emphatically, fearing she'd given Raoul the wrong idea.

"In that case you are well met," he said. "I shall take you to the hospice with pleasure. You were going in the right direction, but I have rescued you from taking the fork just there, if that's where you were headed."

As they rode side by side, Raoul turned his head so that Douce could hear him. "I am a bit apprehensive, I must admit. I know by heart where the place lies, but I haven't been there for many months. It's in one of the directions that I didn't get to before this last hell broke loose, so there's no telling what we'll find. I'll introduce you to the parfaites who run it, Johana and Marda—God willing they are there still. I can't wait for you, though, as I should have been this past hour at the safe house nearby where Brother Lucian is dying. So mind you watch for landmarks as we go."

They rode in silence for a while. Douce, barely able to contain her relief at Raoul's sudden appearance, took it not only as a sign of good fortune but as spiritual confirmation: she was indeed on the "right road." Thus preoccupied, her memory registered no house or barn, no boulder, or any turning in their path. She saw everything around her merely as black, silver, grey, and white.

Raoul turned to face her again. "May I ask why you seek out the hospice? Forgive me, but you know now who I am and where my sympathies lie. Since I am to take you there and introduce you to my fellow believers, perhaps I may know your errand?"

"I had a dream," she said, then floundered, not knowing how to continue. Raoul nodded encouragement. "There were voices," she went on. Was Raoul only humoring her? She decided he was not. Bravely, she pushed forward. "Something happened to me during the dream. I saw an angel in white who refused to give me wings until she caught sight of horns at the back of my head and then she ran toward me with a crucifix. Oh," she gasped, "it won't make any sense to you! It sounds ridiculous, I know. But when I woke I knew I had found my faith, and I had to get to Béatritz's hospice somehow."

The goodman listened, his head bobbing in time with the horse's footfall. Then he turned and said gravely, "I am awed by what you tell me, for it bears the mark of a true conversion. I shall not dissuade you. But please, for your own sake, think of what you are doing. You heard me say to Béatritz that there is an organized group, the White Brotherhood, who is out for our hides. You have seen how Alphonse's troops are inflamed with Cathar fever. You have already witnessed their violence. Are you sure you want to hand over your future to such a fate, to permanent danger?"

After a moment she said, "Raoul, I do thank you for your words. I *have* given this much thought. I am prepared for what comes with joining this church, even the ultimate sacrifice. My life found a new purpose as soon as I entered Béatritz's house."

"Then, Douce de Ventadour," Raoul cried, secretly pleased by her ardour, "Godspeed!"

A short while later, Raoul pointed a finger ahead to their right.

"There it is. Can you see it through the trees?"

"Yes!" she exclaimed as she glimpsed a little house nestled in the fold of a slope. As they turned into the woods, Douce saw that it was whitewashed and moss-grown, exactly as she had imagined it. From the path the riders dismounted into a swamp. Rank vegetation swallowed their feet up to the ankles. Clearly, no one had ventured to clear the place for months. Raoul's expression clouded as they led the horses forward to the door of the hospice.

Happily, their knock brought forth a murmur of voices, then footsteps. The door was opened at a hesitant crack by two figures, one peering over the other's shoulder.

"It's Goodman Raoul!" one of them shouted. The door flew open and the two women rushed forward as Raoul struggled to quiet his startled horse. The women were opposites in every way, one tall and stately (*like Queen Eleanor*, Douce imagined); the other short, with a wide smile and a body to match.

"I have brought you a believer," Raoul said as he tethered the animals to a stout tree trunk. He turned to Douce. "This is Marda . . ."

The taller of the two, a woman of gentle countenance, held out her hand to Douce, who felt the presence of rings on the slender fingers as she grasped it.

". . . and Johana." The second parfaite took both of Douce's hands in her chunky ones. "Welcome," she said.

Marda braced open the door so the travellers could enter. "By what name are you called?" she asked as Douce stepped over the threshold.

"I am Douce, daughter of Count Ebles of Ventadour."

"You are a long way from home!" Johana exclaimed. "Goodman Raoul, do you sponsor Douce de Ventadour?"

"No—" Douce broke in. "Béatritz de Die—would have—sent me here."

"A great friend. We shall miss her." Marda wore a cotte of some plushy substance trimmed with vair, the dress of a noblewoman. *Not black*, Douce thought, *not at all like a Cathar*. She must have been staring, for Johana read her mind. "With so many of us taken," she said, "a disguise has become necessary to avoid suspicion."

"A likely disguise!" Raoul laughed. "Two well-bred women of a certain age, each dressed in silks and furs, hiding out in a tumbledown cottage. There's nothing the matter with wearing all the velvets of Persia—in hall or chambers. But *here*? There's not one Aragonese lout of a soldier who wouldn't smell something amiss!"

"But it's all I have," Marda declared. "Let them assume what they will."

"And you, Johana, not guilty of much frippery, I see." His eyes crinkled at their corners as he addressed the shorter of the two. Douce noticed that Johana's complexion was almost florid and that her eyes were the exact blue of her silk bliaut. "We make no bow to fashion for plainness," she said. "We cannot afford to."

Raoul laughed.

Marda said, "For the same reason, we leave things in the house . . ." she made a gesture of defeat, ". . . as you see them."

Indeed, the main room in which they stood was disheveled. A table upended, and two halves of a smashed earthenware vessel were lying in a corner. The whole entryway showed signs of having been recently ransacked.

"So, they did come here," Raoul said. "I feared as much, but I could not get to everyone in so short a time."

"Do not blame yourself," Marda said. "In any case, we escaped well before they got wind of us. We went farther up into the hills."

"To Brother Lucian," Raoul said.

"Yes," Marda said.

"I am on my way there now," Raoul said.

Johana explained, "Our thought was that if they come again they'll see we weren't overlooked the first time and, God willing, they'll move on to likelier prospects."

Raoul shook his head. "God willing," he echoed. "Now, dear friends, I leave my charge in your good hands. I am off to Brother Lucian's bedside. I hope I am not too late."

"He was able to respond when we read to him from the Gospel of John," Marda said. "But we fear he cannot have much time left."

"Douce," he said, "Stay in God's grace." Looking her in the eyes, he added, "for Béatritz's sake," and then he was gone.

"Come, Douce de Ventadour," said Marda. "Follow us to our place of worship." She lit a flare that cast shadows around her high cheekbones and arched, aristocratic nose. Her hair was fine and silvery; she wore it coiled like Béatritz's, but it rested at the nape of her neck, like a knot that had slid down the back of her head. Torch held high, she went first, the velvet folds of her cotte rippling as she opened a trap in the floor. Johana put a hand on Douce's shoulder as they both followed Marda down a staircase and through a long stone passageway. Douce realized with a tremor of excitement that they were very far below ground.

They came into a chamber with whitewashed walls and a square stone altar. It was sparsely furnished, just two wooden benches and a rough-hewn table of the kind made for a monk's refectory. Johana fetched a white linen cloth, which Marda spread on the altar. Johana then came forward with two wax tapers and lit them with the flare. Marda motioned Douce to one of the benches and sat down beside her while Johana fixed the flare into a wall socket, then joined them.

"So you wish to become a croyant in the Faith," Marda began. She seemed to take the lead in ceremonial matters, Douce observed, while Johana, younger and more energetic, attended to the practical things.

"Have you fasted?" Marda asked.

"No," Douce said. "I have been ill." And suddenly she felt strange, a kind of awe in their presence that made her almost afraid. They were younger than her own mother, and they had been, in fact, Béatritz's friends. Why, then, should she be feeling this panic?

"What is it, na Douce?" Marda asked, using the diminutive.

Douce realized they had sensed her unease, when even she could not explain it to herself. At that moment, an image of bearded priests in their embroidered vestments, clouds of incense, and intonations of Latin scripture—the Church familiar to her as a child—flashed in her mind. There was no remnant of her former faith in this little room.

"We are all . . . women . . . here." The phrase came from her unbidden.

Marda laughed aloud. "It *is* odd, yes. We keep forgetting. You are very new to our ways, Douce, and unused to seeing women like us . . ."

". . . but, Béatritz . . ." Douce broke in. *And*, she thought, *there was Madame Belot*. ". . . still, it seems strange."

"Béatritz was somewhat different. She was not destined to induct you into the faith as a new member, as a believer. She may have led you here, but it is we who will be asking for your responses according to Cathar ritual. With us, here in this room, you are choosing your life, na Douce. That is what makes this a remarkable journey."

Douce bowed her head. Yes, that was so.

Marda continued, "Béatritz may not have told you that our practice is directed as much by women as by men. As you see by Goodman Raoul's example, perfectii may be male or female. Women are often the preachers among us. Men take care for the sick and dying and do it just as ably as the women. Raoul, as you have heard, is on the way to watch over the deathbed of our brother, Lucian."

The explanation was simple and relieved Douce's feeling of strangeness. She sighed audibly.

"Now," Marda said, "let's begin with your instructions." She settled herself against the back of the bench and made a little gesture to Johana.

Johana smoothed the silk of her bliaut across her lap and folded her hands. "Do not be dismayed by our lack of decorum," she said. "These are unusual times. Normally there would be ten or twelve of of the faithful—all in black, robed and hooded, as you probably know—for the ceremony. Everyone participates first in a reading of the New Testament. Then we join hands and bow three times to the altar. After this the responses begin."

"I do not know the words," Douce said.

"Together we shall lead you through them," Marda said. "Johana, while you robe na Douce I will prepare the reading."

"Come with me," Johana said gently. Douce followed the parfaite into a little vestibule behind the altar, where a score of black wool robes were draped over a bench. She held one up for Douce, making sure it would not be too long, then settled it around Douce's shoulders and picked up two more cloaks before joining Marda once again.

When all three women had donned their black robes and taken their places, Douce between them, on one of the benches, Marda opened the Scriptures to the Gospel of John and read, "I am a king . . . To this end was I born and for this cause came I into the world, that I should bear witness to the truth. Every one that is of the truth hearest my voice." The parfaite's own voice was soft, almost a whisper, so low that even the walls of the room seemed to draw close to listen.

After a beat of silence Marda whispered, "Douce, do not be anxious. You need only to speak from your heart." Marda rose and went to the altar, where she knelt briefly. Then she addressed Douce directly, "Please repeat these words: We are come before God, and before you, and before the rule of the Holy Church to receive service, pardon, and penitence for all our sins that we have made, or said, or thought, or acted from the time of our birth up to now; and we ask for pity of God—and of you that you pray for us to the Holy Father of pity—that He pardon us." Douce's voice echoed hers, phrase by phrase.

Marda then asked, "Do you demand pardon for your sins?"

"I do so demand," Douce replied without hesitation, her words coming from somewhere she did not try to identify.

"If you wish to receive the truth of this church you must keep all the commandments of Christ," Marda continued. "Do you, first, renounce the Catholic creed and all the sacraments of the orthodox church?"

"I do."

"Do you promise not to kill, nor to swear oaths?"

"I do."

"Prepare yourself for initiation," Marda intoned at last.

Douce felt a little flame leap inside her. Without being instructed to do so, she rose.

"You wish to be received into the Church of God, to have your confirmation as a croyant sealed with the holy prayer and the kiss of peace. First listen to the words of Saint John in his Epistle: 'Beloved, do not love the world, nor the things that are in this world. Anyone who loves the world and its desires shall pass away, but he who does the will of God shall endure forever.' "

A sudden thrill shot up Douce's spine. Hadn't she heard these phrases from Béatritz, the night of the goodman's visit? Béatritz seemed serenely happy, despite giving up her courtly life with Raimbaut and her father. Hadn't her contentment been what drew Douce to her? *Yes,* she thought, *I can follow her example.*

"Do you possess this will?" Marda asked.

"I do most certainly." Then gravely she added, "And I pray God for the strength to fulfill it."

"May God bless you. May He snatch your soul from evil and bring you to a good end."

So shall Béatritz live on in me, Douce thought.

Both women stepped forth and stood before her. The Gospels were placed upon her head and the kiss of peace—one kiss on each cheek—was exchanged among the three of them. Simple acts, yet Douce felt transformed. Then she knelt alone before the altar, remaining a long time in prayer while the women waited, each shielding a taper.

At last Douce rose. Marda came forward and took both of Douce's hands in her own. "Na Douce de Ventadour, now you are one of us in the Faith." Johana helped her to remove her robe, then slipped out of her own and held out an arm to receive Marda's before returning them all to the vestibule. The two candles quavered as they silently made their way back through the passage to the trap door.

When they emerged into daylight the sky was overcast.

"It is best to take the old Roman road, the *cami roumieu*," Johana said when Douce told them of her plan to stop at Courthézon. "It's used by pilgrims, so you'll not look in any way suspect."

"Remember, always travel in disguise," Marda added.

"Mind you, wear black only among us, not openly, lest you call attention to the Faith," added Johana.

"I can think of nothing more that you should know," Marda said. Johana nodded in agreement.

"Then it's goodbye," Douce said as they stood in the doorway. "I thank you both from my heart. I shall always remember you."

Leaving the stillness of the hospice, Douce felt changed. Her dreams had led her to a peace she might otherwise have searched for all her life. She almost relished the thought that most people ignored such promptings, or went halfway, then retreated in fear. For her, there had been no choice.

A look at the sky gave warning. It was a menacing mauve, the color of storm. Douce retrieved Guilhelma's mare, mounted and turned back toward Montdragon and beyond. Suddenly, she wanted to gallop, so light did she feel. She had short distance when the rain began, first a cool caress, then chasing her playfully, and pelting her. What a baptism! Her heart pounded faster, faster. She breathed great lungfulls of air, as if she might outrun the supply. Water stung her eyes, slanted past her nostrils, entered her ears.

While the storm pursued her with its needles of rain, a sort of relief broke within her and she started to cry, then sob like a child. The road was running with mud and almost unrecognizable. She fought an overwhelming desire to stop and lie down. She was already so wet that it would make no difference to be vanquished by the tearing wind.

But just as suddenly, the sky split open and she saw a rim of cobalt sky at the edge of the horizon. The storm was lifting, for a slice of light was broadening steadily beneath nature's rising curtain. It would soon be over. Her mind fled home to Gaucelm and Guilhelma, though she felt herself to be no longer their concern. She had begun a new life. A bend in the mud-washed road revealed a stone marker; she saw the way back clearly now.

Chapter 19

DOUCE'S CONFESSION

Anxiety about Douce's whereabouts had only amplified Gaucelm's fury. She could hear him stamping and growling before she even crossed the threshold. Strangely, she felt no guilt, no apprehension, nothing but a deepening glow that not even the torrential rain had been able to quash.

"Fever!" Guilhelma cried the moment Douce closed the door behind her. "Gaucelm, she's got the fever again. Look at those burning cheeks!" She ran to Douce, put a palm on her forehead, and swept back the soggy woolen hood.

On the contrary, Gaucelm thought, Douce seemed radiant. The vixen! She was positively blooming though rainwater streamed from her hair, nose and chin.

"And what mischief have you been up to?" he stormed. "Do I have to remind you, miss, that this is the second time you've pulled a trick like this and upset people who love you? We'll be the ones to catch a fever after being out from sext till nones looking for you. All that loud weather coming down on top of us with thunder enough to crack a man's head and agitate his brains into mush! Where were you, by all that's holy?"

Douce gazed at the puddle forming at her feet and moved closer to the door, next to which two pairs of boots leaned against the wall, draining reproachfully. Guilhelma peeled off Douce's cloak and hung it on a hook, where it steamed slightly in the hearth-warmed air. Douce jigged about, pulling at one soft leather ankle shoe.

"I'm going out to the woodpile," Gaucelm announced. Douce did not answer for him. As he edged by her she felt the angry heat he gave off.

After the door slammed behind him, she looked at Guilhelma. "We're not at Ventadour any longer," Douce said.

Guilhelma turned away, shaking her head.

Absently, Douce tried removing her shoes by treading on one heel with the other foot. It was hopeless: they were soaked. She sank to the floor, yanked them off and pitched them by the door with the others.

Gaucelm elbowed his way back inside. Grunting, he carried three great logs to the hearth, where he stacked them to dry beside a pile of older wood.

"We could do with another log on the fire," Guilhelma instructed him, "until Douce dries out. You'll need to get fresh clothes on you, Douce, right down to the skin."

Douce thought about the clothes she had brought to travel in – a rust-colored bliaut of fine-woven wool and silk with a skirt to match – but decided to save them for Courthézon. Instead, she went to the cupboard where Béatritz stored clothing and bedding. She wanted to wear—to feel—something, whatever it was, that had belonged to Béatritz. A long, faded, red silk shift clung to her touch. In an instant she had it over her head and was dragging off her wet rags beneath its tent.

Gaucelm pulled a stool close by the hearth. "Now, Douce, are you going to tell us what happened?"

It would be easy to lie. They would understand if she said she had visited Béatritz's father at the castle and taken him a handful of bread. It was also her right to say nothing; she was not accountable to Gaucelm and Guilhelma. They were not her guardians. But a glance at the sorry lineup of boots by the door made her bite her lip. She went to the table and sat down. She had taken her usual stool, but she was someone else now. Her vows committed her to the truth, to honesty and purity rolled into one. She owed them an explanation.

"I have become a Cathar," she said quietly.

"What?" Guilhelma cried. Gaucelm said nothing, almost as though he hadn't heard. Both came and sat at the table, on either side of her. Suddenly Gaucelm brought his fist up and hit his forehead with such force that his jaw snapped shut. Then he shook his head from side to side.

"Do you know what you're doing child?" Guilhelma asked after a pause.

Douce said, "It's done."

Guilhelma let out a long sigh. After a moment she looked Douce in the eye. "It is because of Madame Belot?"

"No. It . . . was because of me," replied the girl, "and Béatritz."

Another silence. Gaucelm got to his feet. "Now, let me get this straight. First . . ." he cocked a finger at her, ". . . first you run away from home. Alone, with a page in your father's employ. Leaving all of Ventadour castle—not to speak of your parents—in an almighty uproar. You run away from home because you are in love. And this *after* you had heard of your father's plan to have you marry a suitable young man of your own background. Then . . . ."

". . . a *fool* of my own background," she corrected him hotly, sitting bolt upright.

"Then, your *true love*, having died after you spent weeks in a house alone with him . . ."

". . . *not* alone. Béatritz was here," Douce interrupted. She leaned forward abruptly like someone on trial for her life.

". . . your *true love* having died . . ." Gaucelm resumed.

". . . and Béatritz . . ." Douce said, looking down into her lap.

". . . you suddenly decide to become a heretic, thereby placing yourself *and* those who are with you . . ." He made a dramatic rolling gesture with his arm, which included all of them. ". . . in enormous jeopardy. In danger of our lives, in fact." He paused and looked at her.

Douce hesitated, stammering slightly, the fear of losing control welling up in her, but she continued. "You see, I had this dream during my fever . . ."

"You followed your feverish dreaming and became a Cathar. Now what? You will get us all killed. Don't you know there's a war going on, or wasn't that in the dream?" Gaucelm fumed. "My God! if the world followed every fantasy that appeared in the middle of the night we'd all be in a fine mess!"

"All right, Gaucelm, let her be. Poor dear's been through a lot of heartache." Guilhelma pulled her stool closer and drew Douce's head to her shoulder. Douce felt her face grow hot. She dared not cry. Instead she said, "I love you both. But you know I won't go back to Ventadour. I can't ever go back."

Gaucelm gave a sigh that was almost a groan. "All right, then. Douce, you'll have to explain what this means. Are . . . have you, whatever it is . . . taken vows? Have you joined an *order* of Cathars, or what?"

Douce raised her head. "In a way. But it's not the same as within the Church. It's much simpler. The women—Johana and Marda—knew Béatritz. I went to their hospice in the hills just beyond town. They led me through the responses. We gave each other the kiss of peace. On both cheeks. That was all."

As he listened to Douce, Gaucelm's mind flashed to the desolation of Montdragon. "You must know as well as anybody that those heretics are leading themselves to death like sheep to the slaughter, all because they won't hide and they won't fight."

"They *will* hide."

"A Cathar house?"

"Yes. Our religion has safe houses."

"*Our* religion . . . oh my God," Gaucelm threw down his arms in disgust. "Douce, look. I grew up in the Church, but I've never . . . let's just say I've never taken any pope seriously enough even to object to the way he chooses to rule his world. Turning into a resistance fighter, an objector . . ." His hands rose in an arc of exasperation. ". . . it's not my nature. I admire those who do it, who put their lives on the line for it. For a reasoning adult, it's one thing. But for you, barely grown, having seen nothing of the world to speak of. You are throwing your life away in the pursuit of some ideal you probably know less about than I! It's senseless, girl."

"But I was shown the way in a dream. God . . ."

". . . Douce, whether there is a God or not doesn't concern me."

Gaucelm glanced at Guilhelma and gave her a look of reproof as he saw her cross herself quickly. "We're talking about Douce's decision, woman, not mine. But since you look so alarmed, let me explain. Whoever made me, you—the three of us—must have done so for a purpose. Perhaps because nature is economical. Who knows? Anyhow, in fulfilling that purpose, we worship, don't we? And my verses are *my* kind of worship. It's back pay for the privilege of being alive, you see? When I stop making songs, that's the end for me." Gaucelm was not accustomed to talking about God in any language but expletives.

Guilhelma half-rose in her seat, taking Douce partway with her. "And what about the '*Eretria*?" she almost shouted.

Douce opened her eyes.

"What was *that* about," Guilhelma went on, "if not defiance of Church authorities? It got you kicked out of Raymond's court, for the love of Christ!"

"What was the '*Eretria*?" Douce asked.

"Sheer heresy," Guilhelma sniffed. Gaucelm raised a hand in protest. "Some poems that didn't go down well at one of Raymond's banquets," she corrected. "A banquet attended by Abbot Folquet, if I was correctly informed."

Gaucelm gave her an exasperated look. "The '*Eretria*' is a set of *linked verses*," he said starchly, "in thirty-two rhymed coblas. I didn't get to the tornada."

"When was this?" Douce asked

"At Toulouse," Gaucelm said.

"I would like to hear it sometime."

"You will not. I have forgotten it."

Gaucelm lapsed back into silence. He was working something out, arguing with himself over a point he had always taken for granted, until now. He turned to Guilhelma, "You asked why Christ died for us. His death was a warning about evil. It showed us how we might live. But it doesn't mean that I must either live or die for his reasons, does it? That's for others. I have my work."

At that moment Douce, suddenly emboldened by her discovery of the "*Eretria*," bawled, "You might as well worship stones! You are a perfect pagan. Your god has horns and a belly swollen as a gargoyle's." And then, frightened by her own words, she leaned forward onto the table and sobbed, her head cradled in her arms.

"Come now, come," he leaned over and gently stroked her wet hair. "All I mean is that somehow human beings have managed all this time. Before Christ came, men managed. Very well, too. In some way they were more . . . how shall I say it? . . . complete before religion. They had reverence for everything around them, for the whole living, breathing world. They were as full of worship as any poor devil of a Catholic—"

"Gaucelm!" Guilhelma crossed herself again, vehemently.

". . . who would rather kiss a bishop's hems and beseech jewelled crosses for favors than let the Spirit into his life the hard way! Really, Douce, I'd rather pray to a ram's skull or a pile of rocks than to a God who sends army after army out under the sign of His kind of benevolence."

"But I agree!" Douce sat up excitedly. "Oh, I agree. Don't you see? That's why I took the vows. I agree, Gaucelm, but not for your reasons. It may be difficult to worship what you can't see, but the thing far harder is to give your time to tending the sick and the poor, as Béatritz did."

Douce rose and paced about distractedly before she finally came back to the table. Neither spoke. She knew what they were thinking. It was true. She had put them in danger. But she had had no choice, unless she was to go on sacrificing her future to others. She would not do that for her parents, nor for a Comborn. Why should she do it for Gaucelm and Guilhelma? She gazed at their unforgiving expressions, his still stormy, hers a mixture of resentment and resignation. Really, though, she did still love them. Who else did she have in the world, now that Gui and Béatritz were gone? They were her family.

She spoke softly, "Do you understand now why I want to see Lord Raimbaut?"

Gaucelm nodded and said, "Because of Béatritz. But I still don't understand why it is so important to you, why you have taken it upon yourself to deliver the news of this woman's death."

"You would understand if you had known Béatritz."

Gaucelm turned to Guilhelma, hunching his shoulders in a gesture of resignation. A look passed between them.

"Gaucelm, might we leave for Courthézon tomorrow?" Douce asked suddenly.

He heaved a great sigh; he was tired of quarreling. "The sooner the better," he said. "At first light."

Guilhelma gave Douce one of her "we'll have to make the best of it" looks and said, "yes, the sooner the better."

Douce felt warmth rising in her again, but this time it was gratitude. "Then may I kiss you good night?" she said, and gave them each a kiss of peace.

Douce! thought Gaucelm as he pulled off his smallclothes and ducked into the shirt he wore for bed. *That child.* There wasn't a chance on God's sweet earth that she'd turn out like other women. She was a troublemaker of the worst sort, the kind who gets under your skin with her innocence! There would always be something singular about her, some force that would pull her another way, apart from most people. Alarmed as he was by her newfound Catharism, he had to admit his pride in her. From the beginning he had known that they were alike under the skin, sharing something too deep for words. But her revelations tonight showed him exactly what their affinity was: a heedless streak that had no care for what others thought or believed. Pigheadedness, most folks called it.

He turned to look at the girl. She had cried a bellyful of tears that day, he supposed, and he padded over to her, half-apologetic, humming "**non vei una...en ben amar**," only to remember that it was the song with which he had reclaimed Marie's patronage. "**I shall not leave for love of you**," indeed! Would Douce's mother never cease to haunt him?

Gaucelm awoke feeling remorse, like a bad headache. Who was he, after all, to scold Douce for her new faith, to spoil her ardor? It was like taking someone to task for a dream repeated in confidence. Wearing only the shirt under his cloak, he stumbled out into the dawn to relieve himself by the woodpile. Afterwards, surveying the little desmene behind the house, he saw no more promising perch than the flat stone over the well; accordingly, he sat down on it.

The small birds were already at their song-making, soon followed by the crows. He recalled his own voice from the evening's discussion and winced. He had sounded like one of them, as jabbing and raucous as the merchants of Uzerche. He heard those voices from the past sharply: ". . . he thinks too much of himself to learn the trade . . . you can bet a gold besant there's no profit in rhymed verses!" He ran both hands through his hair and sat impervious to the early morning chill, forcing himself to remember snatches of what he had said to Douce. She was young, she was troubled. She was right, of course. This new religion would probably serve her needs far better than the Church had served his. He got up from the stone slab and brushed off his cloak. It would not be of any use for him to make amends. He could only make verses, as the merchants of Uzerche had predicted.

He forgave himself a little as he shuffled back into the house and climbed into bed again. He lay awake, his mind filled with thoughts about what might come next.

Courthézon. Count Raimbaut was a composer of *trobar clos*. He himself never had much use for esoteric verse. In his experience its creators were mincing little men, overfond of their own words. No troubadour he knew was attached to Courthézon, though Raimbaut, being one himself, would be sure to keep a poet's court. Perhaps there would be employment, perhaps not.

Douce hadn't thought out this business at all, beyond getting word to Raimbaut about Béatritz's noble death at the hands of Cathar-haters. How did Douce know that this Count Raimbaut still cared a fig for Béatritz? Were they allowing themselves to be led into folly because of the girl's fantasies about a love affair?

Romantic nonsense! He sat up in bed and looked across at her sleeping form. He'd speak to her the moment she woke up. And yet, he mused, sinking down under the bedclothes once more, he had no better plan. The life of a troubadour was a life on the road. It was his destiny, just as it seemed to be his fate to have womenfolk trailing after him wherever he went.

Ah, but Douce—that was different. Her break with the Church gave him a peculiar satisfaction in spite of all he had said last evening. He fell to thinking about the dogmas that bound his childhood and contrived to protect him from all matters having to do with sex. He saw his mother once more. She had turned away when he asked her *why* the Virgin felt nothing when the Word passed in and out. He would learn the answer in church, she had replied. But he had found out the answer in life—in the Chantier quarter of Toulouse, to be exact—and now as he lay abed he suppressed a laugh. It was Guilhelma who enlightened him. You would have to be the Virgin Mary herself to feel nothing; ordinary mortals were far luckier, he mused. "In church" indeed! He had never learned a thing worth knowing in church.

Would the girl's new vows forever stand in the way of her discovering the miracle of her own body? Sadly, he thought, as he drifted back to sleep, they would.

Chapter 20

THE ROAD TO COURTHÉZON

aucelm sang in the voice he used when composing aloud.
Cant e desport, jois, dompneis e sollaz
Enseniamen, largessa e cortesia,

He boomed the end notes of the first stanza in time with his horse's hoofs: "*Honor e pretz...*" On the third line, his voice trailed off.

"*Esperatz,*" suggested Guilhelma, riding alongside. "Something ending in '*atz*' to rhyme with '*sollaz*'".

"*...e lial drudaria, An si baisat enjanz.*" Gaucelm began again.

"*e mal vestatz,*" Guilhelma added encouragingly.

Gaucelm ignored her. "*C'ab pauc d'ira,*" he fumbled.

"*Non sui desesperatz!*" Guilhelma finished triumphantly. "I told you, '*enjanz*' is no good. It breaks the line."

"Who's composing this song, for the love of St. Stephen!"

"I'm sorry, '*enjanz*' breaks the line."

"Well, your '*desesperatz*' is too easy a rhyme."

"Rudel used it."

"All too often. Who asked you, anyway? Wenches are supposed to wear their learning lightly!"

Guilhelma gave him a fixed smile, her eyebrows raised. She no longer rose to his bait when she knew he wasn't serious.

Douce, riding far behind, was oblivious to their banter. Her mind was on Mornas, around which their route lay. She could not see the town from the byroad, but Goodman Raoul's words, on the night of his visit to Béatritz's house, raised a chill along the back of her neck that she could feel even now. "A great stake will be lit at Mornas," he had warned. That was before Alphonse's men had circled back on Montdragon, and taken Béatritz away. When Douce learned that the *cami roumieu* went straight through Mornas she had persuaded Gaucelm to lead them by another road. The thought of that pillaged place filled her with horror.

"Douce!" Gaucelm called. "When we're at Courthézon Guilhelma will teach you composition. Perhaps she'll even let me instruct you on the lute!"

No answer.

"Guilhelma," he directed, "loosen those reins or that mare of yours will snap them in two." And as she opened her mouth to protest, he added, "Now shush, before the tune's gone clean out of my head. **Songs and diversions, gallantry and joy...**"

Guilhelma reined her horse to a standstill. "Gaucelm," she said, "that sounds *awful.*"

"I know," he replied, "but so what?"

Underneath, he felt an expansive mood coming on. No. *More than that,* he thought, *a mood in which I can accept almost anything, even forgive Douce for her heresy.* And perhaps being on the open road once more blotted out the frustrations he had harbored at Ventadour since Christmastime, followed by the crisis at Montdragon. Now, once again the wide world was open to him! His spirits surged. Perhaps also (and here he acknowledged a faint prick of satisfaction) it was merely being at the head of this little entourage as it made its way deeper into the promised land of Provence. Or quite possibly because he now had his yellow-haired princess in tow, she whom they had rescued from illness and sorrow, though not from her risky beliefs.

"**And soon the month of March will come**..." He sang in the northern tongue out of sheer bravura "...***vei reverdir les jardis et oi les oizelets chanter***—"

"Let's stop and eat something," Guilhelma interrupted, trotting up alongside him.

"An inspired idea. Douce!" Gaucelm shouted. "Are you hungry?" He waited for her to catch up.

Guilhelma, meanwhile, had dismounted. With the reins looped over one arm she walked toward a stout tree and spread her cloak on the ground beneath its branches.

Gaucelm scanned Douce's face as she approached. Her enthusiasm that morning betrayed no resentment of his sharp words the night before. Now she reined in her mare and surveyed the spot Guilhelma had chosen. She was clear-eyed and serene as an angel, Gaucelm thought. Oddly enough, though she seemed untroubled, he was plagued by his harshness on the subject of Cathars. Damnation! She certainly had her own way of infuriating him.

He jumped off the destrier and took Douce's reins, leading both horses to Guilhelma's tree. She was breaking a loaf of bread from her saddlebag into thirds. Douce joined her while Gaucelm busied himself with the horses, sliding their bridles down around their necks like halters so that they might graze with their mouths free of the bit. He then tied them to separate trees, loosened their girths, and came to be with the others. Settling into a groove where two rocks met the great trunk, he reached for his share and munched slowly.

"What's that village?" Guilhelma asked, pointing south across a valley strung with vineyards like warp on a loom. "Douce, do you know?"

"Camaret, perhaps," she replied vaguely. "I've never been there. Béatritz used to say that you get a good wine from those grapes. It's called Gigondas, for the little hills they grown on."

"How nice the names are," said Guilhelma. "Camaret, Courthézon, Montdragon, Sérignan. But Gigondas doesn't rhyme with anything."

"Wine is its own rhyme," Gaucelm remarked.

After they had eaten and refreshed themselves with watered wine, yawned, and stretched, Gaucelm said, "Time to pack up and get this caravan back on the road if we expect to be in Courthézon before nightfall. We've lingered long enough!"

In the saddle he sank back into the destrier's hypnotic trot, a gait so powerful that it left the mares well behind after a hundred strides. Riding always lulled him into another zone of time and space that nurtured the forming of rhymes. The brisk clip-clop, clip-clop of the horse's hooves created a beat he set to music in his mind.

"*Cant e desport,*" he sang softly, taking up where he had left off before lunch.

But as he rode, other sounds drifted in. At first they were random, loud, disturbing. They bore no pattern and would not shape themselves into anything recognizable. Instead of dropping obediently into stanzas as all his verses did, these shards of sound seemed like a frenzied nightmare—the kind of dream that splintered once awake.

In their place loomed shadowy images, the dark figures of soldiers, the sight of smoke rising from campfires, a cloudy skyline pricked by peaked tents. Then, between the destrier's footfalls, he heard the rattle of bits and the rustle of chain mail, the pawing and snorting of horses. He smelled the stench of wine-piss and sweat.

The vividness of the vision startled him, for he had no experience of war. He took a deep breath and let the reins lengthen in his hands. A tune was coming.

The signs were unmistakable now. A single word had lodged in his throat: death. The lament he had composed when Richard Coeur-de-Lion had been killed three years ago surged forth to preoccupy him.

"**Death! that frightening word, terrible to utter**...*estrangz motz, quan salvage a suzir! Ben a dur cor totz hom qu'o pot suffrir!* **Who can hear it without trembling**..." Once he had cleared the imprint of those verses from his brain (but not before savoring their majesty), the coast was clear. What was coming would be another kind of planh, this time for Douce.

Usually he worked on the words first, giving them an instrumental line that lent itself to viol or lute, whichever seemed appropriate, according to the mood of the court or his own fancy. This time, however, he heard something entirely different and solitary, a tambour rising and falling in a menacing rhythm like a snake chattering in the grass: sh-*sha*, sh-*sha*, SHA. Then a steady funereal rap on the belly of the instrument: DUM, da-da, DUM da-da, and quickly the voiced refrain sprang out whole: "**I mourn this war with heart and voice/With heart and voice I mourn this war!**" Only when he had established the musical beat, the terrible drumroll of grief and despair, could he begin to tell the story in words. And then the old, familiar excitement shot through him like lightning and made his head spin. He wanted to dismount and sit on the roadbank until he could get down the whole stanza with its beats and rhymes, whether it ended up first or last or in the middle of what he now knew would be a dirge on the stupidity of war.

"**He who thinks he fights for God, instead abandons all**...*il laissa tot en lansa l'arm' e lo cors, l'aur e l'argen*! **He loses soul and body, his gold and silver as well!**" The words came fast, too fast for him. Damn. It was always this way. He'd be attending to something, anywhere but in his practice room, and the song would arrive unbidden, just like that! He'd have no instrument at hand, no way to mark the phrases. He'd be caught having to memorize the thing, counting the end-rhymes on his fingers like a schoolchild silently reciting sums. But this was even worse—far worse—for phrases were coming in fragments, and the fragments belonged in different stanzas. It was impossible; he would have to get down from this beast so he could concentrate.

A vagrant tree root caught his horse's hoof and almost catapulted Gaucelm over the animal's neck. Righting himself, he glanced behind him to see if the women had noticed, but they were bumping along atop their taciturn mares, heads nodding, oblivious. It had been a narrow escape. Had he continued to compose in that frantic way the planh would have vanished into thin air. Now he settled down to doing it properly, taking his time.

First stanza: **"Those trumpets which had once announced the ancient claims of Aragon are shamed to silence. His hectares cost Alphonse dear in dead and wounded; yet Toulouse lost more: the lives of so-called heretics shall haunt both sides until another set of trumpets sounds—on Judgment Day."**

Second stanza: **"a youth just knighted only to be killed."**

Third: **"sweet Douce robbed of her future."**

Fourth: **"the end of the good Countess of Die."**

Finally: **"all this for what? a smoking pile of bones.** *Il laissa tot en lansa l'arm' e lo cors...***"**

Yes, that was it, much better.

They came within sight of the ramparts of Courthézon well before dusk. The town stood high above the plain, the castle rising four-square at its summit within its own enceinte of warm buff stone. Below, near the main city gates, the top of the church was just visible. Then it all vanished as their road dipped downward. The party of three plodded on across the rain-swollen countryside, each lost in thought.

Guilhelma sat astride her horse, her heels rhythmically ticking its flanks. A picture of what awaited them at Courthézon castle was taking shape in her mind. She saw walls covered in rich tapestries, corridors bustling with company, a great hall alive with nobility wearing brocaded tunics and silk hose from Byzantium. The kitchen would be bursting with confections unknown in the North. Outside would be ladies' gardens with rose borders and a plot below the kitchen laid out in herbs and medicinal plants. She realized that she had let go of Ventadour completely. By what subtle process had she relinquished all thought of returning there? She was not sure, but now that she was here with Douce under her care, she was glad. Who could know what prospects Courthézon might hold for her?

Gaucelm, meanwhile, had finished sketching out the planh and now felt free to think about Raimbaut d'Orange. He searched his memory. He'd heard somewhere that Raimbaut fancied himself a lord high protector of poets; at that idea his heart beat faster. Not since his triumph at Toulouse had he hungered so for a truly cultivated audience, and he let his imagination billow. He saw a court swarming with prodigies of talent: jesters, jugglers, songsters, merrymen, and stern knights, tricksters, troubadours, himself.

From everything he'd heard, Courthézon had a special and sometimes tragic appeal for troubadours. The ill-fated Cabestanh had resided there—Guilhem de Cabestanh, he of the "cooked heart." Poor man, handsome devil of a troubadour that he was, had fallen in love with the enemy, a woman of the Baux family. The lovely Berengère des Baux snagged Cabestanh with a love potion and their passion was evident to all. Her jealous husband killed the troubadour, tore out his heart and had it served to his wife in a stew. Only when she had eaten it did this *jaloux* inform her that she had just consumed the heart of her lover. And then she threw herself over a cliff. That would have been in the time of the third Count Raimbaut.

Now, *there* was a maker of verses! Unlike the other Provençal amateurs, he was the genuine article, born with an understanding of composition in his bones. Some considered him a poet for connoisseurs, a mere virtuoso. As an originator of the *trobar clos* perhaps he *had* pushed artifice too far. Wasn't it he who'd said that the best poems can't be understood at first hearing? All this business about the concealment of the lady's name, weaving it like a silken knot into elaborate verse.

Well, that's not my style, thought Gaucelm. *But there's something to be said for it: once you know the rules you are free to go beyond them. If Raimbaut hadn't experimented, we wouldn't have songs like "When the whole world seems turned upside down...."* And in a low voice he began to sing, "**Ai resplan la flors enversa...**"

But he was too worried about Douce to continue. For her to appear at court as Douce de Ventadour was out of the question. By now, search parties would be flinging their nets in ever-widening circles. She would have to change her name and hide, as best she could, any evidence of her new faith. One slip and she'd be a target for questioning. What disguise could she assume? Lady's companion? Linen maid? He was about to bring up the matter when he heard Douce cry, "Look!"

Before them were the Dents de Montmirail, the famous cliffs that stood straight up out of the plain, exactly like the teeth of a fierce, large animal, though their peaks had been worn by the wind into flattened hooks. Below this dramatic curtain of rock lay an expanse of flatland covered with vineyards; above it the sky swirled with clouds.

The road rose sharply and Courthézon reappeared just before them. Douce, riding last, caught the best view of its profile, silvered in the remaining daylight. *This is the town Béatritz knew so well*, Douce thought. *She never said how big it was. It's nearly a city.* The waning sun performed its alchemy, turning dull stone to precious metal in its dwindling rays, and before they even reached the main gates, Douce knew she would call this place home.

Together, they entered the outer square heralded by an allée of plane trees and passed through the gates with their wood-latticed portcullis. From then on, the way was uphill; even the marketplace was set on a slant. They rode past shops nestled below the church, noticing the sharply angled construction that fit the street's steep rise.

The houses too were angled shoulder to shoulder, one leaning into the next, all built from the same tawny stone. Many were set with sturdy beams over the doorway. How different they looked from the slack-walled piles in the village below Ventadour castle!

Nearing the top of the winding street, Douce noticed roofs spread out puzzle-fashion; here they were piled with "galets," the smooth, rounded slabs of rock brought from the riverbed below to hold down the roof shingles in a high wind.

Aroused by this new chapter in her life, Douce admired the outside stairs, the nooks and little porches, the frail ironwork balconies, the odd windows and stonepiled crannies, the arches and wings and jumble of walls that gave Courthézon the look of a toy village. It was a town for make-believe tourneys and festivals, for games of hide-and-seek in doorways, for leaping the steep stone steps set into the upper reaches of the streets.

The bells of the main church pealed nones as they came to the top of the incline and stopped for a moment to look around. Below them, down the other side of the slope, was the poor section of town with its back lanes sinking toward fields beyond the double city walls. Ahead rose the castle, a straight and dignified bastion, its battlements cutting sharply against the sky. The buff and black banner of the Principality of Orange flew from its central tower.

"Turn round and look down," Gaucelm instructed. They could see the belltower of the big church and the marketplace tipped like a slanted board, all in dizzying perspective. From here, reflected in the setting sun, the rooftops presented a mosaic of brilliants so perfectly fitted together that they could have been the work of some fabulous artisan working in precious jewels instead of slate.

Gaucelm shifted his seat, reached around and pulled a handkerchief from the saddle pouch behind his leg. He wiped his face and neck, removed his cap and ran his fingers through his hair. He passed the handkerchief to Guilhelma. Douce stretched and drank a sip of the watered wine from her flask.

"Ready?" asked Gaucelm. They nodded vigorously. "Then forward!" he gestured in a mock charge.

Once under the barbican their horses' hooves thudded over the wooden boards of the moat-bridge. On the other side, Gaucelm reined in his horse and dismounted, leading the animal toward Douce. He grasped her skirt and whispered up at her.

"And who do you choose to *be*, my girl? You can't enter here as Douce de Ventadour, unless you want to get sent directly home."

"Gaucelm, do try and remember to say *donzella*. I am not your *girl*," she declared firmly.

"Sorry," he apologized. "I mean what name do you want to be called here at Courthézon?"

She thought for a moment. "May I keep Douce? I'll be Douce from the town of Die near Montélimar," she said, pleased with the choice of Béatritz's birthplace for her new surname.

"Good. But what..."

"Does the count have children?" Guilhelma asked as she came alongside. Gaucelm shrugged. "Why not linen maid?" she ventured.

Gaucelm looked at Douce who nodded her assent. "Let's hope they need one," he grunted as he hoisted himself into the saddle. "And Douce?" He swivelled around to catch her eye. "Do not, in the name of God and all his saints, reveal your *faith* to any living soul. And do *not* say anything to Raimbaut about Béatritz's death until we know the man and we are able to get him alone with us."

"Travelers from Montdragon, my lord."
Count Raimbaut d'Orange inclined his torso slightly and brought it back into position again without changing the preoccupied expression in his eyes. His lips smiled, though, as he said, "A pleasure. A pleasure," without seeming to notice whether the trio standing before him was animal or mineral.

Gaucelm stepped forward and whispered something in the ear of the page who had just announced them.

"Gaucelm Faidit!" Upon hearing the name Raimbaut's manner instantly changed to open delight. "What great good fortune brings you to Courthézon? Had I been warned of your arrival I'd have greeted you more civilly." He bowed again before the ladies. "So you have survived Montdragon. Let us hope it takes no more than that victory—and Mornas—to teach Raymond his lesson."

Not a word of what he said registered on Douce. Here was Béatritz's lover, and she stared at him.

"You may go, Yves." Raimbaut dismissed the page and turned to Gaucelm. "I am impatient to hear what you are composing now. I know of the partimen you devised with Richard Coeur de Lion, and your planh on his death is a great work, unique. What have you been up to since then?"

Apparently news of the "*Eretria*" had not reached as far as Provence. *Good*, thought Gaucelm.

"The usual," he replied, uncomfortably aware that there had been no "great work" since the planh Raimbaut mentioned. "A song here and there."

Gaucelm glanced at Guilhelma who stood awkwardly, whereas Douce, confound her, seemed unable to take her eyes away from their host. Gaucelm felt suddenly chilled and weary. He saw that Raimbaut was dressed for warmth in a short velvet cotte which, he guessed, had once been deep blue, but was now a mousey hue from age and exposure to sunlight. Taking note of a pair of magnificent tapestries flanking the dais, Gaucelm decided that this shabbiness of dress was due more to lack of attention than to lack of funds. Not even a wife, he thought, would make much difference. The man was congenitally unmindful of appearance. His face was curious—long, swarthy, with a mobile, fleshy mouth. There was an edge of unease about him, a certain anxiety to please. His grey eyes, fixed at a distance as they mostly seemed to be, announced that he was scornful of small talk.

Count Raimbaut got to the point without delay: first, dinner. "You must promise to report in detail on events in Montdragon. We dine immediately after vespers." Later, he would be pleased to hear more about Gaucelm's travels; for now, he wished to make clear that the esteemed troubadour and his family (as he supposed them to be) were warmly welcome and free to stay as long as they liked.

Douce sensed the Count's eyes upon her and dropped her gaze. She felt little embarrassment in examining him so closely, only the satisfaction of knowing at last just what it was about the man that had endeared him to Béatritz. It was his concentration, his entire devotion to the person or the matter before him—his intensity. She was sure of this. His bearing did not announce itself in any striking manner. Nor was it his dress, which, she saw to her amusement, was rather motheaten. When this man loved a woman, she thought, he was capable of overpowering her.

Raimbaut again addressed Gaucelm. "You may have caught wind of the fact that I, too, am a poet, and one sorely in need of another to converse with. You see," he smoothed the velvet of his cotte, "Miraval took it into his head to embark for Outremer before the winter made passage a hardship. What with this bothersome business in Montdragon and Mornas added to the usual petty concerns of politics, one needs more than ever the solace of poetry, don't you know? Your arrival, Gaucelm, is the answer to a prayer." Raimbaut looked down briefly, then focused hard on Gaucelm. "You are a treasure to be coveted by any court. What brings you here to Courthézon?"

The question was abrupt, but Gaucelm surprised himself. Without missing a beat, he took Guilhelma's arm. "Allow me to present my *jonglaresa*, Guilhelma Monja. We have—all three of us," he gestured to include Douce, "been through our share of the horrors of Montdragon. We left as soon as we buried a dear friend and soldier. When we heard that Mornas was aflame, we skirted it and rode east."

Raimbaut inclined his head in acknowledgment of their difficulties.

"As we are not political refugees," Gaucelm continued, with a wink to which Raimbaut did not respond, "I think we may be of some use to you. Guilhelma is an experienced ladies' companion. And Douce de Die has been a handmaiden in noble chambers and is accustomed to looking after the linen needs of a large household."

"Ah!" said Raimbaut. "Then we are fortunate indeed. My sister Tiburge has need of a lady-in-waiting, if it pleases you . . ." he bowed slightly in Guilhelma's direction, ". . . and Douce must meet the Mistress of the Garderobe at once. But first my steward Bonel will take you to your quarters."

As Raimbaut ushered them forth, Gaucelm asked him, "Did by chance the troubadour Peire Vidal turn up, some time ago, on his way to Marseille?"

"It would have been cause for celebration had he stayed here. But no, I have never met the man. He is known to be peculiar."

Gaucelm only smiled.

Bonel met them at the doorway and led them from the hall. The man's livery was so tattered that the slits of his cotte, far from being positioned to display the contrast of rich stuffs beneath, were created by wear and revealed only the stains on his undergarments. He guessed that Bonel was Raimbaut's old bodyservant elevated to the rank of steward. His appearance was not a promising indicator of the count's financial status. On the other hand, Gaucelm reassured himself, some of the southern nobility were at pains not to display what they had.

Bonel, with the little file of travelers in tow, explained that because the castle was pressed for space—one wing was closed off—Douce would sleep with the house servants. Gaucelm and Guilhelma, it seemed, merited an alcove to themselves. Bonel ushered them into a large common room, then continued with Douce down the long corridor.

After they were alone Gaucelm pointed to a bed well furnished with pillows and a goosedown quilt covered in damask. Raimbaut was no pauper! Extravagantly, he threw his arms wide for Guilhelma's embrace. "See what my fame has brought us!" he exulted, only half in jest. Though neither dared, so soon, to say it aloud, each was thinking, *Why go further than this? Why continue on to Marseille when one is accorded such a welcome here?*

The moment they stepped into the hall for the evening meal, Gaucelm knew which one was Tiburge, Raimbaut's older sister. She stood chatting with him near the head of the long table, wearing a gown of iridescent stuff whose folds changed from gold to green whenever she moved even slightly. Hammered silk, was it? It could not be domestic. He marvelled at the glow of it beneath the torches, and nudged Guilhelma to make sure that she too had identified Tiburge.

To any observer it was clear that this woman was Raimbaut's other half. Like his, her beauty was natural, a matter of familial good fortune. The bones of her face ended in a chin modelled firmly, like the base of an apple. Her fingers were impossibly long, delicately articulated. He thought of master craftsmen with precise tools: makers of musical instruments, chapel stonecarvers. Only someone wise in the secret laws of proportion could have created a being such as this! It was after he and Guilhelma had been introduced to her by Raimbaut and were seated that it came to Gaucelm: She was the very essence of the "*dame lointaine*" of Rudel's songs; she was "*la belle dame sans merci.*"

At table they talked of poetry. Guilhelma had been placed on Raimbaut's left. Though her eyes were wide with the wonder of her own presence at such a gathering, her air of preoccupation told Gaucelm that she was worried about Douce. He reminded himself that Douce would be eating at the servants' table, while here was Guilhelma among the nobility. The irony of this reversal made him smile. She, however—if he read her expression accurately—seemed bewildered by it.

As guest of honor Gaucelm sat to his host's right. He spoke with admiration of the verses of Raimbaut's ancestor.

"He was still alive when I was a little boy," Raimbaut said. "But I am not so enamored of the *trobar clos* as I used to be. It's a form not much in harmony with these times. While he ruled this principality there were no grave political rifts as there are now. None of this business of Aragon and Toulouse both out for our lands. His only worry concerned the Counts of Baux, but by now that's almost a tradition. After all, when it comes to property disputes, being an enemy of your neighbor's friend, as the ancient saying goes, is the rule. Or used to be. Nowadays, it's your neighbor who's the enemy. The world shrinks, does it not, Guilhelma Monja!" he observed, including her politely. "In any case it was far easier to compose arcane verses for a special few in those days. Poetry was a club for the elite. No more."

Bonel appeared at the arched entrance of the hall. At a nod from Raimbaut he ushered in a procession of food bearers who knelt in turn before the dais. Their lord, turning back to Gaucelm, took no notice of them. "I myself compose *sirventes* because politics and war are on my mind," he continued. "Alphonse's victory at Montdragon, for instance: I've been diddling with a song on it." His face clouded and he was silent for a moment. "Many died, of course; many who should not have. That is always sad."

I wonder whether he's remembering the woman Béatritz, Gaucelm thought. Raimbaut's countenance cleared. "I trust your sympathies are not with Toulouse?"

Thank God Douce isn't hearing this, Gaucelm said to himself. Raymond's all-seeing eyes flashed into memory as Gaucelm composed a diplomatic reply: "I have no personal interest in the matter. My sympathies are for a free Provence insofar as it's possible. For that's the only way our remarkable culture will survive."

"Quite so," Raimbaut replied. "Though sometimes I feel that we are on the brink of being eaten alive with the Cathars as bait. It's unfair beyond words that they should be singled out, yet what can we do? The shame of it is that they include some of our noblest families."

A carver appeared, knelt briefly before Raimbaut, then went to the board and, with his knife, cut slivers from each loaf of bread and joint of meat, tasting as he went. It registered on Gaucelm that this curious figure with a long towel draped around his neck resembled a priest in stole and girdle. But, then, everything about this court was different from those he knew further north: the whitewashed walls, the richly painted cloth that hung where a fireplace would have stood if this had been Ventadour instead of Provence.

". . . another sign of the times," Raimbaut was commenting as he gestured toward the carver. "A sad precaution, taking sayes, but a wise one, my steward tells me." It dawned on Gaucelm: poison. Even here one was wary.

Raimbaut began to converse with Guilhelma at his left hand, and Gaucelm saw that he possessed not that studied simplicity which, in one such as Raymond, approached artifice. He had the naturalness of a young man whose attention was elsewhere than on matters of social propriety and dress. The fellow was certainly charming. Could one take what he said at face value? If so, what did he mean by "our noblest families"? Was that not a phrase of inclusive sympathy for the Cathars, and, particularly Béatritz? Instinctively, he thought of Douce. He sighed, resolving to put a check on his own tongue and bide his time. He would be careful not to mention Béatritz's name nor anything at all having to do with Montdragon until he could have a private conference with Raimbaut. Then he might parlay Douce's intentions himself.

Douce, eating with servants for the first time in her life, was on her best behavior. Despite an avid curiosity about Raimbaut and his household, she skirted subjects that might alert her listeners. Politely, she inquired about local events, comings, and goings at the castle. When she was told that a page had passed by only just over a fortnight ago, a boy with straw-colored hair that stood straight up on his head and who spoke a foreign tongue, she nearly spilled her wine. All anyone could understand of what he said was "Ventadour." He was called Pieter, they said, and was heading for St. Gilles, where he would go on pilgrimage to Compostella, then sail for his homeland, far north. This news took hold of Douce with a force that made her shudder. Thank the Lord that he wasn't returning to Ventadour. He had told her the truth about wanting to go back to the lowlands. But it was a close call, hearing this in what she had thought would be a place of refuge. She made no attempt to finish the meal before her with her stomach so in knots. The joint sat in its pool of gravy untouched. She tried to nibble on bread, her head downcast to hide the flush she felt rising to her face.

"Are you a Jew?" a tiny girl asked. She was so thin that the ends of the towel tied about her waist nearly reached the hem of her skirt. She said she was a linen maid and Dorie was her name. "Why do you not eat the meat? Or is the food better where you come from?" Her sister Lucia, equally thin and not less persistent, chimed in, "Where *are* you from, anyway?"

"Near Montélimar" was all Douce could muster, all she dared reply. What she felt was new to her: the flat-out, dark dread of being discovered. What would Béatritz have done? Nauseous and dizzy, Douce looked down at her unfinished meal, closed her eyes, and prayed.

It was partly panic that impelled Douce to seek out Count Raimbaut right away. She had not counted on this sense of unease the day she took vows. The serene countenances of Marta and Johana seemed to preclude the fear she now felt as an undercurrent of every move she made. What if she were caught tomorrow? What if Pieter, discouraged by the hardships of his journey, looped back to seek refuge at Courthézon? What if a messenger from Ventadour arrived in the very next minute? Best to unburden herself to Raimbaut immediately.

It was never hard to find him, Douce learned. He was nearly always in his study. There was no use inventing a pretext; she simply asked Bonel to take her to him the next morning. The study was a small room just off the third landing, about the size of her father's at Ventadour, and equally bare of furnishings: whitewashed walls, fireplace, a standing desk with intricately carved legs, a velvet-covered chaise, an extra armchair—and books piled on the floor in neat, intentional stacks. There were no tapestries and chests as in her mother's solar. Two square windows let in a ration of fierce southern light.

The count greeted her with a nod, but did not immediately move from his desk, where he stood absorbed in a manuscript. Kept waiting thus, she reflected that she ought to be feeling like the servant she had now officially become, but despite his air of abstraction, his demeanor was so kindly that she could not feel ill-used. Besides, seeing that he was wearing the same dilapidated cotte as the night before somehow put her at ease. Finally he came forth with a little bow and gestured her toward the more comfortable seat.

"I have come about Béatritz de Die," she said directly.

He looked at her sharply, his whole body suddenly alert.

"What about her?" he asked, dropping any pretense of ceremony in his speech.

"She is dead. She was rounded up and taken away with the rest of them, with the—heretics—at Montdragon."

He made no reply, but his face seemed to crumble before her eyes. From what Béatritz had said of the man and his political loyalties, Douce expected him to be upset. She did not expect to be witness to a grief that shook his shoulders and made him shield his face until he was forced to get up and hide himself from her. Full of consternation, she sat absolutely still on the velvet-covered seat. There she remained, her hands folded and her gaze lowered, until he recovered himself enough to come out from the anteroom where he had given way to his feelings. There was a hush as he walked across the study and seated himself opposite Douce once more. He cleared his throat.

"You knew that she was a Cathar, then," he said.

"It was what gave her the strength to endure."

"Did she tell you why I had to go to Alphonse's aid?"

"She mentioned a will, a division of property, the Hospitallers."

He did not reply.

"You were kind to keep the baron from harm," Douce added.

Then, seeing that the count was still too moved to speak, she felt it was time to take her leave from him. "Do not trouble yourself," she said, getting up. But he rose and came with her to the entryway.

And then Count Raimbaut did an extraordinary thing. He held out both his hands to Douce and she met them with her own. He bowed his head over their joint handclasp, and said, "I don't know who you really are, but you must be someone very special if you were close to my Béatritz." With this, he kissed her hands and let her go.

IV
COURTHÉZON

1209

Chapter 21

JALOSIA

In Languedoc a storm was brewing. Drought as well as unrest plagued the lands around Toulouse and extended down into Foix, coming as close to the Provençal border as Carcassone and Béziers. In the summer of Gaucelm's arrival in Courthézon, farmers remarked how still the countryside seemed, as though waiting for thunder and lightning to roll in from beyond the mountains and break suddenly out of the sky. The wheat burned to a ghastly brown in the unrelenting heat; cattle died of thirst standing in dried crusts of their own dung; no rain came.

There were few bargains struck at the September fairs that year. Some stalls were empty of goods entirely; some displayed a few skimpy bolts of muslin, a scattering of withered oranges, and winter-stored apples; the pasties were filled with hard cheese instead of meat. Only the wineshops enjoyed a booming trade; men gathered in their cool, dark interiors to drink and discuss the bad season.

Fights began, simmered, and were quelled, but everywhere men set themselves against one another with a strange brooding anger—farmer against farmer, plowman against bailiff, sheriff against reeve.

Near Fanjeaux, a Castillian cleric called Domminic was stirring passions against those who strayed from the true Church. Around Famiers and Gaillac the country people were restive, divided against themselves by parish priests and outlaw preachers proclaiming the new faith. Raids against Cathar families in hilly regions of the Aude and in the Albigeois country made familiar the sight of houses reduced to rubble around a makeshift pyre and its few charred bones.

But the first decade of the new millennium was to bring changes more momentous than a failed harvest and the random pursuit of heretics.

By the end of 1202 the name Folquet of Marseille was known to every court in the South. He and a handful of pious followers had formed the White Brotherhood, and together they raised their voices against the new religion in as many influential pulpits as they could command. At Albi and Toulouse, Folquet publicly proclaimed his intention to purge Raymond's kingdom of those he branded as "infidels worse than Saracens, blasphemers of the Holy See, scourges of civilization." And before three years passed, this merchant's son from Marseille, this failed troubadour and reformed womanizer was made—against all rational odds—Bishop of Toulouse. Thus elevated, he stood on the same exalted ground as his old nemesis and former host Raymond, Light of the World. It promised to be a fight to the death.

In no time, the new bishop had the ear of the Pope. By the beginning of the year 1208, Folquet was ready to bring Raymond to his knees.

First, Pope Innocent III admonished the Count of Toulouse for his failure to suppress the Cathars; then he threatened anathema. Finally, at Folquet's urging, he sent a legation led by Pierre de Castelnau, a Cistercian, one of Bishop Folquet's men. With the flexibility that was the hallmark of his politics, Raymond thought it was the better part of wisdom to pay lip-service to the authorities rather than risk excommunication. For this dreaded writ, far from signalling mere personal spiritual disgrace, dissolved the ties of vassal to lord and could even, by extrapolation, exclude a whole population from religious practice. To Raymond, the consequences of such defiance were unthinkable. Accordingly, he swallowed his pride and on the appointed day in January he swore a solemn allegiance to Castelnau as papal deputy.

The next morning, as the legation set out for Rome, its mission accomplished, Pierre de Castelnau was fording an icy stream with his retinue when he was mortally stabbed with a hunting spear. This single act by some unknown assassin struck terror across the winter countryside. Raymond was excommunicated. Spark had met tinder at last: Pope Innocent proclaimed an all-out crusade against the Cathars, calling on his strongest ally, Bishop Folquet, and on Christian princes everywhere to banish the heretics by force.

This summons to arms brought forth the ruthless northern baron Simon de Montfort, who lost no time in mobilizing his troops. A full scale war against the heretics was about to burst into flames.

By this time Guilhelma was vastly pregnant. Every morning, almost before opening her eyes, she pressed another fingertip against her palm. If her calculations were correct, only the fingers of one hand remained to be counted until her delivery. Over the years she had begun to accept barrenness as her lot, a punishment from on high for the old days in the Chantier quarter, when she'd had to thwart an accidental birth with every possible means. She had eaten macerated wild carrot seeds and steeped countless decoctions of ginger root scented with mentha. She had drunk many a bitter dram of pennyroyal oil. While she had wisely avoided the dangers of hazelwort, she always went back to cloths soaked in vinegar. They were the best protection. She had no delusions about children in those days, not in the Chantier. Then Gaucelm took her away, gave her a different life. After all this time, *En Dieus* had smiled on her. She vowed never to let Gaucelm make fun of His Church again.

She put down her knife and wiped her hands on the towel tucked into her skirt's expanding waistline. Checking the pot once more, she went outside to pull another burdock root and an additional handful of red clover. The kitchen garden at Courthézon was small, but even in the pre-spring chill, everything grew so exuberantly in its acid-green ardor that it was impossible to keep a trim border on the beds. Guilhelma trod the overgrown stepping-stones carefully and yanked a fistful of the dusty pink herb. Before mincing its stems she loved to crush them in her hands for the stain of sweet fragrance they left: it made her dream. Once inside, a glance at the chopping block told her she'd forgotten the burdock. Impatient with herself, she tossed the sprigs of clover with their fluffy heads into the kettle whole.

When the decoction had reached a first boil, Guilhelma picked a ladle from the fireplace hook and plunged it through the liquid surface to make the herbs sink to the bottom. This batch would be potent enough without burdock; the very thought of the nasty root made her mouth pucker. She blew on the mixture until it cooled. Then she tested a drop on her wrist and sniffed it approvingly. She had taken to occupying the kitchen when it was empty these early afternoons, in order to replenish the household stock of medicinals—decoctions, simples, and tisanes—which she kept in supply all year around. There was no one about at this hour, and no sound but the thud and drag from the floor below as the dispenser drew off wine from the cellar barrels for supper.

Gaucelm was out with Count Raimbaut, hunting boar as usual. Guilhelma knew well enough by now that a troubadour with an audience to please will play whenever he's bidden if he's well-praised. Raimbaut had insisted that whether they were on foot or mounted, his hunting parties bagged more quarry when they had Gaucelm's songs for encouragement. Indeed he'd gone so far as to suggest that Gaucelm's voice lured hare, wild hogs, and bucks from their hideouts and brought luck at the kill. So whether the bag was good or game was scarce, Gaucelm always returned from the hunt in a fine glow of self-regard.

Guilhelma put the mixture on for a second boil. She sighed sleepily and sank into a chair close enough to the fire to remove her decoction if it threatened to simmer too low. Then she settled into a sort of rumination which had become her custom of late.

For her this was a time of miracles. She relished these slumberous hours when nothing was required of her, when it was enough just to feed the center of her own being. And how that center had dropped! Her legs felt like stumps, grown round and short, whose only duty was to act as a stool for the child inside her. Child! It was no more than a bothersome growing fruit, at times suspended like a pear, at times crouched, froglike. She rehearsed its birth, the fruit dropping at last, rushed out by a slosh of holy water. A boy, fat and thrashing, with Gaucelm's funny nose and forehead furrows, her own delicious mouth, the periwinkled ears she'd seen on new infants, the blue veins bunched at the temples, the pursed eyelids—and then the blood-red cries of agony that was no agony, but relief at being born.

She was not contemplative by nature, but in her condition she found company trying, and she avoided chatter with servants. Perhaps she was growing lazy as well. "Lady-in-waiting" had such a nice ring to it when first pronounced by Raimbaut, but in fact Tiburge required very little waiting upon. Raimbaut's sister was as self-sufficient as she was energetic and, simply put, Guilhelma's attentions embarrassed her. Now it suited everyone that Guilhelma was absorbed in her new state. Soon she had even looked forward to these regular, unaccountable periods of exhaustion. She was solidly where she had always wanted to be, in the middle of warm, brooding life. Without any doubt she knew that motherhood would agree with her. She was happier than she had ever been or thought she had a right to be.

She marvelled at the succession of seasons that had passed since they delivered themselves into Raimbaut's hospitable keeping, but when she tried to number the years she lost count. They had celebrated Lady Day so many times that living at Ventadour under Marie's brooding custodianship seemed far away, Toulouse further still. The terrible ordeal of Montdragon was long over; gone as well was the constant anxiety of Douce's being discovered, which had cast such a shadow on their first weeks at Courthézon. Once they were well settled in, Douce had sent word of her whereabouts to Ventadour at Guilhelma's behest. Marie fired back a tart reply signalling her acquiescence and, between the lines, her confidence in Guilhelma as guardian.

With Marie's message, Guilhelma had scored her final point: even after Douce's escape, even in her own defeat, Marie had sensed that her daughter was better off in Guilhelma's charge than her own. At the memory, Guilhelma yawned with satisfaction.

Guilhelma displaced her weight slightly forward, off her sit-bones, and sighed. Douce! Trouble was destined to follow her wherever she went, though she did nothing to stir the waters herself. Not long after Marie's message reached Courthézon, the lord Raimbaut himself began to "look after Douce's interests," to use Gaucelm's phrase – a phrase, which by its delicacy, Guilhelma suspected had originated with Raimbaut.

She reflected on how it all started the day after their arrival at Courthézon seven years ago, when Douce, ignoring Gaucelm's warning, had told Raimbaut of Béatritz's death. Gaucelm had been furious. Guilhelma remembered thinking, *It'll do him good, to be disobeyed by a sixteen-year-old with a mind of her own*! Gaucelm had remained cool toward Douce for several days but she seemed completely unaffected. She went about her business, self-contained as usual.

Instead, things took an unexpected turn. When Count Raimbaut recovered from the shock of Béatritz's death, he sent for Douce. "Of course he wondered who I was," she had explained to Guilhelma. "And so I told him—oh, not about my vows," Douce said, seeing Guilhelma's alarm. "I told him that I am the daughter of Ebles de Ventadour."

From that moment everything changed. Douce's first meal at Courthézon was her last in the servants' quarters. Once her station was known, she was treated like any other lady of some—though not exalted—rank. Still, in order to prevent wagging tongues within the castle walls and even graver suspicion without, she was named Mistress of the Linens, and charged with overseeing the supplies of bedding and tablecloths. Raimbaut played the part of accomplice to this game with grace and gentlemanly good humor, taking care never to drop the least hint that might give her away.

And then he began courting her, though never directly. It was through Gaucelm that she learned of it first. Raimbaut began to compose poetry, verses that Douce was not to hear for a long time. Gaucelm reported a period of concentration from which Raimbaut emerged with two finished canson—a record, Gaucelm remarked, for Raimbaut's last completed song dated from seven years ago. In keeping with the great tradition of the *trobar clos* perfected by his forebears, he gave Douce a senhal and kept it secret from all but Gaucelm, whose skill in such specialized matters of the troubadour's art would have led him to discover its meaning in any case. *Ai*, Guilhelma thought, looking back, *it was obvious to any mortal eye that count Raimbaut d'Orange though perhaps a dozen years her elder, was in love with Douce de Ventadour.*

Guilhelma got up from her chair and peered over the rim of the pot where bubbles were forming. Yanking the towel from her waist, she grasped the handle with it and hiked the pot a notch up the ratchet, a little away from the heat. A *senhal*. Not even Gaucelm had gone that far when he was first praising her in verse, tucking a mysterious code-name for his secret love into his lines. But by the Virgin Mary, Guilhelma had gladdened her heart many times with imagining her name disguised in one of Gaucelm's poems. As for the planh he had composed for Douce, it was about politics, not love. Gaucelm had called it his manifesto against all religious warring.

Yet Guilhelma well knew how Gaucelm felt about Douce. She had asked herself many times if she was jealous of Douce. It was almost the only thing that marred her happiness now that she was bearing Gaucelm's child.

Guilhelma had to admit she never did know exactly where she stood with him. But she told herself that it was another Douce whom Gaucelm loved, not the lady of Raimbaut's *senhal*. With Gaucelm it was all games of horseshoes and "princess of the light gold hair" and mock-courtly badinage. And Douce had followed him as children do the village minstrel – until Montdragon. Then she'd grown up, right under their eyes. *How adversity makes quick learners of us all,* she thought. Gui's death had set Douce squarely on her own path, and if anyone had been left behind, it was Gaucelm.

Gaucelm had noticed a difference in the way Douce dressed the spring of their first year at Courthézon. She had a tentative way about her so far from the heedless girl who loved to play games in the courtyard. He began to feel like her father.

"Of course," Guilhelma replied. "Any woman her age pays attention to the way she walks and the clothes she wears. And Douce especially must dress with simplicity without drawing attention to it."

The russet worsted Douce had kept for travel was once again in evidence. That spring, as the weather grew mild, Béatritz's silk bliaut appeared. One night in the great hall when the whole household had gathered to hear the troubadour Raimon de Miraval, Guilhelma knew that Raimbaut d'Orange was in love with Douce. The count could not take his eyes from her, despite the prominence of his guest. And Douce was in thrall, ignoring Gaucelm and Guilhelma completely. Even now, her defection hurt. Even now with the promise of her own offspring.

Thinking back, she had to admit that she had at first regarded having Gaucelm's baby as a mixed blessing. What did she want with a child from a man who once boasted of gambling away his horse and his only suit of clothes in one night's gaming? A man who would ask for the spirit shop before a bath house any day? A man who had spent half his life on the road? What use would he be to her, she who had put down roots at Courthézon by dint of her own efforts? But now she knew that her body had longed for exactly this to happen, had ached to relinquish itself, to expand, to belong to another being, to feel it stirring within. She remembered the moment last summer when, rejecting all herbal promptings, she had come to Gaucelm with a secret flush and the knowledge that she would take away his substance to be tended inside her as she might prepare a potion, a magic brew of two selves that would conjure a life. Alchemy! Then it *had* happened, just as she had hoped, and all her old doubts reversed themselves. She had taken the risk and knew it was right, come what may. Of course, she wanted to marry him. But a wedding ring would never buy the certainty of Gaucelm's love. Love was love, with or without signs. A ring could mean so little. Hadn't she seen that at Ventadour with Marie's gifts of jewelry? No, it was Gaucelm's playful private glances when she helped with service at dinner, the times they sang together in his practice room, the pet names they made love by, even the fights that ended in embraces—these were better than any ring, she was convinced. She was happy with the knowledge that this was no mere jongleur, but a famous poet she harbored in her bed.

But she still worried. Would this creature come between them in some way she could neither predict nor fathom? A child could changes things, Guilhelma knew. And for a woman not tied to any man, having a child could brand her as unmarriageable forever.

Oh, but alchemy be damned! She got up and gave the pot a vigorous stir, jerking it back onto its former hook, where it settled with a grinding, flinty sound. If Gaucelm were to walk into the kitchen this minute and surprise her with a proposal she would be overcome with joy. She wiped her hands on the towel and tucked it into her waistband, yawned grandly to stretch her back, and stood gazing at her decoction, arms akimbo. Then she loosened the top of her bodice and sat down to await the final boil.

Chapter 22

CHAUZIR

Douce knew that Raimbaut, too, had sensed a magical current running between them from their first meeting. Her own heart had fallen into his hands the moment he had kissed them on that day after their arrival at Courthézon seven years ago, the day she had sought him out to deliver the news of Béatritz's death. Blushing now as she thought about it, she supposed her feelings had been obvious to everyone, all these years. Restless in her quarters, she rose from her rush-bottomed chair and went to the window, wishing she had a looking glass like the one on the table near her mother's bed at Ventadour, half-wanting to inspect her reflection. She flinched at her lapse. As a Cathar, she knew she should shun any material comforts or possessions. But life at Courthézon sometimes made that difficult, just as it had for Beatritz, she thought, remembering the milky green stone from Raimbaut that her friend wore on her belt to the last.

She sighed and went back to the chair. In her mind's eye she set on parade a line of figures, all herself, in different attitudes. She tried to fix upon what other people saw when they looked at her. She pictured herself at Raimbaut's table, risking quick glances in his direction. Did she do that? Yes, she supposed she did; she could feel the little muscles in her neck move now as she envisioned the gesture. Before such an occasion she took care to make her hair shine, slipping her comb through it a thousand times, until her arm ached. Did he notice the brilliance of her hair, how a swathe of it fell slightly forward to frame her face before being caught up at the back of her neck? Did he take note of her pink cheeks, pinched sharply by her thumb and forefingers as she stood poised for a moment just before entering the great hall?

For seven years her heart had felt this way and she had been alone with him—really alone—only twice. The second time, when he had summoned her to his study in order to learn who she was, she went gladly. Thinking back on it, she knew that she had been prompted by her need to tell the truth about more than her origins. And partly, she admitted to herself, she had been just plain curious. She was intrigued by this Count Raimbaut.

Once Bonel had shown her into Raimbaut's study she remembered feeling shy, keeping her eyes downcast, her feelings in check. She had not taken any particular trouble with her appearance that day, being preoccupied with the message she had come to deliver. The matter was weighty and fraught with danger: for his sake she thought it best to tell him of the vows she had taken.

She never looked at him as she spoke. Instead, her eyes focused across the room on a writing desk. She was dimly aware of a few graceful objects that stood out against the pale stone walls of the study, but she was mostly conscious of her voice.

"I had to tell you, you see," she blurted out when she finished recounting how she had found the hospice and the two women who had initiated her into her new faith. "Béatritz would have wanted me to."

He had remained standing throughout their interview. Now he nodded and moved away from where she was seated. She gazed at him furtively, as though afraid of having been caught at something forbidden. She saw how thin he was, and might have taken him for a mystic or the gaunt practitioner of self-flagellation if she hadn't already divined his hooded sensuality, if she hadn't know about Béatritz.

His response came slowly, agonizedly. "It must have been as hard for you to tell me as it is for me to accept," was all he said. He made no move to take her hands again, as he had done at their first meeting. He did not thank her. Instead, he laced his fingers together behind his mousey velvet *cotte*, the same one he had worn before, and paced back and forth, tracing a neat rectangle on the floor tiles. Then he went to the window and propped his elbows on the sill, resting his forehead in his hands. She made a little movement to rise. "Please don't leave . . . just yet," he said. There was silence between them for what seemed a very long time.

Feeling awkward, she turned her attention to the room. More objects—a tall pitcher, a stool of dark carved wood—swam into her view, yet she could not put names to them. She wondered whether anyone had ever made such a confession to him. In the quiet it seemed to her that the room's light grew pale. Was there nothing more to be said? She knew she must go.

When she moved to rise this time, Raimbaut left the window sill and came to her. He caught her shoulder and held her for a moment, his eyes fastened on hers. Slowly, a cloud lifted from his forehead and his grey pupils seemed to expand as though with tears. Her lips opened. She could feel herself breathing in and out through her mouth. Then she drew her eyes away from his and, in confusion, left the room.

She flew down the stairs, her pulse beating so violently that she prayed she would not faint. She resolved that she would be perfectly dutiful from then on. There would be no more thoughts of the count. She would behave in absolute accordance with the vows she had just confessed.

For the whole of that first year she was successful. She played her role well, going to chapel like everyone else, but whispering her own prayers into the camouflage of others' murmurings. Following Beatritz's example, she ate no meat. She let it be known that her body's aversion to meat was such that, should she allow herself to be tempted, she was certain to fall ill. After a while no one noticed what she ate or didn't eat. As for Gaucelm and Guilhelma, Douce thought it best to let them go on believing that Raimbaut knew nothing of her religion.

But in spite of herself, the more Douce was aware of Raimbaut's attention, the more she longed to appear in the great hall near him as he presided over his court. And, as though to contradict her mounting attraction to him, she grew more timid in his presence. By contrast, when away from him she was a force to be reckoned with, minutely attentive to her duties, to the supplies of fresh linens, the replenishment of ash and lard. On laundry days, when she could be seen skimming along the corridors with a retinue of housemaids in her wake, she might have been taken for a field commander, focused on nothing but her responsibilities. The task of linen mistress agreed with her, and she quickly gained the respect of the other servants.

Any reason Raimbaut might have invented to see her again in private would have proved too risky in the end. In hall he treated her like any privileged servant, one who, like Gaucelm and Guilhelma, was welcome at his table when there were distinguished visitors. But because of the two canson Gaucelm had disclosed to her, she went about her routine with a flush to her cheeks. She threw herself into playing the role of a Ventadour-in-exile who enjoyed her double life, because the person of greatest significance to her also knew it was a masquarade.

Finally, she had to admit that hers was, in the famous words of the troubadour Jaufre Rudel, an *amor de longh*. She loved Raimbaut from afar. But how she resented it! She felt like a princess trapped in a poem. She envied everyone around her—the carefree Gaucelm, the servants, even, for they had one life only—their work.

Yet lately Douce had seen a change in Raimbaut, a slump of his shoulders, a creasing of his brow. There were stories of what was happening to the north. More murderous rampages in pursuit of heretics. *Like me*, she acknowledged to herself, *people who only want to practice their own beliefs in peace*. Courtehézon had been a welcome refuge after the horrors of Montdragon. When she saw Raimbaut leave the castle and enter the nearby woods one day, Douce knew it was her chance to speak with him alone, away from the eyes of the court. She followed him.

As she drew closer, her instinct was to flee. But his stance was odd, leaning with his back against a great oak. When he did not salute her she noticed that his eyes were closed. Only when the sound of her footsteps on dry leaves reached him did he right himself in surprise. So still had he been, so deep in his own thoughts, that he reacted as one awakened from sleep.

"You look troubled, my lord," Douce said.

"You surprised me greatly."

She summoned her courage. "May I interrupt your thoughts?"

Raimbaut removed the cloak from his shoulders and spun it out over a clump of moss and leaves at the base of the oak. He unbuckled his sword, then motioned for her to sit. His knees made little dry sounds as he first crouched, then let himself down onto the cloak.

Douce hoped she wasn't red in the face. They both looked away, into the forest, saying nothing. A pheasant rose up from the underbrush, squeaking loudly. Somewhere a dog barked. Douce noticed the faintest trace of sweat beading Raimbaut's upper lip. Then he put out his hand. She placed her own in his without hesitation.

He moved to look at her directly and said, his voice lowered almost to a whisper, "I am troubled by events . . . and also," he smiled at her, "by you." His voice broke strangely; he reached for her other hand. She began to say something but instead gazed down in silence at the big hands covering hers.

Raimbaut felt something shift and give way within him. This girl, this Douce, had such serenity—a quality precious to him. Perhaps it was her religion that made its haven in her, that gave her *solatz*. Was that not what he had seen and loved in her these seven years? His need for it, for her, at that moment was as elemental as the need of an infant to be held and suckeled, of a wound to be bound, of pain to be stilled. Confronted with her, the threats and worries—even the certainties—of his own life blurred. Never had he wanted so much what someone else possessed.

Now his hand moved from hers to her head, gracing her hair. For a heartbeat, she had to swallow the impulse to weep. They sat like this, so properly, so uncomfortably, so full of longing, until Raimbaut could bear it no longer. This small creature had disturbed him, haunted him for years. He was bent on having her.

She glanced at him. She knew there would be no struggle. Here, her religion did not exist, nor did Béatritz or Gaucelm or Guilhelma. He drew her down, his breath making a sound like wind through a long, dark tunnel. She thought she could hear the beating of wings as he took her head, cradled it on his chest.

She searched Raimbaut's face, but his look was not upon her. He began to rock her, reaching around through her skirts, to the tender places. She swooned as her skin tingled where he touched. Her eyelids closed. Surely she was going to faint. But instead she gulped for air as something stirred inside her, low and deep.

Douce found herself in Raimbaut's arms saying "please God" out loud, and "hold me" almost inaudibly. In that moment he acknowledged her need as she did his.

Then suddenly her body had its way and she was released from any thought at all. She lay, a part of him, flooded with forgetting, eyes closed. Father, brother, lover, god: there was no use denying that he was everything to her. She was afraid to move lest the moment change.

Slowly, she became aware of a dull pain between her thighs. From far away a horse whinnied and was answered.

Raimbaut reached out and smoothed the hair from her forehead, sat up upon their disheveled pile of castoff clothing, and said, "Shall I sing a canson I made for you?"

She nodded. It was true then, as Gaucelm had said. He had composed verses for her alone. He took her hand and stared for a heart's beat up into the wide fan of oak branches above them with the air of someone unmindful of anything but his own bliss. Then he began,

> *Dona! Pus mon cor tenetz pres*
> *adossatz me ab dous l'amar.*
> *Dieus, aiuda! In nomine patris et filii et spiritus sancti!*
> *Siso, que sera, domna?*

Douce sighed. She turned to gaze at him, preferring to ignore the question in that last line. *What will become of us, indeed?* She thought. "I did not know I had your heart as prisoner," she murmured. "Have I sweetened your bitterness?"

He gave her an open smile.

"Is there more?" she asked.

"Much more. But I must go back." He fished out his breeches from the pile of clothing and pulled them on. He got up, humming still, and straightened his tunic smartly by its hem. Those few gestures transformed him. From a lover, he had suddenly turned into a man with responsibilities.

Douce lay still on the bare ground. She had her answer. She would not leave Raimbaut; not now, not ever. She was afraid to stir, amazed at what she had done. It was true, she thought, something in her had been cast aside forever. Now she knew why Guilhelma once said you couldn't know a man until it came to sex. Much as she had loved Gui she had not, after all, really known him.

Finally she rolled over and looked up at Raimbaut. He had hitched his cloak over one finger. Quickly, he knelt and kissed her, then rose and walked in the direction of the castle. Wordlessly, she let him go.

When Riambaut was out of sight she got up, brushed the twigs from her skirt and pulled her cloak around her shoulders. The wind had come up strong. She could hear it now in the tall trees as she left the woods. It rustled through the orchard and the bordering olives as she walked across the dun-colored fields that separated her from the castle desmene. She began to run, triumphant. She felt that in this moment she possessed everything she wanted. *If only I can get to my room without seeing anyone*, she thought.

Guilhelma awoke to a tremendous clash of metal on stone followed by Gaucelm's voice bellowing "Oh God's eyes! Sweet Jesus!" He was dancing like a bear before its captors, waggling his right hand violently from the wrist. She saw instantly that he had heaved the boiling pot onto the grate without thinking to protect himself from the heat of its iron handle. The whole kitchen smelled like burning tar and clouds of smoke hung in the air just below the ceiling.

"*Dieus*! How could you sleep though that awful stink?" Gaucelm blew on his fingers and shook them out. Guilhelma drew herself to her feet and dragged a bucket of well water along the floor from the pantry. "Put your hand in this," she ordered. As he plunged it in he hissed through his teeth. "Something smelled funny," he said. "I came to take a look."

He sat down on the floor beside the bucket, dabbing his fingers in the coolness and wiping the sweat from his face with his sleeve. "That's better." With his free hand he pointed to the large work table where meat was broken up and poultry plucked. "See what I brought you?" On top rested a brace of hare, the snares still around their hind legs.

"Lucia will take care of those," Guilhelma said, settling back into her chair. It didn't hurt to remind Gaucelm that she was in the kitchen by choice, not duty.

Gaucelm withdrew his hand from the bucket and shook the water off. Guilhelma saw how his eyes puckered to a squint as he examined the burn. Lately she had noticed how, when he peered at something, the crease spanning the bridge of his nose deepened markedly. She wondered whether his sight was growing poor. She still liked the way his nose scrunched up, and even the silvery hair or two that escaped from his nostrils. On the whole, she thought, he had grown very hairy. Two years ago he had started a beard as an experiment and liked it. Now it was full and sported more than a few strands of grey. Even the tips of his eyebrows wore whiskers.

"You missed the baby turning somersaults," she said. Absently, he kissed her on the forehead.

"I've earned me a night off, at least," Gaucelm said, thinking of his hand. "Unless Raimbaut wants a song without accompaniment." He blew another kiss from the door.

Guilhelma thought of her ruined decoction, savoring the comfort of her chair for a moment longer before forcing herself to clean up the mess. She grasped the pot handle with her towel for safety's sake, and lifted it from the hearth. She placed the pot in a tub, rolled up her sleeves and prepared to scrub the pungent sediment from the cooking vessel. It wasn't the cleaning she disliked; it was the odor. The herbs stuck to the bottom of the pot in a blackened mass, giving off a revolting medicinal smell. Grabbing a bundle of twigs, she took a long breath through her mouth and set to loosening the residue.

Guilhelma bent to her scrubbing for what seemed only a heartbeat. When she looked-out the window, she saw Gaucelm and Douce in the courtyard. Something in the way they stood together, unaware of being observed, made her heart lurch. Hardly breathing, she stared at them as though willing them to defy her. Her eyes registered every move: Gaucelm put a hand on Douce's shoulder, turning her away from the kitchen. They began to walk together slowly toward the side entrance. Gaucelm seemed to be showing her his burn, his left hand at the base of Douce's neck, clasping like a torque the bright hair that flowed to her shoulders. When he began toying with it, Guilhelma could bear to watch no longer. It seemed to her a gesture of possession and complicity. She did not stop to think. A harsh, insistent pricking had risen behind her eyes and before the tears came she was in the courtyard, running as fast as her bulk would allow.

She was screaming and weeping at once, her hands in the air before her. When they turned and caught sight of her in that state they halted in mid-course, their faces turned in alarm. She stopped short of them, her towel dangling by one corner from her enormous waist, her eyes wet with tears, her nose red and shiny. She had no idea of what she would say, no real wish for words at all, only the feeling that she wanted to shake and beat the two figures.

Slowly, it seemed to Guilhelma, Gaucelm removed his hand from Douce's hair. "What is the matter?" He reached for her but she withdrew. She could not bring herself to beg him for what should have come naturally—the proposal that should have been hers by right. Nor could she ignore the evidence before her, that Douce had a hold on him still.

"Choose between us!" Guilhelma blurted out. "*Chauzir*! She's your angel child . . . admit it! *Chauzir*!"

"Oh, Guilhelma!" Douce exclaimed in relief, and moved to embrace her. "Did you think . . ." But Guilhelma would not be mollified, and pulled away. She cried on and on, bent over the mound of her stomach, both hands hiding her face. Douce and Gaucelm looked at one another helplessly.

Finally Douce said, "I know I've neglected you, Guilhelma. Perhaps we both have." She glanced at Gaucelm as though to say, *It's your move*. But Guilhelma raised her head, dried her eyes and said in her everyday, sensible voice, "I'm sure it's the baby. They say this happens near to the birth. The humors get out of balance." With that she turned and stumbled back to the kitchen.

Douce and Gaucelm followed at a slower pace.

"What did she mean by 'choose'?" Douce whispered. "She doesn't actually think . . ." Gaucelm shook his mane from side to side in confusion.

"Perhaps it is the baby after all," Douce continued. She's been so cut off, so much by herself. After a pause she said, "And it will be a big change in your life, having a child."

Suddenly she stopped and turned to face him, looking him straight in the eye. "Gaucelm," Douce said, "When are you going to marry her?"

Chapter 23

VIDAL REDUX

The timing had to be perfect. Yves, the page, kept watch at the corner of the stable, while Garsen the cellar steward guarded the trestle board. Vidal, still weary from his journey across the Rhône, crouched in the shadow of the stable wall.

They did not have long to wait. For the last two days, since Guilhelma's move to the women's quarters, Gaucelm had visited her in the morning after his practice session and again before vespers while it was still plenty light enough to save his taking a torch. This morning he was a shade later than usual. Just as sext sounded from the chapel, Yves gave the signal. In a muffled flurry the young men shouldered up the slab of wood with Vidal aboard, propped on one elbow, a hand clapped to his mouth to stifle his glee. Silently, the procession started across the courtyard.

They stole up on Gaucelm from the rear, then came alongside him. As they entered Gaucelm's field of vision and Vidal began to twirl his cap and sing they almost collided. Vidal dismounted abruptly, stood up, and found himself nose to nose with his old friend. The courtyard rang with their cries of recognition, shouts of greeting and slaps on the back. Gaucelm, almost speechless with surprise, tweaked a lock of the black thicket that stood out from Vidal's head. "I can't see your eyes for all that hair! How long have you been on the road?"

Vidal took no notice of the remark. He was captivated instead by Gaucelm's beard. "Behold—it's got *grey* in it!" and his friend's widened girth did not escape a meaningful thump.

"How long can you stay? Off to the barber we go, if I'm to introduce you at court!" Gaucelm said.

"Not so fast, brother oaf! I have much to tell you. *Much!*" Vidal spread his arms wide as if to take in the whole yard.

"Can we find a spot that's private?"

Gaucelm nodded. To his chagrin, he felt the bridge of his nose swell, always a sign of tears. "I thought I'd never see you again," he said, making no attempt to hide his overwhelming joy and, yes, relief at Vidal's reappearance.

"Where can we go?" Vidal asked.

Gaucelm clapped his friend on the shoulder and steered him toward the kitchen. "If you're hungry, it's *this* way."

"You know me well, friend. I'm starving."

Vidal looked the same but thinner. If possible, his little quirks and gestures reminded Gaucelm more than ever of a puppet on a string. But the untroubled brow, the faintly ironic smile about the lips—nothing in his expression had changed over the years. The skin around his eyes was strangely bleached as if by the sun, but the eyes themselves were coal-black, just as Gaucelm remembered them. Vidal's *cotte* had once been rather grand, but now the silk was frayed by years of hard wear. In fact, it was a disgrace, with holes in both elbows and a gap in the left shoulder where the fabric had worn completely away. But there was one improvement in Vidal's appearance: a cap of embroidered velvet sat atop his unruly thatch.

"I'm glad to see you got rid of that mangy old headpiece," Gaucelm remarked.

"Camel mistook it for dinner," Vidal said merrily.

Gaucelm looked baffled.

"I've been to Outremer," Vidal said, as though that would explain cap-eating camels.

"I can't believe you're *here*," Gaucelm breathed as he opened the kitchen door. They paused at the threshold, looking like two mismatched jesters – lumbering bear and sprightly wolf—each with a paw around the other's shoulder.

Gaucelm gestured toward the far end of the room where the kitchen help ate. "Now sit down and tell all," he said.

But Vidal's wiry frame twitched with anticipation as he surveyed the room. "Does the lord of Courthézon keep a good table?"

"Not brilliant," Gaucelm replied. "But I took a tip from you and made friends with the cook."

The kitchen looked as though an army had ransacked it and retreated. There was no one about. Leavings from last night's dinner were piled carelessly on a board perched atop the washing vat, and the fire had dwindled to a few warm embers sitting within the vast yawn of the hearth. No scullery maid had seen reason to abandon the fine weather outdoors for the sake of cleaning up. Gaucelm looked around in disgust, while Vidal went straight for the pile of leftovers and picked out a barely-touched joint of meat.

Gaucelm held up a wine jug he discovered beneath the servants' table. "There's no water to cut this with."

"No matter, we'll have it straight," Vidal said heartily. "And I've found two mugs." He drew a stool up to the table and began working on the mutton joint with his knife.

Gaucelm went to the pantry to fetch bread. He came back with a shrivelled Valencia and some crusty marchpane instead. "Not an elegant meal," he announced.

"It'll do," said Vidal between mouthfuls. "But no lady-food for me, thanks just the same."

Gaucelm tossed the marchpane away and seated himself opposite Vidal. "How did you know I was in Courthézon?"

"I didn't have to ask your whereabouts: your fame has spread in Toulouse like the plague!"

"How so?"

"Folquet."

"Folquet?"

"Folquet, bishop of that fair city. He who churns the air behind him . . ." Vidal got up from his stool and, holding his knife aloft, pirouetted a few steps, swaying from the hips in a form of locomotion more like swimming than walking. Gaucelm shouted with delight at his friend's gift for mime. "The old fart!"

"The old fart in a bishop's mitre," Vidal said, sitting down. "He's got wind of your planh. It has spread across the country, this declaration of yours, although he'd dearly love to put a stop to it. I gather it's against all warring between faiths—a noble sentiment."

"Well, if he's heard my planh, then some good air has blown his way for once!" Gaucelm looked delighted with himself, but Vidal's face grew serious. He abandoned his meat and pushed the stool a little away from the table. He looked squarely at Gaucelm. "See here. You'd better give some thought to disappearing sooner or later. I haven't heard it, mind you, but it seems your little planh contains some reference to a righteous ecclesiastic who dared to flirt with Catharism in his youth. Have you no instinct for caution, man?"

Vidal's remark took Gaucelm abruptly back to what Guilhelma had told him about Folquet in the old days. It had been years since he had thought about Guilhelma's secret, about how Folquet had come to her in the Chantier, full of youthful verses and heretical leanings. Somehow the memory of hearing this had gotten into the planh, in the way things got into his poems almost without his knowing. Now it dawned on him the meaning of Folquet's training at the hands of Marie and Madame Audiarde: The bed-lesson of pain inflicted on self translated with such ease to pain inflicted on others, and then on the enemy at large. It all added up: his shrouded past, his proclivity for silken ties and ladies' knives, and before long, there was a bishop schooled in all the niceties of deviance—a rare qualification indeed for one who would preach a holy war. The delicious irony, Gaucelm reflected, was that in Folquet's case the enemy was the demons of his own past: Cathars. So his task, though Folquet could not know it, was to vanquish his own demons. Folquet, Gaucelm realized with an inspiration like a flood of light, was uniquely fitted to lead this crusade.

"Dieus!" he returned to Vidal's remark. "Is Toulouse to betray me a second time?"

Vidal shrugged, hands raised in an open-palmed gesture of helplessness, and said nothing.

"Ah," said Gaucelm. "I see the way of it, then. Treachery. Papal threats. All that." He took a deep breath, as though to dismiss the whole idea. "Come, you don't really think that fat Folquet will waste his precious time on the likes of me? He has many a bigger fish to fry!" Vidal's expression did not change. "Besides," Gaucelm said, "the reference was nothing more than that. I never named Folquet—it could have been anyone." Suddenly he was furious. "What can he do with me? He can't fry me—I'm no heretic!"

Vidal said simply, "Treason."

Gaucelm put up both hands in protest. "Wait. If Folquet chooses to take that little phrase personally, it's as good as an admission of guilt."

"Treason," Vidal said again. "Who knows exactly what provokes him? But you certainly haven't improved your chances with the planh. To him, not toeing the line amounts to treason."

It took a few heartbeats for Gaucelm to comprehend. "If not being a pious

Catholic is a treasonable offense, every lockup and donjon in the South would be crammed. But if they're clapping poets into prisoner's pits, *I've* not heard of it."

Vidal said, "The heresy, Gaucelm—offense to church and state."

"Who would risk denouncing me as a heretic? I don't even have friends among the Cathars, none that Folquet knows of, anyway."

Vidal ignored the question. "We all have friends who are Cathars, whether we know it or not. Besides, Gaucelm, cut this false modestly. You are plenty big enough for Folquet, as fish go. You're on the list, dear brother oaf."

Gaucelm stared at Vidal. With a surge of incipient relief it occurred to him that his friend might be pulling his leg; that was part of his infamous prankster's charm.

"What list, then?" Gaucelm asked lightly.

"Oh, a sort of roll call of the wayward drawn up by Folquet's henchmen. They call themselves the White Brotherhood. But names find their way onto that list at Folquet's instigation, of course."

"Who else is on it?"

"I am. Everyone who matters. Including Raymond, so we're in polite company. Anyone who ever put forth an unorthodox idea in verse. Any friend of the Count of Toulouse or of his nephew Trencavel. In short, anyone who's thwarted Folquet in any way. It could be anything you've done, political or personal. In my case it was probably a certain lady in Marseille . . ."

"But just how have I thwarted him?"

"By making better songs, perhaps?" He picked up the joint again and reapplied himself to it. "What's in this planh of yours, anyway? And who is the Douce to whom it's dedicated? I can't wait to hear it." He wagged the piece of meat in Gaucelm's direction. "Remember the '*Eretria dels Preires*'?"

"That was *ages* ago!" Gaucelm could not believe his ears. It was as if Vidal had risen from the dead to remind him of his sins.

Vidal said, between bites, "Folquet has a long memory, longer than yours, clearly. Don't forget the little scene you caused in front of Raymond, the night you sang it in court. It still makes my skin prickle." He grinned mischievously. "Folquet called you a heretic, said the Cathars would love you. Then he stormed out, shouting, 'The Pope will hear of this!' Do you remember, or have you blotted . . ."

"But all that was long before . . ."

"Indeed, before he was made bishop. Just so. He bided his time. Folquet puts by his resentments the way a housewife stores preserves. But once he had the crozier in his fat pink paw he lost no opportunity to collect on some righteous debts. Thus the list."

"Folquet is fulfilling his destiny, then, as a venomous nuisance . . ."

"He's having the time of his life. Found his métier at last. Being bishop seems to be the only way to redeem his miserable failure in the songster's trade. That always stuck in his throat, remember?" Vidal held up his knife in the midst of his wolf-like munching and said excitedly, "That fat ass could never put one word after the other. He *belongs* in the Church! You ought to hear what he's composing nowadays – makes you blush for shame." He drained the wine in his mug with a single swallow.

"What sort of thing? Ecclesiastical nonsense, I expect."

"Pitiful stuff. He's gone all soft in the head about Our Lady. Worst of it is, people take it seriously because he's bishop. God, it's enough to turn your stomach! Listen!" Vidal squirmed sideways on the bench and, resting both hands on the tabletop, carefully joined his fingertips together in a gesture of piety. He raised his eyes skyward, then dissolved into peals of laughter. "Be warned," he said, "that Folquet uses phrases of consummate originality. Like this: '**Not for anything would my faithful heart turn from you.**' Then there's, '**No other wish nor command have I but yours.**'"

Gaucelm winced.

"And then this: '**I want your love but know not how to say it.**' An inbuilt confession of verbal ineptitude—isn't that perfect?"

Gaucelm sat forward; his ear had caught something familiar. "How does it go, exactly?"

Vidal obliged:

> *Ja par verjan ni per fuelh no per flor*
> *Mon fin cor maisnon viraray de re*
> *de vos, cui tenc per don'e vuelh amar,*

Gaucelm's eyes widened as Vidal went on, still gazing heavenwards, "*qu'autra el mon non envey ni honor...*"

Unable to contain himself, Gaucelm sang out the refrain, "*e no-s vaira mos cors, e said per que!*"

Vidal stopped abruptly and stared at Gaucelm. "You don't . . . I can't believe . . . is it really . . . *yours*? Did Folquet really dare to copy what you composed?" Vidal sank his small predatory teeth into the last of the joint.

"It seems so . . ." Gaucelm said, ". . . but wait! I have important news of my own. You've arrived just in time for a major event."

Vidal looked up. He let the bone drop and wiped his fingers on the rim of the trencher, then sucked the remnants of grease and loose crumb from each fingertip in succession.

"Well?" Gaucelm said. "Remember the four ducats you won off me the first time we gambled?"

"Christ, you remember that?"

"How could I forget? We were with the stablehands in the courtyard, after you took me through the castle that first day."

"You were pretty wet behind the ears."

"You dried me off well, my friend. But you also put me out of pocket four ducats' worth. I've vowed to win it back from you. Now, I give you three tries to tell me what important event is about to take place?"

"My introduction to Raimbaut, Count of Orange. That's easy."

"Wrong."

"You dare to insult me so? I'll double your debt!" Still hungry, Vidal glanced at the bone where it lay on the trencher. "Oh, all right, I'll play. You've, ah, taken holy orders."

Gaucelm waited.

"You've discovered how to get gold from a pig's turds."

A raised eyebrow from Gaucelm.

"Oh, come on. Out with it!" Vidal exclaimed.

"Have yourself one more try." Gaucelm studied his friend's face. He felt time passing, like the pages of a book turned by the wind. It was unnerving to find Vidal unchanged, while the direction of his own life seemed so uncertain.

"I give up, dammit! What else is there to celebrate, eh? The South is going up in flames, Rai Mundi's been declawed, fat Folquet will swallow Toulouse whole, and you and I will have to take to our heels if we're not to roast on the Crusader's spits. So there. I give up absolutely."

"I am to be a father."

"*You*? Well . . . so there is something to celebrate after all! Good, my Gaucelm, let's drink to the incunabulum. When does it hatch?"

"Soon. Any day. Now, for all I know. Dieus, Vidal, the whole idea is terrifying."

But Vidal seemed to think that the occasion demanded celebration rather than sympathy, and reached for his mug. With it in hand, he saluted the father-to be. "My arrival was perfectly timed, then! I'll help you welcome it into the world, for whatever this world is worth. And who's the wife?"

"Guilhelma . . . though we've never married."

Vidal made a pantomime of fainting in his seat. "Then it's *you* who robbed the Chantier of its most prominent lady of the night! I learned she'd left the stews, but had no idea. So, Guilhelma Monja, from our first evening on the town?"

"The very same."

"I'll be damned! You really are a sport. Does Raimbaut know who she is?"

"My dear Vidal, not even you would recognize her. She's a proper lady now with the best of them, and a good deal smarter than most. You wouldn't be able to tell her from Count Raimbaut's sister."

"By the foot of God, Gaucelm! Where do we begin with the stories of our lives in the ten years since I left Toulouse? This calls for more wine! I've been halfway around the world and back since I last saw you."

"First," grinned Gaucelm, hand outstretched, "my four ducats, please. You're a fast talker but you still lost the bet."

Vidal fished in his pouch, "Here are eight; that should shut you up. First time I've ever delivered double on a loss, but they're for Guilhelma, not you. Now let's do that wine jug justice, shall we?"

Vidal nudged the joint carcass with his knife. "That was a good start. Got anything else to eat?" Without waiting for an answer, he swung a leg over the stool and began rummaging hopefully in the pile of trenchers. "Dieus," he remarked, ramming his own trencher back into the stack. "Not enough here to feed a stray dog." He sniffed his way along the shelves and cupboards, overturning a bowl here, a board there, muttering, "Where do they *keep* everything?" Then, lit with inspiration, he scampered to the hearth where a huge cauldron of congealed mutton stew sat on a hook. In triumph, he heaved it to the floor and dragged it over the flagstones to his place. "Give a hand, will you?" he said, and Gaucelm helped hoist the kettle onto the table. He could barely see his friend over its top, but watched amused as Vidal sat with his knife poised to harpoon the likeliest looking morsel.

"Wine, please."

Gaucelm reached for the jug and poured out for both of them. "Now," he said, "I want an answer. Why did you leave Toulouse?"

Vidal looked puzzled. "Why should I not have?"

"You just disappeared. I was furious, damn you! Just skipped out, leaving me to my fate. Why?"

"Oh, way back *then*, you mean. Smelled trouble. Got fed up with intrigue. Or maybe it was itchy feet, pure and simple. Wanted to see Outremer, travel. You know. The usual reasons. I don't remember, exactly." He added almost as an afterthought, "But I did return to Toulouse last year."

Vidal gave a little sigh. "I was determined not to go to Toulouse actually, but events conspired to take me there anyhow. It's just as well, for poor Raymond, without his knowing, has paid my trip here with what is probably his last stipend."

"Last? How so?"

Vidal raised an eyebrow. "My dear man, don't tell me you don't know. The Pope's threatened to humiliate him again. Promises to have him stripped to the waist and flagellated in public, making his back a map of bloody welts for all to see . . ." Vidal's words tumbled out in a rush, a sign that his blood was up.

"Worst than last year's . . . event, then."

"Much. And I was there in St. Gilles last January. Saw the whole thing. My God, Gaucelm—what a scene it was! The Pope must have planned it for months. It was almost as good as an auto-da-fé with all the fanfare and the delegates from Rome. There were dozens of banners flying from the great facade of the abbot-church, making it look exactly like some imperial arc-de-triumph."

Vidal grew serious. "I've had my differences with Raymond in the past, but it made my heart hurt to see him there, kneeling on the church steps. First he read out his allegiance to the Pope. Then he got up from his knees and was commanded to do homage by bowing to that nincompoop, that papal stooge Castelnau." In a quiet voice he added, "Problem is, of course, the Pope chose the wrong man to eat crow. It only made Rai Mundi more popular than ever among his people."

"Good. Some triumph for the Holy See!" Gaucelm snorted.

Vidal's face clouded with the memory. "It was sad, actually. As soon as word got out that their Bringer of Light was to be bested by Pope Innocent, the crowd pressed in around the walls of the church. I saw some enraged faces, but there were many who wept. It was more like Raymond's funeral than an act of reconciliation with the Church." He paused in thought. "What with the century having turned not so long ago, one would expect some little show of hope nowadays. But instead, all we've had is death and desolation. And just before I left, Bernard's light was extinguished like, like a candle flame. Of course it had been barely flickering for a long time . . ."

"Bernard! Bernard de Ventadour is dead?"

"He died the day before I left. You know, I found myself growing right fond of the old man at the end. Lately he was too sick to be cared for any longer at court. So Raymond had him taken to the monastery at Dalon. I saw him there once or twice. It was pitiful. As you know, he had been sinking for years. He became—how shall I say it—prescient, like a seer, toward his life's finish. He was of some use in old age, after all. We talked. Or shall I say I shouted and he replied. Since Folquet was made bishop he'd felt in his bones that Raymond would be betrayed, that Pope Innocent would have his head. He feared there might even be civil war. He seemed to know all about the White Brotherhood and their list."

Gaucelm could not take in any more of what Vidal was saying. His sudden grief brought his head down upon his folded arms. He could never explain this to Vidal. He could barely explain it himself why he felt his throat tighten, his body coil as though he had been struck. Bernard de Ventadour was dead, the master he had traveled to Toulouse to see, whose presence he had dreamed of since childhood; the poor deaf wraith he'd sung for that night of his first success. Behind Gaucelm's closed eyelids passed the woeful years of Bernard's decline, and then his magical renaissance when Gaucelm could no longer do without his guidance, and the bond between them was forged forever.

Angrily, Gaucelm pushed himself away from the table and with his hand made a quick wave of apology.

"I had no idea Bernard's death would affect you so," Vidal said. "I am sorry."

"We had our time together after you left. We grew close, in a manner of speaking, like a craftsman and his apprentice. The suddenness of this news did take me by surprise. A thousand pardons."

"Forgiven, friend. Shall we set aside Bernard for another time?"

"No. I want to hear the rest."

"Ah, well. The poor man lingered on a while. Perhaps he was merely curious to see how his predictions about Raymond would turn out. After all, it's what had made him a good poet: his audience always wanted to know what happened in the end, and so did he."

Gaucelm glumly got up with the vague notion of locating a new supply of wine. "Full of cheerful tidings, aren't you? How long were you in Toulouse this time?"

"Long enough to see Folquet fume and paddle his way up high enough to knife Raymond in the back. Long enough to watch Bernard's decline. Long enough to be sick of the sight and sound of all of them, really."

"And so you left, your sole mission being to bring me up to date on the happy news from Raymond's kingdom?" Gaucelm roamed about the room. He had already forgotten about the wine.

Vidal ignored his friend's comment. He pushed his stool away from the table and stretched, giving a great yawn that jolted his ruffian's cap down his forehead until it covered his eyes.

Gaucelm came to a full stop beside him. "There's more. There's something you're not telling me."

Vidal righted his cap and sat up. "About why I left? Isn't it enough to have steered clear of Folquet's dear little White Brotherhood, who can't tell a troubadour from a Cathar?" He paused, as though considering something. "Then of course there *was* La Loba."

Silence. Gaucelm led him on by not speaking the words he knew Vidal expected to hear: *The very same lady paid court to by the likes of Rai Mundi and wasn't it—Raiman de Miraval? That La Loba?* No, he would not give him the satisfaction.

"The She-Wolf of Penautier," Vidal said at last. "The notorious La Loba, wife of all that wild country above Toulouse . . ." he broke off, cocked his head. "Heard this?"

> **And if they call me Wolf**
> **I'm not thereby disgraced**
> **— I'd gladly go to her**
> **Through ice and wind and snow**

Gaucelm shook his head.

"No reason why you should. I composed it last week, on my way here," Vidal grinned. "But you are right. That quatrain explains part of the reason for my presence."

"Jealous husband?"

"*Murderous* jealous husband."

Gaucelm had to smile. "I should have known right away that there were more complicated motives than fat Folquet and his list." He added ruefully, "Not that Courthézon can offer much in the way of protection from murderous husbands."

The light was fading. Gaucelm rose. "Let me show you where to put your things. Then I'll look in on Guilhelma." Before they left the kitchen Vidal, more than a little charged with wine, noticed a loaf of bread and pinched it, thrusting it under his arm. Of their progress across the courtyard, Gaucelm would remember only imagining how the company would react to being short-rationed at supper. His brain still spinning at Bernard's death, he was in no mood to encounter Raimbaut, nor to present Vidal to anyone. Neither he nor his friend would sup in hall tonight, he decided.

After collecting Vidal's things from the courtyard, Gaucelm led him to a large, bare room, part of which was partitioned off with hangings so as to afford guests some privacy. Choosing an unoccupied alcove with a window, he shouldered Vidal's saddlebag onto the floor.

"Tomorrow, if Raimbaut isn't cloistered in his study, we can attend to introductions and other such matters of weight and import to court and country. And—fair warning—I'm going to get you barbered beforehand. Now, I'll leave you to unpack," he said, knowing full well that sleep would overtake his friend before he could undo the first strap on his bag.

The verbal flourishes were for Vidal's benefit; they did nothing to cheer the speaker. Nor did Gaucelm plan to visit Guilhelma, not for a while. He would keep Bernard to himself a little longer, let the event sit within him until he regained his equilibrium. It stung him that his joy at Vidal's arrival had been snatched away, or at least clouded by the sorrow of the news he bore. Wandering the castle desmene in semi-darkness, Gaucelm wept openly for reasons both generous and selfish. He wept as well for the memory of his vanished self, that boy of 16 who sought to rise in the world with a teacher's help and then found that he had to do it by himself. He felt betrayed by Bernard's death in the same way that, on that first night in court, he felt let down by the troubador's deafness. Still, Bernard's presence had been assurance enough for Gaucelm that he was on the right path, that some invisible hand was guiding him, that he would amount to something as a songster after all.

Gaucelm crouched on the ground, resting his head on his arms. His past had suddenly broken off in a great chunk and he felt as though he was watching it fall into the sea and float away. It was like the blow of being dismissed by Raymond those many years ago. He had still not forgotten the sharpness of that hurt.

But it had always been different with Bernard than with Raymond. In some way he had become the great poet's heir, though he felt still far from equal to the job. Even during all the years that he had been away from Toulouse, Bernard had been with him as a talisman, a charm, a symbol of guidance and luck. With Bernard gone, he realized, he had no more excuses.

He could feel the words already forming: "***Planher vuelh en Bernard...Ab cor trist...***" *No!* he shouted inwardly, and squelched them. *Not now,* he said to himself. It was too easy to consign grief to poetry, to allow it to be swallowed up and diminished by rhymes. In time, perhaps, but not yet. He wanted to have Bernard to himself, to remember the man and not to have him disappear into meters and stanzas.

Gaucelm blinked the tears from his eyes. He was still the same being to whom Bernard had said, "You have the gift, you will develop great skill." And he had.

Nor had Gaucelm forgotten Bernard's warning against falling into the ease of conventional court verses. Hadn't he said, "What else is a troubadour, a trobar, a finder? Not just someone good at rhyme schemes, but a discoverer, a truth-teller—a *poet*." Had he borne it out? Surely he was on the right path: first the "*Eretria*"; then the planh for Douce. He sensed that some final task was ahead of him, like a grail. Only when he had launched himself on the road toward it would he be within range of the mantle of a Bernard de Ventadour.

Chapter 24

ACORDANZA

Guilhelma was brought to childbed on the following evening as the first stars came out and the church bells announced compline. It had been a day of religious obligation, the festival of Saint Gregory. But in the women's quarters at the castle, the late hours resounded with the fetching and carrying of basins and towels instead of prayer.

Once her waters broke Guilhelma was more comfortable, luxuriating in the attention her lying-in occasioned. The kitchen girl, Lucia, together with the midwife, Dame Berta, rubbed Guilhelma's flanks with oil of roses. For a while the air in the women's quarters smelled sweet. Through the window Guilhelma could hear a nightingale singing in a burst of notes that reminded her of Bernard de Ventadour's famous song.

Then the pangs began and grew more sharp, with less and less respite between them. Dame Berta took charge, banishing Douce from the room but promising that Lucia would call her as soon as there was news for Gaucelm. Dame Berta centered her attention on the patient, showing her how to expand her lungs, slowly drawing in the cool night air, then letting out her breath with a whoosh that made the candle flame next to her bed waver. This deep breathing steadied Guilhelma, but once or twice a contraction caused her to gasp. "I am too old for this!" she cried out once, but Dame Berta said matter-of-factly, "If you're healthy, age weighs but lightly in the balance." Guilhelma released her breath and turned so that her eyes fixed on the flame until it mesmerized her and she grew calm again.

The old midwife anticipated her every discomfort. When Guilhelma began to shiver and perspire at the same time, Dame Berta reassured her, "That's the way of it with some women." When she felt the rise of nausea in her throat Lucia came forward as she was bid and gave her a sip of vinegar and honey. When she grew intolerably hot they sponged her; they brought a chamber pot when she had the need, and a dilution of wine with water when she felt thirsty.

Yet a little knot of fear lay in her, buried deep in some space not occupied by the child struggling to be born—a fear as ancient as mortality itself. It surfaced each time the pangs came on; then she would take long, steady breaths and watch the candle flame flicker. When the pressure subsided, she dozed. The candle's steady flame was there before her each time she woke.

Faintly, the chapel bell rang matins. Guilhelma, eyes closed, breathed quietly. She did not see the midwife yawn, but she was alert enough to hear her say to Lucia, "I'm going to step next door for a bit of shut-eye." "No!" Guilhelma cried, suddenly aroused.

"Lucia will come and get me if you feel the need."

"Don't leave now!" Guilhelma breathed, as a wave of anxiety engulfed her. She was terrified that she would surely lose the baby the instant Dame Berta left the room. Bravely, Guilhelma let the woman go. Then she turned to Lucia for more wine, praying that it would help her sleep as well.

Gaucelm passed the night in Vidal's quarters, picking up first the lute, then the viol, and not succeeding at getting a coherent note out of either. Despite an attempt at insouciance, he was rattled. "I understand why the Church calls childbirth the curse of Eve," he muttered from the bed. "But why don't they talk about the curse of Adam, too?"

Vidal sat on the floor, unpacking, a task he had not felt up to the night before. From his saddlebag he withdrew a winter mantle, a light blue pellice for summer wear, and a yellowed silk shirt. He busied himself with refolding them, then added some linen underdrawers and black wool stockings to the pile. With this stack of clothing clamped between forearms and chin, he rose unsteadily and placed it carefully upon the bed. Only then did he address Gaucelm: "An unconventional view. Aren't new fathers supposed to be ecstatic?"

Gaucelm answered truthfully, "I confess that you find me at a very *pitch* of ambivalence."

Vidal laughed at the expression. "About settling down?"

Gaucelm nodded. "I'm not a marrying man, Vidal. You of all people should understand that!"

"You're on the mark there. But consider, there's a flaw in your reasoning."

Gaucelm looked at him. "How so?"

"You're not me."

"What makes me so different?"

Vidal executed a courtly bow. "Right, then. I shall enlighten you: I leave the women I get with child. You live with the woman whose child you'll get."

Gaucelm laughed. "A nice *cobla* if you could work out the rhymes!"

Vidal, a pair of slippers in one hand and a clutch of red-dyed stockings in the other, danced over to Gaucelm. His face a handsbreadth from his friend's, he whispered, "Marry her, Gaucelm. She's a good woman."

"What kind of life would it be for her? Tied to a troubadour who takes to the road on whim, who moves from court to court, whose eye is caught from time to time by other—"

Vidal put up a hand. "You mean, what sort of life would it be for *you*?" and ducked down by the foot of the bed where there still rested a scatter of belongings.

Gaucelm said, "All right, I take note of your meaning. But Guilhelma is well established here. She and the child would be secure for as long as they chose to stay. If we were wed, I promise you she would want her own house in town."

"And . . ."

"Vidal, seriously—you know the significance of my name, and my name is my nature."

Vidal flapped a hand at Gaucelm. "Significance indeed! We have already spoken on that subject. At length, the day we met: Faidit, son of the road, world-traveler, et cetera, et cetera. *Dieus*—'Gaucelm: the Story of a Strayed Bourgeois.' Your story and mine, remember?"

"But I don't have the added protection of madness. An oversight on my part."

"Marry her, Gaucelm."

"Well now, if I took up the cross, I'd have to, wouldn't I? No one goes to Outremer incommunicate. Would that satisfy your plan for our exile?"

"Worse things have happened to bachelors than marriage."

"On the other hand, thugs from the White Brotherhood might nose me out and string me up before I even got . . ."

"Marry her, Gaucelm."

". . . or Folquet might have his revenge on me for the '*Eretria*' at long last. He promised he would. You were there. You heard him."

"Marry, Faidit."

There were soft footsteps outside the room. The two men fell silent as Douce appeared in the doorway. "Guilhelma was wondering where you were." She addressed Gaucelm, who struggled to his feet. For a single beat the three stood motionless like figures in a charade. Then they all spoke at once.

"Has she . . ."

"Are you . . ."

"I am . . ."

They all laughed and began again.

Douce said, "No, Guilhelma hasn't, not yet. But the baby will come today."

Gaucelm said, "This is my friend from olden days, the troubadour Peire Vidal."

Douce smiled at him and, not missing a beat, recited, "**Ab l'alen tir vas me l'aire qu'eu sen venir de Proensa...**"

Vidal bowed to her deeply, cap in hand. "Merce, *bona domna*. You do honor to my small efforts."

Gaucelm said, "And this, Vidal, is Douce de Ventadour, of whom we spoke."

"The lady of the planh!" Vidal lifted his wine mug to her. Gaucelm noticed how he gazed at her hair. It was no longer baby-fine. Douce now wore it combed behind her ears and bound with ribbons like a sheaf of golden wheat. Her features, as he re-examined them through Vidal's eyes, had been perfected as though by a scribe famed for the purity of his line: her profile from forehead to chin disclosed no fault.

Feeling two pairs of eyes upon her, Douce turned to Gaucelm. "I should be getting back. I'll come for you when her time is at hand." She smiled again at Vidal and left, her skirts brushing the floor.

Vidal looked meaningfully at Gaucelm. "I saw the sparks fly from your eyes," he said. "I could practically hear your heart barking in your chest."

Gaucelm attempted a withering glance in his direction, but Vidal persisted.

"So that is why you will not marry," Vidal said. "May the Lord smite me dead if I lie. You are mightily attracted to this Douce de Ventadour."

Gaucelm hesitated, then snickered. "You've already discredited yourself as a teller of truths."

Vidal shrugged and dropped to his knees beside his open pack.

"Tell yourself lies, then. At least I understand now." He folded the pack shut and shoved it under his bed. "Anyway, I don't like the way you looked at that girl. She's nearly young enough to be your daughter."

Vidal was right, Gaucelm reflected. Whenever he thought about proposing marriage to Guilhelma, Douce crowded into his mind and pushed the idea aside. "She is twenty-three, by all reckoning."

"And you are thirty-three. As I said, she's nearly young enough to be your daughter."

"God's feet and balls, Vidal. I wish you would stop up your mouth! Pull in those wolf-fangs for a bit, will you? They will give me nightmares."

"And so they should. That's why wolves have teeth, to frighten people with. What did I do with that bread, the loaf we brought from the kitchen last night?"

"Not 'we.' You."

"Aren't you hungry?"

Gaucelm shook his head.

"Then what say you to a game of dice, now that I've finished unpacking?"

"I think I'd rather get drunk—this inquisition's set me back a pace or two. I don't take kindly to critiques of my behavior. Life was proceeding sweetly enough before your arrival, not that I'd have missed it for the world."

"Gaucelm, I'm in dead earnest for once. Take my advice . . ."

"And *marry Guilhelma*," Gaucelm thundered, pounding the wall next to him. "Marry, marry, marry her!" he pounded three times more. Then he suddenly stopped. "By all that's sacred under the sun, Vidal, why not? Maybe I will! It might be worth it just to get you off my back."

The wine had succeeded in causing Guilhelma to doze off, for she woke herself with a sudden cry. A great pressure bore down upon her from inside. One look at her face roused Lucia from her nap and sent her running for Dame Berta. Frightened, Guilhelma turned toward the candle, but it had nearly sputtered out, its wick swimming in a pool of hot wax and making jumpy shadows on the wall. The room had grown lighter; from the poultry yard behind the stables a single cock crowed.

Dame Berta came into the room, rubbing the sleep from her eyes. "Start pushing," she called to Guilhelma even before examining her. "Light another candle, Lucia. Put it on the floor—here, beside the birthing stool." Dame Berta placed a hand on Guilhelma's abdomen. Ducking her head under the sheet, she exclaimed, "I see the crown!" Now, wide awake, the midwife sprang into action. From an earthenware bowl on the dresser she scooped a mixture of oil and flaxseed, working it into her hands and up both arms to the elbow. "Lucia," she directed, "help Guilhelma onto the birthing stool. Quickly!" Then she positioned herself before Guilhelma in front of the stool. She waited. In that instant the chapel bell chimed lauds.

To Guilhelma it seemed yet another lifetime before the contractions resumed in earnest, but when they did they seemed almost a blessing. She shut her eyes tight against the pain, which came like a blinding light bouncing from the whitewashed walls of the chamber. She knew she had crossed to a new place where there was nothing to do but to let her own body master and overwhelm her in a way that no man had ever done. She focused on her mighty desire to have this child, crying out rhythmically, "Ahi, Dieus, Maria, Ahi! Ahi, Dieus, Maria, Ahi!" But she was amazed to find that increasingly, as the pain tightened on her notch by notch, she could withdraw from it until it became almost exquisite to her and she could view it as though from afar. If one had to be called to God, she thought, giving birth would be a useful way to go.

Finally, in a flush of effort the baby arrived of its own accord. Guilhelma, her eyes squeezed shut with determination, had to be shaken by the shoulder to see what Dame Berta was holding up before her, still attached by the cord: a solid, howling little boy, all wet and squirming.

"Run and tell Douce to fetch the babe's father," Dame Berta ordered, and Lucia, flush with the good news, dashed from the room.

The bells struck prime as Douce appeared in Vidal's doorway for the second time. Gaucelm somehow knew by her expression that he had a son. Instantly, all the petty concerns of the past few hours vanished. Alongside Douce's rushing skirts he flew to the women's quarters. There, all was calm once more and Douce, with her usual tact, began to busy herself with practical tasks, gathering the utensils used for washing mother and child, so as to leave Gaucelm free to take in his new role as father.

Apprehensively, Gaucelm stared at the figure in bed. They had combed Guilhelma's hair and it was spread out on the pillow behind her head in even mahogany ripples. She lay still. Her eyes were closed, and the candle on the floor cast deep shadows beneath her face, hollowing out her cheekbones. For one terrifying moment Gaucelm thought she was dead. But she stirred, sensing his presence, and moved her head in his direction. He felt his life surge back, his hands and feet tingling with the after shock of alarm at losing her.

When the pinpricks along his skin subsided, he was aware of a little gurgle from across the bed, and heart still fluttering unsteadily, Gaucelm saw his son. His eyes never left the linen-swaddled bundle as he skirted around the foot of the bed. He glanced at Guilhelma almost pleadingly for permission to pick him up.

"Go ahead," she whispered. And then, "It's a boy, Gaucelm!" In wonder he gazed at the blue-pink veins at the infant's temples. Then, awkwardly, he bent over the tiny figure and brushed a finger along the downy cheek. A delicious scent came from the baby's skin, like a sun-warmed white peach. Touching the child's forehead, he thought of Ayen, a village near Uzerche famed for its fruit trees.

Cautiously he picked up the bundle that was his son. The infant's head felt alarmingly heavy, and was rimmed with feathery damp hair. Two eyes widened, blue as the Mediterranean Sea. Gauging his heft, Gaucelm remembered that the birth had come earlier than Guilhelma predicted, but the child was certainly none the smaller for it. On the contrary, he could only be called strapping. The two eyes screwed shut in a grimace. "Ayen," Gaucelm said softly, bringing his lips to the puckered nose, and the blue eyes opened again. Gaucelm was enchanted.

"He cries lustily." Guilhelma had propped herself up against the pillow. "It's a good sign. He'll be a skillful singer when he grows up."

Something swelled and throbbed in Gaucelm's throat and he swallowed hard. He held his son very close against his chest, rocking him, saying "Ayen, Ayen."

The blue eyes remained fixed on his own. He looked over at Guilhelma in a mist of tears. "Don't you think the name suits him?" She smiled to see the two of them utterly absorbed in one another. "It's nice sounding," she said. "What does it signify?"

Preoccupied, he merely said, "I think you'll be pleased."

Guilhelma knew that Dame Berta would not let Gaucelm stay long. Drowsily, she held out her arms for her son. Gaucelm brought the baby to her and nestled him at her side. Then he took her arms, placing them around his neck and kissed her full on the lips, right in Dame Berta's presence. He watched as a flush rose from Guilhelma's throat and spread along her cheeks. He felt nothing but a rich, singing happiness. It was as though he had fallen in love with her for the very first time, at the exact moment he had met his new son. He had fallen in love with them both, and the three of them belonged together.

Impulsively he bent his head and kissed the inside of Guilhelma's hand. Dame Berta loomed above the bed. "The new *paire* ought to go now," she warned Gaucelm. "The infant must suckle and the mother must rest." She folded down Guilhelma's sheet and arranged the baby at her breast. Gaucelm lingered at first like a lovesick calf, but at a nod from Dame Berta became obedient and bumbled backward from the room, unwilling to turn away from the little scene.

Guilhelma's eyes followed him until he was out of sight. Then she fastened her fingers over Gaucelm's kiss as though it were a small, soft bird, and brought her closed hand to her lips.

Chapter 25

PARLEY

Gaucelm reclined on Vidal's bed, his boots just clearing the bottom edge so as not to soil the coverlet. If he raised his head the measure of a fist or two he could glimpse the silvery green puffs of olive trees covering the hills beyond Courthézon. By adjusting his vision closer in, he could view plum and cherry trees standing in the fields, wearing a halo of faint green in the afternoon light. In the coming month, if it didn't snow in this unpredictable part of the world, a hot Provençal sun would pry open their pink and yellowish buds. If he propped himself on both elbows he could see the stableyard, whose rich deposit of fertilizer would eventually encourage the sturdy wild roses to climb along the bailey wall. But he had come to view March's whimsical climate with mistrust.

In the days following Vidal's arrival Gaucelm had taken a small house in town for his little family. He had been prompted by both instinct and a low-rent vacancy. An astonished Guilhelma was overjoyed at having, at last, a place of her own. The move meant that Gaucelm now had only his practice room as a foothold at the castle. But with a second troubadour in court, Raimbaut made fewer demands on him, and he spent more time, happily idle, in Vidal's quarters.

Vidal, on the other hand, was busy earning his keep at almost every evening meal. He found his situation most congenial. "Thanks to you," he had acknowledged to Gaucelm, "I am content with both patron and audience for the first time in years of wandering. No telling how long this'll last, of course, but at least I've proved to myself that, given agreeable conditions, I am clever enough to stay out of trouble for a while."

On this morning he had taken a moment off from practicing to observe a bee hover in sunlight on his windowsill. Suddenly he had an inspiration. Laying aside his viol, he said, "Gaucelm, lend me one of your feet."

"And why should I allow you to take liberties with my feet?"

Vidal shrugged, "If gypsies can read palms, why can't I read soles? Besides, you cannot do it yourself."

"Nonsense!"

"Try it."

Obligingly Gaucelm sat up and, leaning over his belt, grasped an ankle. But the foot resisted his attempts to catch hold and turn its bottom up for inspection. "It's my boot. It's in the way," he puffed, letting the foot fall with a thud onto the floor.

"My dear jolly self-deceiver, it's your *belly* that's in the way!"

Just then the page Yves bobbed his head around the archway of Vidal's quarters. "Gaucelm Faidit! I've been an age looking for you. It seems you know this man?" And there appeared next to him the lean silhouette of Elias d'Ussel. Stooped and shaggy, he ducked his tall frame beneath the arch and raised a hand in greeting.

Gaucelm sprang from the bed and cried, "A thousand welcomes!" Elias nodded, showing no surprise at finding Gaucelm here. Then he ventured a glance at the rakish figure of Vidal, who sat absently drumming the floor with the butt of a bow. His wedge of black hair had recently been hacked at, though by no expert—that was obvious. He seemed to be humming a tune through his teeth. Elias made note: a noisy sort; something odd about him, and not just the hair.

Gaucelm came forward, placing a hand on the newcomer's shoulder. "Let me introduce the troubadour Peire Vidal," he said with a flourish. And then, grandly, "Elias d'Ussel, poet and partisan."

"I know your work," said Elias. "Very pretty, that *Proesna* song."

"You look tired enough to lie down," Gaucelm said, motioning him to sit on Vidal's bed. "What brings you here?" Then he remembered. "But before you answer, allow me to say how sorry I am about Gui."

Elias acknowledged the invitation with a curt nod but remained standing, stiff in his soldier's mail. The hem of his tunic, Gaucelm noticed, was worn ragged. "Has anyone attended to you? Have you eaten?" Gaucelm asked.

"I'm well provisioned, thanks. Though I've had nothing to drink since I left Mornas at dawn."

"So you've come from up there."

"From St. Etienne, actually, all the way up-river. My plan was to head straight back to my brother Pierre, who's with Trencavel at Béziers. But just below where I crossed the river at Sablons, I spotted an encampment of Northerners. Well over a hundred tents, maybe a hundred and fifty. That would mean almost a thousand men. They could only be heading south, and I don't like the look of it. So I rode straight here to warn Raimbaut that he lies just east of their path. Rumor is he considers himself neutral. Is that true?"

"He will tell you. Have you seen him yet?" Gaucelm asked.

"No, as soon as I learned from the page that you were here I came to find you. I want to know the lay of the land before approaching Raimbaut. Neutral—paagh! No southern lord can stay neutral these days!" Elias began striding back and forth like a commander rehearsing a campaign.

"Could they be headed here?" Gaucelm's voice was full of alarm.

"Courthézon?" Elias looked thoughtful. "There's little to tempt them here. There's nothing left for them in the whole area, neither at Montdragon nor at Mornas. Except, perhaps for Orange, there's no fruit worth the plucking until you get to Languedoc. It certainly looks bad down there—bad for Trencavel and worse for Raymond." He paused, chin in the air, like a hound trying to identify a scent. "If only the camp had been on the *other* side of the river, I could be sure. I'd put nothing past them, though. Those brutish Northerners could stop anywhere to rout a heretic or two. You've seen what's happened—even to small villages—all over the South."

Gaucelm thought back to the town of the Cathar buckle. His memory had not obliterated the charred stakes in the little square, or the stench of burned flesh. There were other towns like it, he knew. But that had been random destruction. What Elias was talking about appeared to be full-scale, organized war, and it was officially backed by Pope Innocent.

"How many divisions can Raimbaut call up on short notice?" Elias asked. Not really expecting an answer, he crumpled onto the side of the bed, ran both hands through his hair and stared at the floor. To no one in particular he muttered, "God save the South from learning her lesson the hard way."

"I'll go with you to see Raimbaut," said Gaucelm. "But first, have wine with us and wash up." With a grunt he leaned down and picked up a carafe from the floor. He poured some wine into Vidal's goblet and handed it to Elias. "Exactly how far away are they?"

"A week's march, at most." Elias drank up and held out the goblet to be refilled.

"It's not for nothing that I've had such dreams lately," Vidal put in. Startled, both men turned to look at him.

"Dreams of what?" asked Gaucelm.

"Oh, I suppose you'd call them nightmares. Last night it was a wild black dog in a cage, foaming blood at the mouth, eating grass and offal. Finally a pack of wolves kill him. An old crone is making a sign over him to prevent the evil eye, but it's no good. In the end the beasts tear his head apart and there lies the brain, exposed and torn . . ."

Elias slammed his goblet to the floor. "My stomach may be strong enough for battle, but not for such dreams as that!" He looked askance at Vidal, who resumed idling with his bow.

Gaucelm broke the awkwardness by addressing Elias. "Have you been to Ventadour?" He paused, held his breath an instant. "Any news of Marie?"

"I have not been to Ventadour. My sole concern was Ussel." Elias leaned over and picked up his goblet from the floor. "I can't afford to forget my lands, no matter what else is afoot. My renters think I don't know what they say behind my back while I'm gone. 'He's off raising troops in heretic country, while we work our fingers to the bone on his land.' I *have* to put in an appearance, even if it's just to collect what's due me. That's why Gui was without me at Montdragon, and for that I will never forgive myself." He frowned, studied the goblet in his hand, and took another swallow. "With no son to pass it on to my heart's gone out of keeping the place up."

Gaucelm suppressed a smile. Ussel was in disarray even while Gui was alive; by now, Gaucelm thought, it must have gone to wrack and ruin. He said to Elias, "I should warn you about Raimbaut. His world stops at the Rhône. That's the trouble with these Provençal lords. I also should warn you that he's no soldier. You probably know that he sent troops to Mornas – on Alphonse's side – but he's never once called up his men since, not even for a tourney. I've no idea how many vassals he could summon *if* you manage to convince him."

With a look at Vidal, Elias rose. "Thank you," he said, handing Gaucelm his empty goblet. "Now I'd best knock some of the dust from me before I present myself."

"Where have you left your things?"

"Out by the stables."

Gaucelm ushered Elias down the hallway. "One of the stableboys will draw you some washing water. I'll show you where the latrines are and we'll meet here," he pointed to a high-arched doorway, "just by the great hall."

Suddenly he was sick of politics, sick, even, of poet's talk. What he needed was merely to bask in the toothless smiles of his new son, but that would have to wait until the end of the day.

Gaucelm sent Yves to Raimbaut to announce Elias's arrival, then hurried to the practice room where he kept a change of tunic. He met his visitor by the arch, as arranged. "Tell Raimbaut," he urged Elias, "exactly what you saw, but exaggerate. Make it two hundred tents. Remember—ever since Mornas he's tried to stay out of anything that smacks of a squabble. And Mornas was seven years ago."

"He won't *have* his precious neutrality to worry about before long, unless he's going to go and *fight* for it!" Elias snorted. Gaucelm slowed as they approached Vidal's room. "Vidal's just recently come from Toulouse. Knows the situation there . . ." Elias cut him off. "As you wish," he said curtly, not slowing his stride.

The three made their way to Raimbaut's private chamber where, alerted to their coming, the Count of Orange awaited them. Three chairs had been assembled in front of his own. When the party entered, he looked up from examining the manuscript which lay open on its stand before him. "Welcome." He extended a hand to Elias. "Be seated, pray, and let me know why you have come."

While Elias spoke, Raimbaut remained by his reading stand, fingering the edges of his tunic. Elias took charge, giving a cursory account of his spotting the encampment. Gaucelm listened with misgiving as, true to form, Elias launched into his plea for the southern cause, exhorting Raimbaut to send as many men as he could muster to the aid of Trencavel and Raymond. "Look at the position they are in!" he cried. "One's a mere boy of twenty; the other, a great lord with his hands tied. You will need to call up your knights and vassals. You are not beyond danger, here at Courthézon," he added, hoping to rouse the expressionless count.

Seeing that Elias's words were totally lost on Raimbaut, Gaucelm thought it fitting to step in. "My lord, Vidal has not had occasion to describe to you conditions in Languedoc, which he saw at first hand less than a month ago. Pray let him do so now, for a northern onslaught seems certain, and may soon have repercussions for us."

Raimbaut turned suddenly to Vidal. "What have you to say?"

"Sire," Vidal began, "at Toulouse and at Saint-Gilles I witnessed terrible events, not the least of which was Count Raymond's humiliation before representatives of the Holy Father. I have felt the sting of Bishop Folquet's tongue and I know the extent of the power he wields. This is why I say that he and Simon de Montfort together could spell our doom and that of the entire South, with no regard for boundaries."

Gaucelm stared at his friend in admiration. Though Vidal's talents did not exclude eloquence, he had never imagined this! ". . . and Simon . . ." Vidal was saying. ". . . that man is as merciless a soldier as ever made the earth bleed. He is driven by a fervor that no church with a conscience ought to endorse. He is a madman, pure and simple. Simon de Montfort will stop at nothing. He will not rest content until he has burned and razed our lands from Toulouse to Marseille, and from Courthézon to the edges of Lombardy. Raymond has been silenced for the time being as I have said, and his nephew Trencavel is untried in battle. Between the two—a leader shamed before his own people and the other a raw youth—all of Languedoc lies open to be ravished by the barbarians!"

Raimbaut turned to Elias with a weary sigh. "These troops you have just seen below Sablons, if they originated in Lyons, I have known about them for more than a fortnight. They hold no danger for us. As for Trencavel, he is nonetheless the Viscount Raimon-Roger, liege-lord of Béziers, Carcassone, Albi, and Nîmes. Age matters little when you have a thousand levies at your beck and call."

Decisively, as though the matter had been disposed of, Raimbaut sat down in his chair.

"Languedoc has nothing to do with me. Count Raymond and his nephew are no allies of mine. By what right do you assume that I would want to come to their aid, for surely that is the sole reason you are here?"

Elias said, "It is true that I come as a partisan of the southern cause. I would like to see the whole South united against this northern monster. But if I may second-guess your thoughts, no—I am no heretic. My only heresy is the wish for unity."

"Be that as it may, there is much you do not—cannot—know. Believe me, my lord Elias d'Ussel, these Northerners, Frank and mercenary alike, will not attack Orange. Not now, nor ever." With that, he brought his palms together, as though to draw the meeting to a close.

Gaucelm, stung a bit by Raimbaut's inhospitable manner, could not resist the promptings of his own curiosity. "How so?" he asked. Raimbaut made no reply. Gaucelm continued, traversing the stony silence with what he estimated to be proper care. "Is it not logical to expect that since a war has been declared and an army has moved into the South, that sooner or later . . ."

"Indeed." Raimbaut rose, and paced back and forth for some moments in silence. Then he turned suddenly and stopped. "Well, let me tell you this." He faced the three men with a burning look. Speaking deliberately, as though to half-wits, he said, "Orange will not be taken because it no longer belongs to me. Years ago I ceded my portion of the seigniory of Orange . . ." Raimbaut hesitated, began again. "Look around you." His arm swept the frugally furnished room. "It can't be a secret to any of you that I have debts. Nor am I rich in vassals. By the most optimistic calculation I can count on but twelve knights—and not more than, say, two hundred and fifty men. The Mornas campaign was a disastrous blow to my resources. But even before that," he cleared his throat, "I was forced to dispose of my portion of a city—which has always been a thorn in my flesh—to help right my finances. I see no reason to explain more to you and indeed I would not be disclosing this much were it not that you've given me no choice."

"But Courthézon?" began Gaucelm.

"Oh, Courthézon! Courthézon alone of all my fiefs remains in my hands. But Courthézon. They're after bigger game than this township can provide!"

"I still don't understand," said Elias, his mind on Orange. "Why does your disposing of your princely seat render it immune to attack by the North?"

"Because, my dear man, I reliquinshed it to the North. The only takers were the Knights Hospitallers."

Gaucelm's breath stopped in his throat. He stole a glance at Elias. He dared not utter a word. Raimbaut had sold out to *them*, in order to pay a few debts. So that explained why Raimbaut never spoke the name of the place and never went there, though he was known to all as the Count of Orange.

Vidal gave a low whistle: "You've turned us over to Simon, then," he said under his breath, "by selling your birthright, and you call that immunity!"

"I've done no such thing!" Raimbaut struggled to maintain his dignity. "The arrangement is far more subtle . . ." He broke off, exasperated, and began again. "What do you three really understand of politics? The problems of Provence can be managed only by one born here. Provence has been bought and sold a thousand times in her history. It's not the first time and it won't be the last. My portion of Orange is under the stewardship of Aragon, to whom I am bound as ally. Why else would I have extended a helping hand to Alphonse at Mornas? Do you not see? The Hospitallers do more than collect the rents on my properties until my debt has been paid off. They are my protectors. In this way I've ensured the safety of Courthézon, which is still mine outright. Nobody's lost anything by it, and I've gained time. Is all this beyond the comprehension of soldiers and poets?" He paused, head cocked as though expecting some reply.

"I see," he said. "I'd have done better to keep it to myself. And now my friends, I beg you leave me."

They rose in unison, mumbled some parting words, and embarked on the long corridor with the gait of three men who had just been sold into slavery. When they reached Vidal's quarters, Elias broke the silence. "The floodgates are open," was all he said.

On his way to see Ayen and Guilhelma, Gaucelm's brain beat against his temples. The revelation of Raimbaut's political maneuverings had unnerved him totally. And all this time, knowing what he knew, Raimbaut contentedly played the courtly lord. Could *no one* open his eyes? His own best course, he decided, would be to introduce Elias to one or two of the knights who might see this insurgence in a different light and hope they would convince the count that he must prepare to defend Courthézon.

Before crossing the bridge over the castle's dry moat, he stopped to pluck a few sprigs of savory. To it he added a branch from a bay tree. He crushed the bay with a fingernail and inhaled its freshness. Guilhelma would be pleased; she particularly liked to use the leaf in her mutton stews.

Their new house stood near the top of Courthézon's steepest street, in which one dwelling seemed to sit nearly on the shoulders of the next. Theirs was close to the church of Saint Denis, yet within a few minutes' walk of the castle. Like all the others it was built of stone, but it was squat rather than narrow. It had two stories, unlike its neighbors, which had three. Above each of the windows facing the street, as over the front door, were solid wooden beams. But it was the house's split door that had won Guilhelma's heart. She saw herself unfastening the top half and leaning on the bottom to observe, whenever she had a free moment, all the goings-on in the street. And, because of their relatively high elevation, there was even a second-story view of the hills beyond Courthézon.

At his doorstep, Gaucelm determinedly silenced all thoughts of politics. He did not want to disrupt the peaceful scene which greeted him within—not yet. Nor did he wish to spoil his own delight as he looked into the bright blue eyes of his son. He took pleasure nowadays in seeing Guilhelma care for him, cleanse his gums with honey and rewrap him in his swaddling clothes after a bath. Douce had spent the afternoon with them and was sitting on a stool close by. Guilhelma drowsed, and Douce put a finger to her lips. Gaucelm could sense the awed affection she had for her new "brother." Unlike most womenfolk she spoke to Ayen as to a fellow being, not a babling nincompoop, and this opened his heart to her all over again. He could not deny it. Her presence disturbed him; her secret, serene demeanor haunted him still.

He shuffled about the room feeling a little dislocated. The table, trunk, and extra stool stood awkwardly away from the wall until their placement could be decided upon. The big bed had been wedged into a corner to make room next to it for Ayen's cradle. Piles of linen lay everywhere.

As Ayen's eyes began to close, Douce took him in her arms and sang to him softly. How unlike Guilhelma she was in every way! *And yet*, Gaucelm thought, *by some mysterious symmetry each has what the other lacks*. He glanced at Guilhelma, whose lower lip drooped in sleep. He looked at Ayen in Douce's arms and at Douce, lost in her rocking and singing. There they were, all together – everything he wanted. The idea of this quieted him. He came close and traced Ayen's features with his fingertips. The child was a gift from God, and he knew that from the moment his son was born his own life had changed. Here in Douce's arms lay all the purity of the world when it was new, a *tabula rasa* of absolute goodness, an innocence that Gaucelm, in a surge of desire, realized was within reach: the innocence of his own young self before the world began to knock him about.

He regretted having to break the spell. Bending over Douce's shoulder he said in a low voice, "Elias d'Ussel is here. He came to warn Raimbaut that there are Northern troops up by Sablons."

She ceased singing and whispered, "Was he at Ventadour?"

"No," replied Gaucelm.

"So, no news from there."

"None."

She hummed and continued to rock Ayen as though her sole duty was to ensure his sleep. Gaucelm was amazed that she showed no surprise at Elias's arrival, that this man who was the father of her first love seemed to summon up nothing of the past.

All of a sudden her humming ceased. She leaned forward, her voice, low and clear, "If Elias has come to us it is prophetic. He clearly came in order to convince Raimbaut . . ."

"We have already tried."

"When?"

"An hour ago."

"And he won't listen?"

"Raimbaut has turned over his portion of Orange to the Hospitallers."

Douce continued to rock Ayen in silence. "Then it is even more important that Elias succeeds in getting him to reconsider," she said meditatively. "Surely they will discuss the matter again."

"I doubt it," he said, then added, "This whole state of affairs could put Courthézon in danger. Raimbaut may be forced to call up however many men he has whether he wants to or not. But I fear we may lose Elias before all this comes to a head. He is bent on joining Pierre somewhere near Béziers."

"I will speak to Raimbaut," Douce said.

Startled, Gaucelm could not respond at first. The idea would never have occurred to him. He had to turn it over in his mind. True, she had approached Raimbaut once before. And though she had acted against his admonition, he had been forced to admire the determination that had prompted her, the very day after their arrival at Courthézon, to tell Raimbaut of Béatritz's death. But going to him with a request such as this was perhaps foolhardly, for it amounted to entrusting the future of a kingdom to a woman. Yet he could see, at this point, no other avenue.

"I will speak to him tomorrow," Douce added.

The question of her Cathar vows lay unmentioned between them. When Gaucelm had told her about the Northern troops, a tremor of fear rose and surfaced in her as it still occasionally did. For a brief instant she had panicked. *Have I been discovered? Has someone betrayed me?* she wondered. And then the feeling vanished as she thought: *Impossible!*

"Shall I come with you?" Gaucelm asked, stealing a glance at her. He did not like to think of her using her feminine wiles on Raimbaut. This was a mission of the most delicate nature, one in which religion might play a decisive role. If Raimbaut questioned the motive for her plea, she might be pressed to confess her heresy. But such scruples did not seem to bother her; her expression remained serene. "I'll go alone," she said.

"Then, shall I speak to him first, to prove the way . . ." His voice trailed off. She did not waiver in her decision. The girl confounded him. He wondered, fleetingly, if there was something of which he was unaware in her relationship with Raimbaut.

"No," Douce said. "I'd best go to him alone, in the morning. Beforehand, though, I should talk with all three of you, to know what happened when you met with him."

Sensible girl, Gaucelm thought. He looked at her with gratitude. He bent and kissed her fingertips where they curved around Ayen's shoulders. He watched as she put the sleeping child into his cradle and, with a glance at the snoring Guilhelma, prepared to leave before vespers sounded and the castle gates clanged shut.

Early the next morning before meeting the others, Douce sought out Elias alone. The aging soldier had to peer closely at her features before he could acknowledge that this was indeed the neighbor's child who had been so shy. Now she was grown almost queenly, with the same straight back as her mother and, he noticed with amusement, the same stubborn jaw. But she was charming, with her still-golden hair, and her confident manner.

To Douce, Elias seemed leaner, his face more deeply etched, his manner remote and proud in his soldier's tunic and leather boots with their squared toes. Away from Ussel, he seemed less like the father of her earliest love.

But she did not think of Gui now. Before her was a man secure in the ways of soldiering, a supporter of the Southern cause, and one knowledgable in the ways of warfare. She lost no time in broaching her intent:

"Sire," she said, "Gaucelm has told me how matters stand, with the North encamped near Sablons. I have not known you since Ventadour, but I know that you and Pierre are devoted to defending all of the South against these intruders. And I cannot help but believe that you would include Courthézon in your cause. Please do not leave us until the danger is over."

He looked at her gravely, and began, "Lady . . ." then faltered, gazed at the tips of his boots. "You have taken me much by surprise. I had no idea that you were . . . grown up so handsomely. But I cannot do as you ask, Languedoc needs me."

Douce grew solemn, clasping her hands in front of her skirts. Looking up at him, she sought his eyes. "I was with Gui when he died. For his sake, in his name, I ask you to remain at Courthézon with us until we see what danger we face. We might be in far greater peril than Languedoc at the moment. Look to your son's death as a sign," she said boldly, "and give me your word, Elias d'Ussel!"

His gaze returned to his feet. He seemed to be reconsidering then said bluntly, "Gui has nothing to do with it. My work is cut out for me in Languedoc. I cannot leave Pierre stranded there. It's too much for one man alone. No, I cannot make you any such promise."

"Very well, then," Douce said. "But let us be friends, in any case. Gui meant much to me. You, as his father, deserve to know how it went with him." Elias smiled and turned his head towards her, "I owe you much if, as you say, you were with Gui at the end." He took her by the arm and they stepped into the courtyard as a veiled sun slid from between clouds and cast its first beams on the day.

The four met in Vidal's quarters. Gaucelm was gratified to see the courtesy Elias showed toward Douce: once merely a contentious neighbor's offspring, she was obviously now regarded by Elias as a person worthy of his chivalrous respect.

Elias and Vidal recounted the details of yesterday's parley with Raimbaut for Douce's benefit. When she had absorbed all she needed to know, she rose and went to the doorway. She turned and warned them with a wink, "On no account is any one of you to follow me."

She returned in such a short time that the three men looked up in alarm as she paused in the doorway.

"Raimbaut wasn't there . . ." Gaucelm ventured in a dispirited voice, returning to a complex piece of fingering on the viol which he had brought with him to pass the time. But as Douce approached, Vidal noticed that she wore a triumphant expression. He regarded her, his head cocked to one side, and gave each word equal, dramatic emphasis as he asked, "What did you say to convince him so quickly?"

Elias sat forward on his stool. Douce hesitated, but only for a heartbeat. "There shall be no secrets among us. I said very little. I told him I required his word, before I left his chamber, that unless he would call up the whole Courthézon contingent, I would leave the castle before prime tomorrow and never see him again. He knows I keep my promises."

Chapter 26

ATTACK

At dawn, by torchlight, Raimbaut's vassals and servitors were arming. Talk in the hall was muffled as men slipped into the jingling hauberks held for them by their body squires. Senior men-at-arms, Elias new among them, stood before the unlit hearth, breakfasting on cold roast and an extra measure of wine.

Downstairs, housemaids and pages passed one another in unaccustomed silence. Guilhelma had taken charge of moving the provisions with a steady rain of orders. She had mobilized every serving girl and scullery maid, every poulterer, gardener, cellar man, and dispenser who set foot in her territory—from kitchen to hall—to fill this cask, take down that pot, load this basket to the brim. Two weeks of rest had restored her strength, and she could now leave Ayen in Dame Berta's capable hands. In the courtyard servants formed a chain, passing crates of eggs, braces of chicken, crocks of fat, and dragging jugs of oil, wine, and grain from the postern gate across the cobblestones to the ground floor of the keep, where Guilhelma had stationed herself.

Bonel stood in the middle of the yard shouting directions to those in his charge, his breath billowing in the early morning chill. Perspiration stood out on the foreheads of cooks and carters alike, as all pitched in to help. From the kitchen, iron stewpots clanged and gonged against their loosened hooks as the men struggled to move them to the keep's storage rooms, just below the great hall. In the stables, horses neighed restlessly; cows with young calves raised their heads from their troughs and mooed in answer. Ducks and geese dashed helter-skelter in the yard, squawking and colliding. Roosters crowed in pre-dawn alarm.

Guilhelma had not had a moment to worry about Ayen during the long, frantic night. Lives could depend on how the tower was provisioned. It had happened before that a siege's outcome was determined not by munitions and tactics and other male foolishness, but by how much food and drink the women had been able to store in the castle keep.

In the wavering pool of light cast by an oil lamp, Gaucelm and Vidal crouched on the floor of Vidal's chambers, their heads almost touching as they examined what lay before them. They were already armed and sweating from the weight of their hauberks, from the wine replenished too often by an overexcited page, and from the milling, restless crowding of knights and men-at-arms thudding about on the floor below. On a low table in front of their knees was Vidal's map. "Once again if all fails . . ." Gaucelm began, wiping his forehead with the back of his hand. Moving his arm seemed to him much like hauling up a drawbridge, so unaccustomed was he to the weight of chain mail. "About Marseille: You will have left word at the house of Azalaïs by Easter day. If I'm delayed, I'm to understand that you'll have set sail and I'm to follow on the next ship out. In that case we meet at the house of Lamois in Constantinople. Correct?"

"Correct. Now let's go join the others," said Vidal. "We should attend our gracious lord in order to account for his every action in song, for the benefit of posterity."

"Posterity be damned. If we've got to stand up there on the donjon and sing we'll provide the Northerners with excellent targets and posterity will benefit only from our carcasses. Damn his hide! He'd have us both in full view on the battlements singing like cocks, if he could!" Gaucelm yawned, adding, "Before this mess begins I want to have a word with Douce."

"What's keeping you?"

"I'm not sure if I can get up," he grunted. But saying so, he heaved himself from the bench and rustled toward the doorway.

"You do sound like a rusty catapult," Vidal grinned.

"Let's see what *you* look like when you rise, if you can, sir!" was Gaucelm's reply. He cast an eye at Vidal's theatrical efforts. "Rather like one of those articulated silver lizards that rich Arabs used to favor Raymond with," was his assessment as Vidal stood and attempted a stretch.

Vidal pointed to the table, "Don't forget that." Gaucelm picked up the map, whacked it back into its folds and, with a good deal of sucking and blowing, managed to stuff it into the pocket of his surcoat. "I shall see you atop the donjon tower," said Vidal. "In my lizard's disguise. Toss the lady a kiss from me. War—God preserve us!"

Douce stood watchful, in the courtyard entrance to the donjon. To Gaucelm, she seemed almost aglow. "What possesses you, ladyling?" he asked. "You look ready for battle as any knight!"

Douce smiled at the sound of his old pet name for her, murmuring, "I have been through worse than this will prove to be."

"Have you no fear, then?" Gaucelm's fingers flew to her flushed cheek as though to shield it; she pirouetted half away from him, her skin flaming suddenly. Avoiding a question she did not yet know the answer to, she pressed his hand instead. "And Gaucelm?" She still held his hand in hers, and drew him near. "Gaucelm, if I am captured, send notice to Ventadour along with the request that my dowry be given to the Cathars. This will be against my mother's wishes, but you have always known how to win her over. Will you see to it?"

"I will." There was no point in demurring.

In the torchlight, out on the donjon battlements, Elias d'Ussel's breath plumed. The smaller vats of pitch were starting to bubble at the rim. Behind every other crenelation was a good supply of rocks. The archers could be stationed next. But first he thought he'd better check the fire tubes and the stores of naphta and saltpeter in the charge tower, where he had left Raimbaut. Then he ought to question Bonel about the wells and cistern. He glanced ahead. It was those wall fissures that worried him most; there had not been enough time to patch any but the larger cracks. He spat fiercely and ducked into the staircase, checking arrow loops along the way, counting and re-counting them for the placement of archers.

Douce bumped into him as he bounded from the bottom step. "Elias d'Ussel,

I thank you for staying truly . . ." she began.

"I've no time now," was all he said as he sent her aside and continued, full-stride, to find Raimbaut.

Douce remained at the base of the tower for a moment: the donjon was new territory to her. Resolutely she mounted its staircase, feeling her way with feet and hands at each cold stone tread guided only by the light of a single torch at the top. As she emerged beneath the tarry heat and roar of the torch, her breath came quickly. Straightening up under the archway, she saw that the ground fog had lifted in the northwest to reveal, beyond the town, a field of dazzling white tents, each one flying its pennant of white silk marked with a scarlet cross. The countryside was covered with war horses in blazing mantles, some of them bearing multi-colored plumes. Siege engines, helmets, suits of armor all caught the earliest light of day and gave off their own fire against the rising sun. To Douce, it looked like some gigantic fair. She paused, wishing she had the magic to make herself invisible so as to be able to stay and watch. Instead, she went slowly down the stairs again, and into the courtyard.

The enemy moved on Courthézon just after dawn. At first light an advance guard of twelve knights in grey surcoats marked with crimson crosses rode forth, their banners whipping as they approached the town in a single file. At their head was Hugh d'Harcourt, trusted friend and deputy of Simon de Montfort. He and his knights would be followed by a full contingent of archers, men with liquid fire and lighted brands; by wagons and carts loaded with ladders and ammunition; by pack mules with provisions; by catapult and trebuchet, mangonel and battering ram; and finally by rank after rank of foot soldiers fanned out with unnerving precision. All were at the ready. For now, only the front line moved ahead, flanked by four Order of Preachers priests and a herald.

When the party reached the city gates, the herald was admitted with one of the priests. As they rode through the streets toward the castle, nothing moved but Raimbaut's black and gold standard snapping from the barbican. Overhead, a dense fog moved in. Great clouds spewed from the hills like smoke rolling before thunder. Beyond, the meadows lay in an unearthly, greenish light.

Closer and closer to the castle came the sound of hoofs on cobble and then the herald's sharp cry in the northern tongue: "Surrender in the name of God!" After that, silence. For what seemed a very long time, nothing happened. Gaucelm, standing with Vidal atop the donjon tower, shivered with cold despite the protection of his hauberk. It was impossible to see what was going on below. Around them, every archer was at his station, frozen in readiness, ears alert for the trumpet that would announce the assault. The only sound was the distant crackle of firewood under the main pitch cauldron in the courtyard. Still no signal was given. Gaucelm gave Vidal a look and leaned farther forward.

Suddenly there was a stir beneath them and a figure in long robes moved slowly forward into their range of vision. Gaucelm made him out to be the priest of Saint Denis. He was accompanied by a town elder. So there was to be a parley after all!

For a heartbeat, Gaucelm's heart leaped with hope. He leaned toward Vidal, whispering, "I thought Courthézon would refuse to make terms! Are we going to negotiate after all? Vidal put a finger to his lips in answer. Now they could see the two men gesture at the herald, then turn to each other. The herald sat in the saddle unmoved. As though on cue, the priest from Saint Denis advanced and began to speak. "He's inveighing against taking up arms during Lent, I'll wager," Gaucelm murmured. Vidal's comment was a low, derisory fart.

Gaucelm's mind shot to Guilhelma. She was, he hoped, safely inside the keep by now, with Ayen. His eyes remained fixed on the men who held the fate of the town in their hands. Finally they stepped away from one another as though some bargain had been struck. The elder shouted a word to the main gatesman who passed the command along, and soon, with a roar that could be heard plainly all the way to the donjon battlements, the gates to the town of Courthézon were dragged open. The herald gave a flourish on his trumpet and at the signal the enemy poured into the streets. One or two elderly folk, surprised out of sleep, surfaced like moles put to flight, squealing in alarm. Grabbing what came to hand, citizens could be seen running every which way, some toward the fields, some to the churches, some headed straight for the castle.

Vidal turned to Gaucelm in disbelief. "God's blood! Why was the gate opened?"

"The priest and the elder have betrayed us!" Gaucelm said. "God help us." He crossed to the courtyard side of the tower, but there was no sign of Raimbaut. Then he heard a scuffle, shouts.

He rejoined Vidal, who was hanging over an embrasure to survey the scene in the town. "Look," he turned his head and crooked a finger at Gaucelm. In the streets there was confusion, shouting, running, a thumping of drums. The Northerners had broken rank and were entering houses, grabbing, pushing, striking townspeople with the flat of their bows and swords. Dogs yowled, horses neighed, and chickens squawked in the poultry yards. Gaucelm thought of his little house, its furnishings not even in place yet.

His features were rigid. "Where is Raimbaut?"

In the midst of the mêlée, Gaucelm caught sight of a woman running, her night shift trailing, her feet bare. A grey surcoat was in hot pursuit. She tripped on the hem of her shift and fell back against the outside staircase of a house. He caught up with her before she could rise, forced her down against the stone stairs. In a flash he'd unlaced his breeches and covered her face with her shift. He had her there and then. Her cries were lost in the tumult as he rose and entered the house. She lay, her head turning slowly from side to side, unable to get up.

"Her back is broken," Vidal said, turning to Gaucelm. "Blood lust—it gets them worked up."

Gaucelm's knuckles went white on the edge of the battlement. Just as the rattling and rumbling, the cries and shouts and confusion seemed to reach an unbearable pitch, a second blast of the enemy's trumpet sounded to bring a halt to the pillaging.

The Northerners regrouped to move against the castle. For the first time, Gaucelm could see Hugh d'Harcourt clearly. At the head of his troops he gestured once, a mailfisted punch into the air with his sword arm. In response a war cry went up from his men as they continued their march up the narrow streets of Courthézon. On either side of d'Harcourt's retinue, banners fluttered. His soldiers clattered past the square, past the little Saint Denis now packed with terrified citizens, past the shops, up the shallow stone steps leading to the bridge over the dry moat, and then to the main gate of the castle.

What held Gaucelm's attention was not d'Harcourt, but the sight of his rear guard. Despite the trumpet's warning, in a show of pure contempt for the conventions of warfare, a company of foot soldiers was tossing flaming torches into every building that lined the way of their progress through town. Arcs of fire cut across the morning sky, many setting alight yards, houses, and shops. An alley of sheds blazed like haystacks, filling the sidestreets with smoke. On the battlement, in contrast to below, the silence was uncanny. Still no archer moved at arrow loop or battlement, though everyone was ready to leap at the least sign.

It came at last, that flourish of brass which signalled the defense. A deafening cheer went up, drowning out the final notes of the braying trumpet. Strings thudded on bows as the men scurried to repay the enemy for its calculated lawlessness. From every battlement facing the town a rain of arrows was unleashed on the grey surcoats. Immediately other surcoats began to mount their catapults. They seemed oblivious to the onslaught of arrows. At the castle gate tower, the ladders were being unloaded. First off the carts came the shielding skins mounted on wooden frames. Then the soldiers bellowed in unison as they hauled the heavy ladders from the carts and ran them to the castle walls.

Gaucelm, remembering his own duties, began to shout out the *Reis Glorios*. He was joined by Vidal, and together they seemed to succeed in calming the frantic archers, giving a rhythm to the pull and thrust of their bows, the reloading of the arrows, the settling back and firing. Soon the men themselves began to sing out the refrains, and Gaucelm and Vidal moved on.

They edged along the donjon battlement, winding their way through lines of archers, trying to avoid elbows as the men reached back for fresh arrows, skirting the cauldrons of hot pitch now being poured through the machicolations. Around the next corner they found Elias, supervising the firing of a light catapult. Behind him stood Raimbaut, strangely white, unmoving.

"Get away from that merlon!" shouted Elias at Gaucelm and Vidal, as they tried to pass. "Stay back!" And with a rush, the huge crossbow on wheels slid forward, let go a piece of rock the size of a small boulder, and retrenched with a sickening groan of metal against wood.

Elias rose from a crouch and faced Raimbaut. "Sire, if we could mount another engine we could mow down their front line before they have a chance to bring in their cats and rams . . " Raimbaut waved him aside impatiently; so far as he knew there was no other engine. "Use the archers," he commanded.

Elias, his face set, turned back to his men and gave a signal. Arrows curved into the air and found their marks below or bounced from the skin and wood shields of the enemy.

"Again!" gestured Raimbaut. Some of the archers reached back for replacements and found nothing. Elias called for more arrows. From somewhere a small supply appeared; the archers, in disarray, shot most of what was left, and watched their ammunition scatter brokenly below.

"Again!" shouted Raimbaut.

"We're nearly out of arrows here," Elias thundered back. Was the man blind? He could see the dwindling supplies as well as the dismayed archers. "How can I be expected to maintain a defense without weapons?" Elias exploded.

"Then use flames."

The man was useless. Elias would have to do it his way. He called to his maréchal. "Have the hot oil brought out." Then he wheeled around to face his men. "Flame what arrows you have left," he commanded, and went back to the catapult.

After the first round of fire-tipped arrows had fallen below, Elias called a halt. Staring through a crenelation, he saw what he had feared all along. The enemy had cast aside the few shields which had caught fire from his arrows, dousing them with wine and vinegar from one of the supply carts. The Northerners had used their time to advantage: under the protection of huge wood mantelets, a catapult and a trebuchet were being set up with rapid expertise just below the donjon tower. Worse, to the right, Elias could see that a formation of grey surcoats had wheeled a battering ram over the dry ditch and straight across the bridge to the postern gate.

Elias turned to face Raimbaut. "I can do no more without another engine. I need more arrows. I need more men above the postern gate. Otherwise we'll have the ram at us in minutes!" Raimbaut continued to stand like someone carved in stone. The postern gate, that opening at the back of the castle wall which led over the dry moat and out to the hills to safety, beckoned to him with promise of escape. Even so he had stood nearly all morning watching Elias direct the defense of his castle. The treachery of his town elder and that damned priest! They had broken every code of allegiance to him as their leader and had invited the North to enter Courthézon. Now even in fantasy there was no way out for him.

Treason! Raimbaut wrenched his head sideways, as though trying to wake from a nightmare. Why had God sent him a commander who wouldn't follow orders? And now this ram at the gate. Was he to be trapped in his own castle? He was afraid he might swoon. He turned and walked in the direction of the chapel, whitefaced, like a man in a dream.

"Sire!" called Elias. But it was hopeless. He turned back to his men, cursing the single clumsy catapult, his idling archers and the huge creaking body of the ram which, somewhere down below, would eat away at the castle's rear defenses.

Boom! Boom-boom! The ram sounded with such force from below that Gaucelm could feel its impact in the very soles of his boots. There was no escape from this assault. And the worst of it was trying to sing over all the noise, his nostrils burning with the pungent odor of pitch.

He stopped mid-refrain, aghast. An enemy helmet appeared over the donjon battlement to his left, then another, then another. With shrill cries they poured over the top, through the embrasures, armed with short lances and maces, swinging their axes. They were striking anything they saw, flailing at stone and steel alike, their war cries ringing from the walls. He and Vidal had left Elias and Raimbaut at the outside of the tower while they made their rounds, singing. But now Vidal was nowhere in sight. Gaucelm was alone.

Suddenly, he felt himself enveloped by the scrape and clash of iron. He inhaled the smell of it, could taste metal on his tongue. He drew his sword as a line of grey surcoats crashed by him, the last one splintering an abandoned bow with a single step. They did not seem to notice him. The prospect of hand-to-hand combat sickened him. He pulled on his helmet and fastened the mail neckpiece at his chin, where it tortured the hairs of his beard. With head and throat covered, he felt prepared for the worst.

None of this horror would now be upon him if it hadn't been for that bastard Folquet. Absurdly, his mind went back to Toulouse, his Toulouse of the old days, the open, golden city of his youth. Tears sprang to his eyes, hot tears of resentment and loss. He felt like a child overwhelmed by a great bully. The image formed itself with such clarity that silence seemed to form around him, as though he were within a sphere all his own. His resentment turned to panic. Disorienting sounds came slowly back. He forced himself to move.

They were coming over the wall next to the chapel bell tower, a moving ribbon of grey crossed with red and silver. He heard the cries of blood-lust and the scraping of iron and steel on stone walls. In that instant he understood how it was with war; how it wiped out every thought but that of staying alive; how there was, in the end, so little time for fear. The booming stopped. There was a flare of trumpets below, then a huge cry went up as the postern gate fell. Gaucelm turned away from the outer battlements and crossed to the other side of the tower, drawn by screams in the courtyard. As he looked down, his heart thudded wildly for an instant, then seemed to stop. There was Douce, running across the courtyard crowded with the wounded, a pitcher held aloft in her right hand, heedless to danger.

"Douce!" Gaucelm shouted foolishly, for she was far beyond earshot. He turned toward the top of the donjon stairs to go to her, but his way was barred by a grey surcoat, his crimson cross at such close range that Gaucelm could see no other part of the man. The grey surcoat reached to smack the side of Gaucelm's head with the flat of his lance. Gaucelm thrust his knee into the soldier's stomach with such force that the man crumpled against the battlement wall.

Dumbfounded at first, Gaucelm watched while his victim staggered upright. The little eyes were still screwed shut, the thick pink skin of his face was pouring sweat and the flaps of his bully's neck heaved with effort as he rose.

In a flash, Gaucelm understood he was being offered a chance of survival. This man had got separated from the others who would be at the opposite side of the tower by now, doing battle with Elias's archers. With a ferocity he didn't know he possessed he grasped his sword tightly and, drawn like a magnet to a tear in the man's hauberk, Gaucelm went straight for him again. With all the violence of one bred to battle, he thrust his sword into the man's unprotected midsection.

A howl went up and the figure before him collapsed against the wall. Gaucelm staggered back in utter amazement at what he had done. Shocked, he watched as a pool of blood spread slowly on the stones, the sword locked in his grasp.

A dozen heartbeats ago he hadn't known he could kill a man. Now he had destroyed a living, breathing evil. And yet it was not this . . . sin . . . that stunned him. In some way the notion seemed absurd to him. At that moment, he relished the utter rightness of what he had done. He had redressed the balance against Folquet, vindicated an old and profound injustice. He had felt satisfaction as his sword entered the bare place in the torn mail, as the metal tip drove past the ribs to find its mark. He was even glad to see the man dead, relieved to note the trickle of blood from the puffy lips that was proof of the last breath.

What made him uncomfortable was that he felt like an animal eerily set apart from the act of his own doing. He stepped away from the body to calm his confused thoughts. He said to himself, *I had the chance; I took it.* And having given voice to the words, it was as though the slate had been wiped clean.

With a mixture of triumph and dismay, he descended the staircase of the donjon tower. Only when he reached the bottom step did he realize that the fear, which had immobilized him just a short while ago—the sight of helmets appearing over the battlements—had entirely vanished.

He sensed movement behind him before he heard the exhalation of air. He felt the blow, then everything went black.

Northern cavalry were streaming into the courtyard. Unused to such close quarters, their horses wheeled and snorted and slipped on the paving stones, striking their hooves against broken swords and steel helmets, their eyes flashing in fear. Fresh supplies of arrows had come from the charge tower, allowing Raimbaut's archers to be stationed on every battlement facing the courtyard, which was now enemy territory.

Looking down from the donjon battlements, Elias was struck with a wave of nausea that made his scalp prickle. A store of fire tubes lay to one side of the courtyard. Some suicidal fool—no doubt thinking his action praiseworthy—had put them there. Now all those tubes packed with sulphur and tar, naphtha and saltpeter were sitting in the open, waiting to be blown to smithereens by the enemy. He raced to the stairs, determined to move or destroy the fire tubes before they could be discovered by the northerners.

Douce had decided that to remain in the courtyard, to continue tending the wounded, was foolhardy. She could help somewhere else. She filled her water pitcher at the well and set off, her eyes averted from the bloodied soldiers who lay all around her. An arc of fire cut through the air before her, its flame-tipped arrow lodging itself in a pile of hay not far from her feet. Douce ran and doused it with her pitcher.

As the fire hissed out she glanced up, saw Elias. Without speaking, he drew her to the stores of fire tubes, motioned to her to throw water on them. But she had emptied her pitcher on the hay. Desperate, Elias made for the well, dragging Douce with him. The fighting was so thick there that any access to water was impossible, "I know where we can find some!" he cried into her ear. Pulling her by the hand, he edged along the courtyard toward the charge tower, when there came a loud, insistent sound of hammering on wood from above.

"Look!" cried Douce, pointing up. Elias could hardly believe his eyes: stretching out over the battlement was a large wooden frame. *Whatever type of machine it is*, Elias thought, *it may be our only hope*.

Forgetting their search for water, Elias and Douce climbed to the battlement. They found Raimbaut's engineers at work on the machine. Elias realized the large wooden frame held a springald, an oversized, two-man crossbow. He supervised its moving to the edge of the battlement, and felt grudging satisfaction as a cry rose to greet its presence. Elias, against all his better judgment, began to see a ray of hope. Firing into close quarters was a risk he had to take: if it worked he could disrupt and scatter the tangle of cavalry and foot soldiers within the courtyard. But he knew, too, that one firing would not vanquish the enemy. They would have to repel the Northerners long enough for his men to crank back the bowstring, reload, and fire a second and third time.

"Loaders, at the ready!" he commanded. Bolts stood in a pile alongside the instrument in reassuring supply. Two archers, still wearing their light leather caps, readied the springald. The first strained as he cranked the bowstring tighter and tighter. The second stepped onto the platform, a bolt in his bare arms. But as he shifted his weight, preparing to slide it into place, an arrow seared his neck and he reeled sideways along the rampart.

In a flash, Douce darted out to the machine. Pulling her skirts to her knees, she climbed the platform, bent to pick up a bolt, and reached to put in in place against the bowstring. The second man strained to secure the bowstring into the lever. Douce joined him, pulling with all her might, until she felt her arms would leave their sockets. With the bowstring finally in place, her helpmate stood back, wiping his palms on his leather vest, and glanced in Elias's direction. But this was no time to wait for orders, with the girl up there doing the job of a strong man. His hands came down with hers on the release as he yelled "Fire!" Douce felt the springald jump. The bolt flew out into the yard below. Another man came running to replace her, and Douce climbed down. She sat for a moment to get her breath, her back against the battlement.

She did not hear the roar that arose from the courtyard. Her face and arms were streaked with sweat, her eyes closed with relief and remorse. *I have broken my vows a second time*, she whispered to herself. *In one moment I have undone all that binds me to God.* Numbly she began to cry, not bothering to conceal her face. Elias turned at the loader's insistence and saw, with impossible wonder, the figure of Hugh d'Harcourt, leader of the North, lying flat on the cobblestones, his helmet screwed sideways on his head, his body bloodied by the broken pieces of a bolt. His standard lay across his legs, which were splayed under him, so great had been the force of the hit. A glance at Douce told him what had happened. Elias turned her so that she could see into the courtyard. At the sight of d'Harcourt below, her face brightened, and for one victorious moment she and Elias clung together in an embrace that left them both weak with joy.

Even Elias, seasoned soldier that he was, knew that such moments were few in war, and rarely outlast the redoubled anger of the attacked. So it was for Courthézon. There was no time to celebrate.

"Reload," Elias shouted, and the men sprang into action, preparing the springald to fire again.

Stung with the fall of their leader, the Northerners went mad. One of them, in a savage skirmish near the stables, stumbled on the forgotten tubes of flammable substance and in the instant after he lit a flare to them the whole east wall of the castle rocked with flame.

From yard to tower, Raimbaut's archers and the enemy alike were sickened by the poisonous air. Only Raimbaut and a few of his guards who, with his sister Tiburge were sequestered in the depths of the chapel, escaped the sulphurous cloud which hung above the stables, causing all nearby to vomit and gag.

The Northerners, however, were not ready to call a halt. Their fury seemed to know no bounds. It was Raimbaut they wanted, and they were determined to take him hostage. A group of three Northerners guessed his refuge and, as though foresworn by a pact, made their way into the chapel by the side door, their swords drawn. A single flickering candle on the altar drew them on through the darkness to the spot where Raimbaut and Tiburge knelt praying. As the two rose in alarm, the soldiers struck Tiburge and left her on her back against the floor stones. They bound Raimbaut and his two guards, and marched them out into the courtyard. It was over.

The donjon tower had already cast its black shadow the whole length of the battlement by the time Gaucelm knew where he was. Against its cold stone he stirred, then came to with his head a-blur. A smell of gas, hot metal, blood, and vomit made him stop his nose with his hand and almost cease to breathe. From below came the uncanny cries of hurt animals; above the stables clouds of pitch and gas still hung in the smoldering air. Each time he inhaled he ached below the ribs. Some Northern devil had dealt him a blow, that was certain, but his efforts to remember yielded nothing. He longed to ebb back into his doze, with only the promise of a night in the tower, bedded in his cloak. The sound of fighting—brutal and relentless as the boom of the ram—had ceased, and there was an unnatural chill in the air.

Ayen's name came to him. He had a child! And where was Vidal? In a single, anguished reflex, he totted up all that was meaningful to him: Ayen, Guilhelma, Douce, Vidal. Would they be alive once he could move? Would his own life, miraculously spared, be of any use to him without them? He stirred in agitation, thrust out a leg and flexed it at the ankle. He felt sound enough except for his ribs and an ache above his ear.

Maneuvering his head back against the stone tower, Gaucelm looked up. It was night in the center of the sky only. The rest of the visible world was red and dully burning at the edges, like fire eating a piece of parchment. He expected to have visions, to see prophets, strange creatures of the spirit life. Instead there were the embers of a fiery holocaust. Gaucelm thought, *Now I believe in Armageddon; I am looking at it.* He had contemplated Judgment Day before without heeding it much; he had heard such talk in Uzerche as a child. Even then he had dismissed it, for it was on the tongues of town half-wits and alewives, superstitious folk whose only education had been in church, and precious little of that.

But for Gaucelm all had changed in the course of one lurid night. Not knowing whether he'd be dead or alive for the dawn made him feel reckless. He could believe anything. There was no longer a way to make anything safe—woman, child or friend. Perhaps the half-wits had been the wise ones all along. There could be an end to the world after all.

Gaucelm got to his knees and crawled to an arrow loop. Slowly, what remained of the castle took shape before him: the smoking breach at the postern gate, the charge tower half torn away, its exposed front blackened by fire. Below in the yard he saw a few writhing, dazed soldiers among piles of torn and mangled bodies—the refuse of battle on the place that had been Courthézon castle. He saw the figure of Raimbaut held captive, his head cast forward, his hands bound behind his back. A guard of grey surcoats stood on either side of him. This was it, then, over more quickly than anyone had imagined. He rested his forehead on his fist.

A voice—low, small, familiar—was saying, "*Pretz* and *paratge* are gone from the land. All honor, joy and chivalry have fled." Gaucelm, overcome with relief, threw a heavy arm around his friend's shoulder. Vidal, exhausted, fell silent.

The sound of footsteps, then voices, drifted up from below. As Vidal and Gaucelm watched, the four Preachers reappeared with a new vavassor, d'Harcourt's replacement. He was reading in Latin from a piece of parchment, with a local priest translating the phrases as he proclaimed them. Their progress through this formality was halting, made more awkward by the moans of the wounded all around them. When the proclamation came to an end, Raimbaut was thrust forward by the grey surcoats who were holding him tightly by both shoulders. He raised his head once, in answer to some questions, before the surcoats pulled him roughly back to the edge of the circle of onlookers.

"He'll be handed over to the seculars," whispered Vidal. "Lucky dog. There's hope for him, but not for these." He nodded as another man-at-arms came forth with a group of prisoners, a soldier or two among them. They too were bound, but they hung back, dragging their feet past the miserable refuse about them. Their clothes were torn and ragged, the women moaning, holding their children close to shield their eyes. Some seemed dazed, some merely stared at the ground, plodding along until they were stung awake by the flat side of a lance. On and on they trailed as though driven from behind, like sheep. Gaucelm felt his heart heave at every new face, half expecting to see Guilhelma's, but her familiar kerchief did not appear. There were three dozen at least, he supposed, and more to come.

The vavassor resumed his ranting as the surcoats completed their search. Every gate in the castle wall, every parapet and stairway seemed to yield another prisoner, who was then bound roughly and pushed by the surcoats into the growing band. The vavassor paused, and then spoke to one of his officers. The man nodded and crossed the courtyard, waved an order at a second surcoat, who entered the castle's chapel. In a minute he emerged, victoriously bearing Raimbaut's sword, helmet, and standard. Before him walked the castle's chaplain. And behind him came one last, tight knot of prisoners bound closely together. Among them was Douce.

Chapter 27

KYRIE ELEISON

It had snowed during the night. It was one of those desultory late March snows that subsided before blanketing everything, so that by dawn the black bones of castle and churchyard poked through the thin white dusting. In town it had dampened the smoke-charred house walls and feathered the steep streets. All night long the enemy bonfires had burned in Courthézon's main square. The sun rose slowly, a yellow light behind the clouds.

In front of the church of Saint Denis the Northerners were finishing their work with saw and hammer: a platform stood ready. From the church portals their banner, with its red cross, hung limp. Soldiers idled, playing dice barehanded on the frozen ground or seeking warmth inside the church.

Gaucelm and Guilhelma had spent a restless night in their little house, grateful to have survived the battle. Now, like all the villagers, they were summoned by the church bell to appear in the village square. They walked slowly, whispering quiet words of comfort to one another. They had not seen Douce since the Northerners rounded up prisoners in the castle courtyard.

Guilhelma gasped as they entered the square. There in the center, tripods of poles stood upright, tied together at the top, amidst straw, bundles of twigs, and logs.

"No," she cried, staggering against Gaucelm. "They can't…"

Gaucelm reached for Guilhelma's arm to steady her. Elias came up behind them, shifted his weight awkwardly and blew on his gloveless fingers. Silently, the three made their way into the square.

A full contingent of soldiers marched across the small plaza, their dress helmets, untarnished by battle, gleaming grey in the early light. Some carried torches; some, pennants of red and white. The prisoners followed. As they came forward, the circle of townsfolk leaned toward them, hushed, holding their hands out to touch for one last time the ones they knew. Soldiers elbowed them back.

Gaucelm searched frantically for Douce. *Please, let her have escaped*, he intoned in silent desperation.

The vavassor mounted the platform. The townsfolk pressed in close to listen. A church bell boomed again. As its reverberations died, the vavassor held up a black-gloved hand.

"Do you admit to having embraced the doctrines of that sect of heretics known as the Cathars?" he pronounced in a language few could understand.

"She never preached the heresy! She's no Cathar!" a voice cried out from the crowd.

The vavassor paid no attention. "Do you further admit to having received ordination into their rites?" he continued, then nodded toward the soldiers. The gist of the vavassor's questioning was painfully clear.

Three men stepped forward, grabbed prisoners and marched them to the poles. They pushed the prisoners against the posts, roughly grabbed their arms and, wrenching them backwards, tied them hand and foot to the posts.

"I am no heretic!" one man shouted defiantly.

"He never took the oath! He never harbored a heretic in his house!" a villager sobbed.

"Do you admit to professing and practicing doctrines contrary to the Catholic faith?" the vavassor continued, nodding at the soldiers to take more prisoners to the posts.

Just then Gaucelm saw Douce, shivering in her thin dress. His heart convulsed as he saw her hair, her hands. His dry mouth formed "Douce" over and over, yet no sound came.

"Do you accede to knowing, harboring and encouraging said Cathars in their work of conversion of members of the Catholic faith to their own heretical persuasion?" the vavassor said, signaling the soldiers to take the remaining prisoners. He watched silently as they were tied, several to each pole.

Guilhelma covered her eyes, overcome with the horror of what was about to happen.

A priest from the Order of Preachers stepped joined the vavassor on the platform. Declaring the prisoners to be excommunicate, he proclaimed their sentence for committing treason against French king and pope alike.

"Despairing of your salvation, we have committed your judgment to the Lord's reckoning," he announced quickly. He gave a signal. Two grey surcoats moved toward the center of the square, where the logs and faggots lay ready. With torches they set the pile alight. A third surcoat added pitch to the logs, making the pyre flame riotously.

Vidal squeezed through the crowd to stand with his friend. For once, he had no words.

Flames rose around the prisoners' legs, igniting their clothing and burning their flesh.

Someone in the crowd let escape a terrified cry. Some turned away, weeping. Soon the smoke blinded even those who had the stomach for watching. "***Kyrie eleison, Christe eleison***" wavered through the air. Was it possible that the prisoners were singing? The voices rose and fell as their number diminished. More torches were pitched into the fire to re-awaken the flames. Guilhelma clung to Gaucelm as they tried to force their way out of the crowd. But the soldiers held the townsfolk tightly in place, and there was no retreating from this hideous lesson of defeat and humiliation for Courthézon.

Guilhelma closed her eyes and held Gaucelm's arm tightly. Vidal put his hands on their shoulders. Elias stood with head bowed, eyes shut against the smoke. Flames lofted into the lurid sky as the townspeople coughed and wept.

Gaucelm was filled with such rage that he dared not utter a word. He strained forward, desperate for a glimpse of Douce. The smoke cleared, then billowed again; flames died then leaped anew. "Douce!" he called out frantically against all odds of her hearing him. His eyes found her face just as her head fell forward. He saw a swath of golden hair, curved like a scimitar, in front of her forehead.

He fervently prayed she was gone by the time her body went still, no longer straining against the cords that held it. Then, as the flames devoured her body, the ropes came loose and Douce, changed totally into fire, fell slowly forward.

The day with its numbing progression of events was over. It was the hour in which night turned toward dawn. Gaucelm had tossed hour after hour, dozing fitfully. When his dreams wakened him, he saw fire behind his eyelids, a dark red net of blood beating to the rhythm of his heart. Each time he awoke words came to him in a girl's voice, as though they were spoken by Douce herself, "Why not be wholly changed into flame?"

Had she felt fear? His mind kept returning to the seconds before her brain must have gone blank. Had she felt that? Was she afraid during the long wait? The trial, the moment they bound her to the stake, the lapping of the blue and red sparks at her feet—that would have been the worst part. After that there would have been only pain and the melting of all feeling in the roaring blaze. The pictures in Gaucelm's head would not stop.

She was dead. Why did she continue to torment him? Because he could not let her go. He turned toward Guilhelma like a child needing guidance. He looked at her face as she slept. She was snoring gently, as though she had already absorbed the terrible thing that had happened to Douce, accepting it as she did everything that life brought. He watched her with tender envy, wishing he could be as she was.

He sat up in bed, his head in his hands, trying to sort things out. He listened to Guilhelma and Ayen breathing quietly, their house untouched by the horror beyond its walls. In the shadows Elias and Vidal lay on the stone floor, wrapped in their cloaks, one of them muttering in his sleep. For Gaucelm, sleep was impossible.

It came to him: the fear wasn't Douce's, but the enemy's. It was the grey surcoats who were afraid. What were they afraid *of*? It was no simple mistrust of heretics. It was an older terror by far, one that went back to the roots of human nature: the fear of difference. He wanted to roar with anger and disgust.

Maybe Guilhelma, had been right about letting Douce go. But he could not bear to have her taken from him this way, eaten by fire. He found himself pleading with God, the way he had as a child in Uzerche, as though it were still possible to save her. *I'll let her go, en Dieus, but please not like this!*

He got up, pulled his boots on over his bare feet, and wove his way through the cobbled streets of Courthézon. He looked back at the castle and saw that the walls by the keep and the bell tower had fallen away, exposing the charred remains of the chapel. Ahead of him, the stirring of a grey-cloaked sentry asleep in a doorway reminded him that the town was occupied. He could be arrested for this. He could also speak in riddles or in dialect, make up some gibberish. He could play drunk.

He *felt* like someone who, used to peaceful sleep, is forced to stay awake, subjected to dreams hot with crackling flames. He sensed this nightmare would go on, that many pyres would be lit in this accursed, ill-fated land, this Occitania.

He spat at the cobbles and hurried on.

He came to the spot where she had burned. The cinders still gave off heat. Behind him, the church of Saint Denis was black in the cold dawn. He dared not look at anything around him. He knelt, wove his fingers together, and pressed them to his eyes. "Holy Spirit, help me," he found himself saying. And then to his amazement, he was sobbing. He wept in anger and remorse, rocking on his heels, back and forth, until he felt his insides grow hollow. Then his anger surged forth a whispered vow to her ashes. "With my heart and tongue I will avenge your death until I myself can no longer speak," he murmured. Wiping his eyes, he stared at the ground before him.

Not an arm's breadth away, he caught sight of a familiar shape, ash-blackened but still recognizable. Was this the buckle he had retrieved from another pyre for Guilhelma so long ago? If so, how had Douce come to have it? Had Guilhelma given it to her when they left Montdragon? However she came by it, he hoped she was holding it tightly in her hand at the last. Somehow, that buckle linked the three of them, perhaps forever, he thought. He crawled forward on his knees and furtively reached for the Cathar buckle.

He looked around him for signs of soldiers and, finding all quiet, got up. Then, wretched as a survivor of Armageddon, he made his way slowly back to the little stone house.

Chapter 28

THE MISSION TO MARIE

How very like Marie to keep him waiting. Damn her anyway, Gaucelm fumed as he sat on a bench outside the great hall of Ventadour castle. The feeling was familiar, that of a servant awaiting a potentate's pleasure. At the thought, he arose angrily and, in spite of his fatigue, began to pace up and down the drafty corridor.

It had been a long trip and would have been longer had he not fueled it with his overwhelming impatience. As it was, it amounted to nearly seventeen days' journeying broken only by changing horses. He had been in too much of a hurry to waste even one evening at dice. Instead, he had gone right to sleep every night after his wine and cheese so as to get a leg up on the morning.

Now, here at last after his headlong dash, he was left alone for an interval of time which, he supposed, she deemed sufficient to adjust his wishes to hers. The carefully rehearsed words of the plea that had been ready to burst from him now died on his tongue. *The imperious witch!* he thought. He could read her mind like a clairvoyant: she was determined to have her way with this treasonous troubadour who had left her service in a huff—the ingrate—and had the effrontery to become famous, afterwards, in another place. She would let him know to whom he owed what. And he, come on a beggar's business, was in no position to dictate terms.

The soft tread of slippers crossed the hall. So, she had sent a messenger. The countess would receive him in the morning. He was begged to attend chapel and dinner afterwards, the expected courtesies. Her plan revealed itself to him as clearly as though she had announced it in person. Very well, then, he would play her game one last time. He wanted something; he would wait.

He knew the room by heart. It was one Marie commonly allotted to guests, but when there were none, he had used it as another place to practice. He went to the window. In the waning light two boys in short jerkins were playing bowls, their bare feet kicking up little spurts of dust. He was stung by the memory of Douce at the game of horseshoes, her sleeve rolled to the elbow. He turned from the window and stared at the bare walls, but there she stood out even more brightly, as sharply etched as an illuminated figure in a missal. He caught himself. This was no time to be thinking of her, to go soft with remembrance. He sat on the bed and covered his eyes with his hands.

Ventadour, this room, seemed strangely diminished to him now. Being in these long-ago surroundings queered things, forced him to notice that an almost imperceptible shift had taken place. Perhaps it was that his own life had acquired urgency; time pressed in on him as it had not while he was here. Before Ventadour there had been Raymond and Bernard de Ventadour and of course Vidal. But afterwards, with Douce in his life, he had become a different person altogether. Secret angel! He took the Cathar buckle from his pouch, rubbed a thumb over the worn tracery of its encircled cross. Tears came to his eyes.

There, he had done it, allowed himself to dwell on her for the first time since the awful night he had crept to her pyre. Having begun, he would try to summon her up—but bravely, not sighing, not weeping. Without taking off his boots he stretched out on the bed and closed his eyes. He brought her back in his mind's eye, hoping that if he could just see her clearly she could lead him to understand the rogue part of him that had fallen away with her death and the more loyal part of him that was left. By her example, she had shown him another road, another way of being. And he knew that if he had traveled further down that old road, he was doomed. Was her death a warning or something else? By some evil alchemy, she had been wholly transformed by fire. Perhaps that—being transformed—and not death itself, was the meaning of heresy.

But no, he would not let her memory linger. Ventadour was leading him to revisit painful parts of his past. His duty was not so much to Douce, as to the living: himself, Ayen, Guilhelma. His real life, he reminded himself, lay in Courthézon.

The chapel bell rang for vespers. His stomach rumbled under his cloak. Marie had brought him to a fine state of hunger. Avarice, cold, and an empty stomach were the three punishments he couldn't endure, and she was forcing him to undergo the whole triumvirate at the same time. With a curse he got up and beat his hands together for warmth. Perhaps he'd go to chapel after all, if that was the price to be paid for dinner. Arrive late, stand in the back, see who was there. Deprived of company for so long, he would relish a nod or two of recognition, even the austere grace of the chapel itself.

Entering the nave, he caught sight of Marie's profile ahead of him and a tiny, familiar fork of fear darted at his insides. Still as stone was the outline of her face with its long nose, the angular jaw, the coif strict as a nun's, crowning the perfect economy of her dress.

During the psalms his eyes sought the ceiling, giving his presence an unaccustomed attitude of prayer. Above, the plaster was painted all over with diamond shapes, each one framing alternately a rosette or a single iris. His mind drifted as the celebrant's voice rose and fell. "*Laudate nomen Domini, laudate, servi, Dominum . . .*"

High up beneath the patterned ceiling the air was cloudy with incense and a noiseless host of unseen beings. Perhaps they were the chaplain's words taking flight. Vidal would howl in pain at such a conceit. The thought amused him. "*Homo vanitati similis factus est: dies ejus sicut umbra proetereunt.*" What is man but a passing breath, a shadow? Ventadour had always seemed haunted to him, its real life over and done with before his own stay had begun. But there had been great names. Shutting his eyes to the ceiling, he summoned up the procession. There was Bernard, of course, who had borne the very spirit of Ventadour in its heyday into Raymond's service. There had been the famous monk of Montaudon, whose verses every civilized person knew by heart. And Pons de Capdoill, and Savaric de Mauleon and Giraut de Calanson. Above all, there had been Bertran de Born, the warrior troubadour. After that he lost count.

Beneath closed eyelids Gaucelm saw them file past to the cadence of the

Benedictus Dominus. He had forgotten Raimon de Miravel—where was he now? There hadn't been a verse of his in a decade. Exiled, perhaps—or dead. Ah, but there was the young Peire Cardenal. And Arnaut Daniel, whose songs he admired extravagantly. The air was crowded with names; they pressed in on him, chattering, from the roof of the chapel. And not least was his own, which would take its place somewhere in the starry firmament of Ventadour. As he opened his eyes and gazed upward, the spark of an idea took fire in him. He knew what he must say to Marie in the morning.

While he breakfasted in hall the messenger came for him. The lady Marie was ready to receive him now. *Indeed!* he thought, but abandoned the last bit of bread and followed the page as he led the way. Though Gaucelm knew these corridors blindfolded, he nonetheless felt an unpleasant drumming in his mind.

He had learned while walking to chapel that Ebles de Ventadour had entered the monastery at Grandmont.

"Cistercian?"

"Of course."

"Was he ill?"

"Not ill, just old. Marie is his second wife, you know. And then, he never got over the death of his daughter."

"The one called Douce? I'd heard she just disappeared. Years ago," Gaucelm said ingenuously.

"Oh no, she was killed. Most horribly. Raped, then murdered."

So that was the story. Which one of them had invented this little tale, designed to incur sympathy and maintain the honor of the house of Ventadour? No matter; it would make his task easier, knowing that an excuse had been cooked up for Douce. Though unsuccessful at arranging her marriage, they had, he mused, decided their daughter's fate after all.

Gaucelm stepped into Marie's room. It was as it had always been, hung with precious tapestries from Arras, the bed with its fur throw, the floor strewn with herbs. Marie stood by the window in half-profile as though not quite ready to concede her visitor's presence.

He had decided to be forthright with her, and to get it over with as soon as possible. He fingered the Cathar buckle inside its leather bag. "I have come with some sad news," he began. "Your daughter was burned at the stake as a martyr not three weeks ago."

Marie made no move.

"Douce is dead, Countesa. I am sorry."

"That's impossible. What on earth do you mean!" She turned to face him, her hand still on the casement.

"I mean just that. She was burned at the stake in Courthézon, after the town was taken by Northerners." He watched her as she struggled with the facts, relinquishing little by little her own fabrication of Douce's death. Stalling, she asked, "By whom, exactly? Taken by whom?"

He decided just to answer questions, for the present. "By Hugh d'Harcourt, a deputy of Simon de Monfort." Dieus, but she stood straight as ever. It was only when she turned that he could scrutinize her face, could see how her skin was creased with a maze of fine lines.

"I have heard of them."

"Lady, I have not time to recount the events. You will undoubtedly hear them in detail soon enough. Allow me to put to you the request . . . the last request . . . of your daughter."

"My daughter has been dead to me for years. I have no desire to hear of her. In fact I must tell you that I do not believe you, Gaucelm Faidit. I do not believe what you say."

"Here, madam . . ." He extracted the buckle from its pouch. "I give you this. It belonged to Douce. I recovered it from her ashes."

Marie winced at the word, stretched out her arm toward the object, then pulled back. She waved a hand at the buckle. "I want no proof of her folly! I have said that she is dead to me these past years. For that, I need no proof."

He repocketed the buckle. "Madam, she died a heretic . . ."

Marie's jaw clamped shut. A muscle above her jawbone bulged. He read her expressions: she would give Gaucelm no evidence of her surprise or displeasure.

Marie released her hand from the casement and turned full-faced toward Gaucelm. She asked, "What do you want of me?"

"Douce . . ." he took a breath. "Douce, before she died, charged me with a promise. I must explain to you that she had for years been a Cathar, having practiced the rituals of that faith. She lived quite simply and was happy with . . ."

"Spare me the details, Gaucelm."

He straightened. "She lived with us at Courthézon castle, in the service of Count Raimbaut d'Orange." Marie nodded her recognition of the name. "Elias d'Ussel was with her when she fired the bolt that killed d'Harcourt." Marie raised her eyebrows, causing deep furrows to appear under her coif. Gaucelm, master that he was at arousing curiosity, decided to leave the subject of Douce's heroic action dangling.

"I suppose you have come for money," she said. "Though I cannot imagine in what cause. Did you support . . . her?"

"She earned her keep at the castle by honest labor," he replied, choosing not to elaborate on Douce's humble position there. But Marie surprised him. Suddenly she was all magnanimity and concern.

"Tell me, Gaucelm . . . first let us sit." and she motioned him to a cushioned chair. "Tell me something of your life. You left Ventadour without per-per- . . . without notice." She fanned her fingers against her skirt in self-restraint. I know of your fame. One would have to be deaf not to hear your songs. It is gratifying that your name will always be connected to Ventadour. But your whereabouts, I've heard nothing in all these years. And you look, somehow di-dif- . . . different." That familiar stutter.

"I am older, my lady."

"It is the beard, I think."

"Perhaps. But to tell you . . . well, it would be a long tale, my lady, and I hesitate to begin. I have seen much of war, yet I have been luckier than most. What grieves me above all is to see the South in flames. With God's help some of it will survive, though in what condition is anybody's guess. Perhaps a market town here, a church there will be spared. In any case, the land itself will never forget. Oh, I have many tales to tell, but time is short."

If she could be curt, he would counter with his characteristic expansiveness. They were right back to the old game of chess, he thought, the bartering of words that finally drove him from her court. But this time, he supposed, the game was in earnest; he, certainly, was playing for real stakes. As a first move, he had at least succeeded at provoking her interest.

"No, pray continue," she said, "I am not hurried this morning."

"Soon there will be none of us left, you know. We troubadours seem to be a dying breed."

She rose, spreading the fingers of both hands again, as though to smooth her skirt. A futile gesture: he had his prey. She moved to the window and looked out, as though searching for support in the view outside. He would wait for her to drop into his palm. But she pre-empted his silence.

"If Douce earned her keep and Raimbaut d'Orange pays yours, why have you come to me?"

"It is not for myself that I ask. Besides, Raimbaut has been brought to his knees by the enemy. He is ruined."

"Then out with it! I won't be d- dan- dandled like this!" She turned on him, flushed with a mix of impatience and curiosity. If he wasn't careful, his plan could go to pieces with one misjudged word. He replied with passion:

"I ask for a discreet sum—what is in fact, Douce's dowry. And none too soon. The armies of Simon de Montfort move with demonic speed, devouring everything in their path." The words tumbled from him, there was no stopping him now. "The North speaks a barbaric tongue. When the dust has settled, who will be left to sing the language of the South?" From a low stand near the window, Marie lifted a bowl of yellow winter apples and a pearlhandled fruit knife.

He went on: "We are either old or already plowed under the rubble of Northern skirmishes. God knows who amongst us has perished and it is only the beginning. My lady . . ." The idea that had occurred to him in the chapel overcame him with its urgency.

He leaned forward, choosing his words to win her. "We troubadours are a tribe of laborers in the soil of words; our yield has been a language that is the soul of all southern people. It is fitting that, as you know, there are princes among us, and woodcutter's sons like Bernard, who bore the name of this place. There are farmers, warring knights; we are a democracy, not an effete circle of foppish poetasters weaving a language for one another's delectation."

Gaucelm sat back. It was *his* fight now, not just a vow made to a dead girl. Marie offered him an apple which he waved away, wishing only that she would sit down and focus on what he had to say. Hunched forward again, elbows on his knees, he resumed his plea. "Lady Marie, we have made the voice of the South a living voice. We are a whole race of servants to a tradition, a tradition which you, as much as any patron known to me, have helped carry to its height. Do not let us die out! For when we are gone, and the roots of our ancestors broken up by some new conqueror's plough, our words will no longer remain to mark the ancient ways. The link—for it is such—with furthest antiquity, with ancient learning and with future generations, will be broken forever."

She sat down at last and cut into the apple with the pearlhandled knife.

"Marie de Ventadour, you know this as you know your own name: that in singing about our native land we have helped create it, just as in the making of songs of love we have shown new ways of loving. Lady, I *beg* you to remember what you yourself have accomplished here at court, at Ventadour, for all the world to know. You have housed us, listened to us, encouraged us, in the name of the land you love. We have asked little more from you, for poets are but humble custodians of the past."

A faint sweet cloud of scent rose from the fruit, distracting him even as his words rolled out. "But the past is shrinking beyond our grasp, courage fails us, and the future of our land and its tradition frightens us . . . Marie! Will you allow us to perish, after all you have done? My lady knows as well as anyone alive that, as long as men want their achievements sung, as long as women desire their beauty and generosity praised, the world will have need of poets."

A sinuous golden peel from her apple dropped into the bowl. "Gaucelm, you are eloquent as ever," was all she said.

It was over. He stood. He grazed her rings with his lips and went back to his room, exhausted. *That infuriating woman*, he thought.

He began to pack. As he rolled the last of his belongings into his saddlebags, a page appeared at the doorway. "Enter!" Gaucelm grunted. "My lady sends this," the boy said, handing Gaucelm a scrap of parchment. On it Marie had scribbled, "Since you left no troubadour of note has graced this court. You say the Count of Orange is ruined. Consider my offer to return, Gaucelm."

He looked up as the page left the room, then re-entered with a heavy bundle which he heaved onto the bed next to the saddlebags. As it settled, the rushing sound of coins inside made Gaucelm smile.

Gaucelm slowed his palfrey, reckoning a trot to be the perfect gait for reflection. His mission accomplished, he could take his ease awhile, before the journey back to Courthézon would begin to tax his stamina. It was astonishing how just a few hours in the saddle put things in perspective. He could not have predicted that his eternal tug-of-war with Marie would turn out the way it had. The victory was his—not only in the guise of Douce's dowry, but in his having put Marie in the position of supplicant for the first time. Again he savored her message. Return, indeed!

He was well pleased at how he had earned the coins that rode in the saddlebags behind him. He ran through what he had said to Marie, reviewing with relish its effect on her. He had made the Pope's crusade real before her eyes. *Well,* he thought grimly, *it is real enough, and here I am heading straight back into it.* Who knew where the North would strike next? Truly, the times were turned upside down.

Letting the horse ease to a walk, he recalled the opening bars of *"Ai resplan la flors enversa."* It was the best thing Raimbaut's uncle had composed. Funny how he hadn't thought about *that* Raimbaut in ages. A considerable talent, far greater than his nephew's; must have been a charming man. Gaucelm sang, modifying the rhythm to his horse's hoofbeat:

> **I turn the whole world upside down**
> **I see the plains as little hills**
> **And take the frost and snow for flowers;**
> **My verses make the biting wind**
> **Seem soft and warm as ladies' bowers...**

There it was. That was the poet's power, to overturn the facts. Only verse could perform this kind of magic. He thought of his wounded Courthézon. If only he could conjure up a different ending for the town's fate. Irritated, he switched the reins to his other hand. Could verse extract some meaning from that tragic defeat? At least, he reflected, if it could not explain the horror and the atrocities of war, it could bear witness.

Gaucelm felt his shoulders grow cold as clouds gathered above. He looked up and saw a new moon rising in the east. He thought of Bernard, the *"Eretria,"* the planh for Douce—everything had led him to this point. Why should *he* not be the chronicler of this time of war, of what had happened to Courthézon and of what had gone before? He felt himself ready for a challenge he could give his heart to. *This is what Bernard de Ventadour meant,* he thought. *Bernard gave me a mandate to reach beyond convention, to "find," to "tell" in a new way, and so I will.*

He would go further, he would make what he was to say count: he would write it down. Here was an act to defy convention! No troubadour yet had committed a song to script, not even those who knew how to form their letters. It had always been thus, that after the troubadour had sung his verses the jonglars and jonglaressas would see to it that his words were picked up, carried along, fed into the great stream of cansons which enlivened every market square and village inn and noble court, wherever human beings gathered to listen. If the troubadour's words weren't worth repeating they died a natural death. That was the fate deserved by any craftsman whose work was ill-made.

But a new situation demanded a new set of rules. They cried out for *testimony*. There must be witness to these calamities, even though in committing what he had seen to vellum he would be risking his own future. This was revenge of which he could be master. It fit the purposes of his vow to Douce exactly. And so in place of dread, he marvelled at the thrill that raced through his body like a shock of lightning.

He itched to be forming the letters. He would start by bearing witness to what he had seen, beginning with Bertrand's head, white and staring, on that second morning after his arrival in Toulouse. He would document the charred bones he and Guilhelma had come upon at the base of a burnt-out cross on their way across the country to Ventadour. He would tell about ransacked houses, the horses snorting at the smoke, the dogs wandering in the rubble, and how he snatched the Cathar buckle from the pitiful cinders.

He would recount the deaths of Béatritz and of Gui. He would resurrect the noble heart of Douce. He would tell all, not letting up until the war was over or he was dead. The Pope's outrage against the heretics would be an epic that no one who read or heard it would forget. To seal his vow to himself, he said aloud: "This shall not pass from memory—*en la pena e la dolor e.l martire*—though it cause me pain and hardship and even death, so long as I am Gaucelm."

Here was his chance to be a poet at last, a truth-teller. Bernard's legacy to him felt completely right. It fit well, as though Bernard himself had just dropped his mantle onto Gaucelm's shoulders from heaven.

There was a hush in the air as night came on. The faint breeze died down as it always did before dusk, leaving the spikes of lavender upright in the fields and stilling the branches of wild rosemary bushes so that Gaucelm could identify the scent of each, along with the odor of dense red clay beneath the palfrey's hooves. *Proensa!* Vidal was right: wherever he had been born, wherever he ended, the South was home.

He thought of Guilhelma, and his hand went instinctively to the Cathar buckle, still there in his pouch. Rescued from Douce's ashes, refused by Marie, it came to him that the buckle's presence was a sign: its rightful owner was Guilhelma, and it seemed natural, in the way of things, that he should be bringing it back to her. She was his; he was hers. It was as though some unseen hand had set them beside one another. Somewhere, deeply, he had known that this was so. Vidal and Douce had seen it, plain as day. But he had been all but blind to her, until the morning of Ayen's birth, when he had kissed her and seen the flush rise in her cheeks. He struck his forehead with the hand that held the reins, causing the palfrey to bring his head up sharply in surprise. What a fool he had been! It had taken a battle, a martyrdom, and a journey north to prove to him that he and Guilhelma belonged together.

Now he knew that at the end of this road, the route back to Courthézon, there lay one certainty: he would beg her forgiveness. He would ask Guilhelma to be his wife.

He took a deep breath and glanced up. The clouds had parted and a single star was blooming in the night sky.

His star. He nodded to it.

GLOSSARY

A-B

anathema: an ecclesiastical curse involving excommunication

aquamanile: a basin, often made in grotesque animal forms

arrow loop: slits or cross-shaped openings in castle walls from which arrows could be launched

aubade: song about the parting of two lovers at dawn

auto-da-fé: public penance; punishment of condemned heretics

bailey: the outer wall of a medieval castle, or the wall surrounding the keep

barbican: a fortified outpost or gateway protecting a city or castle; a defensive tower over a gate or bridge

besant: a small gold coin

bliaut: an overgarment with voluminous skirts

bolt: a short, stout, usually blunt-headed arrow

C-E

cami roumieu: Pilgrims' Road

canson: song

caparison: an ornamental covering spread over a horse's saddle or harness

chatelaine: wife of the lord of a castle

chauss: medieval armor of mail or tights for the legs and feet

coif: a hood-shaped cap, usually of white cloth and with extended sides, worn beneath a veil

compline: a service of evening prayers

cortesia: courtly love

cotte: a tight-fitting tunic

croyant: Cathar believer

crozier: a hooked staff carried by a bishop as a symbol of pastoral office

dandled: toyed with

demiard: quarter of a pint of wine

desmene: land attached to a manor and retained for the owner's own use

destriers: war horse

donjon: the inner tower, keep, or stronghold of a castle; the dungeon

enceinte: an enclosing wall of a fortified place

envoi: a brief concluding stanza, a dedication or postscript

épicier: a spice vendor

eyase: a baby falcon

F-K

faggot: a bundle of sticks or twigs bound together as fuel

fermail: a medieval clasp for clothing

gittern: a stringed musical instrument

hauberk: a shirt of mail

jonglaresa: a female entertainer

kalends: the first day of each month

keep: innermost and strongest structure or central tower of a castle

Knights Hospitallers: a Christian military order that was very powerful during the Middle Ages

L-N

lauds: a canonical hour marked by psalms of praise, usually at dawn

laver: a basin, bowl, or cistern to wash in

leveé: a reception of visitors held on rising from bed, as formerly by a royal or other personage

lointaine: distant princess, an ideal but unattainable woman

mangonel: a type of catapult

mantelet: a moving shelter used by besiegers

machicolations: projecting parapets on a castle

marchpane: marzipan

maréchal: marshal; farrier

matins: the first canonical hour, beginning at midnight or sometimes daybreak

medlar: a type of crabapple

merlon: the solid part of a crenelated wall

miniver: a fur of white or spotted white and gray used for linings and trimmings; particularly ermine, used especially on robes of state.

nappe: a length of fabric, which is used as a cover, sheet, or tablecloth

nef: a silver or gold table furnishing in the form of a ship

nones: the fifth of the seven canonical hours, 3 P.M.

O-P

Order of Preachers: founded by a Spanish priest in France to preach the gospel and combat heresy more commonly known after the 15th century as the Dominican Order

palfrey: a stable horse, as distinguished from a war horse (destrier)

paratge: an equality that transcends rank, a recognition of merit

Parfait/Parfaite: a Cathar who has performed a special rite and become a leader among Cathars, known also as the Elect or *perfecti*

partimen: a lyric poem in which one poet states a proposition and the second disputes it, similar to the tenson though shorter and less personal

pelisse: a short - or fur-trimmed

pelisson: dress

pelouse: the grass strip of a castle, inside the outer wall

perfecti: a Cathar who ministers and preaches to others, has taken a vow of austerity, and observes special constraints, including having no physical contact with the opposite sex; also known as parfait or goodman

pillion: a pad or cushion attached behind a saddle

planh: a Provençal elegiac poem, lamentation

poetaster: a person who writes inferior poetry

portcullis: a strong iron grate made to slide vertically and close off a fortified place

postern gate: a back door or gate; a private entrance or any entrance other than the main one

pretz: valor or worth

prime: the second of the seven canonical hours of the divine office, originally fixed for the first hour of the day, at sunrise

Q-S

quatrain: a stanza or poem of four lines, especially one having alternate rhymes

quenelle: a poached dumpling of finely chopped fish or meat

Rai Mundi "Light of the World"—nickname for Raymond

Reis Glorios: the dawn song, Glorious King, composed by Giraut de Bornelh, considered Master of the Troubadours

samite: a heavy silk fabric

seigniory: a feudal domain

senhal: a love poem; the nickname given by the author to the woman he loves

sext: the fourth of the seven canonical hours or the service for it, originally the sixth hour of the day, taken as noon

siege engines: battering rams, catapults and such

sirventes: a poem or song of heroic or satirical character

solar: a room in many medieval English and French manor houses, great houses, and castles, generally situated on an upper story, designed as the family's private living and sleeping quarters

solatz: comfort

T-W

taking says: having someone sample food to assure it is not poisoned

tenson: a Provençal poem taking the form of a dialogue or debate between two rival troubadours

terce: three or third

tisane: herbal tea

trobar clos: closed form; a complex and obscure style of poetry used by troubadours for their more discerning audiences

vair: squirrel fur

vavassor: second in command

villein: a peasant personally bound to his lord for dues and services, but otherwise free

wimple: a piece of cloth draped around the head to frame the face

PUBLISHER'S NOTE & ACKNOWLEDGMENTS

My sister Clara's love for the Middle Ages began early. When asked in a high school history class why knights went on crusades, she replied "because they wanted to carry crosses." She learned Provençal—the language of medieval southern France—in college. It was only natural for her, as a writer, to write novels about this area, and era, that she loved.

Clara and I grew up in a family of writers. Our mother, Emma May (MacIntyre) Grossman, taught English literature in the Philadelphia Public Schools. She made the decision that this was her profession when she was in third grade, and pursued it despite major obstacles. Our father, Louis Grossman, came to this country when he was 4 years old. Although he wanted to be a physician, his family could only afford to send him to dental school. He perfected the technique of saving teeth by endodontia (root canal therapy), but became famous by writing professional papers and books.

Clara and Richard

The seed for the story about the troubadour Gaucelm Faidit was planted when Clara lived in France for a year in the mid-1970s. It germinated and grew slowly, taking more than twenty-five years to come to fruition. Clara and I never discussed her inspiration for this book, but I suspect that our own upbringing played a part. We were brought up as members of the Religious Society of Friends (Quakers). We both graduated from Germantown Friends School in Philadelphia. Similar to Catharism, which grew out of the abuses and excesses of the medieval Roman Catholic Church, Quakerism was born as a reaction to problems in the Church of England.

The rise of Catharism is one of the important themes in *Troubadour*. Cathars eschewed power and preferred a simple, non-materialistic life. In response, the Church mounted the Abigensian Crusade, aimed at wiping them out. Their last holdout was the mountaintop chateau Montségur. In the year 1244, after years of persecution, the Cathars finally surrendered and more than 200 were burned to death in a huge bonfire at the base of Montségur.

For her last research trip to this land she loved, Clara visited Montségur. She was fortunate to have two friends, Marie-Noëlle Hervé and Joy Dunbar, accompany her. This threesome had the goal of climbing to the top of Montségur. Clara had contended with bad health most of her life, yet despite her indomitable spirit, her muscle disease made it difficult to walk, let alone climb a mountain.

Even with Joy and Nollie's help, Montségur was too much for her. Unwilling to give up, they hired a local guide who carried Clara to the top on his back.

As Clara's novel grew, it became too large for a single book. *Troubadour* and its sequel were translated into European languages and enjoyed by many on the Continent. But they were never available to readers in English. Although I have few of the skills that Clara had, I have taken up this quest.

This is the first of her two books. Now that *Troubadour* is published in English, I will move on to *A Troubadour's Tale*. You'll find a short selection from that book at the back of this one.

Clara gave me my start as a paid writer by introducing me to *Women's World*, the magazine you see at supermarket checkout stands. For several years I contributed to the Gynecologist's Column. My principal concern since high school has been human population; this was my reason for choosing medicine as a profession and OB-GYN as a specialty. With this experience I realized that the pen is mightier than the speculum. For many years I have been fortunate to write a monthly column for the *Durango* (Colorado) *Herald* on population.

There is a vast difference between writing about human population issues and writing about 13th Century France, troubadours, courts of love, and Cathars. Fortunately, I have found talented people to help me. Beth Green has reedited the text to make it more readable for a contemporary American audience. Together we have also written a glossary. Mark Stroud, a cartographer, took time away from his usual profession of making travel maps to produce the historical chart included with the book. The book was designed by Lisa Snider. Dr. Shaila Van Sickle and my wife, Gail, helped with proofreading. The cover design was done by Cindy Coleman, of Duck Girl Art, and my son Dave.

What does this collection of people have in common? We all live, or have lived, in Southwest Colorado. I am amazed at the talent in this community!

– **Richard Grossman**

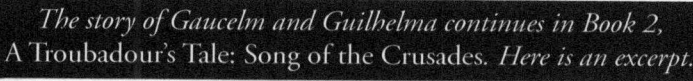

The story of Gaucelm and Guilhelma continues in Book 2, A Troubadour's Tale: Song of the Crusades. Here is an excerpt.

A TROUBADOUR'S TALE: SONG OF THE CRUSADES

PROLOGUE

Matins. It was the hour just before daylight when dreams fly out.

Precisely as the ship's bell struck, Ricard awoke. He felt the boat bellying gently in time with the sailors' chant and the tug of the galley oars. Nearly two months into the voyage, they had come upon the famous adverse currents off Sardinia. For a week they had been drifting about in black squalls on a roiling ocean.

Ricard looked over at his companion. Gaucelm Faidit slept noisily, the breath booming through his nostrils, his face flushed red with fever. That shaggy head, its curls showing gray like an aging Minotaur's, was giving Ricard no peace, even in sleep. That he should be playing keeper to this tamed beast, this troubadour whose fame stretched from sea to sea, was an irony that filled him with awe—and at the same time, something like envy.

For days the mast had rocked naked as a drunken skeleton, its crow's nest poised atop the furled sails like a skull. It was good to see this morning's sky filled with canvas again as a great wind sucked at the sail. High, high up he could just glimpse the Venetian banner and, below it, the snapping pennant bearing the arms of the city of Marseilles.

Ricard reached for the jug by his pallet, dashed some water at his cheeks, and got to his feet. The stench of the night's vomit had lifted slightly with the wind.

All around him were early-morning mumblings, a clank of chamber pots. Men sat up suddenly as though surprised to be alive. Some reached for scraps from last night's dinner, avoiding the pork. One or two ate ravenously, tossing herring bones over the rails for the gulls, which screamed their scavengers' cries in the ship's wake.

Ricard thanked his stars that he had been untempted by any meat on board this ship. By now, however, even the bread was barely edible. Summoning the discipline he had learned in the field, he knelt briefly on deck to say prayers, then went below.

Lauds. Gaucelm awoke in a rage. He didn't expect to die; not yet, by the arm of St. George! He always maintained that a man knew when his card came up, barring an act of God. But if spoiled rations were a trick of the weather, if a deck spilling over with last night's pork was an "accident," then the Venetians were indeed masters of Fate itself. Damned moneymongers! Sold them meat already old no doubt, and for a price. Couldn't care less whether 200 men staggered off the boat at Marseilles or whether only their horses would see the journey through. As for the knights aboard, it was bad enough to discover that fighting for God made good business for merchants whose god was money. For those who had eaten spoiled pork, fighting for God was a game for fools.

Gaucelm raised himself up for a moment to shift his considerable weight against the rigging. Unsettled, he retched and was seized with a sudden fear. Was he going to rot on the deck of this godforsaken ship, in a sea of vomit? It was a disgrace, this continual revolt of a stomach no longer under his control.

Where *was* Ricard? In spite of himself he felt comforted by the youth's presence on this journey.

To be sure, they were strange ship-fellows. Soldiering may have taught Ricard the quick dangers of battle, the sting of pierced skin, the stun of a blow on the hauberk, but he knew nothing of the drawn-out agonies of illness.

Ricard was adept at dealing with delays on land where there were reasons like mud or bad roads. But drifting about in the sea while supplies ran out just made him furious.

Waves of heat overwhelmed Gaucelm, leaving his body in a clammy sweat. He was thirsty beyond measure.

Not that it wasn't a relief to be left unwatched for a few moments. It was positively ridiculous, this overanxious concern of Ricard's, as though he wasn't expected to last another night. Why was he keeping watch?

A thought made him start. Sense of duty, yes; Ricard was a soldier. But there was something in Ricard's manner that he could not explain. Behind those eyes was more than solicitude. Cunning, perhaps? A willful curiosity at least. And then the idea came of its own accord: had he been slipped something in his portion? Even two nights ago the pork had tasted vile, not just rancid. With the thought of it he opened his mouth as though to air his tongue.

Ricard had betrayed him once, after all, in a way that no man would be likely to forget. Ever since that first evening aboard some eight weeks ago, a bonhomie had masked the old anger. At their meeting a slight frisson had raced up Gaucelm's spine; would this be his chance to even the score?

Was it a mere accident that Ricard had been aboard after all? But no, reason told him. The boy was too knock-kneed to be put up to that sort of thing. Besides, there had been ample evidence of Venetian treachery in the air these last few days—too much to warrant pointing a finger in another direction.

No, to be fair, Ricard's heart had probably sunk as low as his own that first night of the voyage. Gaucelm had assumed from the start of the journey that they would be at each other in small ways. He was gratified that it hadn't turned out that way at all.

But recently, he imagined, the man had a hunted look about him, as though he expected something to happen, something he was keeping to himself, something that made him fish for an excuse each time he left Gaucelm's side.

And if indeed it was merely spoiled pork, why was his fever worsening after a day and a night? There was nothing left of him but its heat and a great thirst. He noticed how fever had made him attentive, how he watched over himself as he might over his young son, tenderly. "If I should die before I wake . . ." *Best not to sleep at all*, he thought. In any case, the heat inside his skull left no room for dreams.

Prime. There was a footstep behind him, then Ricard was handing him a goblet filled with some brackish liquid.

"I thought it best to mix a little wine in the water," he was saying.

"Poison to chase poison!" snapped Gaucelm, at once wide awake. "Answer me this boy. Is there some lethal concoction in me beside this rotten Venetian meat?"

The pair of eyes flicked their lashes straight at Gaucelm. "Not that I know about."

The scuttle for breakfast was long over, and the sick passengers quieted. The only sounds were a rhythmic creak of wood as the boat mounted each swell, and the flapping of sail in the wind above.

Gaucelm took short gulps of his wine, each time peering inside the cup as though expecting to find something floating in it. He sat up violently, then doubled over, nauseous. A cold metal object slithered down his chest and he caught at it with his hand, drawing it out at the end of its cord. He gazed at it, cupped in his palm, then stuffed it back inside his shirt and sank back against the rigging.

"Rest now, awhile," said Ricard uneasily.

"I can feel my flesh sagging on its bones, my boy," Gaucelm said slowly. "Don't even bother trying to deceive me. I *know*. I have a poison in me; I'm a marked man, Ricard."

The ship's bell sounded Sext. Soon it would be time for the noon rations and an excuse to get away. It was useless to try and convince Gaucelm of anything as long as he was in the fever's grip. Stiffly Ricard stretched his legs out in front of him, absently scratching his calves beneath their woolen hose.

His mind flew to the gold bullion rumored to be aboard, destined for the captain of the trade commune at Marseilles. A rich cache, this transport held. Ricard could almost smell the oils and beads of myrrh, see the folded silk tents and embroidered stuffs, the letters of credit—all sealed in their caulked boxes, en route to the wealthy families of Marseilles. Well, damn it, he couldn't eat gold! All *he* had were prayers, a starveling's ration of bread and herring, the illness all around him, and dice as his only diversion. He cursed his secret vow and his mission, which was the only reason he was on this ill-fated voyage.

"Go and stretch your legs, boy. And get me something more to drink, but this time leave the water out." The wine already inside Gaucelm was beginning to do its work. The troubadour closed his eyes and drowsed.

Something to drink indeed; more claret had travelled that gullet than Ricard was likely to lay eyes on in a lifetime. Maybe Gaucelm had cut a figure once, but who would know it to look at him now?

Ricard half-rose, then settled in a crouch to study Gaucelm's face. What he first noticed were the rakish, untidy eyebrows curled up at the outer ends, and underneath, those dark protuberant eyes, unmistakably his. It was true, they gave out a smile, even when accompanied by an order. No doubt women liked his famous laugh framed by a burly beard, a laugh which seemed to start from somewhere as deep in him as the bottom of a barrel and then took over his entire body. Whatever it was, it was part of his legend, and the legend had two tunes: Gaucelm Faidit, famed poet, and Gaucelm Faidit, butterbellied troubadour, whoring his way from bawdyhouse to pisspot.

Ricard crooked a finger around the stem of Gaucelm's goblet and stood up. In the course of this voyage he had learned that both Faidits possessed some things worth knowing.

Vespers. Below, a sweep of oars, a pause, and the galley chants began again; it was the rowers, changing shift.

Through the half-light a crewman appeared, carrying a torch and lantern. He bent down near where Gaucelm lay and soon an orange flame rose straight up into the windless air as the oil caught. He left it there on the ship's boards. Ricard reached over, moving it safely away from Gaucelm's pallet, then sat in shadow, beyond the outermost rim of light. Soon the lantern glow mounted and fell to its own rhythm, throwing shadows on Gaucelm's face. The old troubadour pressed his hands against his eyes. "Everything burns."

"Some wine, Gaucelm? I've fetched more for you."

"My poison-chaser, you mean."

"Your pork-chaser!" Ricard declared hotly.

"Oh, don't fence with me, boy. I may be fat-gutted but I'm not fat-witted. How else would you explain this," he gestured at his body, "this fever-ridden piece of flotsam afloat on a barrelstave of a boat? Have you ever seen a man's skin turn grey from mere indigestion? Come, Ricard. I know my own innards. I know them as intimately as I know my nether regions and my useful parts. They would deal with a piece of putrid pork in no time. They've dispensed with more trouble than that in a lifetime of abuse, I can tell you! Trusty old innards don't kick up a fuss like this until the final debt falls due. No games this time, Ricard. I know, and I know *who*. And why."

"Who, then?" Ricard challenged.

"You know as well as I."

He lay back then, Ricard's arm supporting his head. Shadows deepened the ledges above his eyes so that their pupils vanished. He fell silent. Was he awake or asleep? Ricard saw that it hardly mattered. For Gaucelm there was no longer day and night, just a single, fevered dream.

And so Ricard let go of Gaucelm, moved silently to his own pallet, and dropped into sleep. He saw the tavern where long ago he had first met Gaucelm and gamed with him. He could even smell the winey warmth of Gaucelm's breath—this man whose reputation had made him drunk with desire to compose his own songs. He felt again that thrill of throwing dice with a man famed clear across the South, from Toulouse to Orange, a troubadour who had composed a *partimen* with Coeur-de-Lion. It came upon Ricard that that night had warmed him more than his own deeds on the fighting field ever had.

Still young, he felt too late for everything. He had come too late for Toulouse in its high days, for Bernard de Ventadour, and for the rich glories of Gaucelm's prime. But that was all in times long gone.

Soon the ship's bell would sound Compline. His mind snapped to the moment. Silently, taking care that the dying man should not see him caught up in such unsoldierly fashion, Ricard bowed his head and wept.

www.ingramcontent.com/pod-product-compliance
Lightning Source LLC
Chambersburg PA
CBHW030437300426
44112CB00009B/1038